The
Sugar
Rat

A Novel

Gregory H. Bohlen
Jay Bryant

The Sugar Rat is a work of fiction. Although some of the settings are real and it is set in a real time, and the characters make references to real people, it is neither biographical nor historical. The actions and behavior of the characters who appear in the action are purely the product of the authors' imaginations, and should not be attributed to any real person or persons, living or dead.

Published by New Gutenberg, Inc.

ISBN # 0-9774162-0-8

For Susan and Alice

Acknowledgements

No book is complete without the author thanking the people that made it possible to pull it off. First I owe a huge debt of gratitude to my writing partner for his incredible talent for pulling my hare brained ideas together. My sincere thanks also go out to Gary, Meg, JoAnn, Jim, Bev and, of course, Mark. Finally, I would like to thank Alice, who, now that the paperback version is here hopefully can enjoy a good read. She has been the biggest believer in me I have ever known and for her constancy through all that life has thrown at her I owe a debt larger than I can ever hope to repay.

– GHB

If The Sugar Rat *is, as we believe it to be, the best novel ever authored by a team of writers, it is still true that Greg deserves the lion's share of the credit for initiating the idea and doing most of the heavy lifting. Also indispensable were the services of Barbara Roberts, and I would like to express my deep appreciation for the advice of Vince and Jon, and of course, nonpareil Susan, who made important contributions to the book and gave even more valuable moral support to her brother and husband, the authors.*

– JB

The
Sugar
Rat

PROLOGUE

My life was hurtling on a course of my own making, but not of my own choosing. Had I known how it was going to turn out, I might never have done things the way I did. But right or wrong, I had done them, and on that morning I was so scared I couldn't fit the key into the car door lock to begin my morning trip to work.

I usually left the house on the west edge of Wonanonly, Indiana around 6:30 in the morning. Today was no exception, despite the previous night's events.

As I pulled out of the driveway, the field of corn across the road was almost shoulder high. Healthy, green, just starting to tassel, that corn was a daily reminder to me of what my work was all about. The corn had in all likelihood been aided in its growth by one of my company's divisions. Tamson-Long Products made the herbicides that kept the rows clean, the fertilizers that helped the corn grow and the insecticides that protected the seeds from insects. But then again, TLP, as it was known to the locals, made the chemicals that were a part of almost everything anyone could eat, drink or use. It was in fact the world's second largest chemical company. And until last night, the TLP world had been my oyster...I was well on my way to becoming a giant of industry.

I managed to get the car door open, and the car started. When I pulled up to the four-way stop, my eyes were shielded from the red rising sun by the giant grain elevator that stood in the center of town. I noticed our stable hand, Donnie Bradford, drinking his morning coffee and chatting with several fellow townsmen at Steven's Auto Repair. It was a morning tradition for many of Wonanonly's early risers, and the unofficial trading floor for local gossip and area events.

I laughed nervously as I rounded the corner: I didn't know what they were talking about this morning, but I could bet I knew what they'd be talking about the next morning.

My drive time ritual always included checking my answering machine after I turned onto the main highway to Steuben, 19 miles north. This morning I had just two messages. The first call was from Brad Redfoot. In an almost breathless, frightened voice, he told me that he'd received a visit from FBI agents the night before. Brad's voice was cracking with nervousness as he left off with, "What should I do?" He must have made that call before he finally reached me, I thought, erasing the message.

The second message was from Dink Maccabee in Atlanta. He described how FBI agents had come to his apartment when he was not home and told his girlfriend they wanted to talk to him, scaring her half to death. They had left a card with a number for him to call.

It had come to this, then. An utterly innocent young woman in Atlanta was suffering extreme anxiety. Perhaps she had been unable to sleep all night, worrying whether her boyfriend was in trouble with the Federal Government.

He wasn't, but she couldn't know that: not for sure, not even if he had reassured her again and again. She would still be harboring some doubt, somewhere in the depths of her heart.

And it was all my fault.

I wondered how my boss, the Chairman of TLP, had slept. William C. Hargiss was and is the most intense man I have ever known. He was probably hoping his own involvement in the whole mess was still secret, and that his political influence could emerge unscathed. I didn't know then what staring death in the face was like, but now I know it's a lot like facing an irate William Hargiss. Hargiss's son Howard was another story. Howard had not been genetically blessed with his father's intensity, but had instead been given an ample dose of desire to "enjoy" life.

G.T. Binghamton was different in yet another way. I immediately felt pangs of true regret for what I had unleashed on G.T. He had trusted me implicitly. How could I have betrayed the people who had given me a lifestyle I once only dreamed about?

I began punching the buttons on the radio, scanning the news stations. Was anyone reporting on the story? No, which meant the FBI had done a good job, no, a great job of keeping it all quiet; not even the local news had any information about the huge raids that had taken place the night before.

As I pulled up to the first traffic light in Steuben, I began to feel the guilt come crashing down on me in wave after wave. How in the world had I gotten to this place?

This then is my story, told in a way only I can tell it. I apologize in advance for some of the language, but without it you could never understand the culture I lived in at TLP. And I apologize for the ending, for the hundreds of people who got hurt in the end. But mostly I apologize for what we did to you, our customers. I wish I could tell you how it will all end, but sometimes a story like this has a life of its own.

Gary Long
Park Ridge, Illinois
January, 1995

The Sugar Rat

CHAPTER 1

The cocaine in front of Jimmy T was in small plastic bags, $20 a pop. Three hundred of them, about a two-week supply. Jimmy T had driven to the south side of Gary the night before to get them, and it had been after midnight when he'd gotten back to Steuben. He'd planned on sleeping in this morning, but the damned thunderstorm woke him up. He carefully counted out 30 bags and packed them into his pouch, which he took into the bedroom and covered with his Chicago White Sox jacket.

Now that he was up, he was hungry. He walked from the bedroom of the apartment, past the cluttered bathroom and through the living room, furnished with nothing but an old overstuffed chair, a new 27-inch television set and a fancy component stereo set he had put together himself. Electronics was his only hobby.

He went into the kitchen and made breakfast - Cocoa Puffs and Dr. Pepper, eating in front of the TV. Then he went back to bed, leaving the TV on. Another loud clap of thunder sounded, and Jimmy T pulled the covers over his head.

In his own bed across town, Howard Hargiss sat up, rubbing his pounding head, trying to figure out if the thunder was outside the house or inside his brain. Both, he decided. He looked at the sleeping blonde beside him. He thought her name was Trudy.

His father had promised to get him more involved in the company, but today was the September board meeting, and he wasn't invited. "Shit," Howard thought, " I don't know why fuckin' Dad doesn't follow through. I do every damn thing he asks, and I still can't get any respect from the cocksucker. Dammit anyway, Dad." Somewhere in the sentence, he must have started talking out loud, because Trudy or whoever she was bubbled a raspy, "What, Howie?" and coughed before she fell back into her chemically enhanced sleep.

"I don't give a rat's ass how many men you've got on special assignment today," G.T. Binghamton barked over the phone at the Steuben police chief. "I need an escort. Four cars, two in front and two behind." A sharp spike of lightning sizzled across the morning sky.

G.T. – some people said the initials stood for "Go To" – had to get a chemical catalyst chamber onto a flatbed trailer at the Cranford Machine Works and move it across town to the Tamson-Long Products lot. The damned thing was 18 feet wide, and he was supposed to have a permit, but G.T. didn't spend time worrying about permits.

He knew he'd get his escort. He always got what he wanted from the Steuben police. When you were the president of TLP, you could make things happen in Steuben, Indiana.

By 8:30 in the morning, the 70 tons of gleaming stainless steel were on the flatbed. Slowly, the driver inched the powerful truck out of the machine works yard. Lights flashing, two police cars led it onto Market Street. Two others pulled in behind. Any of the officers could have arrested the truck driver for hauling an oversized vehicle without a permit, but none of them did.

There isn't much of a rush hour in a small city the size of Steuben, but what there was suffered under the dual assault of a pelting rain and blocked streets.

A few minutes after 9:30, the convoy pulled onto the TLP lot. The police cars stopped at the gate, and the officers watched as the truck made its way through the gleaming maze of pipes and tanks. Cursing the rain, one of the officers got out of his car and ran to the guard shack. The guard was on his coffee break, and in his place, a balding man who looked like he needed a shave sat on the high-backed stool. The policeman let himself in and stood dripping in the tiny room.

"You Mr. Tully?" the policeman asked.

"Yeah." Andrew Tully picked up a small envelope. He eyed the officer carefully. "You know what to do with this?"

"Chief said you had a letter for him."

"Yeah. Something like that." He handed over the envelope, suppressing a smirk. The officer took the envelope, stuffed it into his pocket and ran back to his car.

"Huhh," G.T. Binghamton said when the phone rang. He always answered the phone that way.

"It's on the lot," Tully said. "You need anything else, 'cause otherwise I'm going back to my room and take a fucking shower."

"Nah, just check in with William later. He may have something. I gotta drive to Detroit this afternoon."

"Oh, yeah," Tully said. "Your dad died. How come you don't take the King Air or something?"

"Fucking board meeting today," he said. "Every plane we've got is picking up silly-ass directors somewhere." Again the lightning sizzled across the TLP lot. That's another good reason not to take a company plane today, G.T. thought.

CHAPTER 2

Four floors above G.T. Binghamton's office, William C. Hargiss wasn't worried about moving equipment around Steuben. As Chairman and CEO of Tamson-Long Products, he left that kind of crap to G.T. Hargiss wasn't even thinking about the board meeting that afternoon, although he would have to turn his attention to it later.

For the moment, he was eyeing three men seated in his office. One of them was Phil McLaughlin, the CEO of McLaughlin Chemical Corporation. The other two were McLaughlin's lawyers.

McLaughlin tried to return Hargiss's stare, but it was impossible. Looking into those piercing eyes was like looking into the headlight of an onrushing freight train. You could feel the power behind them. More than one poor SOB had foolishly dared to stand in front of those eyes, McLaughlin thought, and the receding tracks behind Hargiss are littered with their bodies.

"Okay, what have we got here?" Hargiss mumbled. There was a stack of file folders on his desk, and he picked up two or three and laid them aside. "Oh, yeah, McLaughlin."

The message was obvious. This may be the most important meeting of the decade for you, Phil McLaughlin, it said, but for me, you're just one file folder among many.

"McLaughlin Chemical Company," Hargiss said flatly. "Founded in 1879 by your great-grandfather, Philip." Hargiss looked up and smiled a smirky little smile at McLaughlin. "I've heard tell he was a real son of a bitch."

But you're not. McLaughlin could almost hear the unspoken words at the end of the sentence. For a minute, he thought Hargiss might actually have said them, but it was just his nerves. Hargiss was toying with him, strumming the nerve ends like they were the strings of a banjo. Twang, twang. His body was a twanging cacophony which only he could hear, and he struggled to tune it.

Hargiss got up from his desk and walked to the window, looking at the thunderheads boiling by. "You know, Phil, none of this would have happened if you and Howard could just have found a way to agree on the vitamin thing."

"You mean, if I'd been willing to become part of your criminal price-fixing conspiracy," McLaughlin said, regretting it the moment the words were out. Don't antagonize him, you idiot!

McLaughlin's mind flashed back to the day Howard Hargiss came calling, offering a way out of the sea of red ink precipitated by TLP's entry into the specialty vitamin manufacturing business McLaughlin Chemical had dominated for 20 years.

"Let's sit down and divvy up the market," Howard had said. "You take this customer, we'll take that one. In a few months the price will be back up where it was, and we'll both make good money." McLaughlin told him to get out of his office before he broke his neck, and by the time the front door hit the kid's ass, had called the FTC to complain. For all the good it had done.

Why not? he wondered. What kind of clout did TLP have in Washington? The pictures on the wall told him the answer. By the dozens, it seemed, they showed William Hargiss, handsome with his full head of white hair, eyes smiling as he shook hands with presidents, senators and cabinet officers.

Now McLaughlin watched as Hargiss turned from the window, and without reference to the file folder, made his offer to buy the McLaughlin Chemical Corporation.

Less than two years earlier, McLaughlin had turned down an offer of 75 million dollars. Then the price war with TLP started. As he waited for Hargiss to get to the bottom line, McLaughlin knew it would be a hell of a lot less than seventy-five million. He only hoped it wouldn't be as low as his investment bankers and lawyers had predicted.

"We've looked these numbers over pretty carefully, gentlemen, and I can tell you we were surprised at how much you've lost over the past eighteen months," Hargiss said. McLaughlin could feel the blood rising in his neck. "In spite of that," he continued, "we're prepared to make you a reasonable offer. In fact, we think it's generous. Twenty-five million. For everything." Hargiss sat back in his seat, elbows on the arm of his chair, fingers tapping lightly together in front of his chest.

McLaughlin couldn't quite suppress a gasp. The consensus among the bankers was 30 million. He had allowed himself to think it might be 35, maybe even 40. Twenty-five was a nightmare. They owed almost 20 million on their capital line. They owed another four million on their operating line. That left just a million dollars to split among all the stockholders. By the time the investment bankers and lawyers took their cut, he'd end up with nothing.
McLaughlin felt the heat beginning to build in his face.

Every instinct in him made him want to stand up and punch William Hargiss in the nose. "No. There is no way we would accept an offer like that," he heard himself saying. "You're the reason we're in this position to begin with."

Hargiss leaned back in his chair. "Philip," he began quietly, "I'm going to lay the facts out for you. You can do with them what you want, but I suspect you'll come to the same conclusion we have.

"First, you're losing a million dollars a month, with no end in sight. Second, your plant needs to be updated, and third, you don't have any options. If you don't accept our offer, we'll buy your plant out of bankruptcy for pennies on the dollar. The only reason I'm offering you anything is that we could use the capacity. Let me also remind you that you've got personal guarantees on a bunch of your loans. I can see that big Bucks County house of yours on the market by spring."

McLaughlin stood up. "You can take your generous offer and shove it straight up your ass. You, sir, are the leader of the biggest den of thieves I have ever run across." Then he threw the chair back against the wall and stomped out.

The two lawyers eyed each other uneasily, shuffled their feet and stood up. "Make sure your board finds a way to calm him down," Hargiss said sharply. "They've got big money on the line here."

One of the lawyers paused in the doorway. Speaking softly so he could not be heard by his retreating employer, he said to Hargiss, "You'll get what you want. You always do. The board has instructed me to tell you we have a deal, no matter what Mr. McLaughlin may say."

Hargiss got up from his desk and walked back to the window. The sun broke through an open space between the retreating thunderheads and lit up the scene below him, sparkling off gleaming steel, still wet with rain. He thought about the sun: never-ending thermonuclear reactions, 93 million miles away. Chemistry. It was all chemistry, he thought, and there isn't anyone between here and the sun who has made chemistry work better than I have.

He turned from the window and picked up the direct line to Howard's office. He listened to four buzzes, cursed under his breath and punched another button.

"Huhh," G.T. Binghamton said, looking up from the set of blueprints on the cluttered desk in front of him.

"Where the hell is that stupid-assed son of mine?" Hargiss snorted.

"Beats the shit out of me. You want me to track him down?"

"Well, Christ, I just cut the McLaughlin deal and I thought we ought to celebrate. See if you can find Howard, and get him and Dan Anthony, yourself, whoever else had a hand in it up to the executive dining room at noon, and we'll pop a cork. Get Buffy there too, I want him to scope out the best way to announce it."

"Yeah, sure," G.T. said, "but I'll have to duck out real early. I've got to drive to Detroit for my father's funeral."

"Well, shit, it may be a lousy party, but do it anyway."

"Sure, boss."

G.T. did his best to put the noon party together, but it wasn't easy. He couldn't find Howard anywhere, and for some reason Dan Anthony tried to beg off. G.T. finally had to order him to attend. Buffy Carney was no problem, and G.T. lined up a few others, but he was nervous about the whole thing.

His daughter, Carrie, who worked in the steno pool, stuck her head into his office. She was wearing a pair of white stretch pants and a bright red sweater. "I'm all packed," she said, "what time are we leaving?"

"Jeez, I wish I knew," he said. "I wanted to be on the road by noon, but forget that. Just hang loose, and I'll call you as soon as I can get away."

She leaned over his desk to give him a peck on his growing forehead. Just then, Ralph Sori walked by the door and paused for just a moment to admire the outline of her bottom, tight against the white slacks.

"Carrie," he called to her as she walked out of the office seconds later.

She turned and blushed, walking quickly to his desk. "Hi, Ralph," she said. God, he is gorgeous, she thought. And famous, too, a professional football player just a season ago.

"Hey," he said, standing up. "You want to go get some lunch?"

"It's only eleven."

"So?"

"And we're driving to Detroit for my granddad's funeral later."

"Oh, well, some other time then."

Oh, my God, she thought. I can *not* let this opportunity slip away. Surely we'll have time for a quick lunch. I can't turn Ralph Sori down. "No," she said, "I guess it's okay."

Ralph grabbed his coat and slipped it on.

They had no more than gotten onto the elevator when G.T. walked out of his office. Even though Ralph had nothing to do with vitamin additives or McLaughlin Chemical, G.T. decided to invite him to the celebration. He needed bodies, and at least Ralph was a celebrity.

"Where's Ralph?" G.T. asked Joyce, his secretary.

Joyce bit her lip. There was no way she was going to spill the beans on what she had just seen. "He left a few minutes ago," she said. "I think he may have had a lunch meeting."

"God damn it all to hell," G.T. sputtered. "What's wrong with this place today?"

7

CHAPTER 3

The phone inside Hargiss's desk drawer rang. Somedays he dreaded that ring, but not today. This was not a call for the CEO of Tamson-Long Products. It was a call for Field Resource A3802.

"Let's go secure," a man said. It was the unmistakable voice of Jonathan M. Decatur, rear admiral, USN, retired, Deputy Director of the National Security Agency.

"I'm green."

"Okay, me too. Bill, how are you?"

"Never better, Jon. What's up?"

"Well, I've got some friends in Moscow that need a little help."

"Things must be really hopping over there."

"You bet your ass they are. The whole damn Soviet Union is going down, less than a year I'd say."

"That's good to hear. We've worked a long time for that."

"Yeah, and you've worked harder than most, my friend. Look, here's the deal. We want to have some private business institutions set up and ready to roll as soon as the coast is clear. We figure Number One is a good solid bank that can loan out money, get other companies up and running, start some real capitalism."

Hargiss was frankly amazed and impressed that the agency was thinking that far ahead. "It's that close, huh?" he asked.

"Yeah, Bill, it is. And the thing is, there's going to be all kinds of shady operators getting into the act. They'll deal mostly in currency speculation, that sort of thing, and they'll make fortunes in the short run, but we want to have something that will really work to build the economy, 'cause we figure it's going to be in the crapper once the Communists collapse."

"Well, that makes sense. How much you figure you need?"

"That's the thing, Bill, it's got to be pretty hefty. We're thinking a hundred million."

Hargiss paused. "Well, you're right not to undercapitalize it. But that's a bigger load than we've moved since, what, Teheran in eighty-six?"

Decatur chuckled. "Don't remind me of that fiasco," he said. "Can you do it?"

"Yeah," Hargiss said. "We can use Interoceanic, out of the Caymans.

I've moved the account to Barclays, and I think it's clean as a whistle."

"How much do we have to work with now?"

"Well, the last time I checked it was maybe three hundred or so, total. I'm adding at the rate of about thirty-five a quarter. The diamond money is steady; I'm trying to reduce our need for the, ah, controlled substance source, like you wanted."

"Those are good numbers, and I really do appreciate you're moving us out of the, you know. That's a time bomb just waiting to go off."

"I know. I told you that in the first place, remember? Anyway, the money from TLP is chugging along, and I'm thinking about some ways to ratchet it up even more."

"Good, we may need some cash soon for some domestic stuff. Well, thanks, I'll have someone stop by."

"Do we use the same greeting codes?"

"Yeah, there isn't any reason to change."

"Well, if you hear about something called Tokobank, you'll know it's us."

Hargiss looked at his watch. It was not quite noon. So far this morning, he'd bought a 100-year-old chemical company for $25 million and set up a new bank in Moscow for $100 million. Not a bad morning, he thought.

CHAPTER 4

Jimmy T put on his work uniform: black pants, black and white checked shirt. He tied the cocaine pouch around his chest and put on the White Sox jacket, buttoning it all the way up to cover the pouch. Then he drove through the rain-dampened streets of Steuben to the Steak n Shake, sub-woofers booming all the way.

When he got there, he grabbed a clean white apron from a shelf and took it into the men's room. He removed his jacket, lowered the pouch to his waist and put on the apron. On the way back, he slipped a white paper Sta-Put hat on his head. He was good to go.

"Millie, you sure look fine today," he smiled at the girl who worked the morning shift at the drive-up window. "Why don't you take the rest of the day off?"

"You're ten minutes early," she responded, giggling. She was fat, with a big butt, but she had a pretty face, and Jimmy T liked her. She took off her headset and extracted the drawer from the cash register. Jimmy T put his drawer in its place, fresh with newly counted cash for making change. He slipped the headset on and watched his first customer of the afternoon pull up to the speaker menu.

"Welcome to Steak n Shake," he said. "May I take your order?"

CHAPTER 5

Dan Anthony didn't relish the thought of celebrating the collapse of McLaughlin Chemical. He stood alone by the wall of the executive dining room, watching the small group gather. Where is Howard? he thought. Where is the Price Fixer?

G.T. and William Hargiss walked in together. G.T. clinked a spoon against a glass.

There were ten executives in the room. "Boys," G.T. said, "our chairman has a little announcement to make."

Hargiss cleared his throat. "We have acquired McLaughlin Chemical," he said. Several of the men applauded, and Anthony watched his hands come together soundlessly three or four times.

"We'll announce it by the first of the week," Hargiss continued. "So Buffy," he said, nodding to the preppy-looking young man standing near the bar, "you'll need to get a statement ready for the media. Work something out with G.T. and Howard." He paused, his eyes scanning the room. "Howard had some other business today," he muttered. "G.T., you and Dan need to be ready to meet with their people and figure out how best to integrate their plant into our operations."

He paused, and felt a twinkle in his eye. "And also how many of those candy-assed idiots they call executives we can fire by the end of the month."

Someone shouted, "All right!" and the applause began again. Buffy produced a bottle of champagne from the bar, and each man in turn shook Hargiss's hand and congratulated him on his accomplishment.

CHAPTER 6

Once a year the TLP board met at the corporate headquarters in Steuben. The other meetings were held at more pleasant venues. They would complete their business in the afternoon and then adjourn for a social gathering at William Hargiss's palatial home overlooking the Wabash River.

Randolph Thad was the first director to arrive. He strode easily into Hargiss's office a half-hour before the meeting time. Thad was the one board member Hargiss treated as an equal. Trim and handsome at 50, he had taken an inconsequential Atlanta television station and built it into a communications empire.

The two men had become fast friends over the past ten years; both were on the Forbes 100 list and the "Giants of the Earth," a listing that started out as a joke, but had turned into a news story each year, as the list was updated. There were conspiracy-theory nuts everywhere who believed the group held secret meetings and plotted the destinies of millions. Hargiss and Thad knew better, but of the two, only Hargiss knew how close to being right the conspiracy theorists actually were.

Thad was 25 years Hargiss's junior, but had been the older man's teacher, instructing him in the ways of Wall Street. In return, Hargiss had guided Thad through the power structure in Washington and helped him manipulate regulators in ways Thad had never even dreamed about.

"Well, Bill, the others will be here in a few minutes," Randolph said in his quiet, dignified southern drawl. As far as he knew, he was the only man in the world William C. Hargiss would allow to call him Bill, but, of course, he didn't know about Admiral Decatur. "I'm glad I was able to get here a little early," he continued. "I've got a couple of things to talk over before the meeting."

"What's on your mind?" Hargiss asked. From the tone in Thad's voice, Hargiss decided he was about to get a lecture.

"The next ten billion in revenue's gonna be hard to hit, isn't it?" Thad began.

Hargiss nodded his agreement, waited for the finish.

"You've done a damn fine job of building this company, but even with everything you have in place, if you don't get some value-added lines, you're not going to be able to keep doing everything that needs to be done."

Thad paused for a moment to let the message sink in. "You've got to buy – or build – some value-added lines, take advantage of some of this new biotechnology that's available out there and enter some new product areas."

Hargiss pursed his lips, neither surprised nor disappointed to learn what was on Thad's mind. He fiddled for a moment with a paper clip on his desk. "We're doing stuff in bio-tech. Don't you read our releases? We're finishing up a pilot plant in Memphis. We've acquired some top-notch bugs for Bacitracin and cellulose additives. And artificial sweetener – we'll be in that market in a few months, once the Memphis plant opens. And of course, we've been manufacturing media for years."

"That's not what I'm talking about, Bill, and you know it. You're just nibbling around the edges. You need to do this in a big way. The TLP way. Either buy someone out or form a new division. Become a real player."

"Well, we've looked into the possibility, but bio-tech is so far afield from the kinds of things we do now that I'm not sure we could pull it off. On top of that, the multiples of book are so high right now it just doesn't make sense to try and buy someone." Hargiss had indeed given the subject of biochemistry a great deal of thought; every instinct he had screamed that it was the right thing to do. Still, it was a big move.

"We're picking up McLaughlin, though. I took Phil to the cleaners this morning. We're getting it for a song."

"McLaughlin's got nothing going in biochemistry," Thad said. "They're barely hanging on in their traditional markets."

"All the same," Hargiss said, "we're just crackers, you know." Then he smiled. "Not Georgia Crackers. We mix stuff together and make other stuff. But bio-tech is a whole different animal. Literally a microscopic animal. We don't know anything about animals."

That self-deprecating remark aside, Thad could sense that Hargiss was taking the matter seriously. "It's the future of chemistry," he said. "You know it. Bring it up at the meeting today. Say you want the authority to explore a full-blown bio-tech venture. They'll give it to you." Thad paused and caught the older man's eyes. "Maybe we can put the succession problem to rest as well."

The set of Hargiss's jaw told Thad he had hit a nerve. That's right, Hargiss thought. He had said a "couple" of things.

"Damn it, Randolph, you know what I'm planning to do. Why in the hell do you continue to press me on this?"

"Bill, it just won't work," Thad said. "We need someone streetable, someone Wall Street won't question when it comes time to explain our results and establish plans for the future. Howard just can't pull it off."

It was a touchy subject, and one they had uncharacteristically danced around for the past several months. But Hargiss knew the time for dancing had passed. Besides, he was mad at Howard for missing the McLaughlin celebration. Where *was* he?

Thad studied Hargiss's craggy face for any sign of a reaction, and then added quietly, "Our friends really appreciate the work you've done, but you gotta throw 'em a bone. This succession issue is really important to them. Even you can't last forever, and they feel like all the effort they've gone to could be pissed away without the right combination in place."

Our friends, Hargiss thought. Our friends on Wall Street. The brokers whose personal assessment of the future of the company meant the stock went up or down. If they weren't happy on Monday, Hargiss and Thad could be a hundred million dollars poorer on Tuesday.

"Whoever you bring in to run Bio-tech, you ought to think of him as a potential CEO when you're ready to let go."

Hargiss nodded absently. That means Tully will have to do a fine-mesh screen on the guy, he was thinking. For reasons you, my friend, have no clue about.

Andrew Tully wasn't a friend like Randolph Thad. He was just indispensable. He was ex-CIA, now employed by the Troll Corporate Security Agency, and assigned virtually full time to TLP. Rumor had it Tully had been cashiered from the CIA after screwing up a major operation to catch the leaders of the Colombian Cali drug cartel. What no one knew for sure was whether or not he'd screwed it up on purpose. He had the scruples of a snake, but Hargiss knew he was an invaluable part of the mix. "I guess it won't hurt to keep that all in mind, but I'm telling you Randolph, this is a serious issue for me. I'm not going to be happy with anything that doesn't include Howard somewhere in the mix."

Thad took a deep breath and started to speak when the sound of voices in the outer office caused him to rethink what he was about to say. The other directors were arriving. Thad recognized that Hargiss was firmly in control of the board. Not that they were lightweights. Along with some former and current employees of TLP, and a few members of the Hargiss family, their number included relatives of former U. S. presidents, prominent attorneys, a retired senator, an ambassador. Every one of them owed William Hargiss more than they could ever repay.

Thad noticed that Hargiss was staring at him; he'd won one battle for the day, better to regroup than lose the war. One thing was for sure; he didn't need William Hargiss as an enemy.

"We'd best get to the meeting," Hargiss said.

Robert Aiken was the last of the directors to begin gathering his belongings from the table. The rest of the board was already on the way to the dinner party at the Hargiss house. It was the moment Aiken had been waiting and planning for over the past week.

"Hargiss, that was a good meeting. Picking up McLaughlin is a real coup, and I think you're on the right track looking at some of these value-added things. I'm sure biochemistry is the future. The more you can vertically integrate, the better you'll be able to lower your costs everywhere."

Hargiss pulled his face up into a grin and nodded as his way of saying thanks for the approval. He was sure Aiken wanted something else, and wished he would get to the point. Aiken was the managing partner for the second largest law firm in the United States, and brokered power with the ease of a car dealer negotiating for a used car.

Aiken continued, "William, have you had any thoughts about filling the seat vacated by the unfortunate death of Mr. Carney?"

So that was it. Jim Carney, Chairman of National Industries, had died four months ago when his private jet slammed into the side of a mountain in Austria while on a good will trip for the U.S. The irascible old tiger had been 83 at the time, the only board member older than Hargiss himself. Hargiss had kept the matter of replacing him off the agenda for two board meetings now. He wanted to name Howard to the seat, but knew the reaction that would bring. But if it wasn't going to be Howard, it had to be someone really prestigious, otherwise he'd get no end of grief from his son.

Hargiss had felt closer to Old Man Carney than any to of the other board members. He'd even broken an otherwise inflexible rule he had: he'd given Carney's grandson, Buford, the one they called "Buffy," a job in the TLP public relations department. He hated to give jobs to friends and relatives of board members; it was too hard to fire them when they screwed up.

"Well, I had a couple names, but tell me what you have in mind," he said.

"Our firm happens to represent Ian Howes, the former Prime Minister of Great Britain. He's very anxious to get re-established in the business world. I personally think he'd be a heck of a good addition to the board while we're trying to expand globally." Aiken smiled as he finished.

"Well, that is a pretty good idea. Why don't you set up a time for the two of us to get together and visit?" Hargiss said while shaking Aiken's hand and escorting him to the door.

Damned if it wasn't a good idea, Hargiss thought. He'd met Howes briefly a few times – there was scarcely a world leader he hadn't met – and although he didn't know him well, he knew several things that meant the man might work out.

He gathered up his papers and headed back to his office, where he picked up the phone and dialed a familiar number.

"They're on their way, honey," he said to his wife. "Everything ready?"

"Yes, we're fine," Virginia Hargiss responded, "although I wasn't sure I was ever going to get Madeleine Caldwell off the phone so I could tend to everything."

"What'd she have to say that couldn't wait until your bridge game tomorrow?"

"Well, she's trying to talk John into selling their house. Her allergies are getting worse, and being out in the country like that really bothers her. She wants him to build a new house, with lots of allergy-free technology in it."

Hargiss wasn't particularly interested in the Caldwells' housing situation, but he did have a business interest in Madeleine and her stockbroker husband. "Let her talk about it," he said. "I'll have some things for you to talk about too, at bridge tomorrow."

"Board meeting gossip?" Virginia asked.

"Yes, it'll be something John will find very interesting."

CHAPTER 7

Howard Hargiss drove through the rain toward his house on the outskirts of Steuben. He saw the Steak n Shake ahead, and thought about paying a visit to Jimmy T. He and Trudy had put a real dent in his stash of white stuff. But there were three or four cars at the drive-up window, and he had to piss real bad, so he decided to skip it and get on home.

He hit a puddle and sprayed a blue Dodge Dynasty parked across the street.

In the Dodge, Sid Cox watched the Steak n Shake through the rain splattered windshield. The way it was raining, he could be having sex on the hood and no one would notice.

He felt a little stirring at the thought, and laughed as he realized it was the first exciting thing that had happened to him all day. Staking out a Steak n Shake. It sounded like a stupid song title. And what was their motto? "In Sight It Must Be Right?" How ironic. A month ago, the manager had begun to suspect that Jimmy T was filling some of the black-and-white paper bags with more than burgers. Instead of firing him on the spot, the manager kept his cool and called the FBI, in the person of Sid Cox, special agent in charge of the Steuben office.

After weeks of stakeouts, Cox was sure that Jimmy T was doing a thriving business, maybe even better than the Steak n Shake itself. At least with higher margins, Cox thought. He watched as several cars ordered, received their bags of whatever, exchanged their cash and drove off into the rain. Everyone who was observed enjoying the drive-thru a little too often was then followed by an unmarked Steuben police car and stopped three or four blocks away. If you were looking to bust drug buyers and their supplier, it was perfect. They were going to end up getting 20 or so buyers tonight, and Jimmy T, too.

CHAPTER 8

The dinner at William and Virginia Hargiss's mansion was elegant and convivial. The directors enjoyed a buffet featuring a delicious and spectacularly tender London broil with hunter sauce, served by white-uniformed waiters hired for the occasion.

After the meal, Hargiss sought out Randolph Thad and told him about Aiken's idea of making Ian Howes a director. Thad liked the suggestion. "That stone could kill a bunch of birds at once," he said. Then his face broke into a broad smile. "Y'all sure worked your magic on the board today, my friend. A billion dollars. That's a hell of a lot more than I thought you'd ask for. Why so much?"

Hargiss usually looked forward to the post mortems of board meetings with Thad. Tonight he was still angry about being pressured to pick a successor other than Howard. "Biotechnology's expensive," he said.

Thad was puzzled by his short answer. "Y'all got something else up your sleeve, Bill?" he asked, shifting his facial expression to neutral.

Hargiss mulled over the question, and decided not to answer. Instead, he held up one hand with one finger extended. "If one person knows something then only one person knows it," he said. "If he tells someone else..." He brought up his other hand with one finger extended and held it beside the first one. "...then eleven people know it.

"Add one more..." He put a third finger beside the other two. "...and a hundred and eleven know it." He cocked his jaw and looked Thad straight in the eye, watching the other's neutral face morph into a thin smile. "Anyway, I got the approval you wanted."

"You won't regret it," Thad said. "Today was a pivotal day for TLP."

CHAPTER 9

Sid Cox's career had once looked so promising. He was definitely on the fast track: ten years in New York, a promotion to D.C., and then – boom – one mistake and here he sat in frigging Stueben, Indiana. What a hellhole this place was. Nothing but druggies and petty nigger crimes. The biggest thing he was going to catch tonight was a cold. What really depressed him was how excited the Steuben cops had been. What a bunch of clowns.

Cox yawned and motioned to the car beside him to let them know he was going to head into the restaurant for the start of phase two of the bust. Someone had to watch Jimmy to make sure he didn't try to flush the evidence down the drain when they pulled the plug. Ten of the suspect cars had driven through. If the pattern held, within the hour, another ten cars or so would receive packets courtesy of Jimmy, who had no idea his world was about to come crashing down.

Cox turned on the lights, pulled out of the parking space and headed across the street. Luck of all luck. There was a parking spot right beside the joint. Cox nosed the Dodge into the spot and threw a coat over the radios. The last thing he needed was for someone to spot it as an unmarked cop car and tip off Jimmy T.

Running into the restaurant, Cox cursed as he stepped into a puddle of water and soaked his foot and the bottom of his pants leg. Then, throwing open the door, he jumped inside and shook off the water. He took a seat at the counter, with a clear view of Jimmy T.

Careful not to catch Jimmy's eye, Cox watched his movements. There it was; he kept his stash in a pouch under the apron. Not only was Jimmy a real budding entrepreneur, he was smooth. If Cox hadn't been watching for it, he would never have seen it.

It took almost ten minutes for a waitress named Doreen – hair pulled back, crooked teeth and grease stains on her apron – to set silverware on the counter and take his order.

"How about chili mac with extra red sauce, fries and a large Orange Freeze?" Cox said flatly.

"Sure, hon." Doreen moved off to give the order to the grill man.

Five minutes later the china plate rang against the hard countertop as it was set in front of him. Damn, it does look good, Cox thought, taking a sip of his

Orange Freeze. Just then, the phone rang. The manager answered it and held the receiver to his chest as he yelled. "Jimmy T, phone!"

Jimmy slammed the register shut and walked over to the phone. Cox went on full alert. He watched as Jimmy's jaw dropped. Someone had tipped him off; Cox could see it in his eyes. Frigging car phones. Jimmy coolly hung up and said to the manager, "Hey, I gotta use the bathroom, I'll be right back.

With a move he had practiced in front of the mirror for four weeks at the academy, Cox pulled his gun and badge out at the same time. "Not so fast, Jimmy, get your hands up! FBI!" Jimmy T's hands went over his head and laced themselves together behind it. He's done this before, Cox thought.

"Oh, man," Jimmy T said with a look of disbelief. "How the fuck you guys..." then he stopped. He had almost incriminated himself, but stopped short. He was clearly experienced, Cox thought, with a twinge of regret. He'd hoped to be able to crack this guy and get him to rat out his supplier. That wouldn't happen now. Jimmy T knew the code too well. Cox came around the counter, read Jimmy T his rights, and cuffed him. In what seemed like a scene from a movie, the four squad cars which had begun their day at the Cranford Machine Works descended on the Steak n Shake. Cox handed Jimmy T over to the first uniformed officer in the door, and looked back at his food.

"Doreen!" he called to the waitress, who like the cook and the handful of customers had remained frozen in place during the entire event. She looked up at him with wide eyes.

"Make that to go," Cox said, pointing at his meal.

CHAPTER 10

The rainy season had ended, and the hot sun shimmered over the thatch-roofed huts of the village.

The wailing of the women was earsplitting, but the boy soldiers were deaf to the sound. It was part of every village, and you got so you didn't even hear it at all.

"In the name of God, don't do it!" screamed the man, Monoh. "She is an old woman. She is Auntie Jane to the whole village. You don't have to do it! I will dig for you. We will all dig for you. I give you my word."

The commander of the boy soldiers regarded Monoh with an insolent smirk. "Your word means nothing," he said. He was perhaps 17 years old. Most of the rest of his company was under 15, some as young as twelve. They wore black headbands and carried Russian-made rifles.

Auntie Jane sat, impassive, in the doorway of the hut, shelling beans into an earthenware pot.

The commander knocked her over with the butt of his rifle. The beans scattered, and the old woman's legs flailed onto the dirt in front of the hut. Screaming, Monoh lunged toward the commander, but two of the boys grabbed him and held him back. In one quick motion, the commander sat down, sidesaddle, on Auntie Jane's knobby knees and withdrew a machete from his belt. With three powerful backhand strokes, he cut off her right foot at the ankle. The left foot took four strokes.

Auntie Jane whimpered, but did not scream. The commander stood up. Then he bent over her twitching, shivering body, and wiped his bloody machete on the bright yellow and orange fabric of her dress, which had been sent to her just a month before by her daughter in Freetown.

Monoh was screaming, struggling to get free of the soldiers. They pushed him back onto the dirt that had been mud a few weeks earlier.

The commander pointed his rifle at Monoh's head. "Now, your word will mean something," he said. He waved the rifle at the keening, wailing crowd. "All of you will dig," he said, raising his voice above the din. "We will be back in a few days. It will be best if you have found some diamonds."

He shouted some words in Krio to the soldiers, and they trudged off through the valley, toward Koidu.

In that town, there were real soldiers, men of the Army of Sierra Leone.

Two of them guarded the door of a house on the west side of town. Their orders were to fight the boy soldiers of the Revolutionary United Front, but when a young man with a black headband approached the house, they let him pass inside.

He saw two men in the room: a fat, gray-bearded black man and a wiry Lebanese. They were seated at a mahogany table that, in good condition, would have brought thousands in a London antique shop, but it was not in good condition, not like it had been when its rightful owner had fled the country in 1967. Now, 23 years later, all the promise of those heady days after independence were distant memories – for the young man with the black headband, not even memories; he'd been one then, just a suckling. Everything he had ever known told him that life was nasty, brutish and short.

Now he approached the two men at the table and withdrew a plastic bag from under his shirt. There was writing on the bag: *Pick and Pay*. The black man at the table took the bag, set it on the table, and withdrew a wad of newspaper. He carefully opened the newspaper and spread it out, revealing a small mound of rough diamonds.

The Lebanese peered intently at the diamonds. "Ver' good," he said. "Ver' good."

With that, the bearded man reached into an open cardboard box under the table and withdrew an eight-kilo bag of cocaine, placed it into the Pick and Pay bag and handed it to the young man, who saluted and walked out into the steamy streets of Koidu.

CHAPTER 11

G.T. deeply regretted missing the board meeting. Hobnobbing with the likes of Randolph Thad was one of the real perks of his title, but he had to be at his father's funeral in Grosse Pointe.

At that, he was almost late. First there was the McLaughlin party, then he couldn't find Carrie for another half hour, and by the time he got home to pick up his wife, Cathy, and their son, Tommy, it was after 1:00. Nonetheless, the event went smoothly enough, and G.T. felt his father had received an appropriate honor for his life.

He drove back to Steuben alone, in the brand new Mercedes he had taken delivery on just the week before. G.T. loved cars, and was almost glad that the demands on the company airplanes occasioned by the board meeting had made it impossible for him to fly to the funeral and back. He was also glad that Cathy had volunteered to stay in Grosse Pointe with Carrie and Tommy to clean up the post-funeral details. He had planned to stay himself, but when he called the office for his messages, there was one from William Hargiss. G.T. was expected to be in Steuben bright and early in the morning.

On the drive, he thought about his father, a gentle, debonair man, an architect of considerable talent who, G.T. knew, had always felt he had squandered his life drawing blueprints for skyscrapers. G.T. knew something else about his father few other people knew. In spite of a 40-year marriage to G.T.'s mother, the old man had been a homosexual: discreet and controlled in his *sub rosa* life, he went to his grave believing he had kept his secret. He never learned that his son had discovered the truth. That was good, G.T. thought, as he sped through the darkness.

Now, the next morning, the phone rang before G.T. had a chance to review all of the overnight information. He sighed as he reached over to answer. "Huhh."

There was no mistaking Hargiss's voice on the other end of the line. "Get your ass up here, we need to talk."

G.T.'s office was on the second floor, where all of TLP's operations took place. The trading floor, section presidents, and the majority of the operations staff sat somewhere within eyesight of his office. Hargiss's office was on the sixth floor along with the finance geeks and attorneys, a considerable waste of office space as far as G.T. was concerned. He stubbed out his cigarette and headed for the elevator.

Hargiss's secretary waved G.T. through into the inner office.

"Close the door," Hargiss said by way of a greeting.

"What's up?" G.T. figured it would be something about McLaughlin.

"The board voted to spend a billion dollars to buy or build a couple of new product lines in the bio-tech area. Any suggestions?"

G.T. sat down as he let the news wash over him.

"Whew, no shit? Billion with a B?" G.T. had been arguing for two years that TLP ought to move into biochemistry, but had been unable to raise much apparent interest out of his boss. Hargiss had thrown him a few million to dabble with. G.T. had figured it was just to get him off Hargiss's back, but now it was clear the old man had been listening more closely than he thought. "Yeah, I got a couple of ideas, but nothing firm," he answered.

"You keep thinking about it, do some research, see what you think fits with our products. Somewhere out there is our next line. Tully's looking around for someone to run it. If you've got any candidates, give me a list."

"Yeah, I got one, a guy from Foremost that's trying to do a joint venture with us."

"On what?"

"Hell, I don't know, some kind of bio-tech product that uses something we make."

"Get me his name and what you can find out about the market he's trying to build. I'll pass it on to Tully."

"A billion dollars, no fuckin' way."

"Yeah, and don't spread that number around. The last thing we want to do is get everyone else looking at what we're doing. For God's sake, don't call any investment bankers."

"I'll call you with the name. I'll also get someone working to see what we can find on the marketplace. You're really serious about this, huh?"

"Serious as a heart attack."

What the hell was that guy's name? G.T. asked himself as he rode the elevator down to the second floor. Oh, yeah, Long, Gary Long. Shit, if they hired this guy, people would think he was related to one of the company's founders. G.T. was pretty sure he wasn't, but he didn't know much else about the man. Dr. Gary Long was a young hotshot with Foremost, a British-owned chemical company, and was hawking the latest biochemical conversion technology Foremost had developed.

In a standard chemical reaction, a reagent is used to force a new product to be developed. In a bio-conversion, tiny microbes called "bug" are introduced into a chemical soup called a media. The microbess munch happily away at the vat of chemicals until they eat everything in sight. To put it crudely, the microbes poop the finished product.

For three years, TLP had produced one of the most popular medias for bio-conversions. What had previously been a waste product of their hydrocarbon cracking process had become another valuable commodity. As the bio-conversion industry moved from its infancy through adolescence, it faced the problem of irregular supplies. Gary Long's negotiations were set against that background; the opportunity he saw was the chance to marry a technological breakthrough he and his fellow Foremost engineers had created with two assets TLP possessed: it was a source of the essential medium, and it had a marketing arm second to none. A TLP-Foremost joint venture had the potential to dominate the market for years, and in the invisible hand way of capitalism, benefit the entire industry, indeed the entire world. The self-serving profit motive was ultimately sensible from everyone's standpoint.

CHAPTER 12

One afternoon a couple of weeks later, Hargiss called down and told him, "Tully is here and has a few things for us."

Andrew Tully always looked like he had a two-day growth of beard. "How does he do that?" Hargiss had once asked G.T. "A man ought to be able to look like that only every other day."

Tully wasn't ever jovial, but this afternoon his voice had a little spring in it as called to G.T. at the door. "Good afternoon, G.T., how's the hammer hangin'?" he asked without getting up from the couch behind the coffee table.

"Low and to the right, Tully," G.T. replied. "What the hell's goin' on in your world anyway?"

"Mmm, this and that, this and that, you know, the usual stuff."

"Tully's found some interesting information he thought we might enjoy looking at," Hargiss said smiling. "Tully, give him the overview we just talked about." Hargiss stayed seated at his desk, and G.T. took a chair near the door.

"I got a few names from our friend Randolph Thad," Tully began. "Spent a few days checking them out, and came up with zip. A few slugs, a few sharp business people, but the bright ones were all goody two-shoes types, straight arrows that'd drive you crazy before they were done. Then I checked out the name you sent across. I gotta tell ya, that kid went right off the fuckin' charts."

G.T. stared for a second at Tully, but realized Tully had paused for effect, and waited for him to continue.

"This kid Gary Long was born and raised right here in Indiana, town called Madison, little less than two thousand people thirty miles north of Evansville. Born August one-nine, 1957. Two parents, two brothers and a sister, red brick ranch house on the edge of town. Father's retired now, ran a local car dealership. Daddy was once investigated but never charged with participating in a kickback scheme to get the most popular models."

"Little Gary's a pretty typical kid, played some high school baseball. That's Cincinnati Reds country down there, you know, and I really like this next part: he was a big fan of Pete Rose, you know, old 'Charlie Hustle.' He paused and looked over his papersat G.T. "I've always thought we should put a question on all our job application forms, 'Do you think Pete Rose ought to be in the Hall of Fame?' That'd weed out the goody-two-shoes types right there."

"Well, maybe we'll think about it," Hargiss said, chuckling. "What else you got?"

"Okay, Dad's a car dealer, right, so Gary boy drives a bright red sixty-eight GTO loaded with everything a teenager could ask for: mag wheels, big black tires with wide white lettering, jacked up with air shocks, cherry bomb mufflers and two big yellow flames down each side. You think he couldn't attract some chicks with that?

"The kid never got a ticket, which I figure is strange – probably his old man had an in with the local cops. The county bought lots of cars there. His main squeeze through high school is a gal named Tina Thomas, and she's a looker, a year behind him in school. They even get picked Homecoming King and Queen."

Tully stopped and handed several sheets of paper to Hargiss and G.T. "Then he goes to Iowa State, in agriculture, of all things. He starts showing some good initiative here. He gets into an honors program that allows him to graduate in four years with both bachelor's and master's degrees, works his butt off and graduates Come Loudy.

"Now, let's see, did I tell you that pretty Miss Tina has followed his ass all the way to Ames? Anyway, she did. I mean, Gary Baby is her ticket out of Madison, and she's going to keep her eye on the main chance, even if it means four years in fucking Iowa. So he's finishing up there and it seems like she puts her foot down and says it's time to get married or get on with life. He chooses the former, and they tie the knot on June the sixteenth, nineteen seventy-nine, precisely one week after graduation. Then they head off to Champaign where he's got a full scholarship to study for a PhD in combinatorial biofucking-chemistry at the University of Illinois.

"They get to Champaign and set up housekeeping. Tina takes a job at the mall. So she's putting the bread on the table, and he's cracking the books.

"Gary studies hard at Illinois and doesn't get any B's. He does pick up a role model, Dr. C.E. Bass, Jr. Professor Bass is a workaholic just like Gary's father. He's also got a cute little consulting contract with Technochem, which is apparently why, even before Gary graduates, he gets a job there, and as soon as they finish 'Pomp and Circumstance,' he and the missus are off to St. Louis to begin life in the corporate world. That was January, nineteen eighty-three."

Tully shuffled the papers around on the coffee table and held out some photographs, which G.T. leaned over to take. Blonde Tina looked gorgeous in her high school yearbook picture, perfect teeth flashing a winning smile, long hair pulled to one side and folded over her neck, eyes sparkling. Gary at the same age looked a little gawky, unsmiling, with noticeable sandy sideburns and a '70s sport coat. His current photo, however, radiated confidence. All traces of gawkiness had disappeared, along with the sideburns and the tacky jacket. G.T. looked at the photo intently, trying to find the Indiana boy behind the successful international executive looking back at him. "You get this from Foremost?" he asked Tully, holding up the picture.

Tully scowled at the interruption. "Yeah, from their annual report," he answered.

"Nice-looking guy," Hargiss said, taking the photo from G.T.

Tully scowled again, dropped his eyes to his notes, and resumed his report. "Now, pay attention to this," he said. "I'll get back to it in a minute. In February nineteen eighty-three, Gary becomes an official inventor, applies for and eventually gets a patent on some sort of process to divide a strain of bacteria. So when did he do the research? Must have been while he's at Illinois, which means the patent really ought to belong to the university. But, no, Gary-Boy takes it himself.

"Anyway, he goes to work at Technochem where he works under a guy named Dr. Chuck Kitch – you've met Kitch, G.T., at the association meetings: sharp guy, tall, thin, likes hookers with big tits. Chuck put him to work analyzing something new called bio-reagents.

"Then he gets hired by the Brit outfit, Foremost, and goes to work at their U.S. headquarters in Plainsboro, New Jersey in March nineteen eighty-four. He packed Tina in the Bonneville his Dad gave them as a wedding present and took Exit Ten from the New Jersey Turnpike." Tully looked up from his papers, clasped his hands behind his head and leaned back in the couch. "And you guys think you overpay me. Just think what they could have saved doing a little research.

"Gary and Tina buy a house in Plainsboro and he starts traveling immediately – U.S., Europe, Asia. Every other month he goes to England, where over the course of a year he gets to know the top company leaders pretty well. In April of nineteen eighty-five, they promote him to a job at the world headquarters.

"It was pretty rare for an American to be moved over to jolly old England. Only a couple of other people had ever done it. Somewhere in here, his marriage goes to shit. Tina went with him to England, but came home less than a year later. He was on the road all the time, she started fooling around with some British soccer player, he found out, they had a battle royal – they're in England after all – and before you can say 'cheerio, old chap,' she's back in the States with Mr. Soccer Balls, who is given a contract to play with one of the new U.S.

professional teams. When last sighted, they are cohabiting in Miami."

"Was Gary cheating on her, too?" G.T. asked.

"That's where the story of his patent gets interesting. A couple of the big Asian bio-tech operations are using his patent, and he's collecting royalties. Nothing really big – ten, maybe twelve thousand a year. Then, all of a sudden, they stop. No sign of them in his bank records.

"I figured that was odd, so I had my man in Seoul do a little late-night sleuthing, and it turns out Long's still getting paid, only now the money is going into an account right there in Korea. A joint account. Name one is Gary Long. Two is a Korean woman named Lee Cha. So my man looks up Ms. Cha, and it turns out she's got no husband and a little boy who looks like his daddy might have come from someplace like, oh, say, Indiana?"

"So, you're saying he had a kid by this Korean chickie?" G.T. asked.

Tully gave a little smirk and dug into his folder, extracting another photograph. "You tell me," he said, standing up and handing Hargiss the photo. A five-year-old looked up at Hargiss. There was no doubt the boy had Caucasian blood in him.

Hargiss handed the photo to G.T. and sat back in his chair. Maybe the woman blackmailed him, maybe he just had a conscience. Either way, it didn't really matter. The man had a secret. "I like people with a secret," he said softly, talking to himself. "Especially when I know what the secret is."

G.T. slid his glasses up onto his forehead, and peered at the photo, comparing it with the one of Long that Tully had handed out earlier. "Kid's a dead ringer," he said.

"Anything else, Tully?" Hargiss asked.

"That's about it. In October of eighty-eight, Foremost moved him back to New Jersey, where he kicked the renters out of the house and settled in. Apparently no qualms about wandering around the place he and Tina had shared. Their divorce became final last January. His duties now involve Foremost's acquisitions and joint venture operations in the U. S., which led to his correspondence with you, G.T.

"The word on the street is that this kid may be being groomed to become the president of Foremost, USA. His love life doesn't seem to have fared as well as his career. No new chickies reported, and his phone bills were clean, every number checked out to business or family.

"And that's my report," Tully said, handing out a few more papers and closing his notebook.

"Suckers, Tully, where do you get all this stuff?" G.T. said in amazement.

"You paid me to find a good candidate, that's what I did. I don't ask to get involved in your business, you don't need to know how I do mine," Tully puffed, obviously pleased with himself.

It was Hargiss's turn next. "Well G.T., what we've got here is a hard charging egghead with just a few little cracks. It doesn't get much better, huh?"

G.T. was still more interested in Tully than in Long. "I still can't get over how much information you were able to put together in such a short time," he said. "How many people did you have working on this?"

"Well, in this computer age, it doesn't take nearly as much time as you'd think. Most of the core information is available from the various credit reporting agencies, then all I have to do is fill in the blanks. I did steal a couple of yearbooks from Madison Senior High."

"And hacked into somebody's computer in Seoul," G.T. snorted.

"Which companies were paying him the royalties?" Hargiss asked.

Tully scowled and shuffled some papers. "The Korean outfit is called Daehan Hwa Hak," he said. "The other one's Japanese. Nippon Kagaka."

G.T. raised an eyebrow. "Biggest bio-tech outfit in the world," he said.

Hargiss turned his chair to face away from them and scanned the shelves behind him. "How much do you think it'll take to get Long hired?"

"A couple hundred a year and a car should get him in the fold pretty easily, plus moving expenses of course," Tully replied.

While he spoke, Hargiss stood up and pulled a book from a shelf, watching the shelf fold back into the wall and slide out of sight, exposing a safe door. As he began running the numbers he told G.T., "I've got to make one more phone call before I can say definitely to hire him, but you better get on the horn right away and call this kid. Tell him we'd like to talk further about his ideas, do whatever you have to to get him to come visit us."

Hargiss opened the safe and pulled out a stack of hundred dollar bills with a broad red rubber band around it. He handed it to Tully. "Thanks for your help on this, Tully," he said. "You've done your usual great job."

"Always happy to be of service," Tully grinned, stuffing the money in his jacket.

An hour later, G.T. had Gary Long on the telephone, and ten minutes after that, had convinced him to come to Steuben the following Tuesday.

"Which airport is easier, Midway or Indianapolis?" Long asked.

"Ah, we're about halfway, take your pick."

"All right. I'll try to get in by late morning."

CHAPTER 13

As it turned out, the Midway connection worked best. Gary Long put on his favorite suit, a dark blue tick-weave he'd had tailored on Saville Row when he was living in London, selected a sharp rep tie and took the early flight out of Newark. Landing at Midway, he spotted the yellow and black poster with the picture of O.J. Simpson on it and in a few minutes was behind the wheel of a shiny new Buick and on his way up the Chicago Skyway.

When he saw the sign for Gary, Indiana, he started playing word games. He was Gary, from Indiana, after all. And he was also Long, and on his way to the Tamson-Long company. Whoever Mr. Long had been, he was apparently, well, long gone. Gary had checked. The Tamson family was still around, but he could find no mention of any Longs in the company hierarchy. He wondered about that. Maybe he would ask G.T. Maybe the original Long had been a relative of his. He didn't know much about his father's side of the family. Grandpa Long had died before he was born, and Grandma Long was a distant memory. He thought she had died when he was four or so, maybe five, no more than that.

Anyway, Gary, Indiana is a hellhole, he thought. He took the exit for I-65 and headed southeast. There were no big towns between there and Steuben, just flat as a pancake farmland, row after row of September corn, tall and tanning. Dark brown silk tassels flopped against the still green ears. Interspersed were soybean fields, dappled yellow and green, with brown, almost-ripe pods hanging obliquely from the stalks.

Agriculture still interested Gary; once he could have seen himself as an actual farmer. But of course, Tina would have none of that. She had driven him toward more sophisticated goals, and in many ways, he knew he had her to thank for his present handsome salary and prospects. Of course, she's getting her share, he thought, living with that asshole soccer player, who she'll never marry because then the big alimony checks would stop.

As he came into Steuben, he was struck by how depressed it appeared. Given the phenomenal success of TLP, why didn't the town look more prosperous? That was a puzzle.

He drove up to the main gate at TLP and was pleasantly surprised when a guard offered to take him directly to G.T.'s office. As Gary drove through the large facility, following the guard's golf cart, he was shocked by how plain everything looked. The expected jungle of vats, pipes and low buildings rose from a bed of coarse gravel. Foremost had beautiful landscaping; TLP was utilitarian in the extreme, and for a company that did ten billion in sales, the headquarters was even more dismal than the plant.

The guard ushered Gary into a conference room next door to G.T.'s office. Gary looked around. The room was as luxurious as the grounds had been spartan: a glass-topped conference table on a sculpted marble base, soft leather swivel chairs all around, walnut wainscoting topped by expensive wallpaper, the whole gently lit by recessed lighting. Gary could hear G.T. ending his conversation with whoever was on the phone, and a couple of seconds later the man appeared at the door with a wide grin on his face.

"Good to meet ya', Gary."

Gary stood up to shake hands. "We met once before, at a chemical conference in Bermuda," he said, smiling at the portly, 60-year-old man in front of him, coatless, a silk tie loosened around his thick neck, sleeves rolled up. "I'm sure you don't remember it, but we met at the bar in the Mid-Ocean Club."

"I'm sorry, I don't remember," G.T. muttered, frowning. "I won't forget you again though, that's for sure." Fucking Tully knows what kind of a car the guy drove in high school, but missed this, he thought.

It was Gary's turn to smile. "I'm glad you liked the outline I sent you on a joint venture. I think it makes a lot of sense," he said.

G.T. figured he had two options; he could bullshit for a while and then get around to talking to the kid about a job, or he could go straight to the heart of the matter. If this kid was as aggressive as Tully had portrayed him, he could save a lot of time.

"Well, just being honest, I didn't care much for your proposal. Hell, we've had you guys, ChemIdeas, 3-C and a bunch of others that want to do a joint venture with us. But frankly we've decided, what the hell do we need them for?" Gary's smile had by now left his face. G.T. pressed on.

"All that bureaucracy at those other companies would just cramp our style. Shit, I do our engineering on the back of a paper napkin," G.T. said, his eyes darting around the room as if in search of an actual napkin.

"Why did you want me to come out then?" a somewhat puzzled Gary asked.

"Aren't you tired of commuting through all that fucking traffic around New York? Why don't you come here to work for us and head up a bio-conversion division and we'll just do it ourselves?"

Gary's jaw fell with surprise, and G.T. decided to keep him off balance. "Look, were going to invest over a billion dollars in this division, maybe even twice as much, and we expect it to be the fastest growing division of our company."

Gary just nodded.

"You'd be coming in at a good time; there are a lot of guys in their mid-sixties around here. There'll be plenty of opportunities to move up. A lot of it depends on you."

Gary stammered a bit. "Thanks," he said. "But I'm not really sure what you want to do."

G.T. smiled. "William Hargiss, our Chairman and CEO, doesn't want a joint venture, he wants to build our own division," G.T. said in a slow, singsong voice, arms outstretched, palms open and beating in the air in rhythm with the cadence of his words. It was as if he were explaining an obvious answer to a child.

He stood up again. "Well, hell, why don't we go talk to Hargiss about all of this?" he said. "It's really his idea to try and hire you. Let's see if we can get him on the phone." G.T. pushed the speakerphone button and dialed Hargiss's extension. Hargiss answered and G.T. said, "William, I've got Gary Long here from Foremost, he'd like to visit with you about your thoughts on the new division."

In the elevator, G.T. began telling Gary about the TLP philosophy. "We try to enter markets we can dominate within a couple of years. You know, build it quick with lots of extra capacity, and try to be vertically integrated so we can be the lowest cost producer." The door opened and they stepped out onto the plush carpet of the sixth floor foyer.

G.T. continued to talk as they sat down in chairs outside Hargiss's office. "We keep the prices at our break-even until we eliminate a lot of the marginal players, then we only have the big boys to play with. It generally works out pretty well for everyone." Gary was watching G.T. intently, trying to digest the meaning of what he was being told. Just then Hargiss came to the door and grabbed his hand before Gary could stand up. "Come on in!" he boomed.

Gary scrambled to his feet. The old man's arm was around his back, guiding him through the door and into a velour chair. "I can't tell you how glad I am to have you here talking to us, Gary. TLP is a great place to work. Our managers have a lot of freedom; we move quick because we don't second guess 'em. We don't have any bullshit organizational charts, no budgets, no three-year plans. We just work. Take names and kick ass." Hargiss was standing over him, peering down, sensing the the young man's confusion. "You could be the golden boy around here," he said, dropping his voice several decibels. "None of us has the kind of technical background you've got, and I tell you the field is wide open for you to go a long way if your product lines perform like you've told G.T. they can in some of your proposals."

He moved away now, walking around a huge mahogany desk. Gary watched Hargiss's face become animated as he talked. The old man's piercing eyes were alive with excitement.

"We're gonna make bio-tech the focus division for the next generation. Hell, the board voted to spend a billion dollars without any real proposal in front of them, that's how dedicated we are to doing this."

"Thanks for the confidence," Gary said, trying not to stammer, "but I'm not sure why you want me."

"Your name keeps coming up a lot, so you're obviously well connected in the industry and doing a lot of things right. I'll let G.T. fill you in on all the details, but I can tell you this, I want you here working for us."

The phone rang and Hargiss grabbed it with his left hand, sticking the right out to shake Gary's again as he cradled the phone. It seemed like they were being dismissed. Gary stood up and followed G.T. to the door. "Think about it: how many Fortune Fifty companies can you walk into and visit directly with the chairman?" he heard Hargiss say. Gary stopped and turned, saw the telephone pressed against Hargiss's chest as he talked, almost shouting, as if they were already out the door. "This is something you aren't gonna find every day, Gary. It's a chance to work without all the hoopla and bullshit that go with it. We'd like to offer you a job paying a hundred and fifty thousand a year and increasing that to two hundred in six months, with seventy-five hundred shares of stock options good for five years and a brand-new Cadillac you can go pick out. Whadda you think, Gary?"

Hargiss hunched his shoulders down and leaned over the desk, as though to tell a secret. "For what it's worth, I think you should take it," he said.

Gary reflected before saying anything. He should have been ticked off that he was brought there under false pretenses, but at the same time, they weren't offering a job to the guys from ChemIdeas, 3-C or any of the other companies they had proposals from. It was flattering no matter how you looked at it. "I'd like to see the plant and think a little about it," he finally responded.

"Sure, hell. G.T., have Billie Mitchell show him around." Hargiss suddenly seemed to remember the telephone, clicked off the hold button and put it up to his ear. "Hang on Sam, I'll be right with you," he said, set the phone on the desk and leaned over it again, lowering his voice to the level Gary now understood to be mock-conspiratorial.

"Billie's our senior plant engineer and can answer any questions you have. When you get done, get back with G.T. and work something out. I really want this to happen."

Billie Mitchell proved to be a good choice to take Gary around the plant. A plainspoken, thick-handed farm boy, Mitchell couldn't say enough good things about the management style and how easy the people were to work with. By the end of the tour, Gary began seriously considering the offer. His love life was non existent, so there really wasn't anyone or anything to hold him in New Jersey, but the thought of moving back to the middle of nowhere in Indiana didn't have a lot of appeal either; he'd come a long way from Madison. Then there was the house in Jersey. He didn't want to rent it again, and he knew he'd never get his money back on it. But here it was, the chance to work without all the bullshit, the chance to be the captain of his own ship, maybe even the entire Navy.

Billie dropped him off at G.T.'s office, and G.T. enthusiastically greeted him. "Well, whadda you think?"

"It sure seems like a great opportunity, but I've got this house in New Jersey that I probably can't re-sell quickly."

G.T. didn't hesitate, "How much is it worth?"

"Probably two hundred fifty thousand, but it'll take a while to get it."

"How much do you owe on it?"

"About a hundred and forty"

"Come on up with me, let's tell Zack Brilley, our legal beagle, to prepare an assignment form, you sign the house over to us, and we'll write you a check for the difference."

Darn, doesn't anything slow them down, Gary thought, and before he could react, G.T. moved on. "What's your favorite color?" he asked. "Let's order that Cadillac so it'll be here when you start. Then after we take care of the paperwork on the house, you can take our Falcon 50 back home and give those guys at Foremost notice tomorrow."

Gary replayed the last two minutes of conversation in his head. It was hard not to be impressed.

"I'm supposed to take my rental car back to Midway," he said.

"Oh, shit, Gary, I guess that queers the deal then," G.T. boomed. "I don't know how in the hell we can solve that one!" He was grinning ear to ear, knowing he had caught his fish.

"I tell you what," Gary said, adopting a mock-serious tone. "You get that rental car taken care of and I'll go in to Foremost tomorrow and give my notice."

G.T. spread his arms wide. "Welcome to TLP, son," he said. "And let me tell you, you'll make more money here than you can ever believe." G.T. paused. "As long as you perform." Then he picked up the phone, called Brilley and put the wheels in motion. By 7:00 that night, Gary was back in New Jersey with a $110,000 check in his pocket and a message from a moving company on his answering machine. He never did learn if G.T. got the Buick taken back to Midway or just kept the damn thing.

CHAPTER 14

On October 12, 1990, at 7:30 in the morning, Gary Long parked his Bonneville in a visitor's space, walked through the revolving doors of TLP's headquarters and found his way to G.T.'s office. G.T. looked up from the stack of papers on his desk and quickly extended his hand. "Great to have you here Gary," he said with a grin. "Come on, let me show you your office."

They walked across the trading floor and into a smartly furnished room on the other side. "If you don't like any of this stuff, just tell me and I'll throw it to hell out and get what you want," G.T. said. "But this ought to get you going."

Gary sat down at the bare desk and looked around at the bare walls. "Decorate it any way you want," G.T. said. "Bring in your personal stuff, order anything, don't worry about the cost. Whatever your taste is. We got everything from fine art to fish tanks here."

He took a puff on his cigarette, and as there was nothing resembling an ashtray in the room, walked out the door. Gary followed him, and watched as he flipped his ash into a waste-basket next to an empty secretary's desk. "I'll get a steno up from the pool tomorrow," he said. For today, you can use Joyce for whatever you need. Whenever you find somebody you like, hire her."

Then he turned to face Gary again. "How did Foremost take it?" he asked. "I hope it pissed them off."

Pissing Foremost off had not been on Gary's top ten list of things to do. "Well, I don't think they were happy about losing me, but they understood. They just wished it wasn't TLP. I think they're a little afraid of you guys."

That seemed to hit a sweet spot with G.T. "Woo hoo, damn good," he said. "They should be. Geez, I'd've loved to been there for that conversation."

They went back to G.T.'s office. Here's the fine art, Gary thought, noticing what looked like expensive original oils on the walls. I wonder who has the fish tank?

"What do you know about artificial sweetener?" G.T. asked abruptly, stubbing out his cigarette.

"Well, not a lot," Gary answered, sinking into a cordovan leather chair. "Originally introduced as a low-calorie alternative to sugar...."

"Right, but it doesn't have to be low-cal."

Gary thought he grasped where G.T. was going. "True," he said. "And it can be made with biotechnology. A couple of Asian companies are already doing it."

"Nippon Kagaka, for example," G.T. said, intently scanning Gary's face for any reaction to the mention of one of the companies that had purchased his patent.

"Right," Gary agreed, his face impassive. "They've gotten the price down to where they can compete with the natural sugars and syrups."

G.T. pulled some files from a pile on his desk. "Well," he said, "we're going after their market. William wants to dominate it within two years. We've got a pilot plant in Memphis in operation already, and I'm going to build you the biggest fucking sweetener factory in the world, right here in Steuben."

"Two years!" Gary exclaimed. "You think you can get a plant built in that time, a marketing and distribution network set up?"

"No," G.T. smiled, rubbing his hands in front of him. "I think *you* can."

Gary swallowed hard, but G.T. didn't seem to notice. "You don't have to actually build the plant. I'll do that. I'm the best fucking plant engineer in the world. Just tell me what you want and I'll have that sucker up and running so fast it'll make your head spin. I fucking own the police, the mayor, transportation department, you name it. You focus on getting us ready to sell the product."

"Okay," Gary grinned. "I'm a believer. But remember, the market for sweeteners is incredibly complex, and the price of the raw commodity can be the smallest part of the final price. You've got tariffs, taxes, transportation costs..."

"Yeah, and every one of those factors works to our advantage," G.T. said. "We ought to be able to undercut the shit out of those Asian bastards in Europe and the U.S. As soon as we go on line, the price is going to drop, and we've got enough capital behind this thing to sustain losses for a lot longer than they can.

"Everything we've done is in these folders," he continued, handing them to Gary. "Your job is to take it from there and make us king of the hill."

Gary went back to his office and began to pore over the files. TLP planned to sell its sweetener in the wholesale market under the brand name Sugere. The immediate problem would be determining the level of market interest in the product. They figured to have two advantages. Because Sugere would have, pound for pound, 20 times the sweetening power of sugar, they could compete on a price basis with producers of the natural product. And because they would be producing Sugere in a free-flowing crystalline form, it would have superior handling properties over the powdered Asian-produced artificial sweeteners already on the market. In addition, the crystalline product would have baking qualities identical to sugar, which powdered artificial sweeteners did not.

A market analysis showed that the potential was huge. From cola to ketchup, there was scarcely an aisle in the supermarket that didn't have dozens of products which listed some sort of sweetener among their ingredients. The more Gary read, the more he was impressed with the sagacity of TLP's decision. But the weight of his responsibility also hit home for the first time. They were gambling a billion dollars on him.

G.T. came back into his office, and they spent an hour discussing plans for the new division. Then they went to look at the site for the new bio-tech plant Gary would be running. They took the elevator to the basement parking garage, slipped inside G.T.'s black 500 SL and drove to the west side of the lot. There G.T. showed Gary a spot of bare ground with a construction trailer at one corner. "In a week we'll have concrete poured and in a few months, we'll have the building covered and be working inside," G.T. said. "We build while others are just thinking about it. Then we fix stuff on the fly. It costs a little bit more sometimes, but it lets us get capacity up and in the market quick."

For the rest of the morning, they toured each of the eleven other plant operations in Steuben. As they continued on, Gary became more and more impressed with the advanced level to which TLP had taken vertical integration. Everything fit like a hand in a glove. It was seamless; each component interfaced with the others for maximum profitability, yet each was capable of running alone for maximum dependability. Gary had never seen anything like it.

They climbed back into G.T.'s now dusty Mercedes and headed back to "corporate," as Gary had learned the executive office building was called. "Well Gary, whadda you think?"

"I've never seen anything so well put together," Gary answered truthfully, his earlier doubts about G.T. melting away. As they got out, Gary brushed the dust off his hands and G.T. snapped at the garage attendant, "Don't forget to wash my car again."

They started to walk to the elevator, when suddenly G.T. stopped and whirled around. "Hells bells," he said. "I almost forgot." He grabbed Gary by the arm and led him around to the other side of the elevator stack. There sat a shiny new El Dorado, powder blue with a moon roof. G.T. swung the driver's side door open and motioned Gary to get in.

Grinning, Gary slid into the leather seat and admired the car's interior. "It's all yours, Gar," G.T. beamed. "Biggest fucking engine they make, every goddamn option available. Look, it's even got a CD player and a built-in phone. My Mercedes doesn't even have that!"

G.T. fumbled in his pockets for a moment while Gary gazed at the luxury interior. "Shit, the keys are up in my office," G.T. said. "Otherwise, we'd go for a spin right now."

When they reached Gary's office, a man about his age came out of the adjacent room. When G.T. saw him, his face widened into a grin. "Gary, this is Ralph Sori, Ralph, this is Gary Long, the new president of our new bio-tech division." Then he stopped for a second and grinned to himself. "Can you believe this?" he said shaking his head. "I've got a professional football player and a Ph fucking D sitting by each other. I can't believe we've got guys like that in Steuben." Then he turned on his heel and walked to his office.

Ralph grinned and shook his head. "Ol' G.T.'s a card, isn't he?"

"You played football?" Gary asked.

"Yeah, I played linebacker for the Bears for five years until the knees gave out. I came here about five months ago."

"Well, I'm sure I should recognize your name, but I was overseas most of that time, and I guess I've lost track of football." He was surprised how small Ralph seemed in person; he had figured a linebacker to be bigger. "I like it a lot better than soccer, though," he added, quickly repressing thoughts of the soccer player who had destroyed his marriage. "That's all they play in Europe, and they have the nerve to call it football.

"Nice to meet ya," he grinned. "This is really some place."

"You haven't seen the half of it yet. This is an incredible place to work," Ralph said shaking his head.

At noon, G.T. stopped by and asked Gary and Ralph to join him for lunch. They headed off to the ground floor, which housed the executive dining room. When they arrived, Gary looked around. It seemed to be filled with old men. Most were clearly over 60, and a few looked older than that. Except for the servers, there were no women at all.

Gary couldn't help commenting. "I'd say," he half-whispered to G.T., "that I see what you meant about the opportunity for – he hesitated just a fraction of a second – *guys* our age to move up."

"Fuckin' A," G.T. responded. "When you, Ralph and I walked in here, we lowered the average age of the room by twenty years. Of course," he added, "There is Howard. He pretty much avoids this place. God only knows where he eats lunch."

"Eats?" Ralph asked, sardonically.

"Whatever," G.T. responded.

"But don't sell these guys short," he added. "They're pretty sharp.

Learned their stuff directly from William C. Hargiss University, most of them, and that's a good school to go to in this business – or any business. They built this company, but the challenge now is to keep it growing into the next century. That's where you guys come in."

"There's a young guy," Gary said, pointing to a man sitting by himself at table in the corner. He didn't look 40, with blond hair, horn-rimmed glasses and an expensive, preppy look about him.

"Buford Carney," G.T. said, with an air of disdain. "Call him Buffy. His granddaddy was one of the richest men in the world. Now his daddy is. Someday he will be. Until then, he's cooling his heels in our PR department."

"Actually, I think he's pretty sharp," Ralph said.

CHAPTER 15

"So, have you gotten your biotechnology operations started yet?" Admiral Decatur asked William Hargiss.

They were seated at a polished mahogany table in Hargiss's suite at the Willard Hotel in downtown Washington, just a block from the White House.

"As a matter of fact," Hargiss said, "the guy starts work today. Thanks for running the traps on him."

"You really think this new division is going to be a major new source for us?"

Hargiss took a sip of the coffee on the table in front of him. "Unless I miss my guess, this will be number one for both us and TLP in a couple of years."

"You confident this guy Long has what it takes?"

"He's a hard-charger, smart as a tack and I think he'll play ball. We'll suck him in piece by piece, and we've got the Korean kid as an ace in the hole."

Decatur got up from his chair. He was a tall man, still athletic at 60, with short, salt and pepper hair. He walked to the window and looked out over Pennsylvania Avenue toward the Washington Monument. "You know," he said. "I have access to DNA technology. I could prove paternity if you want to know for sure."

Hargiss took another sip of coffee. "How would it work?"

Decatur turned from the window. "I'd need a sample of Long's DNA. A blood sample would do. If you can get me that, I'll get some from the kid. Then the lab boys do a match."

"If it's that easy, let's do it. It might come in handy."

"Consider it done," Decatur said, seating himself at the table. "Now, let's talk about the situation in West Africa."

CHAPTER 16

Auntie Jane died of her wounds two weeks after the rebels had come to the village. Monoh died the same day. Or at least that was the story the villagers told.

"Someone must go to Freetown and tell what happened here," Monoh had said. "I will go."

"But the rebels know you," Sesay had argued. "When they come back for the diamonds, they will ask questions, and they will torture us."

"We will dig two graves," Monoh replied. "One for Auntie Jane and one for me. You will tell them we are both dead."

While the men were digging the graves, Monoh stole off into the bush. When the rebels came back, they beat Sesay and the other men for wasting their time digging graves when they should have been digging for diamonds.

Monoh made his way through the Loma Mountains, careful to avoid villages. Once, he saw a group of black headbands, but they did not see him. In three days, he reached the Sewa River. From atop a small hill, he saw people digging for diamonds in the gravel beside the river. Three-foot high mounds of gravel marked the progress of their work. All day, he waited and watched.

When it was dark, he carefully skirted the digging grounds, reaching the river upstream from the village. Cautiously working his way down the bank of the river, ever alert for crocodiles, he found what he was looking for: a small wooden flat-bottomed boat. There was neither pole nor oar in the boat, so he looked around, eventually finding a small piece of wood. It would have to do.

"May God forgive me for stealing this boat," he said to himself as he soundlessly pushed the little craft into the river. With his improvised paddle, he steered out into the current. Although he struggled mightily, he could barely keep the boat moving across the river. As it was, the current carried him more than a mile downstream before he reached the other side. Scrambling up the bank, he tried to moor the boat into the mud, so its owner might have a chance to find it. But he tripped on a rock and lost his grip. Sadly, he watched the boat float downstream.

Stopping every minute to listen for the sounds of night animals and spirits, he made his way through the bush for an hour, until he crossed a dirt track leading north and east. He found a spot of soft dirt near the track and slept.

"What are you doing here, father?" he heard a gruff man's voice say, and awoke in the early light to find himself surrounded by a small band of warriors. Two of them had old rifles; the others had sharp spears. They wore no headbands. Monoh had little choice but to answer the man's question.

"I am on a journey to Makeni," he said.

"No," the man replied sternly. "You must join us and become a Kamajor."

So, Monoh thought, they are Kamajors. Tribal warriors come together to fight the rebels, to do the work the Army was incapable of doing, or refused to do.

"I am an old man," Monoh said, rising to a squatting position. "I would be of little use as a warrior. But I must go to Makeni, and then to Freetown, and report the murder of Auntie Jane."

The man rested his rifle on the ground and shook his head sadly. "So many murders," he said softly. "And there is no one in Makeni or Freetown who will care about one more woman."

"All the same," Monoh protested. "I must try. I have risked everything on my journey, not just for me, but for my whole village."

The man rubbed his chin with his big black hand. "Go then, and try. Tell them what happened to Auntie Jane, and that it is happening every day.

"But tell them this, too," he added, drawing himself up to his full height and clenching his fist. "Tell them the Kamajors will never give up until the last black headband is dead."

Monoh stood up. "I will tell them," he said, as if he were giving an oath. "I will find someone who will listen and help us, if I have to walk all the way to London."

The man smiled. "Then I appoint you the Ambassador of the Kamajors to Freetown and London," he said loudly. "May the Spirit of the Mountains go with you, and may you return at the head of a mighty army, bringing rifles and ammunition so we may rid Salone of the black headbands."

"This I will do," Monoh said. "Or I will die trying."

CHAPTER 17

By the end of his first day at TLP, Gary felt like he was making progress in understanding the scope of his duties. His priorities would be establishing a marketing plan, setting up distribution networks and hiring the staff necessary to implement all of TLP's plans.

He asked Joyce to type up several sheets of notes he had produced on a yellow legal pad, and turned his attention to the search for other bio-products that fit the ambitions of the company. He'd brought a stack of literature with him, and was so absorbed in reading and making notes he didn't notice the time flying by. Finally, he looked up and saw Joyce standing over his desk.

"Here's your material," she said, handing him a file folder.

"Oh, thanks," he said, opening the file to find neatly typed pages in front of his originals.

"Look," she said. "It's after six, and everybody else has gone. Since you don't have a key yet, I wondered how much longer you wanted to work."

Oh, God, he thought. She's stayed around just waiting for me. "Let's go," he said. "I think I've done enough damage for Day One." Then, suddenly, he remembered something. "Speaking of keys," he said. "Do you know where G.T. put my car keys? He said they were in his office." No need to drive the old Bonneville one more day, he thought, wondering how much he could sell it for.

Joyce found the keys.

It's been a good first day, Gary thought as he sat behind the wheel of the Cadillac. Ralph had invited him for dinner at the Country Steakhouse, and they set a time of 8:00. That meant Gary had almost an hour and a half to kill, so he decided just to drive around instead of going back to his temporary quarters at the Holiday Inn.

It was warm for October, well into the 70s, with a perfect bright autumn sun, now clinging to life just above the western horizon. In a couple of weeks, the time will change, Gary thought, and it'll be dark by now. He headed the Cadillac east, putting the sun at his back and out of his eyes. After checking out the air conditioning in the car, he turned it off and opened the window, feeling the rush of pleasant air wash over him. The smoothness of the luxury car's ride made it almost seem that car and man were standing still, while the landscape rushed past on either side of the unchanging road.

He watched one house approach on his right, noticing as it drew near that it was abandoned. An unruly vine ran up and over the sagging porch, scrambling for the eaves. Beside the house was a moss-covered apple tree bending with the weight of its fruit.

Unbidden, thoughts of his own mortality entered his mind. What would people say when he died? What would he have been? Gary was used to thinking of himself as a scientist, heir to the legacy of Newton and Einstein. But each year he seemed to morph ever more clearly into a business executive. What would be the next phase? If he made a graph and drew a trend line from scientist to executive, and then extended the line, what would be at the next node? Maybe nothing – maybe this was to be his life, years of Cadillac success until all the red fruit of his being, ripe to the core, fell and rotted into the black Indiana dirt.

He looked into his rear-view mirror and watched the horizon gobble up the sun. When it finally disappeared, he turned around and drove back to Steuben.

Ralph was waiting at the bar when Gary arrived. "Hey, you're right on time, bud," he said.

"Yeah, not much to do to make me late."

A bearded bartender appeared in front of him, and Gary ordered a light draft beer.

"That G.T. is something else isn't he?" Ralph chuckled as the bartender brought Gary's beer.

"Yeah," Gary said, shaking his head. "I figured at first he was a lot of hot air, but the more I see of TLP's operations, the more impressed I am. He can really make stuff happen huh?"

"Yeah, the guy's a legend around the plant. When he and Mr. Hargiss got here, TLP was virtually bankrupt. There's a lot of stories about how these guys turned it all around."

"What do you mean?"

"Most of what they did was just smart management, new ideas and an aggressive attitude."

"And the rest?"

"Well, there's lots of rumors, I really don't know ."

Now Gary's curiosity was fully aroused. "What rumors?"

Ralph leaned back on his barstool and stared at Gary for a minute while he thought about the best way to answer the question. "Let's just say these guys play on a pretty fast and loose track. They keep one step ahead of all the regulations and never really get in serious trouble, but if there's a way to step back and forth over the line between right and wrong without getting caught, these guys'll do it in a heartbeat – if they can make more money. It's all about making more money, right?"

The rest of the night they swapped small talk about friends, family and how they had grown up. By 10:00, Gary was tired, and he begged Ralph's indulgence in calling it a night. The conversation had its effect, however, and Gary tossed and turned as Ralph's words echoed in his mind.

The next morning, Gary looked up when a young man walked into his office. He knew without asking that it had to be Howard Hargiss. He was the spitting image of his father, a little heavier and taller perhaps, but the same angular build and the same face, minus 30 years. Howard introduced himself and asked Gary to follow him back to his office, in the opposite corner from G.T.'s.

"Have a seat, Gary," Howard said ushering him into the office. "I'm sorry I didn't get to meet you yesterday, but I was wrestling some alligators in Cleveland. Anyway, it's damn good to have you here. I can tell you several of us have been arguing for a bio-tech division for a long time."

Gary smiled as he seated himself, noticing the large fish tank beside Howard's desk. Two dozen or more exotic-looking fish circled amid pieces of coral, rocks and seaweed. On the credenza behind the desk, Gary noticed a light, TV and computer. The TV was on, the audio muted. Regis and Kathie Lee seemed to be arguing about something. Something scattered the fish.

"Thanks, it feels good to be here." Gary replied, turning his eyes from the fish to Howard.

"I think you'll find this a hell of a place to work. I focus on pricing strategies, and on hedging our raw commodity ingredients. TLP is something very, very special. I've never seen anything like it. My dad wanted me to come here right out of college, but I wasn't ready, so I worked trading commodities on the floor in Chicago. I made a pretty good living, but this place has more opportunity in it than a Catholic girls school."

Gary snickered at the word picture that Howard had painted. One of the phones on Howard's desk rang and he made the receiver jump up into his hand by hitting it on one side.

"Yeah," Howard said into the phone. "How much room do you see under us?" As he paused, he reached for some fish food next to the tank, and shook a few flakes into the water. "Well, let's lower our bid to three-eighths, a quarter over and give discretion to move another point if we have to, to pick up the numbers we've got authority for."

Financial stuff, Gary thought. It sounded impressive, and Gary would have been willing to sit and listen, but Howard hung up, scowled and said, "Well, shit. That means I've got to get my butt on the phone, but let's get together later, or tomorrow for sure. We should have a good, long chat."

CHAPTER 18

One of Gary's first hires was a man named Brad Redfoot. Redfoot had coal-black hair and a square, pockmarked face that bore a look of intensity bordering on ferocity. He would be Gary's right hand man on the marketing side. Redfoot had been working in St. Louis for Samuran, the American subsidiary of the big Japanese biochemistry firm, Nippon Kagaka. Nippon Kagaka would be TLP's largest competitor in the artificial sweetener business, so Gary decided to try and hire someone with expertise in an existing customer base rather than try to reinvent the wheel.

Gary had just finished hiring Brad and was showing him out the door when G.T. rounded the corner coming out of his office. "Where are you from?" G.T. asked Brad, extending his hand.

"Uh, I live in St. Louis," a somewhat hesitant Redfoot replied.

"Brad Redfoot, G.T. Binghamton," Gary said, a little trepidation in his voice.

"St. Louis! See this watch?" G.T. stuck out his wrist and displayed a thin gold watch. Then he continued, "I bought this watch in St. Louis and I'd tell you what it cost, but if I did it'd make you puke. In fact I liked St. Louis so much that I went back the next weekend and bought a Ferrari. I liked it so much I went back the next weekend and bought another one." It was pure G.T. "Hey it's nice to meet you," he said, grinning. "Hope you come to work for us." Then he was off.

Redfoot seemed a little shocked as he walked out the door with Gary but his encounter with G.T. didn't shake his conviction to be a part of TLP. Gary told the story to Ralph Sori, with whom he regularly swapped G.T. anecdotes. "Oh, man, that's G.T.," Ralph said laughing.

Gary spent day after weary day on the road, but by Thanksgiving he had his distribution network in place. The difficulty had been in getting commitments, because TLP didn't have any product. Luckily most distributors didn't have ready access to the other artificial sweetener sources so that made it easier to get them to agree to come on board with TLP.

Whenever Gary wasn't traveling, he would visit the plant construction site. G.T. had been right, the plant was going up at lightning speed. It had been more than braggadocio when he said he owned the whole town.

The Memphis pilot plant was pumping out five or six truckloads of Sugere per week, and Brad Redfoot was kept busy moving it to food and beverage manufacturers across the country.

Redfoot was telling all his customers about the new source for Sugere they would have in a few months. Interest in the product was running high, and several large companies wanted sample product ASAP for experimentation in setting up their proper mix ratios. TLP was on track to be the largest artificial sweetener producer in the world within a year and a half of breaking ground.

One evening during one of their frequent dinners out, Ralph Sori began to quiz Gary. "Hey, what do you know about G.T. hiring that guy from ChemIdeas, Paul Rodgers?" he asked.

"Well, we hired him away from C-I a couple of weeks ago to help start up a combinatorial vitamin plant. Why do you ask?"

"Well, the rumor is Rodgers brought more than his expertise with him to TLP."

"What are you talking about?"

"I'm told he arrived with a small sample of the bacteria that C-I used to produce their Vitamin C. The rumor is that G.T. paid him a lot of money to bring that sample with him. How much is something like that worth?"

Gary thought about what to say next. This was the first he had heard about TLP having access to the technology. In fact, he had spent much of the day on the phone trying to find a partner to help them engineer a microbe. He'd even told G.T. about his efforts and had been given a grunt of approval. He decided to play it straight and see what else, if anything, Ralph knew.

"Generally speaking, licensing a technology of this sort has an up-front cost of three to five million. On top of that you generally have to pay royalties to the originator of the bug on each pound of product you produce." Then Gary got quiet and reflected. At first, he thought it odd that G.T. would make a deal like that at this time. They were nowhere near ready to begin actual Vitamin C production. But then it dawned on him: by stealing the technology this early, TLP's researchers would have a chance to reproduce the bacteria in some form other than the original, thus wiping out the genetic "footprint" that would lead anyone checking on the process to determine whether or not TLP had independently arrived at a new bacteria that produced Vitamin C.

Ralph quickly dropped the subject and the talk turned to more mundane matters for the rest of the evening, but Gary was determined to get to the bottom of Ralph's conversation.

Gary cornered Redfoot the first thing the next morning. "Yeah, I heard it too," Brad said.

"What do you think I should do?" Gary asked.

"I don't know, you should probably find out if it's true before you do anything," Brad said.

Gary mulled it over the rest of the morning and finally decided to buttonhole G.T. the next day, a Saturday, when there were fewer people around and the atmosphere was more casual.

Saturday morning appearances were mandatory for all divisional managers or higher. G.T. was already at his desk when Gary arrived at 7:00.

"Hey, G.T., got a minute?" Gary asked.

"Sure, come on in, Gary," he boomed back.

"Man, there's a rumor flying around the plant that this guy Rodgers we hired from C-I stole the Vitamin C bug from them and gave it to our research department," Gary said with a voice that was a little squeaky.

"Yeah, it's no big deal," G.T. said smiling. "We got the cellulose bug the same way when we hired that little shit Al Franklin from 3-C. He brought the cellulose additive organisms with him when he came on board. We do it all the time. We know what we're doing here, Gary. Don't worry about it. You let me handle that end of things."

Gary was stunned. G.T. had not only confirmed that it had happened, but that it was normal company policy. He decided to talk to Redfoot about it again, and made his way up to the third floor, where Brad's office was.

"G.T. just told me it's all true, and it seems like it's more the rule than the exception. What the hell do you think we should do?" Gary asked, sinking into a chair in Brad's cluttered office.

Brad pursed his lips and thought a moment before he spoke. "For now, I'd say nothing, just try to get people to shut up about it and we'll figure out what to do about it all later," he suggested, as unsure as Gary was about what they were hearing.

"I don't know," Gary said. "For all the things I really like about this place..." he said, shaking his head, eyes downcast, fingers tapping his knees, not finishing the sentence. Ralph had talked about how Hargiss and G.T. played fast and loose. Now, he had hard evidence, and he didn't like it at all.

"Look," Brad said. "Every company in the world cuts corners. What people like you and I have to do is keep our heads down and make sure we don't do anything crooked ourselves."

Gary wasn't convinced. He couldn't remember anything at Foremost that hadn't been on the up and up. But maybe he was just naive, maybe he hadn't gotten close enough to the top to see it.

"If you insist on purity in the company you work for, you'll never get a job anywhere," Brad said.

That's probably right, Gary thought. He didn't like it, but for the moment he couldn't think of anything to do except try to contain the damage.

First thing Monday morning, Gary headed out to the construction site and located Rodgers.

"Hey, Paul," Gary said, "I don't think you should be telling everyone about what you did and how much you got paid."

Paul gave Gary a blank look for a second and then his face reflected that he caught Gary's point. "Hey, I'm not talking to anyone," he said. "G.T.'s the one blabbing all over town about it."

The construction of the plant was progressing so rapidly Gary couldn't believe it. G.T. ran the operation so well that other than trying to figure out what was going where, Gary really had little to do with it. G.T. would occasionally ask him things like what kinds of bags and handling equipment they should use. Other than that, Gary had little involvement in the building process.

Even so, he spent a lot of time in G.T.'s office. One morning, he arrived to find the door closed, and Joyce scrunched up her nose when Gary asked her who G.T. was meeting with. "Ralph," she said cryptically.

Gary decided to sit in the outer office and wait, and in a few minutes, the door opened and Ralph walked out. When he saw Gary, he grinned, and surreptitiously whistled a few bars of "La Marseillaise."

"I've been promoted," he told Gary a little later when Gary stuck his head in Ralph's office. "Director of Commodity Sales for Europe. I'm off to Gay Paree next week."

"That's great," Gary exclaimed. "You'll love it there. Bummer for me, though. I'll miss you." It was true. Ralph was great company, and always seemed to be in tune with everything going on. They shared one last meal, and Gary gave him all the advice he could think of about living overseas.

CHAPTER 19

The woman smiled at Monoh. "They tell me," she said, "that you are the Ambassador of the Kamajors." She seemed to be taking him seriously. Since his arrival in Freetown, it seemed like no one took him seriously. For a week he wandered the streets of the city, trying to understand it, but it was so different from his village, and even from the provincial towns like Koidu and Makeni. There were so many people.

The people were kind to him, but they treated him like a child. The little money, a few hundred leones, that he had brought with him was long gone, but he spent one day helping load a big wooden crate with burlap bags of coffee beans, under the watchful eye of a white man and the looming presence of a huge steel derrick.

That night, with the money he had earned, he bought a bag of rice and shared it with a man who had a little shack near the Madongo River. In return, the man let him stay in his shack.

Every morning since, he came to the square, where the great Freedom Tree was, and tried to find someone to talk to. Big blue buses circled the square, and there were hundreds of cars and thousands of people. But whenever he tried to talk to one of them, they just smiled and shrugged their shoulders. Until now, no one had spoken to him first.

"It is true," he said to the woman. "I am Monoh."

"You may call me Auntie Pat," she said. "Come to my house this afternoon and tell me your story." She was older than Monoh, and wore a beautiful dress.

She told him where her house was, on the big hill near the college. Then she walked away, and his eyes followed her as she crossed in front of the huge tree. The people she passed smiled at her and bowed their heads. She approached a black car, and Monoh saw a man get out of the front seat and open the back door so she could get in.

She must be the auntie for the whole city, Monoh thought, remembering Auntie Jane and the respect that old woman had had in his village.

For the rest of the morning, he sat under the big tree, watching the sun. When it had passed its high point, he got up and walked off, toward the college hill.

The house was enormous, rising in white, stuccoed splendor behind an iron fence covered with frangipani and jacaranda. At the gate, a man stopped him.

"I am Monoh," he said to the man. "Auntie Pat told me to come."

The man smiled, shrugged, and let Monoh pass.

A beautiful young woman let him in the door. "I am Binta," she said, "Mrs. Salah's secretary. Have you eaten?"

"Not today," he answered hesitatingly, feeling ashamed of his poverty.

The room dazzled Monoh. The walls were yellow, and the floor was made of square stones like nothing he had ever seen, shiny and white. There were soft couches, blue and green, and a profusion of beautiful plants and flowers.

Binta led him to the kitchen. There was a plate of food with waxed paper over it on the counter, and Binta took the plate and placed it in a small oven. She pressed a button on the front of the oven, and a light went on inside it. Monoh could hear a soft whirring sound. Binta motioned for him to sit on a high stool that faced the counter, went to the refrigerator and took out a plastic pitcher. She got a shiny, clear glass from a cupboard, poured cold water from the pitcher into the glass and set it in front of Monoh. "When you have finished eating," she said. "you will meet with Mrs. Salah." He heard the sound of a soft bell, and Binta opened the oven door and took out the plate of food and set it on the counter. It was rice, studded with wonderful chunks of chicken in a savory sauce. Monoh could remember nothing as delicious since the fabulous meals at the mission school, decades before.

He hesitated; was this really for him? "Eat," Binta said, smiling.

CHAPTER 20

At lunch once a week, G.T. and Gary met with Howard to discuss the progress that had been made. G.T. would talk about the plant construction and Gary would talk about the sales and marketing side of the business, bringing Howard up to speed.

One day, as Gary walked into the executive dining room on the sixth floor, a stack of file folders under his arm, he got an especially booming greeting from G.T. "Heard the news from your old employer," G.T. called out. He was grinning from ear to ear.

"Foremost?" Gary asked. He hadn't thought about them for weeks.

"For*least*, if you ask me," G.T. replied, snidely. "Especially now that they've hired your replacement. Guess who it is?"

Gary didn't have a clue.

"Fucking Phil McLaughlin!" G.T. boomed through a broad grin, sitting back in his chair and putting his hands on his balding head.

Gary didn't really know McLaughlin, but he knew that TLP had bought out McLaughlin Chemicals. A staff job at Foremost must have been a real comedown for the former CEO, he thought.

"Well, I wish him well."

"Stupid asshole," Howard muttered, his mouth full of pasta salad.

The next week, Gary got a call from McLaughlin, and they spent a few minutes discussing various projects Gary had left in his Foremost in-box. "You're a tough act to follow," McLaughlin said at the end of the conversation. "Everybody around here thinks you hung out the moon."

Gary chuckled. "Well, they were good to me," he said. "I didn't really do that much." He decided he liked Phil McLaughlin.

"Be careful at TLP," McLaughlin said. "That's a very different kind of company. Keep your head down."

As for William Hargiss, Gary rarely crossed paths with him. The old man didn't seem to spend much time in Steuben, and Gary came to understand that his principal duties involved resolving the many political problems big business inevitably encountered. Hargiss seemed to be almost as powerful in Washington as G.T. was in Steuben, with numerous contacts in both political parties. He spent much of the winter in Florida, and on the occasions that Gary did run into him, Hargiss asked for quick updates about progress toward production and then moved on to other things.

One day, though, Hargiss actually came into Gary's office, which was by now fully decorated, mostly with framed diplomas and other mementos. There was one original watercolor, though, and Gary smiled every time he looked at it. Exquisitely done, it dominated the wall opposite Gary's desk. It showed a boy, who could have been Gary at twelve, reeling in a large walleye pike. Fine art and fish, Gary thought when he spotted it in an Indianapolis gallery. He figured it would appeal to both G.T. and Howard.

Hargiss didn't seem to notice the painting. "I'm getting good reports on you, young man," he said. "So much so that I want to take out a big-ass key man insurance policy on you. You'll have to take a full physical, you know, blood sample and everything. You got any medical problems?"

"Gosh, no," Gary said. "I'm healthy as a horse."

"Well, good. We sure as hell can't afford to lose you now. The doc'll call you in a day or so, set up a time for the physical."

He turned and left the room. I'm a key man already, Gary thought. Pretty darned impressive.

CHAPTER 21

At the annual Christmas party, Dan Anthony shared a few drinks with Gary and then followed him as he headed off to the bathroom. He opened the door, looked under the stall doors, pushed them open to double check for any occupants and then came over to where Gary was relieving himself.

"I hope Howard won't be involved in your operations after you go startup," Anthony said, "because if he is, that means you'll be involved in price fixing."

Dumbstruck, Gary just nodded and said, "thanks for the heads up."

Gary's head spun as Anthony let the door slam shut behind him on the way out. First the stolen technology and now this. He needed someone to talk to, and made a beeline for the last place he had seen Brad Redfoot.

Brad had staked out the food table and made multiple trips to the cheese balls. As he looked up from his latest foraging trip, he saw Gary's ashen face.

Gary pulled him into a nearby conference room and related the conversation he had just held with Anthony. "What have we gotten ourselves into?" Gary asked.

"Well, what have we been asked to do that we think's wrong?" Brad asked.

He had a good point, Gary thought. The answer was nothing. Who knew why Dan Anthony might have said what he did? Maybe he was just trying to cause trouble. Maybe he had some sort of a grudge against Howard. Or maybe against Gary. Maybe he was delusional, paranoid, or just drunk.

"Until they ask us to do something wrong, then we don't even have anything to complain about. These guys may be involved in a lot of dirty work, but it's not our fight," Redfoot concluded.

He was right, Gary decided. It wasn't their fight. Not today, anyway.

In the days to come, though, Dan Anthony continued to warn Gary about Howard, raising the subject almost every time they met in private. Often, Anthony would make some joke about it, but Gary could tell he was concerned.

CHAPTER 22

Kang Pok-tong had never had an assignment quite like this one. Why did they want some of the boy's hair? He couldn't imagine. And how was he to get it? He had to do it without anyone knowing. That much had been made clear. Beyond that, he was on his own.

For the third day in a row, he waited in his car outside the school in the Itaewon district of Seoul. He spotted the house girl, waiting with the others, as before. Then the children came out, bundled up against the cold. He recognized the boy at once, his Eurasian features unmistakable. The house girl took the boy's hand, and chatted with him as they walked down the crowded street. Kang got out of his car, and kept pace with them on the other side of the street. Two blocks, and they crossed in front of him. Two more blocks and then left a block and a half to the apartment building, where they disappeared inside.

The next day, Kang got lucky. The routine started out the same, but after they crossed the street, they continued on; one block, two blocks. Kang was close behind them now, and his heart leapt with joy as he saw them enter the barber shop. He went in behind them, smelling the pungent odor of hair tonic. There was one barber working on a customer, talking about politics. Except for the boy, there was no one else waiting. An emaciated middle-aged woman sat at the back of the little room, a push-broom resting on her shoulder as she smoked a cigarette.

When the barber finished his work, he shook out the sheet that had covered the customer and bowed slightly as the man got out of the chair. The man followed the barber to the cash register at the front of the store, continuing their conversation as the barber made change.

While this was going on, Kang watched intently as the woman rose from her seat, put out her cigarette and took the broom. She swept up the man's hair and pushed it out a back doorway.

The customer put on his coat and opened the front door to leave. The barber stood by, bowing. Then he turned to Kang.

"No, no," Kang said. "The boy was here first." The barber knew that, Kang thought, but he would make the Eurasian child wait.

The barber shrugged and turned to the boy, beckoning him with his hand. The house girl stood up and led the boy to the huge chair. The broom woman appeared suddenly from the back, carrying a smooth board which she put across the arms of the chair, and the boy clambered onto it.

Kang watched intently, his plan now firm in his mind. When the boy's haircut was done, he beat the broom woman to the chair and took a lock of the boy's hair from the floor, rolling it gently between his thumb and forefinger.

"So fine," he said to the barber, who was taking money from the house girl. "Is it very different to cut?"

The house girl scowled at Kang and quickly ushered the boy out the door. "Not much different," the barber said. Kang reached down and handed the board to the broom woman, surreptitiously slipping the hair into his pocket with his other hand. He stood aside while she swept up the rest of the hair and then seated himself in the barber chair.

I need a haircut anyway, he thought, as the barber tied the sheet around him.

Three weeks later, Admiral Decatur placed a call to William Hargiss at home. "Bill, the DNA test was positive," he said.

"Thank you," Hargiss replied, gazing out the window of his study toward the Wabash River.

"You want it in writing?"

"No, no, that won't be necessary."

CHAPTER 23

Ahmad Sesay Salah did not need his wife's report to know that conditions in his native land were terrible. But now, sitting in his office in the United Nations Building in New York, he read the dossier she had prepared carefully. Excellent lawyer that she was, she had done a thorough and compelling job of putting the facts together.

He read the many eyewitness reports she had compiled, including Monoh's, and he smiled at the handwritten note she had taped to that page, for his eyes only. Of course she would hire Monoh to help care for the grounds of the house in Freetown. After all, he couldn't very well go back to his village, being officially dead.

But it was another section of the report that most interested him. Patricia had painstakingly put together an organization chart, showing the trail of diamonds from the innocent villagers to the Revolutionary United Front to a Lebanese buyer in Koidu. From there, the diamonds were smuggled across the border into war-torn Liberia, where they reached the hands of an American, who ostensibly worked at the giant, heavily guarded rubber plant adjacent to the Robertsfield airport outside Monrovia.

That was unusual, and prompted Salah to pick up the phone and make a luncheon appointment with a colleague named Clarence Pettigrew, who worked for the British U.N. delegation.

They met over pompano filet at the Ambassador Grill, a large, aging, placid black man and a nervous, dapper, mustachioed white man. In a room crowded with diplomats of all known shapes, manners and complexions, they attracted no notice.

"It's a bloody shame," Pettigrew said, "what's going on in your country. Everyone had such high hopes."

"Remember," Salah cautioned him. "I am not here representing Sierra Leone. I am an employee of the United Nations, not a diplomat from my country."

"But you *should* represent Sierra Leone," Pettigrew protested. "You should be the President of Sierra Leone. Then perhaps all this fighting could be stopped."

"I just want you to understand," Salah continued. "That I am speaking simply as a private individual, without portfolio."

"Diamonds are to Sierra Leone what the Yellow River is to China," Salah said, gazing off into the distance. "Our joy and our sorrow. We sit on fabulous wealth, and it corrupts our society from top to bottom."

"There's truth in that," Pettigrew answered, chewing his fish slowly.

"For as long as I can remember," Salah continued, "diamond smuggling has been endemic there. Billions of dollars worth have been carried out of the country, with no benefit to the people."

"Yes, yes."

"The colonial government couldn't stop it. The Margai Administration couldn't stop it, the Stevens government positively *directed* it, and now there is no control whatsoever. None."

"I'm sure you're quite right."

"But something new is involved. It's not just the Lebanese anymore, and it's not De Beers, or anyone like that. It's being run by Americans, and whoever it is..." his voice trailed off, and he tapped his fork on the table.

"The Mafia, perhaps?" Pettigrew offered.

"Perhaps. I don't know. But whoever it is, they have an active interest in the instability of Sierra Leone, and they are financing the civil war."

"You don't say!"

"The trail runs through the Firestone plant in Monrovia. I'd like you to pick it up from there and find out where it leads."

CHAPTER 24

As winter set in, William Hargiss began to go on record with journalists about the future of Gary's division. In *Fortune* magazine, he made the remarkable prediction that a third of the company's earnings would come from the newly formed Bio-tech division by the end of 1995.

"Did you write that thing?" Gary asked Buffy Carney, TLP's youthful head of public relations. "Nope, that came straight from the top," Buffy said. "Feeling some pressure from the notoriety?"

"Some," Gary said.

"The other side of it is the clear signal of your importance around TLP," Buffy pointed out.

G.T. had ordered 22 fermenters for the Sugere plant, and had been given no reason to believe the huge, vat-like contraptions wouldn't be delivered on time. Then, just before Christmas, he was told there was a backlog and it would be at least six months before they would receive shipment.

The solution was classic TLP. G.T. heard through the grapevine that an old Technochem plant in California was going to be scrapped. The day he heard about it, he hopped on a company jet and flew out to see it. An hour or so after he arrived, he called back and said, "Hey, Gary, you're going to have that fuckin' plant right on schedule. I just bought everything we need for a couple million bucks."

He acquired the fermenters for ten cents on the dollar. He quickly wrote a check, hopped back on the jet and had 100 TLP semis and flatbeds on the road before he touched down in Steuben. Within a week, he had the whole plant disassembled and sitting in pieces in the TLP yard.

This was business at its finest, Gary thought. No shady deals, no skirting the law – just aggressive, innovative executive leadership that moved with lightning speed to solve problems. Any other corporation would have been mired in the decision process for months, but not TLP. Like perhaps no other company of its size in the world, TLP could turn on a dime. No red tape, no lawyers, no bull, just results.

By now Gary was also making numerous public appearances, talking to groups about the future of TLP: a company that produced more value-added products from basic chemicals than anyone else in the world, and always the lowest cost producer. Gary repeated the message like a drumbeat.

In February of 1991 Gary flipped the switch and turned the plant on. It was great to be in production, but he quickly learned that there was a downside to building a $500 million plant in record time.

CHAPTER 25

Gary headed in to work on a typical Indiana February day, not a cloud in the sky, no snow on the ground, and the air so crisp it practically broke as you walked through it. Eighty hours before, they had flipped the switch that started the Sugere plant, and today the first product was due to roll off the line. Billie Mitchell had the overnight duty and was to call Gary if there were any problems, and he hadn't. That was a good sign, and he felt sure they were well on the road to success.

But when Gary arrived, it was obvious things were not working as advertised. Mitchell was standing in front of Gary's desk with his arms full of papers and a worried look on his face.

"Things don't look so good Gary," Mitchell said.

"Whadda you mean, Billie, what's wrong?"

"Well, there are so many things going wrong I don't know where to start."

"Well, how's the quality?" Gary responded, trying to bracket the problem.

"It's awful."

"How is the particle size?"

"We had to pull most of the screens out. Right now we're turning out two foot by two foot blocks. About four this morning I had to make a choice: either pull the screens or shut the plant down."

Great, this is just what I needed, Gary thought. The biggest day of my career, and it's all screwed up. He had expected a few problems, mostly with getting the right particle size, but he hadn't expected to be turning out chunks of Sugere as big as cattle licks – not very practical for sprinkling into a coffee cup.

"Don't worry, Billie," Gary said, walking around his desk to put his arm on the man's shoulder. "We'll get it fixed."

That message fit the TLP policy perfectly. We build while others think about it – that was the TLP way. As a result, there were always some problems with new plants, but the corporate philosophy was that it was cheaper to fix plants than to waste time with advance engineering. For the most part it worked. TLP was often the first to bring additional capacity on line when margins were good. In this case, in only a year and a half, it had built the world's largest combinatorial chemistry plant. The fact that it didn't work right on day one didn't mean the problems couldn't be solved.

After a lengthy discussion, G.T. and Gary decided to keep a single line going while they tried to fix the problems. That meant they had to do something with the sweetener that was coming off the production line in big blocks. After some hasty conferences, Gary decided to bag the blocks up in burlap sacks to be redissolved and run through the process again once they had everything fixed.

G.T. started calling some of TLP's consultants to see if they could help get the plant up and running. Gary got on the phone to cancel the plant tours they had scheduled. The original plant was designed to put out over a hundred million pounds per year; right now they had a run rate of less than ten million pounds per year, and every bit of it was unusable.

Over the next three or four weeks, a parade of biochemists, engineers, and microbiologists toured the facilities and provided input on how to fix the ailing plant. As it turned out, the three main areas were okay. The fermenters, where the conversion process took place; the ion exchange where purification occurred, and the granulators where the proper particle size was achieved, were all functioning properly, but even so, the needed changes necessitated a major overhaul of the plant.

As Gary watched one Saturday morning, men with sledgehammers broke out concrete they had poured only a few weeks before. It seemed like such a waste, and no single suggestion seemed to cure the underlying problem. In early March, granulated material finally rolled off of the processing line, but the quality was still below the set goals.

Brad Redfoot lined up a couple of generic brand soft drink manufacturers who agreed to take the production in liquid form for a reduced price and not to disclose to TLP's competitors what was going on. This allowed Gary and his team to continue to work on improving the quality and to stop stockpiling the product. By now he was running out of covered places to put the Sugere, and he didn't want to telegraph his problems to the competitors. Still, he knew word would leak out. You can't bring in all those consultants and expect to keep the problem a secret, he thought.

The competition viewed TLP with a mixture of fear and laughter. Many of them had been producing biocombinatorial chemistry products for almost thirty years, and viewed TLP as "crackers," people who fractured air or petrochemicals into products like nitrogen or CO_2, the industry equivalent of "dumb farm boys." Often, the grapevine reported back their snide comments that, "TLP will never pull it off, and even if they do the quality will be awful." For the moment, they were right, but even as they were being roasted around the world as the industry laughingstock, its quality problems began to get solved. Slowly but steadily, quality was improving, although the progress was not fast enough for anyone in the company to feel good about it.

TLP was shipping liquid and crystalline Sugere, albeit of poor quality and at a heavily discounted price. Still, that was a positive. Also, the stockpiles of blocks began to go down as they started redissolving the first product and running it back through the plant. But even with the progress being made, an air of discouragement began to set in.

In May, William Hargiss summoned G.T. to his office.

"G.T., what the hell have we gotten ourselves into. Are we gonna be able to get this right? This is a damn mess. We've got over five hundred million already spent, committed to spend that much again and we can't get any fuckin' product out of these plant lines. What the hell is going on here?" Hargiss slammed his fist on the desk as if to emphasize his query.

"William, this is technical stuff," G.T. answered. "It's a lot different than the other plants we've built. You can't send away mail order and get blueprints for this kind of stuff. We're nearly there, I can feel it in my bones. That's why these kinds of plants trade at a premium. Maybe we should have stepped up to the plate and bought a plant already in operation somewhere just to learn from it."

"Nah, you'll get it, but the friggin' board is gonna want to hear a progress report and I hate like hell to tell 'em we don't have good product coming out the ass end of this thing yet. This has gone on a long time. What in the hell are you doing to fix it?"

"Well, we've had just about every consultant that we think has a clue tour the plant and try to give us ideas. I think it's paying off; we've just got a few more things to change and then we should be there." G.T. hoped to hell he was right. Hargiss's message was clear; get some success fast, or there would be hell to pay. "I know it's frustrating as shit," he said, "but I think you've got to give it more time." G.T. could read the concern on Hargiss's face.

"Get that son-of-a-bitchin' plant up and running, G.T., I don't like looking like a fool in front of my board. I've never asked for this much money for anything, and they didn't even blink when they gave it to me. Don't let me look like a fool."

G.T. unloaded his frustration on Gary. "William just chewed my ass up one side and down the other," he said. "He thinks we may be in over our heads." He paused. "I don't like this," he added. Gary knew how he felt. The pressure was on him, too.

For the next two weeks, G.T. repeated Hargiss's comments at least twice a day, and Gary couldn't help feeling that somehow G.T.'s gloom was *his* responsibility. "He built the plant, you didn't," a self-justifying little voice would sometimes whisper to Gary. No matter. It was his responsibility, his division, and his butt on the line. One thing was dead certain: if heads were going to roll, the first one would be Gary's, not G.T.'s.

Then it happened. All the pipe changes, re-poured concrete and new temperatures began to pay off. The plant achieved 98.5% quality by the first of June. The Sugere coming off the line was as white as fresh snow, and it flowed beautifully. They were still only putting out about a million pounds per month, far short of the goal, but at least the product was good, and the momentum in a positive direction. As the quality problems were solved, they took what was working on the test line, and one by one began to implement it at each of the other fermenters.

By the end of the June, TLP had three fermenters on line, and two weeks of great product. The confidence level increased, and they brought additional fermenters into production. As the volume increased, the mood at corporate began to swing from dark and gloomy to jubilant as the Sugere started flowing out of the granulators.

Buffy Carney came into Gary's office and set a folder on his desk. "It seems to me," he said, "that it's time for us to start crowing a little about our fabulous Sugere operations. That's a plan I've put together. Take a look at it and see what you think."

Gary read the plan that night. First thing next morning, he rang the PR department's extension. "This is really good stuff, Buffy," he said. "Let's go with it."

Brad Redfoot started filling orders for sample product, and orders for quantity shipments followed. "Life," he said to Gary, "is sweet. No pun intended." They both had a good laugh.

Then the virus hit.

A state-of-the-art bacteria will produce a yield of about 97%. In layman's terms, if you put in 100 pounds of bacteria food, 97% of it will be converted to the final product. In the spring of 1992, it was working just like that, but as the summer heat set in, TLP's yield began dropping like a stone. By the end of the month, the yield was 20%, or twenty pounds per hundred of media. Eighty percent of what was coming out was junk. Somewhere in the process, a virus was contaminating and killing the friendly bacteria, and letting bacteria that did not produce Sugere munch away.

Redfoot had to start making excuses to his customers for TLP's inability to deliver on the orders they had placed. The competition, which had been growing more and more nervous about their prediction that the crackers couldn't succeed, had begun to sweat, but bad news travels fast, and word of TLP's problems hit the street almost at once and spread like wildfire. Good work by Buffy kept the whole problem from becoming a total public relations disaster, but even so, it was unsettling.

"I can't hold the bad stories off forever," Buffy told Gary. "I need some good news pretty soon, or we're really going to feel it in the share prices."

With yield so low, it was costing about $6.00 to produce every pound of Sugere that came out of the plant; TLP was selling it for $1.25. It had been costing about five million dollars a month to keep the plant open and running since the first of February.

Gary wondered what the analysts were thinking, but fortunately for TLP, several other product lines had wide margins at the time, and the company was able to disguise the extent of the losses. TLP never disclosed gross profits by product line. Gary had wondered about that, but now it seemed fortuitous.

Ever since the first rumors of TLP's entry into the market had started, the market price for artificial sweetener had been slipping. The historic high had been $1.50 a pound; at the beginning of 1992, it hovered around $1.35. News of TLP's impending entry caused it to drop farther, but Howard remained confident TLP would make money once the production issues were put to bed. The price per pound had never been below eighty cents, well above TLP's projected costs.

For the moment, though, the yield losses were taking a huge financial toll and TLP started shutting down some of the fermenters. The warmer the weather, the worse the yield. Another group of consultants tried to fix the bacteria problems, but no matter what they did, the only thing that seemed to matter was the outside temperature. The hotter the weather, the worse the problem, and this summer was hot in Steuben.

Then, as quickly as the problem had begun, at the end of August it stopped. Everyone scratched their heads and wondered if it was something they had done, or if it was Mother Nature. Regardless, they restarted the rest of the fermenters.

CHAPTER 26

Ralph Sori's phone call from Paris came during the middle of September. "Gary, I'm getting married next weekend back in Steuben; care to stand up with me?" he asked. His affair of opportunity with G.T.'s daughter, Carrie, was well known to Gary. In fact, every time Ralph came back to the U.S., he had stayed with Gary and frequently used the second bedroom in the apartment overnight to complete what he termed, with a wink, strategic career advancement seminars. It had evidently worked. Ralph's meteoric rise in the company was the stuff of legends. In the past six months he had received three promotions and now was in charge of all European marketing for TLP.

"Finally pulling the plug and tying the knot with Carrie, huh?" Gary asked.

"Nah, screw her, I'm marrying Becky, you know, from accounting." Becky Patten was an auditor, and a talented one. TLP sent her around the world to review the books, and she had been in Europe a lot lately. Evidently Ralph had been auditing her assets as well, Gary thought, remembering that her name had come up several times in their recent conversations. There was no question in his mind that she was a better match for Ralph than Carrie in any number of ways, but the news sent warning bells off in Gary's mind.

"Are you sure that's a good idea?" he asked.

"Yeah, well, what do you mean?" Ralph asked in a puzzled voice.

"What do I mean? You've been tagging Carrie for the past year, how do ya' think this is gonna play with G.T.?"

"Shit, G.T. could care less, I'm doing a blow-out job over here, so everyone stays the fuck outta' my way. Are you gonna do it or not?"

"Oh, hell, sure, I'll be glad to stand up with you. Just keep my name out of the papers. I'm still not sure how this'll set with G.T."

As it turned out, it was a small, family affair at Holy Trinity Church in Steuben. Other than the bride and groom, Gary was the only TLP executive present. The day after they returned to Paris from their honeymoon, Ralph was fired. Becky had no alternative but to quit her job as well. TLP's official reason for firing Ralph was the desire to put a French national in the important post in Paris, but it was pretty clear that Ralph's real failing was breaking two important rules of corporate politics. First, don't screw the boss's daughter, and second, if you do, don't stop.

The incident left a bitter taste in Gary's mouth, but the pace of events at the company was so pressing he had little time for reflection on its meaning. Things were happening fast at the new plant.

Everything was going in Gary's direction. Variable costs had dropped to under a dollar per pound and production numbers were improving daily. They were starting to have an impact in the market, taking market share from competitors.

Then the price war started.

For Gary and the rest of the staff it was beginning to feel like a *Jaws* movie – every time they felt they had one problem fixed, something else would go spinning out of control and set them back. By the end of September, the competition knew TLP was in serious production and began to recognize the risk that its entry into the market portended. By now TLP was sending product into Europe, Latin America, even Asia, home turf for its competitors. The company had people everywhere and the infrastructure was already in place to move the product. Crackers they might be, but when it came to marketing, TLP's people were miles ahead of the competition.

The time spent getting the process right had been worth it. Because of the superior handling characteristics of the crystalline Sugere, TLP would get the order nine times out of ten if the price were the same. So in order to compete with TLP, other companies started dropping their prices. By October, the price hit 80¢ a pound, and still showed no signs of stopping its downward spiral. The production process had improved and TLP's cost had dropped along with the price, but because of the increased production it was still losing three or four million dollars every month, and the press picked up on the war.

The trade journals *Chemical Marketing Reporter* and *Bio-Tech Journal* put the price war on their covers. The competition hated TLP and kept repeating the epithet "crackers," while categorizing themselves as the only real bio-tech companies in the combinatorial sweetener business. All the same, TLP was now producing about four millions pounds per month, and Gary could see a clear track ahead. He confidently predicted to G.T. that by February, Sugere production would double, which would just about make TLP the largest producer in the world. Not bad for a bunch of Indiana crackers, but the question remained, would they be producing a product that could be sold at a profit?

CHAPTER 27

Ralph Sori, embittered by his sudden departure from TLP, called Gary at his apartment late one Saturday evening. He had taken a PR job in Chicago, trading on his still-valuable football name. They spent a few minutes in idle conversation and then Ralph got down to the real reason for the call. "I haven't told you about this before," he said, "but I'm so pissed off I'm gonna fill in the rest of something I started to tell you a long time ago."

Gary thought back, but was puzzled about where Ralph was headed.

"Remember when I told you that TLP played pretty close to the line?"

The conversation they held their first night flashed to the front of Gary's consciousness. "Yeah, sure, what about it?"

"Well, I didn't tell you why I said what I did."

"Yeah, well what is it?"

"I had breakfast that morning with Carrie." Gary fiddled with the phone cord. He was beginning to get really uncomfortable with the whole conversation. It was hard to tell who was on what side these days. The last thing Gary needed was to be accused of passing confidential information to a disgruntled ex-employee.

Ralph continued, "She and I were talking about some of the legendary things that had happened at TLP, and she told me one I hadn't heard – about William Hargiss's brother. She told me that this brother got into some kind of a personal financial bind and had given information on some part of the family business to a reporting service to try and get more credit. Hargiss found out about it, and came to see him. He and his brother were alone for a couple of hours, then later that evening, the police were called because his brother committed suicide."

Gary struggled to make any connection. "What does this have to do with anything?"

"Well, it was back in the late '60s, and no one even investigated the possibility that anything other than a suicide occurred, but Carrie put a spin on it like Mr. Hargiss shot him."

Gary snorted, "Jeez, Ralph, you watch too many bad movies. I gotta go to bed."

"Hey, buddy, I'm just tryin to make sure you know all the angles." Then he paused for a moment, and Gary almost had time to close the conversation. But just before he did, Ralph changed the subject entirely. "By the way," he said, " if you're feeling like you're gonna have a job there for a couple a years, I've got something that might interest you."

"What do you mean?"

"Well, there's a house down in my home town you might want to take a look at. I was talking to Mom the other day, and she told me it was on the market."

"Down in Wonanonly?" Gary snickered, relieved that the conversation had turned to something non-controversial. He had always thought the unusual name of Ralph's home town funny.

"Yeah, yeah, I know. But I'm serious. The schools are pretty good there so the real estate values have always been strong. The problem is this house is way overbuilt for the market, so I think you could pick it up for a song. It's fit for a king, or a top TLP exec."

Gary took down the name of the real estate agent and promised to call. "Actually, I've been thinking about finding a real house," he said. "But nothing I've seen has much appeal."

"Yeah, well, Steuben isn't exactly Far Hills," Ralph snickered. "But this is quite a place; you ought to take a look at it."

"I will," Gary said. "And you, my friend, need to get your active imagination under control."

On Sunday morning, Gary called the realtor and made an appointment to see the home on the following Friday afternoon.

The next morning, Tim Johnson, head of the commodity division at TLP, suggested to Gary that they jointly hire someone to handle marketing in Mexico. They had the only two divisions actively marketing there, and Johnson felt it made sense to bring the operation in-house instead of dealing through an independent distributor. "Can you think of someone who lives in Mexico, can speak the language and knows the business climate but isn't Mexican?" Tim asked. "I don't trust those fuckin' spics, they're all lazy goofballs."

Gary started to object to Johnson's ethnic slur, but decided against it. An idea occurred to him that he liked a lot, and it fit Johnson's prejudiced requirements, too. If you wanted to bring the distribution in-house, why not hire the distributor?

Peter Rhyner, an Australian Gary had worked with at Foremost, had formed his own distribution company in Mexico, and had been taking care of the Latin American distribution of Sugere on a contract basis. Gary told Johnson about him.

"Why don't you get him up to Steuben so we can talk about it.?"

Gary broached the subject with Rhyner, who was reluctant to leave his newly formed company and the independence it offered him. "Gary, I just finished purchasing all my equipment, setting up and furnishing an office, and getting my customer base. Why would I think of leaving now?"

"Well, I can think of one reason," Gary said. "We're going to form a division in Mexico regardless, and when we do, it'll obviate the need for your services as a distributor. I don't know what other clients you have, but I'm sure losing our business would take a chunk out of your bottom line."

Rhyner was quiet for a few seconds and then said, "I want to think it over." On Thursday morning, he was in Steuben to talk about the offer.

The visit went well, and by the middle of the second day, everyone agreed he would be a good choice. Rhyner made it clear he would not sell out cheap. "The cost of living is very high in Mexico," he began in his thick Australian accent. "I think I would need at least a couple of hundred to make it worth my while."

He meant a couple of hundred thousand a year, and when Gary looked over at Johnson, who was turning a little green. "Why so much? That seems awful high," he stammered.

Rhyner went through the differences in the cost of living. Gary was shocked to realize how expensive it was to live in Mexico. After 20 minutes of discussion, Johnson asked Rhyner to step outside while he talked it over with Gary.

"It's okay with me. Better talk it over with G.T.," Johnson said.

"I think we've got the authority to close the deal," Gary replied.

"Well, then, let's get him hired."

Then Tim opened the door, motioned for Rhyner to return and said, "Thanks for coming in, I look forward to working with you."

As they left the office, Gary slapped Rhyner on the back and started to congratulate him when Rhyner interrupted him. "Gary, there's one more thing. It is customary when an expatriate exec is hired in Mexico, due to the country's instability, that he gets a year's salary up front as a signing bonus."

Gary stopped in his tracks and thought about it for a minute. It was quite a hit. "We'd better talk to G.T.," he said finally. "I can't make a decision like that by myself."

G.T. was on the phone when they arrived, but the door was open, so they went in and sat down. Rhyner's eyes darted around the cluttered room, stacks of blueprints on the floor, an expensive suit jacket tossed inside-out on a marble bust. Gary noticed Rhyner looking at the improvised coat rack, and went over to it, lifting up the garment to reveal the face beneath it. "Napoleon," he mouthed silently to Rhyner. Then he brushed the jacket with his hand and carefully hung it back on the head of the Little Corporal. G.T. appeared not to notice, and after a couple of minutes, finished his conversation and stood up to shake hands with Rhyner, whom he knew from the sales gatherings.

"How's it going, Gary? You got Peter here on board yet?"

"Well, we've come to an agreement on salary." Gary said.

"Well then what the fuck are you sitting around here for? Get to work," G.T. boomed, smiling.

Gary explained the salary arrangement, that half would be coming from Johnson, half from himself and why it was so high. "There's just one problem; he needs an up-front bonus."

A cloud appeared over G.T.'s face. "Why?" he asked.

Gary and Rhyner explained to G.T. that Rhyner had started his own business just nine months ago, had a lot of money sunk into it he couldn't recover, and that it was customary given the turmoil in Mexico for an expatriate executive to receive an amount equal to his annual salary as a signing bonus. After a couple of minutes of explanation, G.T.'s face began to lighten up.

"Man, it seems like a lot of money," G.T. began to muse, as if he were talking to himself. "But I guess in the scheme of things this is a one-time deal and we're going to be investing a billion dollars, so what's a couple hundred thousand, huh?" He continued talking to himself. "But if I write a check to you for a couple of hundred, you know to someone who is just starting, there are going to be people in accounting or payroll who are going to look at this and say, 'man, here's a guy who was just hired and he's already making more than I am,' and that would be bad for morale. I think the best way for us to handle this is you give us a couple of invoices for some kind of work for the bio-tech division from your company in Mexico, and we'll pay it to you wherever you want and that'll cover it. That way it'll look like you did work for us before we started employing you."

"I see, you are trying not to de-motivate your employees," Rhyner said with a wink.

"That's it. Well, hell, let's do it. Now you can afford the good stuff. Go out and buy yourself a Ferrari and a ten thousand dollar leather jacket," G.T. said, slapping Rhyner on the back as he got up to leave.

As they headed back to the opposite corner of the floor, Rhyner asked, "Is this how things get done around here?" He had a look of incredulity on his face, and Gary could well understand why.

"My flight's not until six," Rhyner said. "Can we get a drink before I have to leave for the airport?"

Gary started to agree, but remembered he had an appointment with the real estate agent to look at the house in Wonanonly. "I'd like to," he said, "but I've got a commitment and I'm already late, so I'll have to pass. We'll get lots of chances to spend time together anyway over the next few weeks. I'll call you first thing Monday to get all the paperwork started." Gary shook his hand and escorted him to the receptionist who arranged for a ride to the airport.

As he was gathering his things to leave, G.T. called to ask how it had gone with Rhyner. "Hey, don't tell that tightwad Tim Johnson what we did on that bonus," he said. "He'd have a fit."

CHAPTER 28

The problem with looking at a house on a Friday night was the feeling it left Gary with.

Everyone had something or somebody to look forward to when the weekend came. Ever since Tina had left, the only thing Gary had to look forward to was work. He had agreed to see the house because he wanted something to do besides work this weekend, this weekend in particular. Tonight was the anniversary of the night he came home early and found his wife in bed with a midfielder.

The drive to Wonanonly took about twenty minutes, through harvested corn fields, the sheared stalks sticking up from the black dirt in neat rows; they reminded him of the stark white tombstones in Arlington. As he drove, the rows, always straight, shifted: diagonal, vertical, diagonal. It was almost dusk when Gary reached the town, but he could see that it was clean and tidy, with a bustling appearance lacking in nearby Steuben. Bright Christmas lights had already been strung across the main drag, and the handful of shops seemed to be doing a brisk business. He looked again at the directions he had scribbled on a scrap of paper, and signaled to turn right at the only stoplight in town. A group of three women crossed in front of him carrying plastic shopping bags emblazoned with the logo of the gift store he could see behind them.

"My gosh," he whispered to himself. "It's Virginia Hargiss." He'd only met Hargiss's wife once, but he was sure it was she. She was immaculately dressed and coifed, perfect snow-white hair framing a face that he was sure must have been beautiful all her life. He had thought before he had never seen a 70-year-old woman with such classic, dignified beauty. She was one of the richest women in the world, and here she was shopping in Wonanonly, Indiana. This town must have something going for it, he thought, watching her and her friends reach the other side of the street and approach a silver Lexus parked on the other side.

A horn beeped lightly behind him, and he realized the light had changed.

He looked at the directions again and drove point-nine miles east, made the referenced jog to the right, and continued east for another half mile before seeing the two story house on the left side of the road. As he pulled into the driveway, two thoughts occurred to him: first, whoever had built the house must have owned the whole damn town, and second, whoever had remodeled it had paid a lot of money to turn it into a modern showplace. It had an air of class about it, that was for sure.

As he opened up the car door, a dust-covered GMC four-wheel-drive pickup pulled in behind him. So, he wasn't late after all. He had promised he would be there by 4:00 to inspect at least the outside of the house before darkness set in. He glanced at his watch and was surprised to see it was already 4:15. Okay, he was late, but the agent was later. Advantage buyer. Buyer? Was he really serious about buying this house? The pickup door opened and much to his surprise a slim female figure jumped to the ground and jogged the twenty feet to his car, extended a hand and said, "Hey, Gary right?" Gary nodded his head, a little stunned by the unexpected beauty of the woman in front of him.

"Sorry I'm late, but I thought that had to be you when you turned the corner at the light. I was filling up on gas – at least you didn't have to wait for me." She said it so fast it took him a couple of seconds to catch up with her.

"Why don't we look around outside first. I'm Jenna, Jenna Potter, Potter Realty."

"You the boss?" Gary asked, grinning sheepishly. Now, there's a line, he thought. What an idiot.

Jenna laughed. "Nah. My dad is. I mostly do the office stuff, but sometimes he lets me show a house, if I'm real good. Let's look around."

Oh, you're real good, Gary thought. Jenna. She was maybe five foot six, with brunette hair, and look at those deep-brown liquid eyes. Blue jeans and a checkered shirt, topped by a suede vest. Thinnish face with an upturned nose and the kind of cheekbones the modeling agencies went nuts over. She turned with a smile and Gary followed her. Cute from all directions, he thought, finally forcing himself to focus on the real estate as she began recounting the history of the property. She led him around the house, pointing out the landscaping, outbuildings and architectural features. She showed him the swimming pool, covered now for the winter. He tried to imagine what it would look like in the summer, with Jenna in a bikini sitting on the edge, splashing her feet in the water.

She moved on. He padded along behind her like a puppy, missing most of what she was saying, focusing on the timbre of her musical voice. They paused in a sort of grotto framed by a pair of flaming maples. A white lattice trellis held an immense rosebush, to which beds of late-blooming asters and chrysanthemums provided a multicolored accent.

"You should see this in summer," she said, forcing him to look away from her. "Spectacular."

When they completed the circle around the house, she bounced onto the front porch. Gary trailed behind her, looking, he was sure, like the biggest geek in the world. Darn, she was pretty.

A man in his middle 50's opened the door and smiled at them. "Jenna," he said, "come in, come in. Madeleine should be back any minute." He turned to Gary. "John Caldwell," he said, extending his hand.

"I think I'll show him the upstairs first," Jenna said.

When the tour of rooms was finished, Gary was left with vague impressions of polished hardwood floors, oriental rugs and tasteful furniture. He could remember an extremely large master bedroom, with a sitting area and a Jacuzzi. There were, he thought, three other bedrooms, but he wasn't sure.

They came to the kitchen last, all gleaming marble countertops beneath expensive-looking walnut cabinets. Mrs. Caldwell was there with her husband. She was one of the women who had been with Virginia Hargiss in town. It makes sense, Gary thought. The owners of this house would be about as close to the Hargiss social set as you could probably find in Greater Steuben.

"Any questions for Mr. and Mrs. Caldwell?" Jenna asked.

Gary tried to think of something, his eyes scanning the kitchen. There was a cooking island with a gas stovetop. "You got city gas here?" he asked.

"No," Mr. Caldwell chuckled. "Not out here in the country. It's propane. The tank is right out in back." I must have walked right past it, Gary thought.

"We love it here, but my wife's allergies are so bad that we've built an allergy-free home on the lake," Mr. Caldwell said.

"Well, about the only thing I'm allergic to is the apartment I'm living in in Steuben," Gary said. "What business are you in?" he asked.

"I'm a broker," Caldwell answered. "Stock, not pawn," he added with a grin.

The rest of the conversation was meaningless to Gary, mostly about taxes and schools. After a few minutes, he and Jenna excused themselves.

"Well, what do you think?" Jenna asked in the now dark driveway.

"Well, it's a little big for just me, but it is a pretty nice place."

"Oh, I love this place, I've always wanted to live in a place like this, but it's a little out of my reach."

Gary wanted to ask her what she was doing for the rest of the evening, but couldn't bring himself to say the words. His social skills with the opposite sex had eroded to the point where he didn't feel functional anymore, and nothing that had happened at the house had done anything to improve his confidence. So he just shook her hand, told her thanks, and asked if he could call her Monday morning to talk more about the property.

"Sure, you've got the number," she said, retrieving her hand. She jumped back into the pickup. "See ya!" she called and with a wave she was off.

His hand still burned where she had held it. As he drove back to the apartment, all he could think about was Jenna. That night he saw her over and over again. When he woke up in the morning, he had forgotten some of the details of her face, but still couldn't get her off his mind.

CHAPTER 29

Howard Hargiss was the exception to the required Saturday morning appearance rule and showed up irregularly at the office on weekends. But on this particular Saturday in mid-November, Gary watched him pass by his office wearing blue jeans and a red flannel shirt. He refocused on the paperwork in front of him but a few minutes later the phone rang. Gary picked it up and Howard's voice jumped out. "Gary, come on in here."

Gary listened as Howard shot the breeze with George Keddy, Vice President of the Agricultural Products Division. He was known as Killer Keddy around the office, because most of the products his division manufactured were designed to kill things: weeds, insects or some other undesirable life form.

A TV with the sound off was playing cartoons behind Howard's chair, and provided the only light in the office.

"Hey, Gary, Killer and I are telling some jokes. Know any good jokes?" Howard asked, his voice slurred.

It had been rumored around the company that Howard was inclined to sniff the white stuff, and although Gary had never actually seen him do it, he had seen him from time to time when he clearly was under the influence of something. This morning, he appeared to be on the crest of a high: his face was lit up, but he did not show the lethargic effects of alcohol. Rightly or wrongly, Gary assumed he was high on coke. Or, he thought, maybe it's something Killer makes on the side.

"Yeah, I know a couple," Gary said in an effort to be polite, but staying near the doorway so he could make a quick escape. Telling jokes had never been his forte.

"Well, don't just stand there, tell us one," Howard boomed.

Gary thought a moment. "You guys hear the one about the young farm boy who got bored one hot afternoon and decided to chase the chickens for fun? He got bored with that after a few minutes and decided to chase the hogs. His momma had been watching him out the window and yelled for him to stop and come inside. When he did, she told him because he had chased the chickens he wouldn't get any eggs for breakfast, and because he had chased the pigs there wouldn't be any bacon either. About then his pa came up all hot and sweaty from working in the fields. As he started up the steps he kicked the old farm cat out of the way. The boy looked up at his momma and said, "You gonna tell him or you want me to?"

"That's it?" Howard said. "I don't get it." That evoked a loud guffaw from Killer.

"Aw, leave him alone, Howard," he said. "Let me tell you the one about the old guy that married the twenty-five-year-old woman."

Gary felt a little embarrassed that his effort had been so poorly received. He listened to Killer's joke, and the several others that followed from Howard, laughing energetically. They're good at this, he thought. Finally, Killer stood up and excused himself. "Turkey Day's around the corner, gotta get home and help the wife get ready," he said, and then slipped past Gary and out the door.

"Gary, sit down here," Howard said pointing at a chair in front of his desk. "That Killer is sure a good shit, isn't he?" he said, phrasing it as a question but stating it as a fact. "That guy's been around here for twenty or more years. This is a neat place, isn't it Gary? Guys like Killer and me, we've kind of grown up in this thing together. How do you like it here, Gary?"

Gary sensed that Howard's remarks were rapidly changing direction, but he hadn't found anything in his conversation yet he couldn't agree with, so he nodded and said, "It's great. I really like it, there's no junk. I like the way we get things done quickly. It's one of a kind."

Howard nodded in agreement, grinning. In the dim room, the light from his cigarette bobbed up and down, reminding Gary of a cop's flashlight directing traffic after a ball game

. "Man, you've got to loosen up. You take yourself way too fuckin' seriously Gary," Howard said, making another quick rhetorical turn. "Don't worry, though, it'll come with time. Hell, Killer didn't even go to college. When you've been around here as long as we have and you've learned the system, you'll take it easy too. We don't worry about degrees. You learn the system and you won't worry about degrees either. That PhD you got from Iowa ain't worth shit." As he took a breath, Gary told him his doctorate was from Illinois, not Iowa. "Well, it's the same goddamn difference," he said. "Another fucking flat I-state, just like this one."

Howard was puffing like a fiend, and the clouds of smoke were beginning to bother Gary's eyes. "Gary, how much you make?" he asked suddenly. As in any corporation, there were rules about discussing your salary with other people in the company, but Gary knew Howard could make one phone call and get the answer. He probably already knew it.

"Uh, right now I'm getting close to two-fifty, plus the options," Gary said, less sure of himself than just a minute before.

"Ah shit Gary, that's gonna be a drop in the bucket before this is all over with." Howard paused, leaned back in his chair and glanced at the TV where Bugs Bunny was pulling Yosemite Sam's beard. "In spite of your being a PhD, I like you. You're a quick learner, but you take yourself way too goddamn serious and I guess we're going to have to knock the shit out of ya," he said with a smile.

Gary was now fairly confident that Howard's rough words were masking what would turn out to be a pat-on-the-back session, but with Howard it was sometimes hard to tell, and his current state of mind could not be considered lucid. Gary liked pats on the back as well as the next person, but at the moment, all he wanted to do was get out of Howard's office and back to the safety of his own desk.

"You ever heard of some of the perks around here besides salary and options?" Howard asked, again slurring the end of his sentence and finishing it on a high note.

Gary paused and thought before he said anything. "Well, I saw G.T. give one to Peter Rhyner a month ago." Gary's curiosity was aroused and bells were beginning to go off in his head. He didn't know what to expect, but was pretty sure what was about to happen would be enjoyable. If Howard made another turn at this point, he was certainly a mean drunk, or addict, or whatever the heck he was.

But there were to be no more turns. Howard had gotten to where he wanted to be. He was about to deliver the mother of all pats on the back. "You've done a damn good job getting this whole bio-tech thing started," he said. "I'll talk to G.T. about working out the details after the first of the year. He's better at this shit than I am but Gary, this shit is tax free. We want to pay you a bonus equal to your salary. I'll have G.T. work out the details to start the new year off right." Howard paused and took a drag on his cigarette.

Holy cow, Gary thought. He couldn't believe what he was hearing. The house in Wonanonly suddenly began to look more appealing. Gary was speechless.

Howard glanced at Gary's face and figured he could see everything he wanted to know. As Gary stammered, "Thanks," Howard dismissed him with a casual wave of his hand and said, "Now you son of a bitch, get your ass out of here and go make us some fuckin' money and don't say anything to anyone about this." Although it was said gruffly, Howard had a twinkle in his eye.

After Gary left, Howard picked up the phone. "Dad, he took it," he said.

"Good work," Hargiss answered. "Call G.T. and pass the news on to him."

Howard felt good about his father's approval. Words of praise from William C. Hargiss were rare. He stubbed out his cigarette and pulled a small black notebook from his desk. "I think I'll see if Karen is free for the afternoon," he said, picking up the phone.

Gary sat at his desk in a state of shock. What the deuce is going on? he thought. My division is losing three or four million dollars a month, and the price of Sugere is down to 70¢ a pound. I know these guys are worried. G.T.'s been riding my butt every day, and telling me how concerned William C. is. It was true that Howard had never gotten on him about the problems; he had typically just shrugged his shoulders and said that's what happens when you enter a saturated market.

Maybe I'll never understand this place, he thought.

CHAPTER 30

Later, Gary called Jenna under the pretext of wanting to see the house again that afternoon. Then he began engaging her with small talk. "Have you always lived around here?" he asked.

"Yeah, pretty much, except when I was in college and a few years after."

"Where'd you go to college?"

"Missouri."

"Tell me about what you've done since you finished."

"Well, that's a boring story. Did the usual, graduated, got married, moved to Indianapolis, had a couple of kids. Turned out he wasn't exactly a one-woman man, and one night I caught him. That pretty much ended any thoughts of happily ever after. So I moved back to the old hometown and started working for my dad."

"And took your maiden name back," Gary said. He was staring at her business card.

"Not officially. Because of the kids. But it's useful in the business. I mean your name is Long. I'll bet you find that works wonders around Tamson-Long."

"Sometimes I don't really know what works around Tamson-Long," he said, regretting it as soon as the words were out. He didn't need to be telling tales out of school.

"For the record," he added, "I'm not a member of the family. Just an ordinary hick from southern Indiana. Look, is there any chance I could see the house again and then take you out for dinner after?" Gary couldn't believe he was saying those words. He hadn't intended to ask for a date. It just came out.

"Well, you can come and look at the house, but I'm kind of tied up this evening."

Gary felt his heart sink to the floor. All of a sudden, he realized he wasn't very interested in looking at the house again, but it would be embarrassing to back out now. "Sure, I understand," he said flatly. "How about meeting me there at oh, say, three or so."

"I'll call the Caldwells and make sure it's okay, but if you don't hear back from me, I'll just meet you there."

Gary toured the house the second time, forcing himself to pay much closer attention than before, making notes on a yellow legal pad, taking pictures.

He went into an upstairs bathroom and turned on the faucet to check the water pressure. He talked to Madeleine Caldwell about whether or not the curtains in the living room would convey. He asked John how old the furnace was, whether there had been any problems with the pool, and also inquired about Caldwell's brokerage business, hinting that he might be looking for a broker himself. Good psychology, he thought. With Jenna, he was careful to avoid any personal talk. Somehow, he felt it was important that he convince her that he really was interested in buying the house. Of course I am, he thought. I am not doing this just to impress her, to hustle her. Then he took the thought to a deeper level, and wondered why he cared what she thought. Was his businesslike posture just part of the hustle?

He asked her for the name of a local inspector, whom he called on the spot and hired. No-nonsense direct action, TLP style all the way.

He couldn't quite avoid those brown eyes when they said good-bye, but he tried. They didn't shake hands. No touching.

"Have a nice Thanksgiving," she said as he climbed into the Cadillac.

"You, too," he mumbled, shutting the door.

CHAPTER 31

His Thanksgiving was depressing beyond words. He got up early and drove to Madison, had dinner with the whole family at his sister's, showed everyone the pictures of the house, watched a little football with his dad and the other men, gave each of the women a small package of Sugere and drove back to Steuben. The time in Madison was tolerable, except for the reaction to the house pictures. Nobody really said anything, but somehow he sensed that they thought it extravagant, maybe even gaudy. Only his kid brother, Bert, seemed enthusiastic. But of course, Gary thought, Bert is always supportive of anything I do, and with good reason.

The six hours on the road, going and coming, were pure melancholy, especially the return trip. He felt a growing distance from his family, and worried about his mother. She looked frail, he thought. In his ideal world, she was the one who fixed Thanksgiving dinner, in her house. That was how it used to be, but now the torch had passed to the next generation. He thought about Tina, the Thanksgivings they had spent together, in Madison and elsewhere. He was embarrassed about his feelings toward Jenna. He was worried about the price of Sugere. On top of everything else, he had an upset stomach. Damn wine, he thought. That stuff is poison to me.

On Tuesday, he got the inspector's report, and after reading it, called Potter Realty and asked for Jenna. "I'm sorry she's on vacation," the secretary said. "Her father's here though, can he help you?"

Gary had every intention of making an offer on the house, but after visiting with Bud Potter for a few minutes, Gary put it off. "I'm probably going to make an offer," he said, "but I've got to work on it a little." He put his file on the house in his desk drawer and forgot about it. He had lots on his mind at the office, and today's chore was finalizing his choice of a secretary. Ever since he'd arrived at TLP, he'd been making do with a series of temps from the general pool. One of them was head and shoulders above the others. Her name was Leigh Curtis, and she had worked as an executive secretary at TLP back in the 1970s. Then her husband had been transferred to Denver and she left. Six months ago, he had died and she returned to Steuben, taking the only job available at the time. She was in her 50's, with a matronly figure, salt-and-pepper hair, and a quiet competence Gary admired. He hired her.

Two weeks later, Leigh stuck her head in his door. "It's someone named

Jenna," she said, giving a teasing grin when Gary's eyes lighted up and he eagerly grabbed the receiver.

"I just got back from vacation," Jenna said. "Dad told me you were thinking about an offer."

"Well, yeah," he said, "but I've been really busy and I just haven't been able to focus on it."

"What is it exactly that you do?" Jenna asked, changing the subject. "Your card says 'President, Biocombinatorial Chemistry Division.' What's that mean in words a girl from Wonanonly, Indiana could understand?"

He launched into a short lecture on combinatorial chemistry and its applications. Then he told her about some of the products that were on the drawing board. "It's not as complicated as it sounds, but to me it's exciting."

"It is pretty interesting," Jenna said. "Maybe you could tell me more about it over dinner sometime."

Gary couldn't believe his ears. "How about tonight?" he asked.

"Um, sure, I'd like that."

"Great, I'll pick you up at your house. If you'll give me directions, that is. Seven o'clock?"

"Sure, that'll work."

Gary hung up the phone. Okay, he thought, it's probably just good business on her part. A potential client who hasn't been heard from in a couple of weeks. Schmooze him a little, coax an offer out of him. Don't get your hopes up again. On the other hand....

The hands on the clock moved at sub-glacial speed all afternoon. Finally, at 6:35, Gary pulled the house file out of his desk and flipped off the light switch. The phone rang. He started to ignore it, but then decided maybe it was her and picked it up in the dark. It wasn't her. It was Rhyner, wondering about a supply problem. Gary gave the shortest answers possible, slammed down the phone and left the office. He sped out of the garage and through the lot. Cursing, he pulled to a stop at the first light, which had just turned red. He went through the second light on yellow. Out on the open highway, he ignored the speed limits, passing two cars en route to Wonanonly. For all of that, it was still 7:05 when he pulled into the driveway of a small frame house on the west edge of town. He got out and went up to the door, finding a knocker almost hidden behind a Christmas wreath. A boy who looked to be about ten, his eyes dancing with mischief, opened the door. "Mommy, he's here."

Jenna came around the corner dressed in a bright blue skirt and white blouse. She was even prettier than he remembered. "This is my son Justin," she said. "His brother, Mark, is around somewhere. The baby sitter isn't here yet, so we'll have to wait for her."

"Justin," she said to the boy, "go find Mark."

The younger boy was six, blond and shy. He didn't want a thing to do with Gary, and hid behind his mother.

Then the doorbell rang again and a freckle faced teenaged girl rushed through the door as Justin opened it for her. "Sorry I'm late," she said, dropping books and a bag in a heap.

"Gary, this is Kris. Kris, meet Dr. Long."

"Ooo, are you a real doctor?"

"Nah, if you pay fifty dollars extra to the University of Illinois they give you the title." Kris, who could tell her leg was being pulled, made a funny face and sat down on the couch.

Jenna picked up Mark and deposited him next to Kris on the sofa. "Show Krissy the ornament you made," she said, moving to a closet and retrieving her coat.

"I'll show her mine," the rambunctious Justin shouted, leading babysitter and brother to the tree in front of the bay window.

"Let's beat it," Jenna said to Gary, hustling him out the door. "You guys behave," she called back.

They had dinner at the Olde Coach Steak House in Hardin, the only town between Wonanonly and Steuben. Gary had noticed it on his several trips and thought it looked nice. It was, but Hardin was a dry town, so there were no drinks. So much for getting her drunk and taking advantage, Gary thought. He shook his head as if to cast off the unseemly fantasy.

"What's the matter?" Jenna asked.

"Oh, nothing," he said, and then chuckled. "I'm just clearing my head for the important business transaction we're going to do."

"Are you going to make an offer?" she asked, quickly adding, "on the house?"

"Yeah," he said softly. He told her what he had decided. It was somewhere between lowball and what the Caldwells wanted. He thought it was fair, given the extremely limited number of potential buyers for a property like that. "You think they'll go for it?" he asked.

"Only one way to find out," she said, reaching into her handbag. "Here are the forms. We can fill them out right now if you want."

The waiter arrived with their salads, giving Gary a moment to think. "Why don't you just give them to me and I'll fill them out in the morning and fax them back to you?"

"Works for me," she said, handing him the papers. Then she carefully pulled three pale cucumber slices out of the salad and set them on the side of the plate. She looked up to find him staring at her. "I hate cucumbers," she said, blushing. "You want these?"

He leaned back and smiled the most genuine smile he had let cross his face for months. "No, that's all right," he said. "And it won't do the starving children in China a bit of harm if we let them go to waste."

"Did your mother tell that one, too?"

"Over and over."

"I think it's a Midwestern thing."

So Gary talked about Madison, and she talked about Wonanonly.

"Where'd you go on your vacation?" he asked her

"Puerto Rico. And I don't want to talk about it. It was terrible."

Fair enough. "You know Ralph Sori?" he asked.

"*Everybody* knows Ralph Sori," she said firmly.

Oh, Jeez, he thought. Maybe she dated him. Maybe he even...but the thought was too horrible to contemplate, and he banished it to the recesses of his mind.

"He dated my sister for a while," she said.

"Wow, you mean there's more like you at home?"

"No, not at home. Rachel's out in California – something to do with cable television."

"She a star?"

"No, I think she sells time."

"Selling time," he said. "Now there's a metaphor for modern life."

"Philosophy," she grinned. "From a man who sells artificial sugar."

They both laughed.

The waiter took the salad bowls, brought the entrees, and took those plates when they were finished. He asked if they wanted to see the dessert menu, which they declined, and brought two rounds of coffee. The whole process took almost two hours, and it was hard for Gary, thinking about it afterwards, to figure out how they had managed to eat, so nonstop had their conversation been. By the end of the meal, Gary was more comfortable than he had been with anyone in recent memory.

She was beautiful, smart and witty, and he seemed finally to escape the geek syndrome and display at least a little charm. He was sure Jenna was having a good time and he hated to see the evening end.

A light rain had started to fall, and they ran, laughing, across the parking lot to the car.

"Thank you for a wonderful evening. Can we do it again soon?" he asked as they drove into Wonanonly.

Jenna paused before answering. "Look, I'm just in the process of breaking up with the guy I've been seeing for the past year. We went to Puerto Rico together, and we fought like cats and dogs. I've done that scene, and I'm not ready to do it again."

"Well, his loss, that's for sure."

"Thank you," she murmured. "Gary, I had a great time tonight, and I don't want you to think I'm a tease, or anything like that. It's just that...right now I'm scared to start something. My mind is a muddle. I keep going back and forth, back and forth. When I called you, I knew it was a risk, but there was always the chance I'd think you were a jerk and then it'd be over, or maybe you'd even say no, but we had to meet anyway on the house, so I took the chance." The words were rushing out, helter skelter.

"Well, at least I think you're saying I'm not a jerk," he said softly. They were parked in her driveway now.

"Oh, no, no, no. I think you're..." She paused and looked up at him. The light from a lamp post shone softly through the windshield onto her face. Looking into her eyes, Gary could almost see through them into her mind, almost sense her left brain proposing adjectives which her right rejected one by one. "I think you're sensational."

They were separated by the center console, and Gary's mind flashed back to his old high school GTO days. For the briefest moment, she was Tina and he was sixteen. But the GTO had a bench seat, and whenever Tina was hurt or scared, she would snuggle up to him and he could put his arm around her and comfort her with a hug or a kiss. How he longed to kiss Jenna right now, to soothe her anguish. Bucket seats are the curse of the world, he thought.

"Look, can I at least call you?" he said.

"Of course," she said, reaching across the console to touch his shoulder. "I'd like that."

It wasn't what he wanted, but it was better than what he had.

They talked on the phone almost every day after that, sometimes about the deal on the house, more often about nothing much at all. The Caldwells countered his offer, and TLP-like, Gary had decided to hold firm. Three weeks later, Jenna called him at work. "They've agreed to your price," she said. "I guess you were right not to counter. How soon can you close?"

By then Christmas had come and gone. He had decided not to go home, and had taken several large boxes of presents to UPS for shipment to Madison. He bought a box of cards and sent them to friends in St. Louis, New Jersey and London. One day when he knew Jenna would be at work and the boys in school, he drove to Wonanonly and left a package on the front steps, a book for Justin, a model dinosaur for Mark, and for Jenna an elegant Ulysse Nardin watch. Then he drove to the airport and flew to Salt Lake City for a few days of skiing. He spent Christmas on the slopes, an odd solitary figure among happy vacationing families and couples. When he got back to the apartment, there was a small pile of packages and cards waiting for him. The package from Jenna had been mailed the day before he left, and contained a nice pair of leather gloves. There was also an overstuffed letter, mailed the day after Christmas. In it were handwritten thank-you notes from the two boys, and one from Jenna complaining that the watch looked far too expensive for her to accept. He thought at first she was serious, and perhaps in a way she was. But the tongue in her cheek became apparent when he read on to learn that she had decided to keep the watch as a business bribe for her cooperation in securing what she called in the letter his "absurdly cheap" offer on the Caldwell house. "On personal matters," the letter continued, "I am utterly scrupulous, but what the hell, business is business." She'd fit right in at TLP, he thought.

Now, in early January with a light snow falling, Jenna's question about closing on the house brought him up short. His offer included a large down payment, which he figured to make out of the bonus Howard had promised him "right after the first of the year." Since then he had heard not a peep from either Howard or G.T. about the bonus. Gnawing in the back of his mind was the sinking feeling that the whole thing might not be real. Maybe Howard had just been babbling. Maybe it was just the cocaine talking. Maybe he had completely forgotten the offer and had said nothing to G.T.

He could still afford the house, but he'd have to redo the loan proceedings if he didn't get the two hundred grand.

"Look, it's going to take me a little while to move the money around. Let's set it for March 15," he said.

A heavy, wind-driven snow was falling when he left the office that night, his mind filled with a thousand complicated thoughts. With the cold January weather, the production process was steadily improving, although not nearly enough in Gary's mind. It was taking six pounds of media to get one pound of Sugere when the ratio should have been two and a half to one. Still, that was a lot better than it had ever been, and even though Gary felt they should be doing better, everyone else seemed satisfied.

His car phone rang, startling him. He almost never got any calls in his car, and he fumbled a minute picking up the receiver. His mind distracted, the car skidded in the snow. "Hang on a minute," he said in a small panic, dropping the phone onto the passenger seat and returning both hands to the wheel. In a few seconds, he had the skid stopped. Pulling to the curb, he picked up the phone again.

"Sorry about that," he said to whoever it was. "It's a little slippery out here."

"Gary, it's William Hargiss. You okay?"

"Mr. Hargiss," he gulped. "Yeah, I'm fine. It's snowing like crazy."

"Can you pull off or something?"

"Already have. That's what I was doing."

"Well, good. It wouldn't do for you to have an accident."

"No worry, I'm fine now. What can I do for you?"

"Sounds like you need a break from the weather, and I'm just the guy to give it to you."

"I accept," Gary chuckled. "Where am I going and how soon can I go?"

Hargiss was chuckling into the phone as well. "Well, you're going to have to work for it, but here's the deal. The board is meeting Monday, on Longboat Key in Sarasota, and I'd like you to fly down and give them a report on how things are going. I've been stalling them for months, but from what G.T. tells me, you've got production moving in the right direction, so we ought to be able to sound real positive about things. Get young Carney to help you put together some remarks and a slick-looking document."

The snow was nearly horizontal in the wind. Gary looked out the side window. He knew there was a bowling alley right across the street, with a huge neon sign, but all he could see was a faint red blur through the blizzard. Longboat Key sounded terrific. "Well, the numbers are nowhere near where I'd like them..." he began.

"I know, I know. That's why you're good at what you do," Hargiss said. "You won't be satisfied until everything's perfect. But the board gave me a billion dollars to win this race, and you're the horse I placed the whole damn bet on. They deserve a look at you. So get with Buffy and then get your butt down here Monday with a report that sounds like we're going to win. You don't have to entirely cover up the problems, just make sure it comes out like most of them have been solved and the others will be in two shakes of a lamb's tail. You got the picture?"

Gary was staring at the red blur. The wind paused for a moment, and the snow switched directions. B-O-W-L, he could read, just barely. "I've got it," he said.

"Good. Now get home safely and fix yourself a hot toddy. I'll see you Monday."

CHAPTER 32

Clarence Pettigrew prided himself on his work. For 15 years, he had skillfully built his reputation within MI-6, serving the intelligence needs of the United Kingdom, even as the sun was setting on the British Empire.

He'd been right about the Falklands, even though no one had believed him at first. Then when the crisis hit, his reputation soared, and he was moved out of his Latin America-Caribbean beat to New York. Now, he was heading home, to London, with new and enlarged responsibilities.

Before he left, he owed it to Sesay Salah to give him a report on what he had found out about the new Sierra Leone diamond smuggling operations. The problem was, he couldn't tell him the truth. The truth was far too sensitive to share with an African diplomat, even one Pettigrew liked as much as he liked Salah.

Pettigrew had found the American in Liberia, a certain Roswell Cleveland. Firestone was paying him $50,000 a year as a personnel manager. But a search of his bank records revealed that Cleveland was being paid twice that much by a company called Interoceanic, registered in the Cayman Islands.

Pettigrew knew all about the Caymans, and understood all too well that any company operating out of that offshore banking haven was likely to be involved in business that was, if not downright illegal, at least highly secret.

Twice a month, even during the worst of the Liberian civil war, Cleveland managed to send a package by courier to Antwerp. There, the packages were delivered to a diamond-cutting operation run by a man whose MI-6 file identified him as an operative of the American National Security Agency. The profits from the diamonds, which were huge, went into a bank account in Switzerland which bore the name of Tracinda.

The most interesting thing of all was that the signatory on the Tracinda account was exactly the same as that on the Interoceanic account in the Caymans – William C. Hargiss, whom Pettigrew's research showed to be the multi-millionaire CEO of the American chemical company, Tamson-Long Products.

So, Pettigrew concluded, one of the world's largest corporations, in conjunction with the U.S. intelligence community, is smuggling diamonds and fomenting civil war in West Africa. But why? And what were they using the profits for? This was a matter he definitely would keep researching when he got back to London.

He arranged lunch with Salah at the Ambassador Grill, and made his way to the restaurant through a wet snowfall.

"I can confirm your information about the man at Firestone," he told Salah. "But beyond that, little is certain. The operations are definitely being directed from here in America, and are undoubtedly criminal, but I'm not sure it's the Mafia."

It wasn't much, but it was all he could really say.

Salah shrugged. "Please keep looking," he implored Pettigrew. "I particularly need to know if the group has political connections here. If not, I may be able to get the American government involved, but otherwise...." He let his voice trail off, as a waiter brought them bowls of steaming vegetable soup.

"I will definitely keep on it," Pettigrew said, shaking a generous supply of pepper into his soup. "But I will be doing it from London. I'm being sent home next week."

Salah just nodded, sadness etched in his face. He set his spoon down and withdrew a snapshot from his vest pocket, handing it to Pettigrew.

The picture spoiled Pettigrew's appetite. It showed a footless young black man, bandages around the stumps of his ankles.

"Please do what you can for my countrymen," Salah said softly.

CHAPTER 33

The TLP board meeting was held at The Colony on Longboat Key. Gary flew to Sarasota on Sunday afternoon, picked up a rental car and drove through town and across the bridge to St. Armand's. The first time around the traffic circle, he missed the turn for Longboat Key and had to make another complete circle. When he arrived at The Colony, he checked into a luxury suite overlooking the tennis courts. A pro was helping some teenaged girls practice just outside his window.

He called the operator and asked for Mr. William Hargiss's room. There was no answer, so he left a message that he was in his room. On the desk beside the phone there was a brochure for the resort, and on the cover was a picture of a man walking on the beach carrying a beautiful woman piggyback. She was laughing, her bare feet spread out on either side of him. She looked like Jenna. He thought about calling her, but decided against it. For the moment, he was the handsome man on the beach, and she was riding on his back, laughing. If he called, it would probably destroy the fantasy. He didn't want to do that.

Instead, he opened his briefcase and took out the report he and Buffy had prepared for the board. Half an hour later, the phone rang.

"I see you made it," Hargiss said.

Fifteen minutes later, he knocked on the door of Hargiss's suite. It was at least twice as big as Gary's, with a large table in one corner. There were three other men in the room. Gary recognized Ian Howes immediately. Hargiss introduced the others as Robert Aiken and Randolph Thad. Gary had studied the biographies of all the board members. Thad was the famous cable TV magnate. Aiken headed one of the largest law firms in the world, and Howes was the former Prime Minister of Great Britain.

"I have lived under your governance," Gary said to Howes. " When I was with Foremost, I lived in London for a couple of years."

"I hope you didn't find the heavy hand of Downing Street unbearable," Howes said.

"Not at all."

"Pity you couldn't have voted."

"England's loss is TLP's gain."

Howes dipped his chin just a bit in acknowledgement of the compliment.

"Well, speaking of TLP's gain," Hargiss said. "I trust the report you will give in the morning will show evidence of that."

"I've brought a copy with me," Gary said. "Do you want to go over it?"

"Not right now. Leave it with me and I'll look at it later tonight. These gentlemen and I have some business to discuss over dinner, but I wanted them to have a chance to meet you before the meeting. We have twenty minutes or so. Can I fix you a drink?"

Gary accepted a gin and tonic, and a seat at the table. I might not be good enough to go to dinner, he thought, but it ain't bad to be sitting in a Longboat Key luxury suite with four of the most powerful men in the world.

They talked about sports for a few minutes, but the discussion seemed to bore Howes. When a pause came, he changed the subject. "Say, fellows," he said. "It looks like the Democrats are going to run this awful chap from Arkansas."

"And we'll probably lose again," Thad snorted. "What's your politics, Gary?" he asked.

"None in particular," Gary replied. "I guess I've moved around too much to ever get involved. My family was mostly Republican," he added.

"Well that makes me the only Democrat in the room again," Thad said, smiling.

"For what it's worth, Randolph," Hargiss said softly, "I think your boy will win the thing."

"Oh, you can't be serious!" Howes looked appalled. "The man has the morals of a barnyard animal. Surely the Republicans will make a mockery of him by November."

"I don't think so," Hargiss said. "Their campaign is being run by a bunch of second-stringers. I predict they won't lay a glove on Clinton. And they completely underestimate the brilliant venality of the man.

"In truth," he added, surveying the surprised looks on the faces around the table, "it wouldn't be bad for us with Clinton in. We can do business with him."

"Ah," said Thad, "but can you do business with his wife?"

Hargiss chuckled. "Don't think of her as his wife. What they have is not a marriage. It's a small, two-partner law firm. A sleazy one, perhaps, but with very big potential."

When Gary got back to his room, the light on the telephone was blinking. He called the desk and asked for his messages.

"Mr. Binghamton called at five fifty-three," the operator said. "He asked you to call him in room 165. Would you like me to ring it for you?"

"Gary," G.T. boomed enthusiastically, "you called just in time. Cathy and I were hoping you could join us for dinner."

Gary knew that G.T. had flown to Florida two days before the meeting, bringing his wife with him for what he had described in the office as "a little R and R."

Howard had teased him about it. "You pussy-whipped old fart," he had said.

"Well, I'll tell you something," G.T. had responded, "if you ever get married – and this goes for you too, Gary – you'll learn that a few days in the sun can do wonders for a man and wife. I'm here to tell you these old bones of mine will get the best rattling we'll have all winter once I rub a little beachside Coppertone on the old lady."

"Like I said," Howard responded, speaking directly to Gary. "He's a pussy-whipped old fart."

Gary recalled the exchange as he and the Binghamtons ordered dinner at Marina Jack. He had met Cathy only a few times, and always with other TLP people around. Now, in this intimate setting, with a piano playing jazz in the background, he saw a side of G.T. he had never seen before. There was not a hint of the usual boisterous crudity. He examined the wine list with the eye of someone who knew what he was reading, disdaining an '85 French Sauternes, asking politely for an '88, and when that was not available, settling for an '86. He ordered orange roughy, and Gary tried to remember if he had ever known G.T. to eat seafood before.

Cathy was a tall, well-proportioned woman, with shoulder-length blonde hair, an infectious laugh and bright blue eyes. When it came her turn to order, she quizzed the waiter at some length about the ingredients in the various dishes, eventually ordering the small-portion prime rib, rare, a baked potato with sour cream, and a diet cola.

"I'm sorry to have to be so fussy," she said to Gary as the waiter left, "but I'm a diabetic, and I have to be careful in restaurants. I'm afraid their sauces aren't on my diet list.

"Now," she continued, looking at Gary with a sparkle in her eyes, "George tells me you are the very brightest star in the TLP galaxy."

Gary blinked before responding, partly out of modesty at the compliment, and partly because he had never heard anyone call G.T. George before. "That's very kind of him," he said. Kind? G.T.? It seemed like an oxymoron. "Your husband has built a very remarkable company," he added. "I don't know of another corporation in America that is managed with such boldness and skill."

G.T. beamed.

"He's done pretty well," Cathy said. "You know there were lots of people who said he couldn't succeed in top management, being an engineer and not trained in business administration."

Gary had never thought about that. No doubt the Randolph Thads of the world would have preferred someone with an MBA as company president. But then, he thought, no MBA would dare operate a company the way G.T. ran TLP; it would go against everything they had been taught. G.T.'s MBA, Gary thought, was from William C. Hargiss University.

G.T. himself had a more mundane explanation. "Actually," he said, "chemical cracking is very much a margin business. The key to profitability is being the lowest cost producer and a substantial part of that is in engineering. The other thing is, I've always had a knack for spreading costs."

That was certainly true, Gary thought, remembering the report he was going to give in the morning.

The pianist began a melodic rendition of "Stardust."

"That," G.T. said softly, "is the finest popular song ever written." He paused, deep in thought. "I've often wondered," he continued, "if the coarseness of today's music isn't somehow a necessary cause of all the violence of the younger generation."

Again, Gary was taken aback by this unexpected G.T. He had used the phrase "necessary cause," and Gary had to assume he meant it to be understood in its technical sense: not a sufficient cause, but a necessary cause, meaning – Gary strained to recall his logic class – that the music wasn't enough to bring about the violence all by itself, but without the music the violence wouldn't have come about. He was trying to decide if that was right, but Cathy interrupted his thoughts.

"Do you have children, Gary?"

"No. Perhaps someday." Thoughts of Jenna floated back into his mind.

"Well, I hope so," Cathy said. "For all the trouble, they really are treasures."

"Carrie is really doing well in her new job in Indianapolis," G.T. said. Gary hadn't thought about the Binghamton's daughter since the trauma of her having been jilted by Ralph Sori. In TLP language, he thought, they must have shipped her out of town to avoid the embarrassment. But now he could see it in Binghamton family terms, too, and it was somehow touching that G.T. would find a way to speak well of the girl, whom Gary had always considered vacuous.

In any event, it was a subject he didn't want to pursue. "And how's your son?" he asked, remembering the photo on G.T.'s desk of a young man playing basketball.

"Tommy's a champ," G.T. said, breaking into a broad grin. "If we weren't here, we'd probably be in Kokomo watching him play tonight. He's pretty good. Good rebounder, usually gets eight or ten points, mostly in the paint. I try to get to as many of his games as I can, but it isn't easy."

"He's the student in the family, too," Tommy's mother said. "All A's and B's."

"Sounds like TLP executive material," Gary said.

"Oh no," G.T. said. "Not in a million years."

"Tommy's thinking about pre-med," Cathy explained, "when he gets to college."

"It's his choice, of course," G.T. added, "but medicine has always been an honorable and rewarding profession. I think for someone his age, the real opportunities will be in geriatrics. Think of it, Gary, all you millions of baby boomers, and one day you'll all be senior citizens. The doctors of the 2020s and 2030s are going to be more important than they've ever been."

The next morning, before the meeting, Hargiss didn't say a word to Gary, which he took as a vote of confidence in the report. When it came time for him to speak, Hargiss introduced him in glowing terms as the quarterback of their bio-tech team. The presentation itself was a touchdown. Gary charmed them with amusing anecdotes about the problems they had encountered and overcome. He impressed them with his thorough knowledge of biochemistry. He encouraged their optimism with carefully constructed graphs showing sales and production increases. He confidently predicted that the price of Sugere would soon stabilize and start upward again once their capacity allowed the strength of their unequalled worldwide marketing power to exert itself.

When the meeting adjourned for lunch, Hargiss gave Gary a surreptitious little thumbs up, and left the room quickly. He needed to go to his suite and call his wife. There would be good news for her to pass along to her friend, Madeleine Caldwell.

That afternoon, on the plane back to Chicago, Gary realized the risk he had assumed. He had raised the board's expectations with his bold optimism. If it didn't happen, they now knew exactly whom to blame.

CHAPTER 34

When Gary stepped off the plane in Steuben, the sun was shining brightly, but it was bitter cold.

The day after he got back, a man named Dink Macabee came to interview for the position to head up the North American sales division. North America counted for about half of total Sugere sales and Howard hoped to be able to maintain that percentage of usage as production ramped up. Dink had signed a three-year contract with TLP and was earning about $250 thousand as an independent distributor in Atlanta. Gary knew they couldn't justify paying him that much in salary, but Dink was in the same box Peter Rhyner had been in: TLP was going to hire someone for the job, and if Dink chose not to take it, a large portion of his income would go dry once his contract ended.

Gary made sure Dink understood the consequences of not taking the job, and then tried to come up with a carrot or two, so the offer wouldn't be all stick. "Dink, there are a lot of old people here, and a guy like you can move up quickly through the ranks," Gary told him. "Besides," he added, "wouldn't it be great to have health insurance, and all your expenses covered?"

Maccabee was still not convinced. He could buy a lot of insurance with the 150 grand he stood to lose.

After listening to Dink moan for a few minutes, the thought struck Gary that maybe they could give him a bonus like they had done for Peter Rhyner. The one-time tax-free payment definitely piqued the man's interest.

G.T. agreed. "Just make sure," he said, "that you have him bill us before he comes on board, and do it through an overseas company, if he can. That makes it better for everyone."

G.T. stopped for a second. "Oh, yeah, goddamn it, I almost forgot, I owe you two hundred thou too."

Gary had been on pins and needles about the bonus ever since he had made the offer on the house. Now he felt a soothing rush of relief. But the casualness of it all amazed him. How could someone just forget about a $200 thousand bonus, unless it was going on all the time?

"Howard mentioned it to me back in November, so work something out for yourself. Hell Gary, you've earned it. You're doing a great job and we're glad to have you."

Gary left G.T.'s office and floated back to his own. This place was beyond non-bureaucratic; it was almost completely unstructured. It violated everything he had ever been taught about business, yet through it all, things got done. Hargiss and G.T. had been running the company their way since before Gary was in kindergarten, and while they obviously hadn't been able to throw money around like this in the early years as they struggled to rescue TLP from bankruptcy, it was clear to him that freewheeling financial practices had gone on for a long time. He wished he knew the whole story.

Dink quickly agreed to the offer; he even knew a British company he could bill the bonus through.

That night, G.T. gave Gary a lesson in how to prepare the paperwork for Dink's bonus. By the end of the night, Gary was swimming in a sea of numbered accounts and fake contracts.

"Now," G.T. said to him, "you've got to work out your deal the same way."

"But I can't think of a company overseas I would dare bill it through," Gary complained.

"Well, hell, just make one up then," G.T. said. "Get yourself to Switzerland and open up an account for yourself that sounds like a business of some kind. That's where you put the bonus check, and bingo, no taxes, no trouble."

"No taxes, really?" Gary asked. "Is that legal?"

"Absolutely," G.T. snorted. "That's the whole point of taking profits offshore. That's what places like Switzerland are for, for Christ's sake!"

In the middle of the next week, G.T. stopped by Gary's office. His face wore the look of someone who was not enthusiastic about what he was doing. "Hey, Gary," G.T. began in a quiet voice, "I want to give you a heads up on something. Howard is going to stop by to talk to you about working closer with him on the pricing, you know kind of like a mentor situation."

All the warnings Dan Anthony had given Gary over the past few months came rolling in waves to the front of his mind. Shit, shit, shit. They were going to try to fix the price of Sugere, he thought. These bastards want me to cross the damn line. No wonder they haven't been worried about profitability. "I've kind of been warned about this G.T., and I don't really like it," Gary said defiantly.

"I know it's going to eat you up, but goddamn it don't let it," G.T. said. "He doesn't want to learn what you know, he just wants you to learn from him, learn how to do business the TLP way.

"Fuck, Howard's a pro and he's been here twenty years, so he knows how we do this goddamn stuff around here. He's not just the boss's kid, Gary, he's really sharp on this stuff, and it's important for you to learn what he knows. It will definitely be an advantage, not a disadvantage. Believe me Gary." His tone was deadly serious and flat as he looked at Gary for signs of a reaction.

A whirl of thoughts ran through Gary's mind. So this is why they wanted to give me that bonus, he thought. It all made a perverse kind of sense. He wasn't being rewarded for his performance, he was being sucked into the system. All those warnings and here he was with what amounted to no choice at all.

He had just accepted the bonus a week ago, and now they wanted to set the hook and make sure he fell into line. Damn it anyway, he thought, why did I allow myself to get to this point?

He knew he should quit on the spot, but how could he? He had a house closing coming up. He fell back on a technicality; Howard had told him the bonus was for the work he had already done. That meant he'd already earned it. But he didn't *have* it, and if he left now, he for sure would never get it. Besides, if he quit, he sure as heck couldn't stay around Steuben, and that meant backing out on the house altogether. And Jenna. I've got no choice at all, he thought. I've got to gut this one out.

As G.T. left Gary's office, he said, "You and Howard sort this out later, but this is an opportunity, Gary, not a demotion."

"What was that all about?" Leigh asked as she replaced G.T. in the doorway, handing him a small stack of phone messages.

"Oh, nothing," Gary said.

As the day wore on, Gary began the process of self-justification. The warnings he had received from Dan Anthony notwithstanding, he had not, at least not yet, done anything illegal. He could always quit later if he was asked to do something wrong. Suppose Anthony had never said anything to him? He wouldn't be suspicious of Howard's motives; curious perhaps, but he'd never suspect price fixing. And maybe Anthony was wrong.

The next morning, after a sleepless night, Gary still had not settled on a course of action. At mid-day, Howard called and asked Gary to come to his office. As usual, he was casually dressed and smoking like an old diesel truck. Oblivious to the foul air, the fish swam contentedly in their tank. "Gary, you're doing a fine job – hell, you're doing a great job," Howard began. He paused and blew out a puff of smoke. "I know G.T. has already talked to you about this mentor arrangement, but I want to tell you again that we view it as a positive move. We want you to get experience in some of these market negotiations. Gary, we've got a lot of older guys around here and we see you as one of the younger guys that we want to groom. We see this as a positive."

Howard paused as Gary felt a wave of fear and excitement run through his body. Why were they being so defensive about the whole thing, unless they knew it was the start of trouble? And they had to know that he knew, too. Or at least suspected.

"Gary, you're going places," Howard said. "And we wouldn't give you the things we do unless we believed that. Now it's time for you to move up to the next level. This isn't forever, we just want you to learn how to be a TLP kind of guy," he finished with a smile that seemed almost kindly.

"Monday morning, be prepared to tell me who the competitors are in the artificial sweetener business, where their plants are located, how much they are producing and what the capacity of each of those plants is. We're going to turn this thing around to where we're making good money." Howard paused and lit another cigarette.

Over the weekend, Gary compiled the information and Monday morning at 7:30 sharp, was in Howard's office to report on the three other producers: one Japanese, one Chinese and one Korean. He told Howard the capacity of each of their plants, how much of that capacity they were using and how much product they were selling.

After reviewing the details, Howard stubbed out his cigarette and took a deep breath. "Well, the problem is pretty simple, isn't it? You've got about twenty or thirty percent more capacity than what the market is using, so we have to sit down with these guys." He paused for a second. "Gary, do you know them, I mean well enough to pick up the phone and invite them for a visit?"

"Well, I know who they are, at least," Gary answered. He thought for a quick moment about his other relationship with two of the three companies. Nippon Kagaka and Daehan Hwa-Hak were still paying royalties for using his patent, but that wasn't relative to anything he was doing at TLP, and in any event, he hadn't seen any of that money for years. Thinking about the bank account in Seoul suddenly, for the first time in a long time, something occurred to him: somewhere in that bank, he was listed as a co-signatory on the account, along with Lee Cha. He didn't have to pay taxes on that money; he presumed she did, Korean taxes. Which meant that maybe G.T. was right about overseas profits, and if Switzerland didn't have income taxes, then it probably was legal for him to take the bonus, just like G.T. said.

Howard interrupted his thoughts. "You've got to get hold of them as quickly as you can and get them here to see us. We need to sit down with them, separately if possible."

"It's already evening in the Far East," Gary said. "I'll call them tonight – tomorrow morning their time."

"Fucking slant eyes," Howard said. "They can't even get the time of day right."

Gary left the office at 6:00 and drove to his apartment. He had some leftover Chinese food in the refrigerator, and he heated it up in the microwave. Here I am in Steuben, Indiana, he thought, eating Chinese food and sick to death because I have to call some guy in China.

Actually, he had two calls to make, one to Shanghai and one to Tokyo – homes of the two biggest companies in the artificial sweetener business. The Korean outfit was much smaller, and Gary figured that if he could get the deal cut with the two big boys, the Koreans would follow.

He planned to make the calls about 10:30 on the special OPX line the company had installed in the apartment. He finished the leftovers, lay down on the couch and tried to watch television. He didn't have a clue about what he was watching. Then the phone rang.

"Hey, guy, whatcha up to?" Jenna said.

His face brightened at the sound of her voice. "Indigestion," he said. "Courtesy of General Tzo."

"Ah, you've been to the Canton Palace," she said.

"How'd you know?"

"Well, maybe it was woman's intuition. Or maybe because I know there are only two Chinese restaurants in Steuben, and the other one doesn't serve General Tzo's Chicken."

"Is there no limit to your knowledge?" he asked, chuckling.

"Actually, yes. There's one thing I've never been able to figure out."

"What's that?"

"If they ever got together, what sort of military strategy would General Tzo and Colonel Sanders come up with?"

He burst out laughing. "I don't know," he said. "But it'd be hell on chickens." God it was good to talk to her.

"There's one other thing I can't figure out," she said.

He sensed a change in the tone of her voice. "What's that?"

"Why we never see each other any more."

"Aaaaaaaaa, I think it has something to do with a girl who needed some space."

"Well, maybe now she needs some companionship."

"If she can hang on until tomorrow night, I can put that deal together.

Say seven o'clock?"

"Okay. Don't be late."

And you thought this was going to be a bad day, he said to himself as he hung up. He looked at the clock. It was just after 9:00. I've got to focus on these Asia calls, he thought. He picked up the folder he had brought home and stared at it. But all he could think of was Jenna.

The hour and a half dragged by interminably. Finally it was 10:30. He picked up the phone and dialed the long string of numbers for Nippon Kagaka in Tokyo. The operator spoke perfect English and put him through to the office of Sumiko Numata, General Manager. Numata expressed total confusion as to why Gary was calling and complete skepticism about his invitation to come to Steuben. There was no question that Gary was making himself understood; Numata had been educated in the U.S. and had a very good command of the English language.

So the confusion and skepticism were real, and not a matter of failed communication. Gary told him that TLP wanted to discuss forming an association of artificial sweetener producers that would promote artificial sweetener usage. He explained that TLP had been part of such an association for petroleum distillers for almost 25 years, and he wanted to see if it made sense to put together a similar association for sweeteners.

Numata's response was wary, measured and perfectly understandable. TLP had taken almost half his company's sweetener business; a product that had once been profitable was now hemorrhaging money from their bottom line with no end in sight. When you think about it, it's amazing he would even talk to me at all, Gary thought.

The second call, to Song Dian-Nuan, chairman of New World Chemical Corporation, the Chinese company, produced, albeit with much greater difficulty, the same result. It was difficult to get the call through, difficult to find anyone among the clerical staff who spoke English, and difficult to explain his purpose to Song, whose own English was marginal at best. At the end, though, Gary was pretty sure he had been both understood and rebuffed.

When he finally hung up, Gary realized he had an odd feeling about what had just happened. He had just failed miserably in his assignment. But somewhere deep inside him, he wasn't disappointed at all. He went to the refrigerator and opened a can of beer. Suddenly, he realized why he didn't feel upset at his failure. If the Asians wouldn't agree to meet, there couldn't be a price-fixing deal. Maybe, he thought, that should be my strategy. If I screw this up, I won't have to do anything illegal. He downed the beer and went to bed feeling really good about the day.

Howard was unfazed when Gary relayed the conversations to him the next morning. "Well, hell, Gary, let's see, if they don't want to come to Indiana, why don't we go over there?" he proposed.

When he got back to his desk, Gary had half a dozen calls to return. One was from Jenna.

"Bad news," she said. "They've just taken my grandmother to the hospital, so our date is off. Mom and I are leaving this afternoon for Ft. Wayne to be with her."

"I'm sorry," Gary answered.

"She's eighty-nine," Jenna said, "and hasn't been well for months, so it wasn't unexpected." She paused. "What I'm sorry about is... well, you know what it is."

"I'm sorry about that too," he replied. "Call me the minute you know when you're going to get back."

"I will, don't worry," she said.

CHAPTER 35

As it turned out, Jenna's grandmother died the next Monday, and the funeral was set for Thursday. When it was over, the family spent three days sorting out a huge household full of possessions. "It's a damned disaster," Jenna told him on the phone the day the old woman died. "I'm not going to get home for a week!"

It was a week of telephone tag frustration for Gary, but eventually he reached both Numata and Song Dian-Nuan and won a reluctant agreement that they would see TLP if Gary and Howard made the trip across the Pacific. Song ultimately suggested a meeting in Hawaii, with a game of golf included, and Howard jumped at the chance when Gary told him. "Hell, that'll be great, Gary," he boomed. "See if the Jap guy will go for that!"

It didn't work. Numata was very cold and still insisted that if they were to get together, it would have to be at their offices in Tokyo, and so they agreed. The meetings were set for mid-April.

On Friday, G.T. came to Gary's office, looking very agitated. "I just got a call from William," he said. "The fucking President of France called him personally, all pissed off because some idiot consumer types over there are spreading rumors that Sugere causes cancer, and their fucking congress or parliament or whatever the hell they have is all up in arms."

"I've had some reports," Gary said, "but I had no idea it had reached that level of importance."

"Well, it has. And William wants your ass in Paris on Monday to handle the damage control."

Monday! The day Jenna was due to return from Ft. Wayne. Of all the rotten luck. But if William C. wanted his ass in Paris, his ass would be in Paris.

"There's one good side to it," G.T. said. "When you finish, you can bop over to Geneva and open your new bank account!" He slapped Gary on the back in a vain attempt to cheer him up.

Night was falling on Sunday when Gary cleared Customs at Charles de Gaulle Airport, and was met by Armand Pomerleau, the man who had replaced Ralph Sori as head of TLP's European marketing operations. Pomerleau did not appear confident. "It's a mess," he told Gary.

"But we've done the tests," Gary protested. "None of them showed any hint that Sugere had any carcinogenic effects."

"Ah, *monsieur*," said Pomerleau, smiling. "Tell that to René Beaulieu." Beaulieu was the leader of the Green Party in France, and chief instigator of the Sugere cancer crisis. "Your problem, Gary, is that you are being logical. This has nothing to do with logic." He paused and handed Gary a small piece of paper. "You are to call Mr. Hargiss at this number before leaving the airport," he said.

"Mr. *William Hargiss*?" Gary asked. Looking at the number he already knew the answer. It was the Washington, DC area code.

"But of course," Pomerleau said.

The phone conversation lasted all of 30 seconds. "I want you to remember one thing," Hargiss told him. "It's a city: Calais.'" There was no further explanation, and the click on the phone told him Hargiss had moved on to other things.

When they walked into the lobby of the Hotel Crillon, a small, immaculately dressed man approached Gary. "*Monsieur* Long?" he asked.

"*Oui*," Gary replied, "*c'est moi*."

"Monsieur Long, what is your favorite city in France?" the man asked.

Gary stared at him, confused. His favorite city in France? Then he it hit him. "*Calais*," he answered. "*J'adore Calais*."

The man reached into his pocket, handed Gary an envelope and disappeared into the crowd.

"What was that all about?" Pomerleau asked.

"Beats the heck out of me," Gary replied, pocketing the envelope.

When he read its contents in his room a few minutes later, Gary realized that the damage control strategy was going to be very different from what he or any of the other TLP executives who would be in the room had anticipated. He also realized again the extent of William C. Hargiss's resources.

In the news conference Monday afternoon, Pomerleau read a statement in which he accused René Beaulieu of being secretly in the pay of the International Sugar Company of New Orleans. By noon Tuesday, the comptroller of that corporation had confirmed the accusation and resigned his job. The crisis was over. Six months later, the comptroller was hired by Randolph Thad's cable television network.

Tuesday afternoon, Gary took the Eurorail coach to Geneva. G.T. had suggested that he set up an account with Union Bank, but the next morning, Gary noticed a branch of Swiss Bank Corporation across from his hotel. It wasn't the bank G.T. had suggested, but there it was, so Gary simply walked across the street, introduced himself to a receptionist and said, "I want to open an account."

He was ushered to a waiting area and within a few minutes was escorted to an elevator and sent to an office on the second floor, where he was met by two men. After a few minutes of chatting, they asked to see his passport. One of the men wrote down some information on a form as he looked over Gary's documents. After four or five minutes, his passport was handed back to him and he was given an account form to sign. That was it.

CHAPTER 36

When Gary got back to Steuben on Thursday afternoon, it was bitter cold and he was jet-lag exhausted. He went straight to his apartment, called Leigh to make sure there wasn't anything he had to do that day and went to bed.

The next morning, he had a bad cold. He bundled himself up and went to the office.

"You're very much in demand today," Leigh told him. "I think they're planning a party for you, given all the smiles around here." Then she looked at him more closely. "You look terrible," she said.

Howard and G.T. walked into his office together. "You sure kicked some butt in Gay Paree," Howard said, slapping Gary on the back.

"Way to go, Gary," G.T. added. "And I can assure you that William is just as pleased as we are with the way you got things handled."

"Thanks, guys," Gary said. "William did all the heavy lifting."

Leigh walked in carrying a teacup and a file box filled with medicine. "Can't you see this man is sick," she scolded Howard and G.T. "Let him alone now while I tend to him." The two men looked at each other, shrugged, and left the room.

"Now," Leigh said, placing a steaming cup of honeyed lemon tea on his desk. "Drink this and take two of these and one of these." She picked out two bottles from the file box and set them beside the cup. "You'll feel better."

"Yes, nurse Curtis," Gary said, counting out the pills.

An hour later, he felt well enough to call Jenna.

"Can we get together tonight?" she asked.

"Its fine by me," he said, "but I hope I don't give you my cold."

"You don't sound good."

"Believe me, I don't feel good, either."

"Well, I've been waiting a long time for my companionship, and I don't want to wait any longer. Are you well enough to travel?"

"Seeing you would be the best medicine I could think of," he said, looking out through the open door to make sure Leigh wasn't listening. He didn't want to offend her by appearing to put her remedies in second place.

"Why don't I drive up to Steuben?" she suggested. "We'll have dinner at Wisner's and you can get home early and get some sleep."

Leigh brought him some chicken soup for lunch, and as he was eating it, G.T. reappeared.

"Gary, how do you feel about meeting with the Japs and Chinks?" he asked.

"All right, I think we've got the appointments set," Gary said, less than enthusiastically.

"This thing has really got you down hasn't it? Are you getting discouraged?"

"I'm not discouraged, I'm just confused," he answered honestly. "I mean, what's the need? We've really been doing pretty well on our own. We've taken thirty-five percent of the world market in one year, production is improving, and I think they'll have to back down sooner or later on pricing anyway."

G.T. nodded, and Gary could tell that he was in agreement. It surprised him.

"Gary, Howard likes all this psychology bullshit," G.T. said. "Me, I just like to kick ass and take names. I really agree with you, we should just go out and kick ass. We are the low cost producer in almost everything we're in, and I'm sure over time we will be in this, too. When you think about it, why in the hell are we making deals with people that we should be kicking the ass off of? But hell, Howard calls the shots, and his father backs him up. I'm in charge of managing production and they're in charge of the business end."

The sight of Jenna cheered him up when she walked into Wisner's, but it couldn't do much for his throat or sinuses. He ordered a pasta dish and regretted it the moment the waiter set it in front of him. The closing was coming up in two weeks, and Jenna filled him in on the latest details. He talked briefly about his trip, but didn't feel he could tell her what really had happened. She relayed some details of the funeral and complained that her house was a mess with all the junk she had acquired. Try as they might, neither of them could be witty. All in all, it was an unsatisfactory evening. In the freezing cold of the parking lot, she gave him a little kiss on the cheek and told him to get better fast.

CHAPTER 37

In March, the market for Sugere continued to erode and the price fell to 58¢ per pound. TLP's production costs had also continued to fall but still remained above the selling price. They were still losing money. The engineers said TLP could expect costs to reach a low of 50¢ per pound when everything was working right. They were still a long way from that however, and who knew what the price would be by the time they got there?

Gary and Jenna saw each other once or twice a week, and while none of their dates was as disappointing as the dinner at Wisner's, they remained curiously dispassionate. Gary got his $200,000 check and sent it to Geneva. The house closing came off without a hitch on the fifteenth of March, and Gary moved in the following Saturday, renting a U-Haul trailer to move the few belongings he had at the apartment. He could have put it all in one room. Jenna brought a bottle of champagne and helped him unpack a few boxes while Justin and Mark raced through the empty house. When they left, she gave him a kids-are-watching kiss, and then he was alone. He wandered through the rooms, wondering why in the world he had bought the place. It needs furniture, he thought, that's all. No, he thought again, it needs Jenna. So why was he holding back? She wasn't being aggressive either, to be sure, but he knew the fault for the slow pace of their courtship – if that's what it was – was really his.

What was bothering him? Truth was, he knew the answer. He had crossed a bridge in his life; he was now a bought and paid-for member of a criminal conspiracy. He could count the number of days before the crime would actually be committed, and it was driving him nuts.

The middle of April came far too quickly, and the time for his and Howard's departure to Japan was at hand. Finally, one Friday night he flipped the calendar over to the page that had "Trip to Japan" marked on it. Gary turned off the lights feeling a sense of dread.

For Jenna, the past several weeks had been equally maddening. The depressing cold weather hung on, Mark was having trouble at school, and the Caldwell-Long closing was the only one Potter Realty had made since the first of the year.

As for Gary, she just couldn't figure out what to do. She left the office early that Friday – there was no reason not to, with nothing going on – and on a whim stopped at Shapiro's Jewelers. "Sammy," she said, taking off her watch, "how much is this worth?"

"Whew," the old man said. "Don't see many like that around here. Let me look it up. He turned away from her and began riffling through a stack of catalogs on the credenza behind the counter. Finally he found the one he wanted. He slid his glasses down on his nose and peered over them at the fine print, running his finger down the column of numbers. He paused, looked at the watch again, and closed the book. "Retail price, seventeen hundred and fifty dollars," he said.

She swallowed hard, told Sammy thanks, put the watch back on and walked out of the store.

"Good to see you, Jenna," the old man called after her.

At Shapiro's, you can buy a watch for $20, she thought as she walked back to her GMC. He also has really nice ones for $300 or $400. But she was willing to bet that no one else in Wonanonly had a $1,750 watch.

And I don't care if he is the president of some division at TLP, she thought, you don't give a girl a present like that if you aren't nuts about her.

So why did he seem to be backing off now? She thought about it all the way home.

The boys were still at school when she got there. She set the ironing board set up in the dining room; ironing was always good for thinking. Probably it was all her fault for putting him off in the first place. Then she totally screwed up their fantastic first date. Then when she finally got up enough courage to fish for a second date, she had to cancel it. Why wouldn't he back off, given how her attitude seemed to change from day to day?

She heard the school bus pull up, and a moment later, the boys burst into the house. That is, Justin burst in. Mark trailed behind, seemingly hesitant even about entering his own home. They were the flesh of her flesh, and she suddenly saw herself as both of them combined. Some days she was Justin, aggressive and hard-charging. Other days she was Mark, shy, confused, unsure of what to do.

"Look, Mom, I got an A," Justin called to her.

She called Gary that night, sensed that his depression was even worse than usual and asked what was wrong.

"Oh, nothing really. I'm just getting ready to go to Japan, and I hate traveling there. It takes so long to get there and come back; besides, I really hate the food."

She doubted that was the whole truth, but damn it, it was time to be Justin.

She laughed and said, "Well, I'll tell you what. When you get back, I'll make you a real American dinner you won't forget. Maybe that'll give you something to look forward to."

She fell asleep that night determined to get an A this time.

Gary fell asleep that night wondering if he could figure a way to flunk Price Fixing 101.

CHAPTER 38

Howard spent the night before the trip to Japan with a waitress named Sandra and had her drive him to the airport.

"It must be exciting to fly all over the world," Sandra said as they rolled through the empty streets of Steuben in her Honda.

"It sucks," Howard replied. "And for Christ's sake, shut up. I've got thinking to do."

What he was thinking about was the flight itself. There wasn't much planning necessary for what to do when they got to Tokyo. Just play it by ear. But Gary was likely to pepper him with questions on the plane.

The boy is not quite ready, he decided. He's a little more goody-two-shoes than Tully had thought, and that fucking Dan Anthony had spooked him. He should have fired that candy-assed son of a bitch two years ago, but he hadn't, and now it didn't really matter much. As they neared the airport, Howard decided to Sphinx it on the trip. It was probably the best policy anyway. There was always a chance of being overheard on an airplane.

Through the plate-glass windows, he could see Gary sitting in the company lounge waiting for him when they pulled up. Howard grabbed his luggage from the back seat of the Honda. "Take care of that ass," he said to Sandra, "it's your future." He slammed the door and walked up the sidewalk to the lounge. The co-pilot rushed out the door to meet him and carried the bags to the King Air that would take them to Chicago, where they would catch the non-stop to Tokyo.

"Ready to go?" he said to Gary.

"Ready as I'll ever be," Gary replied, rising quickly when he saw Howard enter the lounge.

Howard didn't stop, walking directly out the back door and across the tarmac to the plane, Gary falling in behind him. In seconds they were rolling toward the runway.

The second best thing about traveling in the company plane, Howard thought, is that you don't have to put up with any stupid safety instructions. The best thing is that the whole fucking cabin is the smoking section.

He knew the 13-hour flight to Tokyo would be non-smoking, and he had brought some nicotine gum with him to ease the problem. But in the 35 minutes to Chicago, he could get in, what, about seven cigarettes, he figured.

It'll drive fucking Gary nuts, he thought.

The two men didn't say a word to each other on the short flight. Gary was reading the morning paper, his air vent full open. Howard looked out the window as he puffed, watching as the greening fields were replaced by sprawling suburbs and then the Chicago skyline, half obscured by a layer of smog. The yellow fog that rubs its back upon the windowpanes, Howard thought.

"We may be the only white people in first class," he said to Gary as they checked in at O'Hare. "Fucking slant-eyes are everywhere."

Gary just nodded.

As soon as the 747 was airborne, Howard pulled a book of crossword puzzles out of his briefcase. He liked doing crossword puzzles and he was exceptionally good at it. It was something that gave him confidence that he was not just a dumb kid who had only gotten where he was because his name was Hargiss.

A few minutes later, Gary nudged him and asked, "What do you expect out of these meetings?"

Howard stared at him for a moment. "We'll make our visit, we'll see what their attitude is, you know, look them in the face, eyeball 'em and see what's possible." It was the only business discussion they had during the entire 13-hour trip.

They ate, drank, watched the movies and took naps. Howard chewed gum and did his crossword puzzles. Gary read a Tom Clancy novel. Howard had already read it, and thought about discussing Clancy with Gary, but decided against it. When they spoke to each other, it was mainly to complain about how long the flight was. The flight attendants came in two types: male and ugly. Howard decided that was all right with him. He used to flirt with pretty stewardesses, but had concluded there was no point to it.

When he wasn't reading, Gary tried to distract himself by thinking about the future. He had a great house, and money in the bank, and things with Jenna were looking up. But he couldn't banish his sense of foreboding. He certainly didn't relish the thought of becoming involved in price fixing. He tried, as he had lying in bed the night before, to think of some way he could throw a monkey wrench into the proceedings, but nothing occurred to him.

It took almost an hour to clear Customs at Narita. Howard complained about how rinky-dink the airport was and how much he already disliked the country. When they arrived at the Palace Hotel, Howard and Gary headed to their rooms to freshen up for their dinner meeting with Sumiko Numata.

They met Numata in the lobby. He was a short man, in his mid-50s, with boundless energy that belied the professorial look suggested by his thick black-rimmed glasses. He escorted them to a waiting car and they were driven at breakneck speed through the streets of Tokyo, eventually stopping in front of a restaurant. Upon entering the building, they were quickly escorted to a curtained-off section where two other men awaited them. They took off their shoes and Numata introduced his associates: Masahiko Yamasaki was Numata's assistant, and Keizo Okada was the Japanese equivalent of a U.S. executive secretary. Numata barked orders to the waitress and the men began the task of learning more about each other. It was not easy: the Japanese were clearly on edge, and Howard and Gary were exhausted from the long flight. As a result, it took a great deal of effort to communicate and at best each side probably understood no more than about half of what the other said.

The atmosphere became less strained as the night wore on but stopped well short of congenial. Most of the courses were various types of sushi. Gary could imagine Howard's disgust at the raw seafood, which frankly was no favorite of his, either. They both downed several glasses of saki and toward the end of the meal fried foods began to appear, which Howard and Gary devoured with eagerness. Around 11:00, Numata summoned the limo, rode back with them to the hotel, told them the car would come around to pick them up at 8:30 the next morning and disappeared.

"These people are as cold as that fucking fish," Howard grunted. He was not enjoying his maiden voyage to Japan one bit.

It was now almost midnight and they both desperately needed sleep. As Gary walked to his room, he wondered why Howard would expect anything but a cold shoulder. TLP had caused the price of artificial sweetener to plummet 50% in a market Nippon Kagaka had dominated for 20 years. Maybe, just maybe, he thought, I don't need to do anything for Howard's plan to fail.

CHAPTER 39

The next morning, a gleaming black Lincoln Town Car arrived, and they were driven to a tall modern building about five minutes from the hotel. Howard and Gary signed in at the reception desk and Okada, the secretary, appeared and quickly escorted them to a shiny elevator. Although there was a gaggle of people waiting for elevators, no one got on with them, and they made no stops en route to the top floor. When the elevator stopped, the doors noiselessly parted, and they stepped through a small vestibule into a stark white conference room. Yamasaki was seated on one side of the conference table waiting for them. He stood up, bowed and then shook their hands. Reseating himself, he asked if they minded if he smoked. Finally, Gary thought, Howard had found some common ground with the Japanese.

As Numata entered the room a few minutes later, they all stood, bowed and shook hands. After taking their seats Yamasaki and Howard lit up.

Seconds later, they rose again, as a distinguished-looking man in his 70s entered the room. It was Sadaaki Hamanaka, Nippon Kagaka's Managing Director, the Japanese equivalent of a chief executive officer. It was evident that the Japanese viewed this as an important meeting.

Interesting, Howard thought. The real stuff should begin now. But he was wrong. The small-talk phase was not yet over. The subject turned to golf, and once Howard knew he'd hit common ground he was off and running. "I took lessons from one of your players over here," he said smiling.

"Ah, who might that be?" Hamanaka asked, with a sudden spark of interest in his eyes.

"Hiroshi Nokumura." That brought oohs and ahs from everyone present at the table.

Never one to miss a chance, Howard reached for his wallet and pulled out a snapshot of himself and Nokumura, which drew nods of approval as it was passed around the table.

For the next hour they talked of nothing but golf. Hamanaka excused himself after about 15 minutes, but the golf talk continued. Howard recalled some of the shots he had learned from Nokumura and while he talked Gary could see the air of national pride reflected on the faces of the Japanese executives. For someone who had never done business with them before, Howard was a quick learner. The ice that had surrounded the previous evening's conversation began to melt and Gary could see their hosts' reluctance to trust them begin to crumble, all because of a game. Numata invited them to play at his club and Howard eagerly accepted.

"What have you come to see us for?" Numata said, finally ready to get to the point.

"Well, for one thing," Howard began, "we want to get to know the people that we're dealing with. For another, I tell you what, in a lot of our key business areas like petroleum products, there is an association that works together to help promote the product." Howard paused and looked around the room. "You know, like the dairy producers promote milk, and that helps all the producers, you know, because it educates the customers.

"You all know," Howard continued, "the artificial sweetener industry has lots of extra capacity, but if it were promoted properly that additional capacity wouldn't be a challenge."

He paused, and the Japanese began conversing among themselves in hushed tones, looking at the Americans from time to time with puzzled faces.

Japanese culture is very ancient, Gary thought. They probably think of themselves as the premier culture in the world. Sure, we kicked their ass in the war, but they see that as similar to the barbarians whipping the Romans. To them, we're like a bunch of cowboys shooting from the hip. He studied the faces carefully. Numata seemed to grasp the concept, to be trying to convince the others.

The others are confused, he thought. But none of them trusts us.

Howard, on the other hand, was sure they all understood perfectly what was going on, even if they liked to play dumb. He thought back to the briefing his father had given him about business in Japan. It was customary for Japanese producers of commodity products to meet and even to fix prices. The government took a see-no-evil-hear-no-evil approach. As long as the price fixing was not egregious, no one seemed to care. MITO, their version of the FTC, was far more flexible and willing to look the other way. But they weren't buying this deal, at least not yet. Either they were afraid of the American government, or they just weren't willing to let Tamson-Long in on their secrets. Regardless, they weren't going to proceed on anything quickly.

But, Howard thought, they are also under pressure to do something about their margins. Would that, in the end, overcome their reluctance? It was too soon to tell.

After another hour of shadowboxing, the meeting ended with the Japanese asking simply if Howard and Gary could send them some information on TLP's existing associations. Then they were packed out the door for lunch and an afternoon at the country club.

Numata and Yamasaki joined them for lunch at a nice restaurant with lots of fried food, which came as a relief to both Howard and Gary. "At least this shit's cooked," Howard whispered to Gary at a break in the conversation. During lunch, Howard explained how TLP was structured and the chain of command for reporting. "Gary runs all our biotechnology operations," he explained. "We both report to G.T. Binghamton, our President."

Numata's eyes narrowed, and he asked quickly, "Why are you here then, what do you have to do with Sugere?"

Howard was not expecting the question, and he stumbled for a second before replying, "I've been at TLP for 25 years, and I'm helping to show Gary the ropes, plus I oversee the pricing of all our products and I've been involved in setting up a couple of associations like this before."

After lunch, they headed to the golf course where Howard and Gary played in their suit pants since they didn't have time to go back to the hotel and change. The golf course was an hour away, and as they traveled through the city and into the countryside, the scenery became breathtakingly beautiful, a true glimpse of the paradise Japan must have once been before it became so heavily populated. After their arrival, they were escorted to the first tee where two sets of clubs arrived for them, pulled by a Japanese woman with a scarf over her face.

Howard backed up his claims of golf expertise by scoring in the 70s. The Japanese hosts took the middle ground and duffer Long brought up the rear with a less than impressive score over 100. After the game they relaxed in the clubhouse, had a drink, and then headed back to the hotel. On the ride back, the conversation flowed more smoothly. By the time they got to the hotel, the Japanese had expanded their general request for information to include a proposed structure for the Artificial Sweetener Association, as well as a set of bylaws for the existing Petroleum Products Association. "We get back to you in a month after we have chance to think over," Numata said.

It still wasn't much, but it was all they were going to get. Thanks to golf, Howard had made some progress, but Gary could still hold out hope that the whole thing would collapse. The only problem was he still couldn't think of any way to help it collapse.

Gary had a telephone message when he got back to his room. It was from Song Dian-Nuan, and Gary had a sudden sinking feeling that perhaps Song was going to tell him that New World was backing out of their meeting in Hawaii. Covert strategy or no, he had been looking forward to Maui, and he knew Howard would be furious if the meeting were cancelled. Then he noticed that the number on the message was a local Tokyo number. That made the call even more mysterious. What was Song doing in Japan?

He dreaded the call, anticipating no end of language problems, but in fact the secretary who answered spoke perfect English and put him right through to Song.

"Ah, Dr. Long," Song Dian-Nuan began in his broken English. "Am in Tokyo on way to Hawaii. We have office here. Was thinking you and Mr. Hargiss can see us here in morning before flight."

Gary quickly agreed to the meeting, and called Howard.

In the morning, a limo took them to the New World office. It seemed like they only went a couple of miles, but the ride lasted about an hour and a half through the crowded streets of Tokyo.

Song Dian-Nuan greeted them very warmly, unlike their reception the previous day at Nippon Kagaka, and ushered them to a starkly furnished meeting room on the eighth floor. They were introduced to Bai Ken-ren, general manager of the food additive division, who was waiting for them at the conference table. Mr. Bai was large for a Chinese, with strong hands and a boyish smile.

The meeting proceeded quickly. Howard spent about 20 minutes selling them on the concept of an association; the remainder of the hour was spent on golf.

Toward the end of the meeting, Howard explained that they had given the same proposal to Nippon Kagaka. "I'm not sure they're very eager though," he explained. Bai gave Song a knowing nod. "We can help you get them to agree to such a proposal." He said it with so much confidence Howard was convinced they already had an association in place, and that the discussion between the two companies would not be on whether to set one up, but on whether to allow TLP in as a new member.

"We'll pick you up at the airport in Maui," Gary said as the meeting ended. Bai consulted a notebook and gave them the flight number, and the Americans headed back to their hotel.

When they entered the lobby, Howard looked around and quietly said, "Here's how I see it. These guys are a lot more interested in our proposal than the Japs. Why? Because Nippon Kagaka has an extensive and diversified biotech product line, but for Bai and Song, sweetener is their primary product. The last six months of the price war has been devastating to their bottom line. That's why they seem friendlier, and why they may be our ticket."

"Do you think Nippon Kagaka briefed them after our meeting?" Gary asked.

"After and before," Howard said. "The only reason they're in Tokyo is because they were told to be here. I figure old Hamanaka was on the phone with them while we were having lunch with the other two. But don't think this thing is one-sided. The Japs are bigger and to some extent they call the shots. But they need New World just as much as New World needs them."

"Why?" Gary asked.

"Cover," said Howard. "You can't extradite a Chinaman."

CHAPTER 40

After he finished packing, Gary checked his voice mail for messages. A few of the problems could wait and a few needed immediate attention. He added his responses to each of the messages and forwarded them to the appropriate people, or to Leigh. The last message took him by surprise. Jenna's voice jumped out of the receiver. Jeez, Gary thought, as he felt his heart pounding. Even the sound of her voice makes my pulse race; get a grip, boy. Jenna asked when he would be back in Steuben. She said she had a little paperwork left over from the closing, something the settlement attorneys had messed up, and she needed his signature as soon as possible. She hoped he could see her the day he got back. Gary shook his head. All business, he thought. No mention of the promised dinner. Things sure went up and down with this woman. He punched a code into the phone and got Leigh's voice mail. "In addition to the other stuff, would you call my realtor, Jenna Potter, you've got the number. Tell her, just a second, let me check my tickets....we should be back in Steuben at the airport around seven-thirty Friday night. She can meet me in the lounge if she wants."

"Man, I'll do fuckin' anything not to have to come back to this bucket of shit country," Howard said as he and Gary rode to the airport in the Nippon Kagaka limo. "Make sure if we have any more fucking meetings we do it somewhere else."

Once they were on the plane, Howard's mood improved. In the quiet of the cabin, his mind shifted to the future. Golf on Maui in April – that was just about perfect.

They had a two-hour layover in Honolulu, which they spent on the telephone. By the time the scheduled departure for Maui came, Gary had talked to enough people to feel like he was back in the loop. "Oh, yeah," Leigh said as he was ready to hang up, "Miss Potter said she would meet you at the airport."

They flew in a small ten-seater prop plane to Maui and rented a Lincoln Town Car that seemed almost as big as the plane they had just left. They drove through fields of sugar cane, with the huge mass of Haleakala on their left and the spectacular Iao Mountains on their right. Suddenly, the blue waters of Maalaea Bay appeared before them. Gary checked the map and turned right, following the coastal road through Lahaina to Kaanapali and the Ramada resort. They had barely checked into their rooms when Howard knocked on Gary's door and insisted it was time to hit the course and play a round.

"Look," he said. "It's time for me to get serious about my mentoring. I mean you really stunk up the course in Japan. It was an embarrassment to TLP. So I'm going to give you a golf lesson."

The afternoon was actually enjoyable for both of them. Howard's tips were definitely helpful, and by the end of 18 holes, Gary was already showing improvement in his swing. There was, after all, something useful he could learn from his forced association with the man.

The next morning, they had a big American breakfast and drove to the airport to pick up their guests. When they arrived, both Song and Bai were already sitting outside on benches waiting for them. Song was no more than five foot three, and so thin Gary would have been surprised if he tipped the scales at a hundred pounds. He was already dressed for the golf course with green slacks and a yellow shirt. Bai, a head taller and nearly twice the weight, was wearing a Hawaiian shirt and a pair of gray slacks. Gary grabbed their bags, threw them in the trunk and took off toward the Ramada.

After checking the Chinese in, the group inhaled a quick lunch from the salad bar and headed off to the first tee. They paired off, Gary with Song, and Howard with Bai. Howard won the first hole easily, and when they got to the second tee, he looked Bai in the eye and challenged him, "If Gary and I win this hole, then we get to sell an extra two thousand tons in Thailand."

Bai smiled and chuckled, but didn't answer. As the hole played out, Gary and Song both made bogey. Howard had an easy par and Bai sunk a long putt for his par. On the third tee, Bai piped up while Howard was setting his ball on the tee. "We tie last hole," he said. "No winner. But if we win this hole, then you not sell any product in Japan."

They all laughed, even Gary. It's out in the open now, he thought. Golf and business. Fun and crime. What a crazy world this is.

For the rest of the holes, they played for countries and volumes. The jokes flowed freely back and forth and an air of joviality, even silliness set in. Howard was playing well, and as Gary was beginning to learn, Howard was always in a good mood when his golf game hit its stride.

They got back to the hotel about 6:00 and then headed off to a seafood restaurant where they sat outside under a coconut-palm-leaf thatched roof. Howard was downing Dewars and soda with a twist while the rest of them sipped fruity tropical drinks in coconuts with parasols. After the meal, they moved into the disco bar filled with dancing vacationers.

Midway into the second round of drinks, Howard started kidding Gary.

"Hey, Gary," he teased, "look at all those pretty girls out there. Why don't you go dance with one of them?" The Chinese joined in the chiding.

"Mmm, I'm pretty sure I want to remain virus free on this trip, and it looks like there could be some pretty nasty social diseases represented here," Gary said.

Howard laughed and said, "I didn't say anything about trading body fluids, for Christ's sake," he said. "Just dance."

"Yeah, well, once a girl dances with me, I pretty much own her body thereafter," Gary said, taking a long sip of his drink. "I'd hate to leave a trail of broken hearts."

Howard laughed and sneezed "horseshit" into his cupped hand. "Gary here is our resident geek," he said to the Chinese. "All work and no play."

"He playing tonight," Song said, and they all laughed. Gary was feeling the effects of the booze.

A few minutes later, Song and Bai excused themselves to go to the bathroom, and Gary leaned over and asked Howard why he hadn't brought up price fixing yet.

"Because you're drunk, and I'm not in a hurry," Howard said. "If we go too fast we'll scare 'em off. Just follow my lead on this."

The next morning, they met at 9:00 on the golf course. The overnight coolness was evaporating as the sun announced its presence with tropical authority. No matter how uncomfortable Gary felt at the purpose of the trip, Hawaii was magic, and he felt a twinge of regret that this would be his last day there before heading back to bleak Indiana.

As Gary stepped up to the tee, Bai said, "Hey, Dr. Geek, if I get par on this hole, okay I get half your business this year?" Without missing a beat he had picked up two separate themes left over from the day before.

By the third hole Howard decided it was time to advance his agenda. He leaned over to Song and said, "This sweetener situation doesn't look too good, does it?"

"Oh no, oh no, doesn't look good, not good," Song Dian-Nuan replied.

"I think it look like shit," Bai added.

Howard paused, and teed off before continuing. "I know Nippon Kagaka is the biggest in the business, and even though we talked to them, they still were pretty cold."

Bai drove his ball, and then turned to Howard. "They in business a long time. They think TLP too aggressive, build too much too quick."

Howard thought for a second, then sat down in the cart and said, "You know, if we could do this association thing, we could expand everyone's business by working together."

Nobody spoke for the next three holes. While they were teeing up at the seventh hole, Howard broke the awkward silence. "If I get par on this hole, we'll sell Kagaka's sweetener for them, too."

"Sure. They in business thirty years and you gonna sell for them?" Bai shot back. "They still not over you stealing Brad Redfoot from them." Howard didn't respond and they played the hole in relative silence.

On the 12th hole, Song said, "We will talk to Nippon Kagaka for you about joining this association." As Gary watched Song's face, he knew the diminutive Chinese man understood the code word; the purpose of the "association" was to fix prices. He also knew that Howard had succeeded. He looked over at Howard, who winked at Gary as if to say "gotcha!" That was the last time business was discussed, and Howard started giving golf lessons to them as they finished the round. After lunch, they helped their guests into an airport limo, and Gary went for a walk on the beach.

When Gary got back, Howard met him with a smile. "Hey, whatcha been doin'? Out cruisin' chicks again? I need to call G.T., and you ought to be in on it." Howard reached G.T. at his home and gave him the lowdown. "These Chinks are our ticket, G.T. We've got a long ways to go for things to work out, but these guys are our ticket."

After the phone call, Howard turned to Gary and said, "I wanted you here because this is your business." Gary didn't answer him, but he thought to himself, it may be my business, but right now, you're running the show.

CHAPTER 41

Jenna woke up with a knot in her stomach. She hadn't stopped thinking about Gary since he left for Japan. She had committed herself to take their relationship to the next level, and had given him a strong indication in her offer of "a dinner you won't forget." Her thoughts went back to that first day, showing the house. She recognized his initial reaction to her; she'd seen it before. Always it was flattering, always scary. Probably he had been embarrassed by his own thoughts. That was why he had pulled back. And as for her, why had she pulled back? She was coming off a bad marriage and a bad love affair, that was the answer. How could she be sure this wasn't just a rebound of a rebound?

Trust. It was all about trust. She didn't trust her ability to know who to trust.

But Dr. Gary Long was a cut above the other men she had known, probably a cut above anyone she had ever known. Who could she compare him to? None of her college friends. Certainly no one in Wonanonly. He was handsome, well educated, personable and fun – at least most of the time. He had one of the best jobs in the whole state. And, she thought, stepping out of the shower and looking at herself in the mirror, he eats up your act.

She put on the little bit of makeup she habitually wore, just eyebrow pencil and a touch of lipstick, and thought about doing something fancier. No, she decided, he likes your face just the way it is. Then she went to the closet and pulled out a stone-washed denim jumper, quickly got dressed and hustled the kids out the door.

Darkness was falling when the King Air landed in Steuben. As Gary opened the door to TLP's private terminal, he saw Jenna stand up to greet him. The jumper she was wearing did nothing to flatter her figure, but it still looked good on her. "This is quite a place!" she said.

Howard walked up beside them, a smirk on his face.

"Jenna, I'd like you to meet Howard Hargiss," Gary said. "Howard, this is Jenna Potter, the realtor who sold me my new house." He noticed Howard was still smirking. "Apparently there is some time-sensitive paperwork I've got to sign before I'm even allowed to set foot in the county," he added, trying to dispel the smirk.

"Miss Potter," Howard said, taking her hand. "Had I known there were any realtors so beautiful, I would have been buying a house a week."

Jenna giggled as Howard nodded his head and walked away.

"I've got the papers you need to sign. Is there somewhere we should go?" Jenna asked Gary.

"Nah, we can do it right here." Gary motioned toward a coffee table in the center of the room that was surrounded by four couches. Jenna spread the papers out on the table and Gary glanced down at them. Then he looked up again. "How have you been?" he asked. "How are the boys?"

"Fine, fine," she said nervously. "How was your trip?"

Gary thought about his response. "It was, well, interesting," he said. Jenna cocked her head a little to one side. As the hair fell across her face, she brushed it back behind her ear with one hand. Gary tried very hard to turn back to the papers in front of him, but it was a losing battle. She was just too beautiful.

He picked up the papers and set them on the couch beside him, putting his feet up on the table, and started talking about the trip. He told her about his misadventures on the golf course, and kept Jenna giggling the whole time. Tired as he felt after the long trip, he didn't want to let her go. Maybe, he thought, I should offer to take her to dinner. But *she* had promised *him* dinner when he got back – not that she said it would be the first night. He kept talking all the while, trying to sort out in his mind what he should do next. He was about to run out of stories he felt he could share, when the flight line manager came up and asked, "Do you need anything else, Dr. Long?"

"Nah, I'll be out of here in a minute."

"If it's okay with you, I need to leave to make an appointment."

"Sure, I can lock up."

"No need to do that, sir, the doors will lock behind you, but are you sure I can't do anything else?"

"No, thanks."

He turned back to Jenna, but he was out of ideas and initiative. "Here, you've probably got things to do, and I've kept you away by telling you all these stupid stories," he said.

"Oh, no, I love to hear your stories. Always. But you do need to sign those."

He took a pen out of his pocket and began signing the papers. "You're not even reading them," she said with a note of exasperation. "You're supposed to *read* the papers."

"If you're gonna take advantage of me, I'd prefer it would be in other ways…but I don't think you'd do anything to cheat me," he said. Jenna looked a little panicked. Then, with a shrug of her shoulders, she stood up. Don't stop now, she thought. It's now or never.

She ran her eyes around the room. They were alone. A car drove by outside the plate glass windows, its headlights shining in his eyes. Behind him, she could see the door to the hangar. "You know, I've never seen the inside of a business jet, do you have one here I could look at?" she asked.

"Sure, at least I think there are a couple here, " Gary replied, turning to the hangar door and opening it. He saw that their largest plane, the Dessault Falcon 50, was sitting with its door open on the other side of the hangar. "Come on, let's take a peek."

He followed Jenna into the plane. "Wow, this is incredible," she said. The plane was appointed with leather chairs, a workstation and a wet bar.

"Care for something to drink?" he asked.

Jenna laughed and said, "No, thanks," as Gary sat down in one of the swivel chairs and swung it toward her.

Jenna watched his face and focused on his deep blue eyes. She lifted the hem of the jumper, and sat down on Gary's lap, facing him. She watched the blue eyes fly open with surprise, then narrow slightly, quizzically. She stared deeply into them, looking for something to tell her to stop, but saw nothing of the sort. She leaned forward and kissed him lightly on the lips.

He put his arms around her and held her close. The kiss was no longer light. She slid toward him. Their lips separated and they stared wordlessly at each other for a long moment. Then she stood up and slipped out of her loafers. Reaching under the generous folds of the jumper skirt, she removed a pair of black panties. Holding them up and giving a mischievous grin, she twirled them around once and flipped them onto an empty seat.

In an instant, Gary's mind was clear as a bell. No more confusion, no more indecision, no more jet lag, game-playing or evasions. He wanted her – not just right now but always. He wanted to see that grin every day for the rest of his life. He wanted those kisses every night.

He reached for his belt buckle, barely getting it undone in time, and again she sat on his lap, the loose jumper falling away on either side.

All his senses seemed scrambled: tactile moans, perfumed embraces, all conducted by a rhythmic ponytail. Finally, Jenna collapsed on his chest.

"If that was my dinner," he said softly over her shoulder, "I truly will never forget it."

She straightened up and looked him in the eye. "That was not dinner," she said, with mock sternness. "That was sex."

She stood up. "Furthermore," she said, "if you had bothered to read the papers I brought, you would have seen that they were one hundred per cent BS, except for the part where I wrote out a very clever invitation to you for dinner at my house tomorrow night.

"Since you didn't bother to read it," she continued, pretend-angry, "and therefore would not have shown up, I had no choice but to advance the agenda."

Gary was laughing. "Well, I did sign it, so I guess I'd better show up," he said. "Can I have a copy of the invitation so I can read the particulars?"

"You can have the original," she said. "Now, does this fancy plane have a bathroom?"

"It'd better," he said, suddenly aware of how ridiculous he must look at that moment.

CHAPTER 42

Gary was at his desk by 7:00 the next morning, several piles of paperwork stacked neatly in front of him. Howard popped his head in about 7:30, and said, "G.T. wants to see us." Gary joined him immediately and together they headed to G.T.'s office. He greeted them at the door. "Hell, I was wondering what was going on. I didn't think you guys were ever coming back," he grinned. Then the grin left his face. "Tell me in detail how it went."

Howard told how he broke the ice with New World by making bets on the golf course, but confessed he had gotten little accomplished with Nippon Kagaka.

"They feel like they own the industry," he said. He reaffirmed that New World was the ticket to get a foot in the door with the Japanese. Without really leaving anything important out, he summarized the whole week in five or ten minutes, and Gary thought the ratio was just about right. They had taken a week to mine a lode of coarse rock containing five minutes of gems. Evil gems.

"What's the next step?" G.T. asked.

"We've got two things to send them," Howard said. "The Petroleum Refiners bylaws, which I have in my desk, and an outline of how the proposed new association would be set up. I made some notes on that on the plane, and I'll dictate a more complete memo this morning. Gary, you can fax it all to Numata and Song this afternoon."

"And then?" G.T. asked.

"Then we wait. We need to get everyone together, but it can't happen until we hear from one of those guys," Howard answered. "Shit, I sure hope we don't have to do it in Japan! I don't ever want to go there again, and I especially don't ever want to eat dinner there again."

Gary smiled to himself at the mention of the word "dinner."

CHAPTER 43

Gary had been back from Japan and Hawaii for about a week when William Hargiss stopped by his office. It was only the second time he had been there, and as before, it was a surprise visit.

"Well, Gary," Hargiss said as he pulled back a chair and seated himself in front of Gary's desk, "I heard from both Howard and G.T. about your trip to Asia and about you playing around in Hawaii while we were here working our butts off. Sounds like it's possible for things to improve."

Gary didn't say anything but nodded his head in surprised agreement. "What's your feeling on fifty-eight cents?" Hargiss asked. "Think we're stuck there forever?" Sugere prices had been hovering at 58¢ per pound for the last several weeks.

"I don't think so William," Gary replied deliberately. "We've taken a third of the market and someone will have to crumble soon. I don't think the Chinese can take much more of this market."

Hargiss dropped his eyes to Gary's nameplate and toyed with it for a second. "G.T.'s got production costs as low as he thinks he can get them for a while. We can't continue to lose three million a month forever."

"Obviously that's the reason we went there," Gary countered, trying not to sound sour.

"Howard did well, didn't he," Hargiss phrased it as a question, but intoned it as a statement.

This was dangerous territory, Gary realized quickly. He didn't feel like flattering the boss's son, and was still disgusted by what he had taken part in, but only a fool would speak out now. "Pardon me?" Gary asked in a quiet respectful voice.

"You know, making deals, scaring competitors." Hargiss's voice drifted off. He could read the discomfort written all over Gary's face. "You hang in there, buddy, we gotta have you. If Howard asks market sizes, you have the answers. You're the one who knows all the aspects of the business."

He paused again for a second, got a faraway look in his eyes, then focused back on Gary. "You remember that bonus you got back in January?"

"I certainly do, Mr. Hargiss, and I really appreciated it," Gary said, pointedly adding, "I worked hard getting the plant built and the division set up. It was nice to know it was appreciated." I'm on the record, he thought. That's what the bonus was for. He hadn't even been sure Hargiss knew about the bonus, but he obviously did, and if he was going to tell Gary it had anything to do with price fixing, Gary wanted to stake out his position up front.

What Hargiss said next floored him. "Well, I've got something here for you, and that's the real reason that I'm here this morning. "G.T. and I have been talking. You're a quick learner and you move fast. You did a hell of a job in Paris, and you played the board like a violin down at Longboat Key. I'm impressed. We see big potential here for you, especially with Howard's help. I know he's rough around the edges, and maybe that's my fault, but the truth is, I'm damned proud of what he's done. Nobody's perfect – not me, G.T., Howard or you. But with the right training and the right incentives..." The old man paused for a moment. "With the right training and the right incentives, the right *people* rise to the top. The key to what I do is to pick the right people and then add the other things. That's what TLP is all about."

Where was all this heading? What did Hargiss "have" for him? Gary's mind spun in circles.

Hargiss got up from the chair and turned his back to Gary. He seemed to be studying the painting of the boy fishing. Or maybe he was staring right through it. Gary couldn't be sure, and he shifted nervously in his chair.

"This won't happen at the next board meeting," Hargiss said, "because we have to prepare some other people for it, but we are going to give you some added responsibility and make you a corporate VP. We want you to take on some other things beyond the Bio-tech division, especially after you get the Sugere problems ironed out.

"It'll happen sometime this year, though."

Gary was listening, but not really paying attention because his mind was racing ahead trying to sort out what it all meant. He would be by far the youngest corporate VP, putting him squarely in the lead for management advances

"Anyway, there's one thing I can do right now, and that's to give you a little money to say thanks. In fact we want to give you a million bucks." Hargiss turned again and his piercing eyes focused directly into Gary's.

Gary was dumbstruck. The interview had begun with Hargiss complaining that his division was losing millions every month, and now he was offering him a gigantic bonus. It was weird. Finally, Gary stammered, "Will this be like in...stock options or like cash or...or what?"

"You'll get more stock options when you become a corporate VP, but this is cash just like you got before." Hargiss paused again and then continued, "By the way, don't tell anybody; this is just between us. There are a lot of guys who have been around a lot longer who are still important to us so we're going to have to walk this pretty delicately.

"This is a big bonus, too, Gary. Very rarely have we given a bonus this big and we have never given one to anyone this young and only two years with the company. It's a big deal and you should be honored. We think a lot of you, Gary."

Those eyes, Gary thought. Those eyes, boring holes in mine. What do I want them to find? He let loose of them, and dropped his gaze to his desk, shaking his head. "I'm flabbergasted," he said. I should quit right now, part of him thought. Are you crazy? the rest of him replied. Who quits on someone who's just given him a million dollars?

"I...I just want to understand," he stammered. "This promotion, and the bonus, are based on what I did in Paris and Florida, and what I've done to build the division?"

He steeled himself and raised his head, trying his best to meet the challenge of Hargiss's eyes, trying to stand his ground. What if Hargiss said, no, it's an advance on the price-fixing you and Howard are going to do? Then he'd have to quit. He'd *have* to.

But, incredibly, Hargiss blinked, and raised his eyes, looking over Gary's head at the diplomas on the wall. "Sure," he said.

"Just take it and enjoy it, shit it's worth double that amount because it's tax free." Hargiss got up and rubbed his chin. "Let's see, where did you take that last one – Europe?" Gary nodded.

"Well, on your next trip to Asia just set up an account there and do it through someone there this time," Hargiss barked.

"Okay," Gary mumbled.

He was numb. What a bizarre place this was. Just when he thought nothing could surprise him, bam, another shot comes in from left field. Where would it end?

Hargiss started to leave the room, but then turned and sat down in the chair in front of Gary. "I'm seventy-five years old," he said. "At best I've got maybe another ten good years. Think big picture, Gary. You could sit at my desk one day. You really could."

With that, he got up and left. As soon as Gary was sure Hargiss was gone, he put his elbows on his desk and clasped his head tightly in his hands. A new thought entered his mind. He could sit at Hargiss's desk. He could run TLP. He, Gary Long, could get rid of all the corruption and shady dealing, all the price fixing and technology stealing. He could clean up the company, keep the aggressive, no-red-tape style, and make everything perfect. He'd retire G.T., send sleazy Howard packing. He'd bring Ralph Sori back, and Becky too, promote sharp guys like Brad Redfoot and Buffy Carney. He would become, truly, the Long of a new Tamson-Long.

Hargiss headed back up to his office and called G.T. on the phone. "I just gave the kid a million bucks, but you've got to stop the bleeding. How're the quarter numbers?"

"They suck, fuckin' analysts are gonna have a lunch on our asses this quarter," G.T. responded.

"That's what I thought," Hargiss said. "Well, it's all up to Howard, now. I think he'll put it together. My only worry was that our boy Gary wasn't committed enough to keep from screwing it up. That's why I had to move on the bonus sooner than I might have wanted. We're in big shit trouble on this whole bio-tech thing unless Howard and he get the deal with the Japs put together. We can't take any chances on that. Meantime, we'll just have to fake our way through. Let me know the numbers as soon as fuckin' Kincaid gets 'em to you. I'm sure as hell going to need to pull some money in this quarter."

"Yeah, okay," G.T. said. "But it sure seems like we've been drawing a hell of a lot more on that well than we've been putting in lately."

"Sometimes that's the price G.T., sometimes that's the price," Hargiss said. "Bottom line, we've got what we need in a player. How much is that worth?" He started to hang up, but put the receiver back up to his head. "Your next bonus is about due, too, isn't it?"

"Uhh, yeah, next month," G.T. replied.

"Well, why don't you have Gary attach it to his?"

CHAPTER 44

Gary ate lunch alone, trying to make sense of the morning's conversation, and to turn his new found goal into an actual plan. He was still in a daze when he got back to his office.

"What's wrong?" Leigh asked.

He shook his head and looked at her. "Why do you think something's wrong?" he asked.

"Because you didn't say those two little words, like you always do."

"What two little words?"

Leigh did an impression of Gary walking into the office. "Any calls?" she said in her deepest voice.

Gary couldn't help laughing. "Nothing's wrong," he said. "Believe me. Now then, Ms. Curtis, are there any calls?"

"No," she said, giggling.

They both laughed. "I'm sorry, I couldn't resist that," Leigh said. "Actually, it's almost true. There was only one, from a Mr. John Caldwell. I didn't recognize the name, but he said you would know who he was."

"He's the guy I bought the house from," Gary said, taking the phone message from her hand.

"I was just thinking," Caldwell said after he and Gary exchanged greetings, "It's almost time to open up the pool, and I don't believe I gave you the name of the man I usually hire to do that. "He usually charges about two hundred dollars," Caldwell added hurriedly. "Of course, you can save the money and do it yourself, but I always thought it was worth it to know the job was done right."

"I think I can afford the two hundred," Gary said.

The spring weather was indeed starting to warm up, but Gary had been so consumed with his job he'd almost forgotten he even had a pool. He got the name from Caldwell, called the man and arranged to have him do the job on the first Sunday in May.

That day was forecast to be the warmest of the year so far, and Gary called Jenna as soon as he got up. "Can you come over?" he asked, and she and the boys showed up a few minutes after the pool man arrived.

While Justin and Mark watched the uncovering of the pool in

amazement, Gary and Jenna examined the freshening spring growth in the yard. Bright red and pink azaleas were already blooming on bushes around the house.

"What are these other ones?" Gary asked, pointing to some taller shrubs with large, waxy leaves.

"Rhododendrons," Jenna told him. "See these pods. In a couple of weeks they'll be huge purple and white blossoms that will take your breath away."

"You take my breath away sometimes," he said.

"Sometimes?" she teased.

"Okay, all the time," he grinned.

She led him around behind the house to the grotto. The maples were in full leaf, and the trellised rosebush had hundreds of tiny buds that promised a dazzling summer. "What color will they be?" Gary asked.

"The deepest red you've ever seen," she told him.

They sat on a stone bench facing the trellis, and he put his arm around her shoulder. "I remember the first time you showed me this spot," he said. "It was less than six months ago, but somehow it seems like forever, so much has happened."

"I remember it, too," she said, looking into his eyes. "You seemed pretty uninterested. I really didn't think you'd ever buy the house."

"It wasn't that I was uninterested. I was just distracted."

"By what," she giggled. "As if I didn't know."

"By some real estate agent's cute ass in a pair of tight jeans," he said. "As if you didn't know."

"And is that all you think of me, a cute ass in blue jeans?"

"No," he said, suddenly serious. "You shouldn't ever, ever think that. You've become my best friend, my only happiness, my solace from a business world that's so full of pressures I sometimes can't stand it. If I lost you, I think I'd lose my mind."

She bit her lower lip to stifle the emotion building inside her. "I'm not that good," she said finally. "I'm just a country girl with a checkered past and a couple of kids, peddling real estate in a one-horse town in Indiana."

He stood up and took both her hands, pulling her up to face him. "Who's kind and caring and smart and witty and beautiful and classy and strong...I know you've been through a lot, but look at what you are now, in spite of it or because of it or whatever, I don't know and I don't care, I only know I love you more than I ever thought I could love anyone."

"Oh, Gary, I love you too," she said, smearing his face with her tears as she kissed his neck, cheeks and mouth.

When their lips parted, she wiped her eyes with the heel of her hand. He put his arm around her shoulder and they stood silently for a moment. At length, he noticed some green shoots thrusting from the ground around the rosebush. "Look," he said, "those bushy flowers that were here last fall are coming up again."

She followed the line of his gaze and bent down on one knee. "No," she said. "Those were asters and mums. They won't be up until much later. These are your summer flowers, coreopsis, rudbeckia, bee balm, I think. The brown stubble in between are the asters and mums. Caldwell cut them down to the ground after we were here, so they'd come back strong."

"So there's work involved in taking care of it all," Gary said.

"Oh, sure. And there are places where you should put out some annuals, too."

"I'm an absolute dunce about this stuff. I think I need to hire a gardener."

"I know someone who dearly loves this yard, and she works cheap, too."

"Okay," he said, kneeling beside her. "But if she's got a cute ass, I might not be able to control myself around her." He cupped her chin in his hand and kissed her.

A moment later, they saw the boys racing toward them, Justin in front, screaming, "Mommy, Gary, come see!" while Mark tried to catch up.

"Come look at the pool!" Justin cried, taking his mother's hand and leading her away. Mark hesitated just a moment, and then grabbed Gary's hand and led him off behind the others.

The water sparkled like diamonds in the bright sunshine, and Gary could hear the hum of the pool machinery set back behind a bush beside the pool house. "She's all ready," the pool man said. "Came through the winter real good."

"Can we go swimming?" Justin shouted.

"Yeah, swimming!" Mark echoed.

"Not today," the pool man chuckled. "For one thing, the water's so cold it'd turn you into two big ice cubes. And for another," he turned to Gary at this point, "it's full of chemicals right now. But I've got the heater started and it should be warm enough in a day or so. By that time the chlorine level will be down to just about right, too.

"Do you need me to show you the maintenance things you have to do over the summer?" he asked.

"Yeah, I'm a real novice at this," Gary said. "Why don't you show my, ah, gardener here, too."

After the man left, Gary, Jenna and the boys hauled chaise lounges, tables and other stuff out of the pool house and arranged them around the deck. Justin kept asking if he couldn't just take his shoes off and put his foot in the water, but Jenna kept saying no until he gave up and contented himself by racing around the yard, with Mark in tow.

Gary and Jenna stretched out on chaises. "My father always said he thought living in a house with a pool would be like living in a resort," she said. "I think I can see what he meant."

CHAPTER 45

Later that week, Gary made a fast trip to Hong Kong to set up the account for the bonus. He didn't tell Howard or G.T. about it until the last minute, because he was worried Howard would want him to do a side trip to Tokyo. Not only was he concerned about having to conduct another price fixing meeting, he also couldn't bear the thought of being away from Jenna one day more than necessary. He hadn't told her anything about the bonus, but since his conversation with Hargiss, it seemed like scarcely a minute passed when he didn't think to himself, I'm a millionaire and I'm in love with the most wonderful woman in the world.

When he got back to Steuben, he took the Authorization For Expenditure form to G.T. to be signed, and got another surprise when G.T. told him to redo it. "Make it for a million and a half," G.T. told him. The extra five hundred grand is for something else." When Gary brought him the second AFE, G.T. signed it without a glance. "We'll take care of the wire later," he said.

Gary went back to his office dazed and confused. Leigh was at lunch, and when the phone rang, he picked it up himself. Jenna's voice floated out of the receiver. "Hey, whadda you think about dinner here tonight? Let me cook up a meal you won't forget."

"The last time you said that, I didn't get a thing to eat," he said.

"Oh, you poor baby," she said. "Were you terribly hungry?"

"Man does not live by bread alone."

"I know, he must have peanut butter and jelly," she laughed. "Well, I'll tell you what. You show up tonight and I guarantee you something to eat."

"No peanut butter."

"I promise, it won't be peanut butter."

My real life has surpassed my fantasy life, he thought. "Well, okay, I'll be there," he said. "Look, I know you'll be busy in the kitchen, but is there any chance you could do a little shopping for me and pick out a few things for the house?" he asked.

"Your tastes or mine?"

"What?" Gary asked, puzzled.

"Well, I wondered if you wanted me to pick out things I think you would like for the house, or if you wanted me to pick out things I would like."

Gary laughed. "Is this gonna be our first fight?"

"I hope not!"

Gary could detect a giggle in Jenna's voice. "Good, because I think we should get married. Then whatever you want will be what I'd want, 'cause I want you to be happy."

There was silence on the other end of the line. Maybe he shouldn't have just blurted it out. Maybe he should have waited until tonight, or tomorrow, bought a ring, gotten down on his knees. He certainly hadn't been planning to ask her over the telephone, but he was on such a good roll he figured he would try to extend it.

"I can't believe you just asked me that," Jenna said finally. Then the line got quiet again. In almost a whisper, Jenna said through a tear-choked voice, "Yes, I'll marry you Gary Long." His roll was still rolling.

The next morning, he got a call from Roger Kincaid, TLP's top accountant and comptroller, who asked him to come up to his office. Gary finished up his list of phone calls and headed up to Kincaid's fourth floor office. His secretary was away and Gary tapped on his door.

"Hey, Gary, come on in," Roger said. A trim six-footer in his late forties, he could have passed for an athlete. Only a pair of wire-rimmed glasses hinted that his life was dominated by ledger sheets. He was considered one of the brightest people in the whole corporate structure. He was one of seventeen corporate VPs, the youngest, pending announcement of Gary's appointment.

"Gary, I got this invoice today for a million and a half for this company called FES," Kincaid said, waving the AFE. "What's this all about?"

Gary had figured that Kincaid knew all about the money transfers. He hadn't questioned Rhyner's, or Dink Macabee's, or for that matter, Gary's first bonus. Maybe he doesn't bother with small change under a million, Gary thought. In any event, he wasn't about to put his foot anywhere close to his mouth on this one. He made eye contact, held it and said, "You talk to G.T. yet?"

"No, it's in your division and I wanted to ask you about it first," Kincaid said, not smiling or breaking his eye contact. Gary decided not to play any games. "I think you know what this is for, Roger; you know how some of the key executives are paid here at TLP. My recommendation is that you talk to G.T. if you have any questions; I'm just doing what I was told to do."

Kincaid came up out of his chair like he had hit an eject button. "I wish G.T. Binghampton would quit doing this shit and start playing it straight around here. We're too large a company now to be doing this stuff," he said, more to himself than to Gary. He forcefully stamped the paper, threw it onto his desk and sat back down. Gary got up to leave without saying a word. Whether out of jealousy or anger, for the next few weeks, Kincaid would barely look at him. But Gary didn't return the anger. Instead, he made a mental note to include Roger Kincaid in the new TLP.

Toward the end of May, Leigh buzzed Gary to say that a Mr. Song Dian-Nuan was on the line. His heart sank a little as he picked up the phone. "Mr. Song, how nice to hear from you," Gary said. A short pause ensued as the message made its way through the myriad wires to its destination in Shanghai.

"Dr. Long, I reply to proposal made by Mr. Hargiss regarding association." Song Dian-Nuan paused, then continued, "We would like to meet to discuss with TLP, Nippon Kagaka, and New World all together in Mexico."

Here we go, Gary thought. The three companies responsible for more than 80% of the artificial sweetener production in the world are about to form a cartel.

"When would you like to get together?" he responded.

"Soon. I am proposing early June at Nikko Hotel in Mexico City."

Gary didn't want to say another word without Howard on the line, so he said, "Mr. Hargiss is a few doors down from me. Can you wait while I go get him to be in the conversation with us so we don't have to go through this again?"

"Sure, sure, I wait," Song Dian-Nuan said. Gary stuck his head in Howard's door and told him what was happening. Before he had a chance to finish Howard stood up and said, "Let's go!"

Back in his office, Gary switched the phone to the speaker setting and asked Song Dian-Nuan to bring Howard up to speed. The Chinese executive repeated what he had just said to Gary and waited for a response. Howard pulled out his pocket calendar and set the time and date. Song Dian-Nuan added that Nippon Kagaka wanted to have a representative from their French division there as well.

Howard agreed wholeheartedly.

Howard's face was covered with a grin from ear to ear when the conversation ended. "Let's go see G.T.," he said as he stood up. For the next couple of weeks, the mood around the office bordered on jubilation as G.T. and Howard breathed a collective sigh of relief.

Gary and Jenna set their wedding date for the 15th of June. Jenna wanted a small, private wedding, so the arrangements were easily and quickly made. Gary would have a couple of weeks after Mexico to get everything in order before he took off on his honeymoon.

On June second, the day before they were to leave for Mexico, Howard stopped by Gary's office and said, "Let's go get our marching orders from G.T."

"There's not much we can say now," G.T. said. "Let's see what they throw on the table."

Howard pressed him. "We gotta have a minimum that we'd be willing to agree with; after all we built this big-ass plant. Can't we find some base to work from?"

G.T. was still unwilling to commit. "Let's get a real good feel for what they're thinking and move accordingly," was all he would say.

The next morning they hopped on the King Air, headed to Chicago and caught a direct flight to Mexico City. They landed in the late afternoon, and were met by Peter Rhyner as soon as they had cleared Customs. Rhyner offered to take them out to dinner, and Howard agreed, stipulating that he got to choose the place. "I hate Mexican food, and I hate the goddamn Mexicans," he said. Gary looked over at him and said with a grin, "If it's not a steak or hamburger or a cigarette, it's not much good is it Howard?"

Rhyner found them an Argentine steak house, and they had an excellent meal. Back at the hotel, Gary asked Howard what he thought the meeting would bring. Howard just shrugged his shoulders and said, "Why even talk about it if we don't know what they're thinking?"

They met for breakfast at 8:00 the next morning and went up to the meeting room. Song Dian-Nuan was already there, along with Bai Ken-ren, and Jacques Coté, President and CEO of Nippon Kagaka's French subsidiary, Euro Dolce. The rest of the Nippon Kagaka contingent, consisting of Sumiko Numata and Masahiko Yamasaki, arrived moments later. Everyone took a chair around a big conference table.

In one corner of the room was a flip chart on an easel and in another was a small table that held coffee and water. After a few minutes of chit-chat while everybody got comfortable, Yamasaki cleared his throat and said, "We interested in your proposal, but we not clear on what purpose is. We hope we can talk with you today to find out purpose of association."

Howard coughed, put out his cigarette and said, "Well, the best way I could explain it is to say it's a way to promote the product, but the best way for me to show you why we need it is to put down a few numbers." He stood up and walked over to the flip chart.

On the top of the chart he wrote the word "Sweetener" in red marker, and underlined it. On the left side in descending order he wrote "TLP," "New World" and "Nippon Kagaka," at which point he paused, looked back at the group, and said, "When I say Nippon Kagaka, I'm including the French partner."

"Gary, what's the name of that Korean producer?" he asked.

"Daehan Hwa-Hak" Gary responded.

"How do you spell it?" Howard asked.

"Just put Daehan. D-A-E-H-A-N."

On the right side, Howard started filling in each company's production capacity. He already knew what TLPs total was, but he wanted Gary to say it, and so he asked.

"About two hundred fifty million pounds," Gary said.

"It would probably help if we could put the figures in metric tons," Coté said, and the Asians nodded. Yamasaki took out a calculator. "That's about 113,000 metric tons," he said. Someone in the group coughed. Howard ignored the implied comment and put the number down.

Song Dian-Nuan spoke up next. "Our number is 74,000."

Howard stopped looking at the chart. "That number seems a bit high. Could that be right, Gary?"

"If you add in their plants in Canada, Mexico and Japan, then it's probably close," Gary responded. Then Howard said, "Sumiko, what about your number?"

"Put us at 100,000," Numata said firmly. There were some muffled coughs and choking sounds around the room, and finally Bai Ken-ren said, "I think your number too high."

"I think everyone else's number is too high," Numata snapped back.

Howard quickly stepped in to referee, "For now let's just keep going. Gary, what about Daehan?"

"Well," Gary started, "their president, Kim Jungwoo, is claiming forty thousand, but it seems to me like they are selling more like 30 or 32," Gary said. There were murmurs of accord around the table. After a few minutes of discussion, there was a general agreement that for various reasons the Korean company might be having problems reaching their capacity, but they decided to put them in at forty thousand anyway. Howard asked, "What's that total up to?" Yamasaki began furiously entering numbers on his calculator. "Oh, that should be 327,000, Mr. Hargiss," he said.

Howard flipped over to a clean page. At the top left hand corner he wrote the word "Usage" and underneath that he wrote "Countries." Under the Countries heading he wrote: U.S., Europe, South America and Asia. While he was writing, he said, "This is how we do it in petroleum products." Then he looked up from the chart to Gary and asked, "What's the usage in the U.S?"

"About a hundred and twenty million pounds." Gary replied.

"That about 54,000 metric tons," Yamasaki said. Howard thought for a second and crossed out "U.S." and put in "North America." "That would be about 60,000 tons," Yamasaki said. Gary agreed and then the rest of the group gave Howard numbers on Europe at 60,000, then South America at about 20,000. The remainder of the world, which included Asia, Australia and New Zealand, came in at 45,000 metric tons. It reminded Gary of a giant Risk game, dividing the world and establishing values for each territory.

After a few seconds of mental calculation, Howard drew a line under the Asia figure and wrote in 185 underneath it. "Well gentlemen, I think we've found the fuckin' problem. The users worldwide are using a hundred and eighty-five thousand tons." He flipped back to the first page, "And we can produce 327. I got another exercise for you. Let's take this hundred and eighty five thousand metric tons..." Howard flipped to third blank sheet. "Gary, give it to me in pounds." Gary told him it was about 407 million pounds.

"What was the price before we entered the business?" Howard asked.

Song quickly weighed in, "A dollar thirty a pound."

"Well, then, take the price today, 58¢, from the previous price of a $1.30, then take that times the total usage. Gentlemen, that's two ninety-four."

Howard let this new information sink into the group for a few seconds. Then he lowered the boom. "There it is friends, we just gave our customers $294 million in one year. We all spent hundreds of millions of dollars building sweetener plants and we left $294 million dollars on the table. That's almost $300 million, gentlemen, which we have given away to our customers. Perhaps you can understand now why our motto at TLP is 'the competitor is our friend, and the customer is our enemy.'

"That motto comes from the top," he added.

For the next few moments, the only sound in the room was the gasps around the table. The reality of losing almost $300 million was sinking in. People were mentally calculating what percentage of that figure would have belonged to them. Eyes were darting around the room to see how others were reacting. Howard sat down like a lawyer who had just rested his case.

Song Dian-Nuan was the first to speak. "One thing we agree with you. That the customer has benefited and we have not, but we really challenge and have problems with what you say your capacity really is. We believe that you are less than half that capacity."

Howard fired back without hesitation, "I tell you what: you are welcome to come to our plant and bring your experts and engineers and let them see for themselves."

Numata jumped in, "We should bring some technical people, too, would that be a problem?"

"Come on, bring them too," Howard snapped. "Come together or separate. Our president, G.T. Binghamton, will be delighted to show you our whole operation. We'll put you up overnight at the Chemical Club at our expense."

Song Dian-Nuan summed up the situation. "Until we go through and see your plant and see for ourselves what your capacity is, we won't have anything further to discuss."

A short pause ensued while everyone digested this pronouncement, and then Numata said, "I met your G.T. Binghamton once, before Gary Long and your Bio-tech ever started."

Howard and Gary exchanged nervous glances. They had no idea G.T. and Numata had ever met, and Numata's tone reinforced their instant concern that the meeting had not been a pleasant one. What in hell had G.T. done?

"Right after TLP made the announcement of their coming entrance into the Bio-tech market in eighty-nine, I saw your Mr. Binghamton in San Francisco. I told him this was a very complicated business, unlike the petroleum cracking you TLP are familiar with. I told him this was a very high tech business and needed lots of technical people, and that we were the best in the business and we had been there thirty years and we started it."

Howard and Gary looked at each other dumbfounded. "Your Mr. Binghamton said to me, 'you should find another business to get in because TLP has the raw materials for this business and we are going to be very big.'"

Howard and Gary's were speechless. How could G.T. ever say anything like that and then not even tell them about it? Damn.

"I told our people in Japan what Mr. Binghamton said and they did not like it."

Now things started to fall into place. No wonder the Japanese were so cold to us when they first came to see them, Gary thought. They had been pissed off for a long time because of G.T.'s insensitive stupidity.

Eventually, Howard broke the silence. "Whatever has happened in the past, let today be a new beginning," he said. It seemed to satisfy the group. Everyone had seen their embarrassment, and it was punishment enough, at least for the moment.

"Well, is there anything we can discuss?" Howard asked. "We understand you need to verify our capacity, but we all came such a long distance...isn't there anything else we can accomplish while we are here, assuming our capacity is confirmed, which we see as just a formality?"

Jacques Coté spoke up for the first time in almost an hour. "If you want to sell that capacity, there will never be any kind of peace in this market," he said.

Numata picked up the point. "Yeah, what is your suggestion, Mr. Hargiss?"

"I tell you what," Howard began, "I know we have to confirm capacity, so let's get that resolved first." For the next few minutes the group decided that they wanted to come separately along with their technical and engineering people, and set rough dates. Then Howard continued, "We wrote down 113,000 metric tons, and I know our management expects to sell our full capacity, but with all this money left on the table, I would be willing to go back and propose something other than full capacity if I had some kind of indication that it would affect our bottom line."

"But, you see," Coté said, "if everyone tries to sell these capacities, I cannot imagine prices going up."

"Jacques make good point," Numata said, "but it is also true that the price has dropped not just because of production, but because customers have grouped together and driven the price down farther. Mr. Hargiss is right to get us to think about that."

Numata now held the group's rapt attention. "For example... because TLP is so big and so quick in business, if they offer customer X a certain price, say sixty cents a pound, we go to customer and they say, 'we like your company, but TLP just come here and offered 58¢ a pound,' when really you offered 60¢ a pound. But our sales people believe them and match the price. This is a big customer trick."

Once again, there was silence in the room, as the men digested Numata's point. Once again, Howard got things started again. "I think we ought to do two things," he said. "If the customers are lying and ripping us off then there is nothing wrong or illegal with trying to protect ourselves from customer tricks." He waited for this to be absorbed by the group and then continued, "In other words, if Gatorade got an offer from us at 60¢ and if they're telling you it's 58¢, then it's fair to talk to Gary to try and protect yourself...there's nothing wrong with doing that.

"My recommendation is the following: first, that we get the Nippon Kagaka and New World people into our plant to confirm our capacity; second, let's exchange home phone numbers – that will allow everyone to move instantly regardless of the time differences – and whenever you think you spot a customer trick, you call and find out if the offer's real before you match the lower price."

After a short discussion, everyone around the table concurred that Gary should be the contact and that calls should start immediately. They agreed to call whenever they heard a price quote lower than what they had previously heard in the market.

Howard stood up to signal that the meeting was over. "Let's get you guys to make the visits as soon as possible and then let's see if the prices start going up. Personally, I think they will. And if they do, that's just an indication of what we can accomplish if we work together. My guess is, we'll be up in the 75¢ range by fall. If that happens, then we will see if we can be flexible on our volume."

Everyone got up and started shaking hands, commenting how this meeting had been a good step forward. Howard seemed to be well on his way toward accomplishing his goals. Gary walked over to the easel, tore off the sheets that Howard had written on, and stuffed them in his briefcase.

He and Howard went to Howard's room. "This is not looking bad, Gary," Howard said. "We're still a long way from home. Obviously G.T. is going to agree with a lower volume but to help with our negotiating position, we've got to tell them that he's pretty inflexible. It may turn out to be not so bad that he insulted them. Good cop, bad cop, you know. Let's call and give him an update."

Gary dialed the number and handed the phone to Howard. "Things are improving, G.T.," Howard said. "I've got an interesting story for you though: these guys said they saw you once." By the end of the story, Howard and Gary were rolling in laughter as G.T. tried to remember the meeting, and then tried sidestepping to avoid talking about it. "We've got to keep you inside and away from as many people as possible," Howard said, laughing.

CHAPTER 46

"Man, sounds like you guys had a great trip. Way to fuckin go!" G.T. exclaimed to Gary and Howard the morning after their return.

"We're not there yet," Howard cautioned him, "but it sure as hell was a big step forward. I told the slants if prices went up we'd be willing to come back to management and try to get you to lower capacity, and we all agreed to work together to keep the customers from playing tricks on us – with Gary here as the point man."

"Sons'a bitchin' customers," G.T. replied, grinning. "It's a shame we have to have 'em. They're really the ones driving the prices down. Fuck 'em."

Gary was trying to put bows and ribbons on the day when John Caldwell phoned him.

"I wanted to see if you'd had a chance to establish a relationship with any brokers since you moved to this area," Caldwell said. Gary replied that he had not.

"Well, I'd sure like a chance to talk to you about your portfolio in the next week or so and see if there's a chance we could do some business."

"Well, John," Gary said. "Thanks to you I found a house and a wife. The least I can do in return is give you some business."

Gary had looked at his statement just a few days before and was surprised at the amount of cash he had in his account. "It's probably a pretty good time to put some money to work before Jenna spends it all on furniture," he said.

They set up a lunch meeting for the coming Thursday.

When Gary arrived home that night he was beat. The stress of the trip and of briefing everyone finally had caught up with him, and after calling Jenna, he collapsed into bed before 10:00. The first edges of sleep were starting to overtake his consciousness when the phone jarred him awake.

"Dr. Long, this is Song Dian-Nuan. I wanted to call you about a customer problem like we talk about."

"Yeah, go ahead," Gary said, shaking the sleep from his head. "What's up?"

"One of our salesmen in St. Louis call to say you offer fifty cents per pound to Goody's Cookys in Arkansas. Is that true?"

Gary did a quick mental calculation, remembering it was 15 hours ahead of their time in Shanghai; that made it 1:00 p.m. and meant Mr. Song would have arrived home only a few hours ago. Gary was surprised he had called so soon; and in truth what he was reporting had to be an actual customer trick. "No way, Mr. Song," Gary told him. "Our lowest price anywhere is fifty-eight."

"Ah, Dr. Long, thank you very much, I appreciate this."

CHAPTER 47

Gary's next week was filled with trying to make sure he could spend his week-long homeymoon without having to worry about the office.

He did keep his lunch appointment with John Caldwell, asking him to put together a recommendation for a $500,000 portfolio, with a concentration on growth stocks. If Caldwell was surprised at the amount, he didn't show it. The experienced broker was used to the fact that TLP executives always seemed to have a lot of money; that was why he courted them as clients. Still, Gary was glad he hadn't revealed the full amount of the cash he had sitting in Geneva and Hong Kong.

That done, he hurried back to his office and worked late into the evening. He got everything he could think of done, and went home pleased that he would be able to take Friday off and help pick up his family at the airport and give them tours of TLP. His father, who had been skeptical, seemed genuinely impressed with the acres of gleaming stainless steel tanks and pipes, and even more importantly to Gary, with what his son was accomplishing. All in all, it was very satisfying for Gary and he felt he had finally found his place in his father's eyes.

It was good to see his brothers and sister, too, and their families. Jenna had not met any of them before, and she quizzed Gary about their lives.

"Okay," Gary told her. "Ken is the oldest. He runs the car dealership now that Dad has retired. He and Cheryl have one son, Ken, Jr., who's fourteen."

"Got it," Jenna said, closing her eyes and giving a nod as if to slide the information into place in her head.

"Maria is a year younger than me." She was in Tina's class, he thought, angry for allowing the name to cross his mind. "She married the local State Farm agent. They don't have any kids.

"Bert is the baby. He's really a decent guy, but he's had it tougher than the rest of us. Had a hard time in school, served a hitch in the Army, came home on leave and got Mary Lou pregnant, married her, got out of the Army, came back and worked for Dad a while, and now welds boat trailer frames together for a living. That's a big business in southern Indiana."

"And they have – you told me this before, I know – two girls now, right?"

"Right. Kim and Kandy. Dad bought a house, which they rent from him, although I don't know how regularly they pay the rent. It's been tough for them."

The next morning Gary arose as usual with the sun and watched while his mother made breakfast in his new kitchen. "Gary, this place is so beautiful, and Jenna has done such a wonderful job of decorating it. Your father and I are very proud of you and what you're doing. Jenna seems so nice, I really like her." It all came out so quickly that Gary felt tears coming to his eyes.

"Thanks, Mom, I really feel like everything's going good for me right now."

"Well, remember, Gary, things won't always go so smoothly in life. It's important you find your center and keep it. You lost a lot of it before with Tina."

Gary silently thought about Tina and how their life had been torn apart. "Mom, I know I can't predict the future, but I really want this to work. I know it means sacrificing somewhere else, maybe even work," he said, wondering as soon as the words were out why he had put it exactly that way. What did he mean by "maybe even work"? What in his subconscious had brought that out?

Gary's mother turned to look at him, fixed her eyes on his and said, "Work has to be the second priority in your life. You've got a family to take care of. Regardless of whose kids they were, Justin and Mark are yours now. You'd better focus on doing *this* job now."

A pang of guilt ran through him as he thought about what he was being forced to do at TLP. Jenna and the boys hadn't bargained for an international price fixer as husband and father.

His mother had always had a plentiful supply of woman's intuition. How many times, when he was a boy, had she sensed problems he was going through before anybody officially told her anything? Maybe she sensed something amiss here, too. Gary certainly did. Could his mother tell that? Suddenly, the memory of his father's brush with the law flooded back into his mind, and for the first time in his life, he made the connection between their sudden affluence and the alleged kickback scheme his dad had been investigated about. For the first time, too, he felt a pang of doubt. It had been presented to him as gospel that the allegations were completely unfounded. Now, suddenly, he wondered, and with those doubts came another thought: how had his mother dealt with all of that in her heart and mind? Had she believed unquestioningly in her husband's innocence, as Gary had always supposed? Had she had doubts? Or did she know a forbidden truth? And if the father really was guilty, what did that mean for the son? Was there a bad gene in the Long heritage?

Mom may have gone through hell then, he thought to himself. Was he about to put Jenna through the same sort of hell? He had never talked about any of TLP's shady dealings with Jenna, nor had the subject of his source of cash been discussed, but he was sure it wouldn't be long before it was the topic of a late night talk. He already felt safer talking to Jenna than to anyone else he had ever known; she didn't judge him, and just seemed grateful to be inside his head whenever he opened up. It had been a great comfort to him. Now he wondered if his comfort was only a prelude to her distress.

He looked into his mother's eyes intently, seeking some sort of answer. But it was just Mom: sincere, compassionate Mom, looking after her boy as always. "I know, Mom," he said.

Jenna had planned a simple but elegant wedding, and it all came off without a hitch. Gary marveled as all the details, from the ceremony to the flight to St. Thomas the following afternoon seemed to glide effortlessly into place. Jenna snuggled into his side on the plane and fell into an exhausted sleep.

When they landed, they piled their luggage into a taxi van and made the bumpy uphill and down ride to the east end of the island, where they boarded the ferry for St. John. At the Cruz Bay dock, Gary left Jenna with the luggage and following the directions he had been given, walked two blocks to the St. John Rental Company, where a grizzled New Yorker rented him a Suzuki jeep. "Drive on the left," he warned Gary, tapping a dashboard decal with the same words on it.

"No problem," Gary said. "I lived in England for two years."

He drove back to the dock and picked up Jenna and the luggage. "Next stop, Caneel Bay," he called out to her as she jumped in.

For the next two days, they did little but make love and lie on the beach. The third day, they drove to Cinnamon Bay and rented snorkel equipment. Later, they returned the equipment and lay by the water's edge, dozing. As the sun dipped below the mountains to their right, Gary decided it was time to tell her about his financial affairs.

"Jenna, we really haven't talked much about money," he said hesitantly.

She was half asleep on the rattan mat beside him. It sounded to her like a confession was coming. She had thought about it some already. The big down payment on the house, all the new furniture, the Cadillac, the expensive watch he had given her – she knew top executives at TLP must have good salaries, but she had decided that perhaps he had really stretched himself. She had prepared herself for some belt-tightening.

"Well," she said, "I figured if I keep on working, I can at least contribute to the effort."

To her surprise, he laughed out loud, grabbed her and pulled her into a long, deep kiss.

She struggled to free herself and playfully punched him. "What's that all about?" she asked.

"Jenna, I've got almost a million and a half dollars in savings. That's what I wanted to talk to you about."

Jenna was silent for a second. "How have you gotten that kind of money?" she stammered.

"Well, TLP has an overseas bonus program for their executives. That's where I got the money to buy the house."

"I was kind of surprised you made such a big down payment, but I never dreamed ..." Jenna paused and turned sideways to look at Gary. "Overseas? You mean like in some tax-free Swiss bank account?"

"Yep, I've got one, and no, I don't pay taxes on the money that goes into it. It's apparently quite legal; TLP does it all the time. G.T. said I wouldn't get a ten ninety-nine on it, and I wouldn't have to declare it."

"I've heard about people like you, earning millions and not paying taxes," Jenna said playfully. Then she grabbed his hand and pulled him on top of her.

The beach was deserted in the twilight. She grabbed his bathing trunks and practically ripped them off, rolling him over and leaving him lying on his back on the mat. Standing, she put her left hand on the bow holding her bikini bottoms at her right hip. At the same time, she reached behind her back with her right hand. In one coordinated motion, she pulled both strings and the two pieces fell off at the same time, leaving her standing naked above him. An almost full moon bathed her in a soft pastel. She fell on top of him and they made love with reckless abandon. When it was finally over, they lay exhausted, entwined together on a single mat. As the curtains of sleep fell over Gary's eyes, he congratulated himself on the wisdom of his decision to tell her. It had already been worth it.

For the rest of the honeymoon, Gary kept quiet about work. He decided there would be time enough to tell her his concerns about price fixing. By the end of the week, Gary was ready to head back to TLP. It felt odd being away from the phones. The vacation had been perfect, but a pang in his gut told him it was time to get back to business.

The last night on St. John, Gary and Jenna walked on the beach and talked about their plans for the future. They packed early the next morning and headed for the airport. The minute they cleared Customs and reached the gate area, he made a beeline for the phones.

He had almost half an hour of messages to wade through. Most were from well wishers, but several were customer trick reports. There were no panic production calls; the plant seemed to be taking care of itself for now. The best news was Brad Redfoot's report that Sugere prices were inching up.

They got back to Wonanonly before midnight, and the next morning, Gary was up and out the door by 6:30. Jenna woke up when Gary called at 8:00, threw on some clothes and quickly drove to her parents' house to pick up the kids. Justin was watching for her at the window, and ran out the door, jumping into her arms as she crossed the lawn. Even Mark seemed enthusiastic about seeing her, running to the door to hug her around the waist.

They were taking all of this pretty well, she mused. Gary had made the transition as easy as possible, there was no doubt they loved the new home and each had his own separate room, a real bonus. In fact, the boys seemed to adore him. Their father, Bobbie Sholes, had long since vanished from the scene, never visiting his sons, and making only infrequent payments of child support.

How she had agonized when the support payments failed to come in! How many times she had reproached herself for her folly in such an early marriage! How completely she had convinced herself that her judgment in men was simply terrible! Now all that seemed so distant.

She felt like she was living in a fairy tale, half in reality, half outside it. The revelation that she and Gary were literally millionaires had come as a total shock. She knew he had done well and was respected by the people with whom he worked. Leigh Curtis had confided to her that Gary was considered on track to be the next president of TLP.

She hadn't planned to marry a rich man, only a loving one, but by gosh, she'd done both! As she set breakfast in front of the boys in their new house, she began telling them about St. John and some of the things she and Gary done and seen there. She gave out the presents they had brought back for each of them, and spent a little while showing them how to work the various gadgets Gary had picked out. She had gotten each of them a straw hat with the words, "Hey, Mon" stitched on the front. The vendor offered to stitch the boys' initials on the back, and she quickly agreed, then just as quickly changed her mind. Gary and she had talked about his adopting the boys as soon as possible, so their initials would change. She had settled for hats with no monograms.

She left the boys wearing their hats and playing with their toys and went up to the master bedroom. What a glorious room it was, she thought, even messy with mostly unpacked luggage lying all around. I'm on top of the world, she thought, and began humming that tune as she unpacked.

They had decided to keep her house in town to rent out, and her main job for the day was to begin the process of getting it in shape to rent. With the suitcases unpacked and the washer sloshing away, she spent the morning getting bids for the painting and carpet cleaning work. She had asked Gary about doing the work herself, but he reminded her, "You're going to be kept busy doing things an executive's wife has to do."

CHAPTER 48

Gary got a customer trick call at home almost every night. On occasion, TLP's sales people would pick up a story similar to the ones they were reporting. When that happened, Gary would call Bai Ken-ren or Masahiki Yamasaki, but in truth, they were calling so often that he usually just waited for them to call and discussed the information on their nickel. G.T. and Howard were enthusiastic about the number of calls he had been receiving. Moreover, the system was working. Prices hadn't risen significantly, but the downward spiral had definitely ended. Maybe, Gary thought, just this agreement will be enough. Maybe there won't be a need for actual volume agreements and price fixing.

But with the warming of the summer months TLP again developed production problems that became steadily worse as the temperature rose. By the end of July they were losing money at the rate of seven million dollars a month. William Hargiss called G.T. into his office late one Thursday afternoon. "G.T., damn it, I thought we had this shit fixed. What in the name of tarnation is going on in that plant?" he demanded.

G.T. was shocked by the tone in Hargiss's voice. "Fuck, we've done everything we know to do," he replied bravely. "I guess we'll have to bring the consultants back in."

"You know the minute you do that, every damn body in the world will know we're in trouble again," Hargiss sputtered.

"I know, I know," G.T. pleaded. "That's why I haven't done it before now. But our in-house people have looked at it till they're blue in the face, and we can't figure it out."

"All right, all right," Hargiss said, his voice softening. "Tell me exactly what the problem is, cause I'm gonna have to explain it to the board."

"Well, to sum it all up in a nutshell," G.T. said, "we're getting seventy to ninety percent contamination when the industry average is around three. I can't believe we're getting contamination problems of this size." He shook his head and stubbed out a cigarette butt.

"Let me ask you something," Hargiss said. "Didn't we hire a couple of guys from Samuran? Is it possible they're sabotaging the process somehow?"

Leave it to the old man to see a conspiracy, G.T. thought. Hell, he's masterminded enough of them, no wonder his mind runs that way. Still, it was a possibility. G.T. was desperate and more than willing to grab at any straw around.

"Yeah, that's a thought," he said. "I'll talk to Long and see if he thinks it's possible."

"Just get that fucking plant on line and fixed. I don't care how you do it, just get it done. By the way, Howard tells me Gary's really coming up to speed on arranging better prices for us. How do you feel about him?"

"Smart. Got the market figured out. Got some new products to fit our back-door integration plan. I'm impressed, and he seems pretty grateful for the bonuses."

"I probably should start spending a little more time with him. The stock picker hymies in New York are falling all over themselves when we talk about the value-added coming on stream."

"Yeah, well, I'll leave that stuff up to you. I'll let you know what he thinks about your idea."

G.T. walked down to Gary's office and stuck his head inside. "We've got a hell of a problem here, kid. The fuckin plant's not up to speed, and the old man is about to shit. He just asked me if we had someone inside the plant causing the production problems. What do you think the chances are?"

Gary's brow furrowed. "It's possible, I suppose. But it'd be pretty difficult to do. In order to get the results we're seeing, you'd have to be directly inoculating every single batch of bacteria, which means inside access around the clock. No one person has that kind of unlimited access."

"Well, think about it a little bit. See if you come up with anyone you think is a likely candidate, and start with those guys we hired from the Jap company."

The parade of consultants started again, trying to solve the contamination mystery. By now they were falling behind on orders, and costs had soared to over a dollar per pound. Customers would place orders expecting that Sugere would be shipped on Monday, and often they were unable to ship until Thursday or Friday. Rumors of the problems began circulating through TLP's customer base, and Gary was sure it was reaching the competitors.

While the consultants sampled, measured and studied, G.T. turned his mind to the sabotage possibility. He knew Gary didn't believe it, and in his heart, G.T. too figured it probably wasn't possible that anyone was contaminating production, but if Hargiss believed it, it was simple cover-your-ass mentality to investigate. At a minimum, an aggressive anti-conspiracy plan would give him additional time. He went to Hargiss with a plan.

"William, I'm not sure," he began, "but I don't think we can discount the possibility that someone inside is contaminating the process. Maybe we ought to have Tully look into it."

"Tully can't handle this by himself," Hargiss mused. "I'd better get him some help."

As soon as G.T. left his office, Hargiss picked up the phone and dialed a familiar number in Ft. Meade, Maryland.

"Admiral Decatur's office," the voice on the other end of the line said.

"This is William Hargiss, is the good Admiral in?"

Jonathan Decatur was jotting notes on a report from one of his assistant directors when his secretary interrupted him with the news that Hargiss was on the line. Decatur had joined the National Security Agency after leaving a career post with the Office of Naval Intelligence. Arriving during the turmoil of the late 1970s, he had seen his share of change in the political winds, but nothing had ever crossed his desk like what he was looking at that very minute. Never before had he seen such a blatant attempt by a foreign government to interfere in an American election. Shaking it off, he picked up the phone to talk to one of his closest friends.

"Bill, good to hear your voice. How are things in Indiana today?"

"Fine, fine. Well, actually I have a little problem, and I need some help with it."

"Sure, what've ya got going on?"

"Well, we think we may be being sabotaged by one of our foreign competitors."

"No kidding. Give me the details." Hargiss told him everything he knew.

Decatur let a low whistle escape. "You sure do have a problem. Is this the market you're trying to set something up in?"

"Yeah, we think we're getting close, too. Maybe another six months or so and we'll have the whole thing up and running."

"All right, I'll make a few calls and see what we can find."

Decatur didn't even set the phone down. He just punched a few buttons and spoke a few sentences. The wheels were in motion. William Hargiss didn't ask for much, he thought, not compared to all the things he did for his country.

CHAPTER 49

The weather in Indiana cooled off as September approached, and the production problems cooled off with it. Hargiss's "conspiracy" was certainly a strange one, Gary thought. It only operated in hot weather. In any event it was good to see the production numbers moving up again, all the more so because it was time for the competitors' visits to Steuben.

The Nippon Kagaka contingent was the first to arrive. G.T. had instructed Gary to follow up on the offer Howard made in Mexico, about TLP putting the delegation up overnight at the Chemical Club, but Numata declined, saying they would be in and out the same day. Both G.T. and Howard seemed disappointed at that, and Gary wondered why, but didn't ask.

Numata brought along the chief engineer from their Samuran plant in Iowa, a Dr. Obuchi.

They met in the executive conference room on the second floor and Gary handed out some papers and photos. After a brief question and answer session, he and Billie Mitchell took them on a tour of all the plants, just to give them a feel for the size of the Steuben facility.

Mitchell had no idea who he was taking through the plant, and seemed surprised by the kind of questions that were being asked, about vat sizes, valve specifications and dozens of other technical questions. Gary understood the common thread in all the questions: what was TLP's capacity to produce Sugere? After the tour, he brought them back to corporate, where everyone ate lunch. Howard stopped by to say hi, and started quizzing Numata.

"Now do you believe what we told you about the size of our facility?" Howard asked.

"Very impressive, Mr. Hargiss," Numata said.

"Since you've had a chance to see our plant, how about us paying a visit to your operations in Thomasville?" Gary asked, looking at Obuchi.

He hadn't planned the question, but Thomasville, Iowa was the site of Samuran's largest American plant, and had been the subject of much discussion at TLP. Gary had hoped Brad Redfoot could supply information, but Brad said he had never been to Thomasville during the time he had worked for Nippon Kagaka in St. Louis. The opportunity for a reciprocal tour seemed like a natural.

"Oh, sure," Obuchi responded. Gary thought he noticed a quick look of chagrin on Numata's face, but he couldn't be sure.

"Yeah, we'd love to take a look at it," Howard said.

"We are going there now, could you come this weekend?" Numata suggested wanly.

They checked calendars while they ate, and decided that G.T., Mitchell and Gary would tour the plant on Saturday.

On the plane ride to Thomasville, G.T. told Mitchell that the main point of the trip was to assess the plant capacity. They discussed the questions they would ask.

The plant was located right next to a corn processing facility, owned and operated by Universal Chemical, from which Samuran received the raw materials needed to produce the dextrose the sweetener bacteria thrived on. Gary wasn't sure what to expect from the tour, but it was certainly more than they got. In fact, they got nothing.

"We don't allow people through this plant unless they are employees," Numata said quietly.

So the vaunted inspection visit turned out to be little more than a tour of the loading facility. As the three Americans looked over the site, they could tell that there were three fermenters, but little else was gleaned from the trip.

Mitchell tried to ask some of the questions he and G.T. had discussed, but it was clear that reciprocity had been thrown out the window. Why, Gary wondered? Were they embarrassed by the smallness of it, compared to TLP's operations? Were they in the middle of some revisions they didn't want to show? Was Numata still smarting from the memory of his first meeting with G.T.? Whatever it was, they wouldn't answer any of Mitchell's questions. After a few minutes, he whispered to Gary, "This sure is a waste of time."

On the flight home, G.T. burst out laughing at the size of the plant and the audacity Numata had in not showing them anything. "It's a piece of shit," G.T. said. "Fuck these little guys." The day had truly been a complete waste of time.

On Monday, Howard stuck his head in Gary's office and chuckled as he said, "Hey, I heard you saw a nice plant on Saturday." Gary grinned and shook his head; there wasn't anything else to say.

Bai Ken-ren came to Steuben the following week, accompanied by a New World technician, an American from a plant they operated in Canada. Gary and Billie Mitchell gave them the same thorough tour they had given to the Nippon Kagaka team.

After the tour was finished, Howard came in for a short visit while they were sipping sodas and coffee after lunch. Cordial greetings were exchanged, and everyone chit-chatted for an hour or so, among other things, comparing notes on the price of artificial sweetener. It was up over 70¢, and Howard took the opportunity to boast about the prediction he had made in Mexico. "Be sure and remind Mr. Song," he said, "that I predicted this would happen once we started working together."

Bai clapped his big hands together and smiled. "I will tell him," he said. "We are not where we need to be, but we are going in right direction."

But Gary thought he sensed a little apprehension in Bai's manner. Like Numata before him, the Chinese man would never admit that TLP's plant was much larger than he had supposed, but Gary had read the astonishment on his face. It was like he had seen a monster.

The next day, Gary was visiting with Buffy when he received a call from Dr. Obuchi, the Nippon Kagaka engineer who had visited the plant with Numata. That was unusual. Why would an engineer be calling me? Gary thought. He didn't have to wait long to find out.

"Ah, Dr. Long, when we visited your plant, your people said that the granulating process was patented. Could you confirm that for me?" Obuchi asked.

Gary was taken back by his request. Either this was a bold attempt to steal the granulator technology or this guy was on a fishing trip, but for what? Gary replied guardedly that he would look into it.

He called Zack Brilley, the TLP lawyer, later that afternoon and asked about the patent.

"We never did file it in order to not disclose the technology. If we file it, someone will make a small change and get around the patent," Zack told him.

Gary called Obuchi later that day with the news. "What did you think of the Thomasville plant? Were you impressed?" Obuchi asked.

Gary decided to be nice and confabulate for a few minutes. "Oh yeah, it was a very interesting plant," he politely lied.

"You had visitors from New World, huh?" Obuchi asked next. He must have talked to Bai, or perhaps his engineer, Gary thought, wondering what else he knew. Suddenly an idea hit him. Why not joke with this guy about having moles in TLP's plant, just to see what his reaction would be? If by any chance there was truth in Hargiss's conspiracy theory, Obuchi just might know about it.

"Yeah, they were here. Hey, by the way, you don't happen to have a guy working for you in our plant do you?"

There was a momentary dead silence before Obuchi said anything. "Could you say again more slowly?" he asked eventually.

Maybe he didn't understand, Gary thought. So he repeated the question for him more slowly.

Finally Obuchi responded. "Why do you say that? What do you mean by that? I do not understand."

No, Gary thought, it sounds like you understand perfectly. He decided to press on. "From time to time, we have had problems with our production and we always joke and say that we must have a guy from Nippon Kagaka in our plant." Again there was a momentary dead silence on the phone.

"Not good joke," Obuchi said.

Language may have been a problem, but Gary felt sure it was more than that. Maybe Hargiss and G.T. had been right all along and the contamination problems were sabotage. Obuchi never answered Gary's accusation and made an excuse for a quick exit. At any rate, Obuchi's pause and lack of denial planted seeds of doubt in Gary's mind.

The next morning, Gary rendered an account of the conversation with Obuchi to G.T., who listened thoughtfully at first and then became amused. "You don't really believe they have anyone here, do you?" G.T. said grinning.

"I don't know how," Gary said shaking his head. "But he didn't deny it and it was almost like he was in shock that we'd found out. Something is definitely wrong with all this." Gary knew Hargiss's conspiracy theory was far fetched, but after Obuchi's call he was beginning to wonder.
A few days later Gary's phone rang at home and he heard Obuchi's voice on the line. "What was question you asked me again, please?" Obuchi asked tentatively.

Gary repeated the question for him.

"You do have two of our people working for you," he said.

Gary instantly knew what he was talking about. "No, no," he said. I'm not talking about people who *used* to work for you, I'm talking about people on your payroll right now secretly sabotaging our production process," he said, firmly. There was no way Obuchi could think he was joking this time.

Again there was a long pause, but this time Gary broke it. "It sure would be worth a lot to us if we could find out who it is," he said.

Gary talked to G.T. again the next morning. "G.T., I tell ya, this guy sure isn't denying they have a mole; in fact it seems like he is more interested in the fact that we think there is one."

G.T. rubbed his chin. "You know Gary, think about it. We got our bug all legally from Genotype. You've got Nippon Kagaka that has been in the business for almost thirty years. They have engineered and massaged their bug for thirty years and it would be so strong that it would resist almost any contamination. Agree?"

Gary agreed that Nippon Kagaka most likely did have the strongest bacteria currently in use. He suddenly realized what G.T. was driving at. If TLP had Nippon Kagaka's bug, the summer contamination problems would be over.

He hesitated to take the conversation further, but the temptation to find out for sure just where G.T. was heading was too strong. "Of course," he said. "So? I mean," he added, "we don't have it."

"Not for lack of trying," G.T. said, looking intently at Gary's astonishment. "Meet me in Howard's office in ten minutes," he added. "I've got an idea."

When Gary got to the office, Howard and G.T. were already there.

"Here's a little fable you may find interesting," Howard began, leaning back in his chair and gazing into the fish tank. "You've been to Thomasville, Iowa," he said.

"Yeah," Gary said. "They give the worst damn plant tours in the chemical industry."

"Right," Howard said. "As you and G.T. and Billie found out. But think for a moment about your impressions of the community. A rinky-dink burg if ever there was one. It makes Steuben look like a metropolis, wouldn't you say?"

For the life of him, Gary couldn't figure out where this was leading. "It's pretty much a dump," he said, honestly.

"Right on," Howard said, turning to face Gary. "Now, if you were looking for some really high-class hookers – I'm talking about top of the line pay-per-view pussy here – would you expect to find it in Thomasville?"

"Well, not that I *would* be looking for such a thing," Gary responded, "but if I were, no, I would not go to Thomasville."

"Good answer," Howard said. "But Gary, my boy, there was a time not long ago when the whores of Thomasville would rival anything in New Orleans, Las Vegas or Chicago. In fact, that's where they came from. A half dozen of them, tits, ass, miniskirts and all, and they all landed in Thomasville at the same time, stayed for a few months and left."

"Why?"

"Why? Because our dear companion here, Mr. G.T. Binghamton, arranged for it to happen, that's why. He and his friend Mr. Andrew Tully put the whole operation together. Have you ever met Mr. Tully?"

Gary hadn't, but he had heard the name mentioned. "Isn't he a private investigator?" he asked.

"Ah, and much more," Howard replied, turning back to the fish. "Tell him about it, G.T., you fuckhead. Admit to at least this one of your great failures in life."

"Ah fuck, Gary," G.T. said. "I had Tully take care of this little idea I had, it was no big deal. When we decided to open up the Sugere pilot plant in Memphis, we obviously had to have a bug. I hate to pay the going rate for shit like that, so we hired these hookers and sent them to Thomasville to go and meet plant workers at the bars around the plant and try and find someone who might be willing to sell the Samuran bug to TLP."

No shit, Gary thought, these guys are unbelievable, but nothing really surprised him anymore. These guys were corporate Mafia. What was he a part of?

"But we never found anyone with enough access to the bug to be able to steal it, so we closed the operation down and bought a legit bug from Genotype."

"It happens all the time in this business," Howard said, noting the shock on Gary's face.

"Anyway, Gary, we're telling you all this because your discussions with your friend Obuchi have suggested another approach," G.T. said. "You know how much that bug would be worth to us: millions and millions of dollars. Plus, having it would solve our production problems, sabotage or no sabotage. We sure as hell don't want to go through another summer like the last two.

"Now my idea is that this Obuchi is a senior engineer for those guys, couldn't he get it for us?" He paused and lit a cigarette, inhaled deeply and started speaking as the smoke came back out. "We could make this guy very rich if he could come up with an answer for our contamination problem. Gary, you gotta try him on this."

"See if you can make it happen," Howard said.

Oh, shit, Gary thought as he stepped out to leave.

G.T. called after him. "Just think what it would be worth!"

Gary stopped, turned and said, "If the guy calls back, I'll try it."

He was pretty sure Obuchi would never call back; at least he hoped he wouldn't. He didn't relish the thought of being involved in trying to steal someone else's technology. But like an episode out of *The Twilight Zone*, late in the afternoon a week later, Leigh buzzed him on the intercom.

"It's Dr. Obuchi for you," she said.

Gary was about to leave for the day, and wasn't mentally prepared to take the call.

"Tell him I just left," he said. "Have him call me in the morning." Then he changed his mind. "No, have him call me at home in an hour."

He spent the drive home rehearsing what he would say when the call came. When it did, he swallowed hard and jumped in. "Hey, Obuchi, you know we sure would be interested in having you as a TLP employee." There was silence, and Gary could imagine Obuchi pondering, trying to be sure in his own mind that he had heard Gary correctly. "If you are interested, we'd sure like to have you doing some of the things for us that you do for Nippon Kagaka." Would he bite?

But his pause was shorter this time. "No, no, I been here for hundreds of years."

Well, that didn't work, Gary thought, let's try to do the deal the other way. "Another thing we would be really interested in is the bacterial organism that Samuran uses. If there could be some way we could buy it, G.T. would sure make it attractive for whoever sold it."

Gary hadn't said anything incriminating so far, and the next move was clearly Obuchi's. It's kind of like making an arrangement with a hooker, Gary thought: neither party is completely sure the other isn't a cop, so they both dance around the subject matter. Obuchi knew from their previous conversation that TLP had contamination problems, and that they thought there was a mole in Steuben. After a few moments of thought, Obuchi said, "I am really loyal to my company. It sounds to me like you guys have a big contamination problem, just like they are saying."

Was he talking about their production problem or their ethics? Gary couldn't be sure. In either event he was right.

Obuchi and Gary conversed for a few more minutes, but the engineer made it clear he was insulted by the attempt to buy him off. Another bullet dodged, Gary thought. Another potential crime averted. How long could he hold out?

When he reported to G.T. the next morning, G.T. took it grimly. They still hadn't solved the problem: TLP's advantage in raw materials cost was being lost through the inefficiency of their bug.

Gary headed down the corridor toward the bathroom. On the way, he passed the door to Dan Anthony's office.

"Gary, come on in," Anthony called, spotting him.

"I'm on my way out to get my mail and take a pee." Gary countered.

"I heard about you taking your buddy on another one of your price fixing excursions," Anthony said, paying no attention to Gary's more immediate problem.

"Well, I didn't do anything but take notes, and do what I was told to do." Gary responded.

"Yeah, I feel bad for you. Be really careful of this stuff. These guys ride the waves," he said, leaning back in his chair.

"They sure do. Well, I'd better get going."

"I've been telling you this for a long time," Anthony said as Gary left his office. It was true. He was the one who warned Gary about Howard in the first place.

As Gary walked into the bathroom, Killer Keddy was standing at the urinal. "Hey Gary," he said, "I heard you and Howard are traveling pretty heavily together."

"Yeah, yeah, no big deal," Gary responded.

"Well, Howard's no chemist, so is he helping you on your Sugere price, little buddy?"

Cripes, everyone and his brother knew about Howard! What had G.T. done, taken an ad out in the *Steuben Daily News*?

Keddy snorted as he zipped up. "Well, be careful," he said. "It's a shame we have to do business that way, but I shouldn't talk. We're doing the same thing in our products."

Gary was sick of hearing about price fixing, hookers and stolen technology. He couldn't wait to get home. He had to talk to Jenna. He dreaded the conversation, but he needed to vent. The day had been building to a horrible climax, and Gary was at the end of his rope. Everyone at TLP seemed to know about everything; sooner or later, somebody's wife was bound to say something to Jenna. Gary knew she deserved to hear it from him.

That night, he waited until the kids were in bed before broaching the subject. She was sitting on the couch in the family room, watching *Cheers*. He sat down in the chair across from the couch.

"This working with Howard isn't any fun," he started. Carla was cracking a joke at Norm's expense. Jenna waited for the punch line and then turned to look at Gary. When she saw the expression on his face, she reached for the remote control and clicked the power switch off. That was the end of any cheer for the night.

Gary gave her a short explanation of price fixing, and what he had done. "I don't really think I've done anything illegal yet, but it's surely in the gray area. The way things are headed though," he said, "it's getting closer to black than gray."

Jenna began probing to gain a deeper understanding of what was going on, and once she had a handle on it, all shades of gray disappeared for her.

"I don't care how good the job is; nothing's worth going to jail for," she said, softly but firmly. "You can't jeopardize everything we've planned by doing something stupid like that. Get another job or refuse to go through with it. Something, anything, but don't for God's sake...." Jenna didn't finish, but collapsed in the chair in a sea of tears.

"Jenna, I know this is tough," he said. "I'm trying to think everything through carefully and rationally. The shady stuff aside, I've never had a job this good, and I'll never find another job this good. I love what I'm doing. And the thing is, I think maybe in the long run I can do a lot of good here. If I leave, everything will go on the way it is. But if I stay on, maybe I can find a way to stop it, to keep the aggressive style without the bad part. If I play along for a while, maybe I can be the one to clean up the mess. If I don't do it, I don't see anybody else who ever will."

Jenna looked at him through tear stained eyes. "Rationalization, rationalization," she said, with sharpness in her tone. Then her voice softened again. "Don't you understand?" she said. "You've got more than yourself to think about now, Gary. If I have to work, then I'll be glad to do it. Please don't do something that could put you in jail."

She clung to him in bed through the night, not lovingly, but desperately. Over breakfast the next morning, Gary tried to find a way to assure her that he wouldn't cross the line, but with the boys needing their normal school morning attention, it was difficult to hold a serious discussion. As he left for work, he promised they would talk again that evening.

As if he had a direct pipeline to news on Gary's life, William Hargiss called shortly after Gary got to his office to say that the announcement of his promotion would be made that very afternoon. The board was in the middle of a two-day meeting in New York, and had agreed to his personnel proposals the night before. In an almost whispered voice, Hargiss also informed him that Howard would be joining the board as Vice Chairman.

Buffy poked his head in the door a few minutes later. "The old man just told me to write up a release on your promotion," he said. "Way to go, Tiger." Leigh overheard him and quickly arranged a divisional celebration for the afternoon. All day, people kept calling or coming by to congratulate him. Only two people seemed cool to the news: Jenna, when he called to tell her, and Dan Anthony.

"It seems to me," Leigh said, "that Anthony's ticked off you got it, and he didn't."

CHAPTER 50

While the rest of the board enjoyed a fine luncheon in a private room in the Plaza Hotel, William Hargiss sat alone in his penthouse suite and enjoyed the moment. He'd pulled off Howard's promotion with almost no resistance. The price fixing in the various markets in which TLP had managed to set up associations had made it possible for Hargiss show his fourth straight year of record profits, in spite of the big losses in bio-tech and the fact that other companies in the chemical industry had been forced to cope with weakening margins. The board, expecting the worst, had sat in disbelief when he announced the third-quarter results.

Hargiss had of course softened up several members by making a few deals earlier in the month, but when he proposed the promotion plan, it met with wide acceptance, drawing almost nothing but favorable discussion even by the minority of the board he hadn't spoken with. Even Randolph Thad made only the most perfunctory objection to the moves.

A ringing telephone interrupted his pleasant moment, and he crossed the room to pick it up. "Mr. Hargiss, Admiral Decatur is calling," an efficient-sounding female voice said. Then after a brief pause, he heard Decatur's familiar voice.

"Bill, how are you?"

"Plum dandy, Jon. If I was any better, I'd be two people."

"Sounds like you got through your board meeting huh?"

"Yeah, the board is really pleased with the numbers we've been able to post. It always makes for a nice meeting when you're making good money."

"Great. And Howard's appointment?"

"Smooth as silk. Thanks for your help on a couple of those details."

"Glad to help, which brings up another subject. Your problem at your bio-tech plant. I ran it through channels and we actually had a few men checking around. One of the guys revolted a little and reminded us that we weren't supposed to be doing any work for domestic corporations. That made the Director a little nervous and he asked us to forward all the investigation files to the FBI, and follow up with them. We'll pledge to give them assistance, but we can't take the lead. Sorry about that."

Hargiss let the line run silent for a second before replying. "I'm not sure how comfortable I am with having someone else involved. Do you feel comfortable with it?"

Decatur responded quickly, "Bill, these guys don't need to know anything other than information about the plant. You know, stuff like who works there, what the process is, background information you have on the hires, just basic information. The rest of their work will be outside the company. Besides, you've dealt with the audits for years; there's nothing that can affect what we're doing on that level, right?"

"Okay," Hargiss responded, still a little edgy about the proposition. "Go ahead and send it where you need to. I'll make sure they get what they need from us. You just make sure you contain it from your end."

"I don't see that as a problem. Let's see if we can catch some SOB doing the dirty work. I'd love to pin something like this on China. That'd be the end of their favored-nation hopes."

"Let's find something. This problem is gonna eventually eat into our savings account if we don't get it cleaned up."

"Yeah, well don't worry, we'll make sure it gets the priority it needs."

That night, Gary pleaded with Jenna for more time to sort things out. He thought she might be finally beginning to relent, when the phone rang with another customer trick call. They were coming almost daily now, but this one was different, the first Gary had to take with Jenna knowing what it was all about. He felt a red flush rising on his face as she listened to the call.

"What was that, another price-fixing call?" The pleading look her face had held for the past day vanished, replaced by a sternness he had not seen before.

"Yeah." It was the only reply he had.

"Can't you see how deep in you are already? Come on, Gary, get out before it sucks you in like a giant vacuum cleaner."

They talked some more. He promised not to go one step farther if she would give him a little more time to sort things out.

The next morning, Gary got a call from G.T. "Meet me in the purple room," G.T. said. That was pretty unusual, Gary thought, and so was G.T.'s voice. It had an unfamiliar air of tension in it.

The executive conference room had a large table in the center surrounded by purple chairs. It also had a VCR, TV, and a large credenza. Sitting on one side of the table was Howard, and on the other side sat G.T. An unshaven man in horn-rimmed glasses and a rumpled suit was sitting beside G.T.

G.T. quickly made the introduction. "Gary, this is Andrew Tully. From time to time he does a little work for us."

Gary moved forward to shake his hand. Tully stood up and said, "It's nice to finally meet you Gary. I've heard a lot of good things about you."

"Well, I've heard a lot about you, too," Gary replied. What the hell is he doing here? he wondered.

"Gary, sit down," Howard said quickly and in a hushed voice. "You're not gonna fuckin believe what my damn dad did. You know when we were having those production problems and we talked about the possibility of sabotage?" Gary nodded his head: the famous conspiracy theory. " T e l l him what he did, G.T."

"Well," G.T. began, "it seems the old man decided to take things into his own hands, and called a friend of his at the National Security Agency. The NSA guy felt like it was worth looking into and contacted the FBI in Washington. They got hold of the local FBI guy here, and Howard and I just met with him," G.T. said, careful not to mention his own role in advancing the process.

What does this mean and why does it involve me? Gary thought. "What happened?" he asked.

"Well, we only met with him a few minutes and I told him that I really didn't have much to do with the division, and that you were the person he should really be talking to," Howard said.

The picture suddenly came into clear focus, and Gary didn't like it one bit. They were hanging him out to dry.

"Yeah, anyway this FBI guy, Sid Cox, wants to meet with you at two o'clock today at his office at the old First Bank Building. Tully will go with you. Dad sure got us into a hornet's nest this time."

Howard sat back in his seat and looked for a reaction. Gary's heart was in his throat.

"The important thing for the next few minutes here is to think about the last trip and some of the people you've been talking to. Where did you last talk to that engineer from Nippon Kagaka, Obuchi or whatever his fucking name is?"

Gary thought a moment and then said, "From my home. Well he called me first at the office, and then at home."

"Do you have an OPX line?" G.T. asked.

"Yeah."

"Have you ever talked to the Japs on that OPX line?"

"No, no, I haven't. They don't have that number, just my regular home phone."

G.T. sat back and lit a cigarette. "Good, good. So there's no way any of them would ever call you on that line. Now, Gary, did Obuchi ever bring up selling you the technology?"

"No, G.T., we asked *him* about it. You're the one who suggested that I bring it up to him."

Howard looked over at Tully. "Well, Gary, the problem is I just told this Sid Cox guy two things and we have to be consistent," he said. "The first is that *they* tried to sell *us* the technology and not that we tried to buy it, and the second, Gary, is that you need to say that you talked on the OPX line because they want to hook a recorder onto it to record the next time the guy calls. I told him that was the line to bug, because I was pretty sure it wasn't, and we sure as hell don't want the FBI listening in on any of our customer trick calls."

Over the next hour, they grilled Gary on what to say and how to say it. "You're in here with us, aren't you Gary?" G.T. asked at length.

Gary must have nodded, because G.T. continued, "Don't bring up Howard as a part of Bio-tech at all. Remember that. We sure don't want Howard brought into this mess or questioned on anything."

Gary thought about saying, "Yeah, you dipshit, you should have thought of that last November," but he kept quiet as G.T. finished, "Good luck; you'll do fine. You and Tully get your asses back here the minute you're done and tell me how it went."

Gary went back to his desk, and returned a few urgent phone calls, but his concentration was wrecked.

After an unsatisfactory lunch, Gary called Jenna from a conference room and told her what he was going to be doing that afternoon. She didn't sound worried at all, and Gary became frustrated because she didn't seem to understand. She kept saying, "You haven't done anything wrong so you don't have anything to be worried about. Just tell the truth."

CHAPTER 51

Sid Cox was alone in the spartan office on the fifth floor when Gary and Tully entered. He offered coffee. Gary couldn't remember ever meeting an FBI agent, at least that he knew of. The man was poorly dressed in a sport coat, tie and slacks, and had the kind of hair that went all over the place. He sniffled as if he had a bad cold. The coffee maker sat on a gray metal table at the side of the room. Some paper towels served as a tablecloth, spotted with brown stains and littered with stirrers and empty sugar packets. A tower of styrofoam cups in a torn plastic wrapper teetered beside the machine.

"You take anything in it?" Cox asked.

He's the farthest thing from intimidating, Gary thought, as he watched Cox sit back at his desk and shuffle through his papers. Every few seconds, he would take his hand and kind of push the hair back up off his forehead. He was singularly unimpressive, and Gary began to relax a little.

"Why don't you tell me in your own words what all has gone on?" Cox asked.

Gary took a deep breath and launched into the party line. For the next 45 minutes, Gary told him about the contamination problems they had been having, and the calls from Obuchi in which, Gary reported, Obuchi hinted at a willingness to sell them the bug technology. As Gary told the lie, he watched the corners of Tully's mouth turn up into a smile, the first Gary had seen.

"Actually," Tully said, "I understand the contamination has stopped. Isn't that right, Gary?"

"Seems to be," Gary said.

"Now, you first met this Obuchi when he was here with his boss from Japan, right?" Cox asked. "What were they doing in Steuben?"

Gary swallowed hard. He could see Tully across the desk, and the smile had completely vanished from Tully's face, replaced by a look of pure panic. They hadn't rehearsed an answer to that question, hadn't even thought about it. Cox hadn't asked it in a way to challenge Gary, but it posed a challenge nonetheless, one Gary hadn't counted on. Gary developed the story as he talked, half truth, half lie. "There is an association, an amino acid association that gets together to promote the usage of artificial sweeteners like Sugere, and it was our turn to host it. It's the same thing as milk producers promoting milk: we try to get people to use more of our product."

Cox didn't seem to have any problem buying it and Tully was surreptitiously wiping sweat off his brow, so Gary was pretty sure he'd dodged the bullet.

"He calls you on the OPX line at your home, right?" Cox asked next.

"Yeah." Lie, lie, lie, Gary thought.

Cox spent a few minutes looking over his notes, but didn't have any other questions to ask. "Well, I think there are a couple of things that we'd like to do. First, we need to get a recorder on your OPX line. It will have a switch that you can turn on when you want to record a call. It won't come on automatically. I'd like to put it in this afternoon."

No, that won't do, Gary thought. He had dinner that evening with a visiting TLP distributor and his wife from Venezuela. It was on Jenna's schedule, too, and the plan was for them to meet at the Steuben Country Club. He suggested that tomorrow would be better. Cox thought about it for a minute and then set his jaw and said he really wanted to do it today. Gary proposed doing it later in the evening. "We should be home by nine-thirty or ten," he said.

Cox pulled out a pocket calendar and, after a few seconds of flipping pages, agreed. Gary gave him his Wonaonly address and the directions to his house.

"The second thing," Cox said, "is this: do you have some people who are working for you that you think could be doing this?"

"Well, we have hundreds of people in the plant, and I don't know all of them personally. We do have a couple of people who came from Nippon Kagaka." Gary replied.

"The best way to handle this is in the next day or two give me the phone numbers of all the people in the division, not their home phone, just their office phone and their names. All right?"

"No problem," Gary said.

"Good. Well, I'll see you tonight around ten o'clock."

Gary was very nervous as he got up to shake hands. He knew that he'd lied and gotten away with it for now, but he also knew the charade couldn't continue forever. Tully stepped into the elevator with Gary and turned to face him once the doors had shut.

"You were excellent; you were cool and calm, and quick on your feet. This will all be over in a couple of weeks." Then the door opened. Gary felt like running to get outside into the fresh air; he was scared to death. This nightmare has got to stop, he thought.

For the first time, he wished he'd never heard of TLP.

CHAPTER 52

Sid Cox put away his notes, but he couldn't put away the nagging feeling something just didn't add up. He'd gotten the referral from Washington two days before, and had been told to make it his top priority. Along with the referral paperwork, all he'd received were some notes made by an agent from the National Security Agency, where the case had originally landed.

That was puzzling. If it had been the CIA, he could understand it. One of their operatives in Tokyo or Shanghai might have picked up something and passed it along. But the NSA? Cox didn't claim to know a lot about the inner workings of that agency – who the hell did? – but in all his years with the Bureau, he had never seen a referral from them. Their gig, as far as he knew, was big-shit geopolitical stuff: electronic bugging, code breaking. How in hell, he wondered, had they come across something like this?

Top priority. That meant someone very big cared a lot about this. In Steuben, there was only one very big someone, and that was William C. Hargiss. If some Japanese company was sabotaging an American company like TLP, that was certainly a big deal. But the younger Hargiss and G.T. Binghamton hadn't acted like it was a big deal at all, and the security guy, Andrew Tully, said the contamination problems had stopped. It sounded to Cox like a false alarm. If there ever had been sabotage, TLP had already cracked the case, but didn't want to admit it. Or else the people on the ground here knew there was no sabotage.

Cox had spent 15 years in the high-profile world of New York before being banished to Steuben, where his days consisted of nothing more significant than catching petty drug dealers in Steak n Shakes. He had hoped this case really was something big, something that would cause the suits in the Hoover Building to re-elevate his fallen angel status and get him somewhere nice, like Florida perhaps, where he didn't have to fight his sinus infections and cold weather. Damn, he hated cold weather. Now the case was looking more and more like another dead-ender.

Well, shit, who knew what would turn up? He at least had to go through the motions and put the phone recorder in place. Better call the wife and tell her I'm going to miss another meal at home, he decided.

Howard was waiting for Gary when he got back to his office. "Tully says things went just fine," Howard grinned. "These assholes'll find something better to do real soon. It's a shame they've got time for this kind of bullshit when they could be getting drug dealers and murderers off the street." Yeah, right, Gary thought sarcastically. With Howard's reputation for cocaine use, it was absurd to hear him say something like that.

Later, sitting in his office, Gary tried to sort things out. He called Jenna and told her that he didn't want to talk on the phone because there might be a problem, but he wanted to meet her at least half an hour early for dinner that night.

He sat back in his chair and re-thought the possibilities. His first option was to tell Cox everything he knew, including how he had been coached to lie. That might clear his conscience, but it could also land him in jail. Even if the customer trick calls didn't constitute price fixing, lying to the FBI surely was obstruction of justice or something like it. Maybe they'd let him go in return for coming clean, but then again, maybe not.

The second option was to put himself completely in bed with Howard and G.T. Forget about providing the list of employees' names Cox had asked for, and just stonewall everything. Maybe, like Tully had said, it would all be over in a couple of weeks and nothing would happen. Then he could get on with his plan to take over TLP and clean it up. But in the meantime, he would be a card-carrying member of the TLP Mafia. If Cox cracked the case, Gary would land in jail. His marriage, his new family, his whole life would be over. He could never live with himself if that happened.

The third option was to give Cox the list and adopt a wait-and-see attitude. But who knew what would happen when Cox started talking to hundreds of TLP employees? If Killer Keddy was so flip as to discuss price fixing while taking a leak, there was no telling who might spill all the beans.

For the life of him, he couldn't see a course that didn't carry a huge downside.

Leigh broke his concentration, or lack of it, and said, "You sure look bad. What's wrong?"

"Sometimes life around here can really get you down," he said. It was an unguarded slip, and he regretted it the minute the words were out of his mouth. To his surprise, Leigh looked him straight in the eye and said, "I know. Believe me, I know."

"Is there something you want to tell me?" he asked.

She closed the office door and sat down in the chair in front of his desk. "When I came back to Steuben," she began, "I did it because all my family is here, and I really needed them after my husband died. But I vowed I wouldn't work for TLP again. Then there weren't any jobs anywhere, and I figured it would be all right to do some temp work. Then you came along, and you were so different from everyone else here that I decided it would be all right."

"Have I done something to make you regret that?" he asked. Something was obviously troubling her.

"Oh, no," she said quickly and with obvious sincerity. "You are so far above the rest of these clowns, it's unbelievable. I love working for you." She paused a moment, and Gary waited to see what she would say next. "But on days like today, it seems like they're getting to you, too, and that worries me."

"Leigh, why did you get turned off on TLP in the first place?" he asked.

"I'll tell you just one story," she said. "I don't know if it's still going on or not. My old boss is long gone. He died back in the eighties. But one of the things he was in charge of was making arrangements for important visitors to the plant. TLP kept – still keeps, I guess – some special rooms at the Chemical Club. He had me take care of the details, and in the course of it all, I learned that the rooms were bugged. They were taping everything people said in their rooms."

"No kidding?" Gary asked. Another piece of the puzzle had fallen into place.

"No kidding," she said. "I went straight to my boss and complained. He told me not to worry about it, that G.T. and Andrew Tully had set the system and I shouldn't give it another thought.

"Needless to say, I've given it a lot of other thoughts," she added.

"That's an incredible story," he said.

"Gary, be careful," she said, her eyes reddening. "You are the one and only hope for this company."

With that, she left, and Gary buried his head in his hands. He was bone tired. Thank God this day will come to an end soon, he thought. In truth, it was going to last much longer than he knew.

He had to tell somebody about his FBI meeting, and he decided to risk calling Jenna again. He told her about the meeting, and that they were sending a man to tap the OPX line at the house. Then he dropped the bombshell. "Hon, when I met with the FBI, I kind of had to lie to them." Gary said.

"What are you talking about?" Her voice was filled with incredulity. Gary told her about the day's events and how Andrew Tully was at the FBI meeting to make sure he followed through on what had been rehearsed. As the complexity of the situation dawned on her, she calmed down a little bit, but complex situation or not, she didn't budge from her firm stand. "Gary, you have to tell the FBI everything," she said. It was the same tone of voice she might use in lecturing Justin when he did something very bad. And in truth, Gary felt like a small boy being lectured on the essentials of right and wrong. Only grown-up rights and wrongs were so very complicated.

"Maybe I could tell him tonight, when he comes to the house," Gary said, playing with the phone cord, trying to decide if he had the courage to go through with it. Courage? Was that what it was? Or insanity?

"Good idea," Jenna said. "With no Andrew Tully around, there'll be no excuse." He couldn't argue with her logic, but he wasn't ready to decide yet. "I don't know if I can do it," he said.

"You have to, Gary," she implored. "We'll talk more about it before dinner."

Gary said he'd see her soon, hung up and tried to gather his wits.

The world, he thought, does not operate on goody-two-shoes principles, however much innocents like Jenna thought it did. Not for car dealers in Madison, Indiana, and sure as hell not for multinational corporations like TLP. TLP had provided an incredible opportunity for him, and made him a rich man already. For all their faults, the people he was working with were the smartest people he had ever known. The potential of biochemistry was almost limitless, and the products he was developing would be of incalculable benefit to mankind. If he threw a monkey wrench into the machinery now, in all likelihood none of it would ever happen.

No, no, no, he thought. I can't let myself fall into the trap of believing that the ends justify the means. I can't put Jenna through what Mom must have gone through, only on a much bigger scale.

But your dad got away with it, some evil angel whispered to him. And the profits from his kickback scheme put you through college. No! his mind screamed back at the evil angel. You don't even know that for sure!

In the car on the way to meet Jenna, another fact struck him. If he spilled the beans to the FBI, he would incur the wrath of the entire company, starting with William C. Hargiss – one of the most powerful men in the world, brilliant and unscrupulous. Cripes, Gary thought, suddenly remembering the story Ralph Sori had told him, he may even be a murderer. A cold sweat broke out on his brow.

CHAPTER 53

Jenna was waiting for him when he arrived. She looked worried, apprehensive, scared. A maitre d' in a tuxedo showed them to a table, its crisp, white linen tablecloth a background for four place settings, bone china with dark red and gold stripes around the rims, heavy silverware, a bouquet of fresh flowers. In all Steuben, this was the most elegant place for dinner.

Jenna leaned over the table, her normally quiet dark eyes pleading. "What are you going to do, Gary?" she asked.

A waiter poured water, handed them menus and left.

"I don't really know," Gary said. "I mean, I know what the right thing to do is. Believe me, I understand that. What I'm not sure is whether you understand the cost of doing it."

"Forget the money!" she whispered, sternly.

"It's not the money," he told her. "Look, if I turn on these guys, and they're as evil as you and I are coming to believe, they might do anything to get back at me. In a lot of ways, they're like the Mafia. If I cross them, our lives could be in danger."

Jenna stared at him. In truth, she hadn't thought about that. In her analysis, the cost of turning on TLP was only material: his job, the money, probably the house. She had considered that they might have to move to another state and start over. Those sacrifices she was more than willing to make, and she expected him to make them as well. Now, he was complicating the picture immensely.

"Do you really believe they would...?" She let the question trail off.

"In my opinion," he said gravely, "Andrew Tully is the kind of a man who would have no qualms about anything, especially if William Hargiss ordered it."

He looked up to see that their guests had entered the room. "Rats," he said. "Time to act normal." He stood up. "Manuel," he called. "Over here."

As they ate their dinners, Gary could do little more than pick at his food. Manuel couldn't help but notice, and after a few minutes whispered in Gary's ear, "Do you feel okay?"

"Yeah, I'm fine," Gary said. "But I've got a lot on my plate right now," he added, meaning the mess he was in and not the food in front of him. "Plus I've been traveling so much overseas that I think it's finally caught up with me."

Jenna and Gary both tried to be as friendly as they could, but it was obvious how distracted they were. Finally the ordeal was over. As he walked the Venezuelan couple to their car, Gary figured he hadn't done the company any good at all that night. What he couldn't figure out was whether he cared.

Because Jenna had driven up from Wonanonly to meet him, they had both of their vehicles at the Club. As she watched Gary saying good-bye to their guests, Jenna thought they should leave her truck there, and worry about it the next day. We need to talk, she thought. But by the time Gary got back to where she was waiting, she had changed her mind. In light of what he had said about the physical danger they could be in by talking to the FBI, she needed to think. So they drove home separately, Gary leading in the Cadillac, Jenna behind in her GMC. She stared ahead at his tail lights, trying to collect her thoughts. By the time they arrived home, she had found the flaw in his argument.

The boys were already in bed. Jenna paid Kris for the babysitting, and as soon as she and Gary were alone, they sat at the kitchen table, and she began to speak, calmly but firmly.

"What's done is done," she said, "and we can't escape the fact that our lives now have to be lived with the possibility of danger. That's true no matter what you do tonight. Nobody in the Mafia is safe. Ever. If I have to live with that, I want to do it knowing it's because the man I love did the right thing, not the wrong thing."

He looked at her, blinked his eyes twice, and said, "I love you, Jenna."

At precisely 10:00, the doorbell rang.

There are places around the world where a late night visit from the national police strikes terror in the hearts of innocent people. Tonight, in the heartland of America, Gary Long felt that terror.

He composed himself and greeted Sid Cox, who was standing in front of their door in a winter coat. It was actually warm for November, and had it not been for a light breeze, long sleeves would have been enough for most people. Gary knew the temperature would drop quickly as the night fell, but if he went ahead and told this man everything, the heat of the conversation would be intense.

Gary introduced Cox to Jenna, and then took him upstairs to where the OPX phone was. He could hear Cox's car running outside, and started rationalizing that the FBI man was probably in a hurry tonight; maybe he should give Cox a call tomorrow instead of bothering him now.

It took Cox all of three minutes to hook the recorder up and show Gary how to use it. As he started to head back down the stairs he said, "If this guy calls again, we'll get him." Gary followed him down, and as he started to open the front door, he could see Jenna across the room.

Time was up.

Jenna followed them onto the porch. "Sid, can I talk to you about something?" Gary asked.

The agent stopped and turned to face Gary, noting that Jenna was now standing beside her husband. She had placed her hand on his elbow.

"Sure," he said, his training helping him read the body language. "What's on your mind?"

"Maybe we could go to the garage to talk," Gary said. Mark's room was right over the porch, and Gary didn't want him to hear any of this conversation. The three of them started to cross the lawn to the garage. Then Cox stopped.

"I'd better turn my car off," he said, walking away from them.

Gary and Jenna looked at each other. "I'm proud of you," she whispered.

When Cox returned, Gary unlocked the garage door and ushered them in. Then he turned on the lights. A gust of wind blew the door closed with a bang. It sounded like a bank vault in Gary's ears, or perhaps a cell door. His mind went blank.

"What's up, Dr. Long?" Cox asked with a quizzical look.

Gary had no clue how to start. Finally, haltingly, he asked, "Have you heard of anything strange going on at the executive level at TLP?"

"What do you mean, strange?"

Gary could tell his question hadn't really registered anything with the agent. He had to find a way to open the conversation up. "Look," he said, "Steuben is a small town full of gossip. Surely a man in your position would have heard about things that may be illegal going on at TLP."

Cox's brow furrowed. This man is scared, he thought. He ran through the collection of petty rumors he had heard about TLP executives. Every one he could think of involved some violation of state or local law, stuff the local police winked at because, well, because TLP was TLP. As a Federal agent, such matters were of no concern to him. "Well, you hear things," he said, "but people talk. Sometimes it's true and sometimes it's not, but there's rumors going on all the time."

He was either a good bluffer, firmly under the control of William Hargiss, or he genuinely didn't know. Gary hoped to high heaven it was the latter, because he was about spill his guts.

"For example, have you heard about some of the guys who have been around here for a long time doing price fixing around the world?"

The fat was in the fire now, and Cox's already deep furrow deepened further. International price fixing? That was certainly a Federal matter, he thought. At least this guy wasn't wasting his time with penny ante misdemeanors. "No. Why don't you tell me what you're trying to get at?"

Gary knew he had to fish or cut bait quickly. "Well, I do have something to say, but I don't know exactly how to get at it."

"Just go ahead and say it." Cox's brow returned to normal.

"Well, at TLP, price fixing is one thing that goes on." Now Gary had his attention. He could tell by the change in his posture and the new expression of interest on his face.

"What do you mean by that?"

"You know, price fixing. Competitors get together and set prices and allocate volumes to one another."

Cox thought for a second. "Are you doing this in your area, Gary?" he asked.

"No, not yet, but the stage is being set for one of my key products, Sugere. There's been discussion with competitors about a deal, but it hasn't actually happened yet. But it has happened with other products at TLP for a long time."

Cox looked thoughtful and sensed Gary had more to tell. "What else is going on Gary?"

"Well, we've hired hookers to try and steal biotechnology from a Japanese company."

He could read the astonishment in the detective's face. "You're serious," Cox said.

Gary nodded.

"Why are you telling me all of this?"

"I wanted to tell you this afternoon, but Andrew Tully was in the room and I had been coached for an hour and a half to tell, well, less than the truth. That's the reason Tully was there, to make sure I said what I was coached to say. My ass would have been grass if I'd done anything else."

Cox backed up a step and cocked his head to one side. "You've got my attention," he said. "Let's keep moving. What were you coached to say that was different than what you would have said?"

"First, that machine you just put on the phone. I never got a call from the Japanese guy on that phone; G.T. and Howard didn't want that machine on my other line. That's the one where the price fixing calls come in."

"From this Japanese guy in Iowa?"

"Obuchi? Naw, he's just a red herring. The important calls come from his boss, in Japan. And the head of another company in China."

"I see. What else did you lie about this afternoon?"

"Well, the technology we said Obuchi was trying to sell us...there was nobody trying to sell us the organism. We were trying to get him to steal it for us."

"Are you telling me TLP is involved in corporate theft?"

Gary hesitated for a second before he said, "Yeah. All the time."

"For example...can you give me another example, Gary?"

Gary told him about Al Franklin, Paul Rodgers, and the bugs they had stolen.

"What do you think these technologies would be worth?"

"Mmm, somewhere between three and five million dollars each I'd guess."

"Holy mother. This is unbelievable, I gotta start taking some notes." He reached into his briefcase and pulled out a black, fake leather-covered three-ring notebook.

It was getting cooler, and Cox asked if Gary and Jenna were comfortable or not. "I'm feeling chilly myself," he said. "Maybe I'm coming down with something, I don't know."

Gary tried to think of somewhere else they could go. The house was out; he didn't want the kids waking up to hear this. He decided on the pool house. In addition to serving as an equipment storage shed, it had a little sitting area, and an air conditioner that also had a heat setting. John Caldwell had put the unit in because he liked to enjoy an evening cigar, and, with his wife's allergies, there was no way he could smoke in the house. The room was dusty and full of junk, but Gary and Jenna pushed enough things aside so the three of them could sit at the round glass-topped table, with a hole in the middle, where, when the table was pulled out beside the pool in the summer, a bright-colored umbrella was placed. Gary turned the heater on and looked at his watch. It was almost 11:00.

"Before you even start," Cox said, spreading his notebook on the table, "I want you to know that you're doing the right thing. Lying to me this afternoon, that's obstruction of justice, Gary, and you are certainly doing what you should do by telling me now."

One desperate thought kept coming to Gary's mind and he could push it back no longer. "Before I say anything...I mean here I am, vice president of the whole company. I've got a great career going here and we like this place and this town. What's going to happen to me if we tell you everything?"

"Gary, look, you're doing the right thing," Cox said.

Gary realized he hadn't made his point. Cox seemed to take Gary's welfare for granted, and Gary wanted to make sure Cox understood the risk he was taking by talking to him. "If you go to the company tomorrow, I'll be out on the street before you hand your visitor badge back to the front desk. These people are brutal."

"Gary, that's the last thing we're gonna do."

"They've got a lot of connections."

"Well, I'm not one of them."

That made Gary feel more comfortable. He spent the next few minutes telling Cox how he had come to TLP from Foremost and how impressed he was with the lack of bureaucracy and the quickness with which TLP moved.

"You'd hate working for the Government, then," Cox said laughing. He was very unassuming and easy to talk to. "President of a division is pretty high up, isn't it?" he asked after they stopped chuckling.

Gary told him it was and then launched into the full detail of what he knew about Paul Rodgers and stealing the Vitamin C bug from ChemIdeas. Then he talked about the Thomasville hookers, how G.T. had come up with the idea and Tully had implemented it. Then he told him the story about Al Franklin and stealing the technology for cellulose additives. "That all happened before I got here," Gary said.

"Who else knew about it?" Cox asked.

"Billie Mitchell, G.T., Howard Hargiss, maybe Andrew Tully."

Cox was writing furiously. "What about William Hargiss?" he asked, looking up at Gary. Gary could see he was keenly interested in the answer he was about to give.

"On the organisms, I don't know. He's not really involved in the day-to-day operations, but I assume since he sees all the big expenditures, he knows what they're for. On the other stuff I'm going to tell you, I'm sure he does." Gary talked about Howard's mentor relationship, and what Dan Anthony and George Keddy had told him about price fixing.

"And you're sure William Hargiss would know about all of this?" Cox asked.

"I don't know that I can prove it, but I'm sure of it, yes."

"Are Anthony and Keddy really in a position to know about this stuff?"

"Well, Anthony runs the specialty products division. Keddy heads up ag products, you know, pesticides, herbicides, that sort of stuff. That's why they call him 'Killer.' They'd have to know if price fixing was going on in their own areas, because they'd have to meet a volume quota."

Either the heater or the heat of the subject matter was starting to have an effect, and Cox stood up and took off his coat, suit jacket and tie. Without a word, Jenna took them and laid them on top of the pool filter. "What else?" Cox asked, sitting down again.

Gary told him Leigh Curtis' tale about the bugged hotel rooms at the Chemical Club.

"Is that still going on?" Cox asked.

"I have reason to believe it is," Gary replied, "because G.T. wanted to have the Nippon Kagaka team stay there when they came to Steuben last month."

It was almost midnight.

Jenna, who had been quiet during the entire session, taking everything in, announced she was going to bed and both of them told her goodnight. She had done her duty – staying at Gary's side long enough to make sure he did his. In a way, her going to bed was a vote of confidence in Gary, a sign he had passed the test. After she left, Cox took his cellular phone out of his briefcase and called to tell his wife he was going to be very late. Then he turned back to Gary.

"Anything else?"

As Jenna walked to the house, she felt like she was going to be sick. Hearing the details about TLP's crimes made her stomach churn. How could such a big company be involved in so many dirty things? It didn't make any sense, but she knew Gary wasn't lying.

When she got to the top of the stairs, she heard Mark crying softly in his room. That meant he was having one of his nightmares. She went in and caressed his sweating brow with the back of her hand. It seemed to calm him a little. "Mommy, I'm scared," he murmured softly in his sleep.

Back in the pool house, Gary told Cox how G.T. bragged about owning the police in Steuben, and claimed he and Tully had covered up a hit-and-run accident, where a TLP executive had almost killed somebody. Then he told him about how they had moved the catalyst chamber with a police escort, even though it was both overweight and oversized.

Cox didn't care as much about that. Way back when the conversation started, that sort of thing was what he had been expecting. "Sounds like a state problem to me," he said. "Can you tell me more about the price fixing?"

It was hard for Cox to understand how price fixing worked and why it was done. Gary spent the next half hour telling him about TLP's entry into the artificial sweetener market, and the ensuing price wars that occurred as its competitors fought TLP's attempts to secure volume. He also talked about Howard's use of vitamin additives as an example to show the Japanese how it could work for Sugere. "In the vitamin additives situation, they literally drove McLaughlin Chemicals out of business when McLaughlin wouldn't go along, and bought the company for a third of what it was worth," he said.

Gary paused a moment, to get his thoughts back on track. "Anyway, in February I was told that I would be working closely with Howard," Gary said. His tone must have conveyed the apprehension he felt at the time.

"The mentor arrangement. You brought it up earlier. What's so bad about it?"

"Well, Howard has never asked me one thing about the business, never asked me who the people working for us are, never asked where our plants are. The only thing he has ever cared about is who our competitors are, where they are, and how soon he could see them."

"Did you? See them, I mean?"

"Did we ever."

Then Gary detailed the story about the trips he had taken with Howard. He started with the calls leading up to the trip to Japan, who all the players were, what companies they represented and what had resulted from going to Japan and Hawaii. As he was talking, Gary felt a real cleansing begin.

Periodically, Cox would interrupt to ask questions, and Gary tried to bring him up to speed as well as he could. Eventually, Gary got to the June meeting in Mexico City.

When he got to the part about Howard charting out the capacity of the various players and the current markets, he remembered something he thought might be important. "In fact, I still have the charts in my briefcase," he said.

"Are you kidding me?"

"No, let me get them for you. They're in my car." Quickly, he retrieved his briefcase from the Cadillac, returned to the pool house and pulled out the sheets.

The look on Cox's face was beyond description. Gary thought he looked like a kid who opened a package on Christmas day and found the one present he wanted most, but was sure he'd never get.

"Has anyone else touched these besides Howard?"

"Yeah, lots of people at the meeting. I pulled them off the flip chart and brought them back because I didn't want them to fall into the wrong hands."

"This is unbelievable," Cox said shaking his head.

Gary explained the figures on the chart, as Cox looked it over. Then he talked about how the others didn't believe TLP's plant capacity was as big as claimed, which was why they came to Steuben, not for an association meeting like he had said that afternoon.

"That makes sense," Cox said, excitedly. "This is really starting to fall together. This is huge Gary, huge. What hotel did they stay in when they came?"

"No hotel, they both came in and were back out the same day. Remember, I told you G.T. had me try to get them to stay at the Chemical Club."

"Oh, yeah. That's right. In the bugged rooms."

"That's what makes sense to me."

"How'd they travel?"

"Numata and Obuchi flew in on American Eagle, and the New World team drove up from Indianapolis."

"Well, we should be able to get the airline records pretty easy. What was the date?"

Gary looked it up in the pocket calendar in his briefcase. Then he moved on, explaining that Obuchi had really called about the granulator patents, not to sell the Nippon Kagaka bug, and how Howard had asked Gary to try and get Obuchi to defect so TLP could get the bug and solve its contamination problem.

"So the contamination problem is real?" Cox asked.

"The problem is real enough," Gary said. "But the sabotage theory is a figment of William C. Hargiss's imagination. And somehow, Hargiss got the idea that the Obuchi situation was part of it. My guess is that Howard probably didn't tell his dad the right story, or he wouldn't have called the CIA and he wouldn't have had me lie," Gary finished.

"It wasn't the CIA, it was the National Security Agency," Cox corrected him. "For our purposes, though, it's the same difference."

Gary spent another half hour going over various phone calls and conversations. "Then this morning, you show up in the office and the next thing I know, Howard calls me into a conference room and says, 'Holy Shit! You can't believe what my dad just did.'"

"Well, I thought he acted a little nervous," Cox said. "Heck, I didn't even get to talk to him for more than ten minutes, and when I did, he claimed he was naive about everything." Cox started looking back through his notes. Everything that had puzzled him about the attitudes of Howard, G.T. and Tully made perfect sense now.

Gary looked at his watch; it was already past two, but he wasn't tired at all, and neither was Cox. Gary could see the excitement in his eyes.

"I know I said this before, Sid," Gary said. "But I'm still worried about what happens if TLP finds out about this discussion. If you talk to anyone there...you know, try and get them to confirm what I've said or whatever...my goose is cooked."

Cox studied his face for a second, and replied, "Gary, believe me, I'm not going to talk to anyone at TLP about anything.

"Remember," he added, "they didn't want the Bureau in here. They may not even have known the NSA referred the case to us. I know you're worried about their clout, but they don't control the FBI." He paused and looked back at his notes and closed his notebook. "I'll tell you something you really do need to be worried about. Tomorrow you're going to walk back into the office, and Andrew Tully will be waiting for you so he can ask you what happened tonight. If you tell them I was here for four hours, they'll hang you."

He stopped for a second and appeared lost in thought. Then he continued, "You gotta lie, and they are gonna want all the details. You gotta lie and you gotta deny. I was here for five minutes. I didn't even turn the engine off in my car. You could remember that. That's a nice touch. Telling them anything else doesn't help me, and it only hurts you. That's the reason they coached you for an hour and a half. Think back now – you've got to pretend that I just walked out the door after the installation and drove off. There was no conversation whatsoever after that."

Now the FBI is coaching me to lie, Gary thought. What was the difference between them and TLP if they both want me to lie?

"I'm gonna call Tully and tell him I put the recorder on and left," Cox said. "You gotta say the same thing or they'll destroy you."

At 2:30 a.m. it seemed clear to Gary. Now he was lying on the side of the law. That was different from lying on the side of the criminals. He decided to trust Cox completely. They finished up the night with a short drill on how to answer questions Tully and Howard might ask.

As Cox started to pack up, he said he would have to talk to his superiors about everything Gary had told him and that he would get back in touch with him in a few days. "I'll tell you one thing though, Gary, you definitely did the right thing here tonight," he said.

As Gary watched him drive the blue Dodge Dynasty away from the house, he stood on the steps for a few minutes. The cleansing effect he had felt earlier waned as trepidation began creeping in. The night had grown quite chilly, but the deeper cold he felt stemmed from the realization that his life had taken a sharp turn and he had no idea where this new road was leading.

Of course Cox was right, Gary realized. But the leaves on the tree of deceit were growing thicker and thicker. Now he had a new coach, a better coach, a more honest coach, a coach who was not trying to cheat anybody or break the law. But even so, he was still being coached to lie.

The minute his feet crossed the threshold of their bedroom, Jenna sat bolt upright. "I'm sorry I couldn't stay up; what happened after I left?"

Gary sat on the edge of the bed. "I told him everything, I mean I told it all. The stuff with the charts, cocaine, price fixing, bugging the Chemical Club, all the fraud, everything."

He could see the relief on her face, but then she caught his arm as he started to stand up. "Is he going to confront TLP with what you've told him?"

"No, he said definitely not. In fact, he told me to lie to them about the whole night." Then he explained what Cox had said at the end of the conversation and what he was told to say to Tully and Howard. "You need to say the same thing if you're ever asked," he concluded.

She nodded and said, "Gary, please, let's just leave. We can't ever be happy here now. Let's just pick up and go somewhere else."

They talked for a while longer.

"Jenna," Gary said at length, "let me tell you something Leigh said to me today. She said I was the last hope of TLP. What we've done tonight could be the first step in getting this company cleaned up. Let's wait it out and see what happens. Let's trust Cox. Maybe we can get TLP cleaned up once and for all."

As Sid Cox drove back to his house, he replayed bits of the conversation in his mind. This case, he thought, could be my ticket out of Steuben after all.

CHAPTER 54

Gary woke up later that morning in a cold sweat. The night's events were still swirling around in his head and it was hard for him to believe he hadn't just awakened from a bad dream. The fog in his mind started to clear as he pulled himself out of bed. He had spilled his guts to the FBI, and they had been replaced by a cold lump somewhere deep inside him that acted like a thought magnet. If he tried to think of anything else it instantly sucked him back.

Was the lump malignant? Would it spread and consume everything he'd worked for?

The drive to TLP wasn't nearly long enough. Gary set the radio to a top 40 station, but not even the blare of rock music could drown out the cacophony in his brain. There was too much static there. His heart jumped in fear every time the question of what Cox was going to do with all the information he had given him crossed his mind. If Cox went to TLP, Gary knew he would be fired on the spot. Gary wasn't ready to leave yet. He had accomplished a lot since coming to Steuben. He had seen how a big corporation could operate without bureaucracy, how it could give managers the freedom to make decisions. It cannot be, he thought, that a management style like that has to be corrupt. Maybe, just maybe, he could be the man to clean it up and make it run right. Or maybe not.

He arrived at the office around 7:45 and tried to focus on the upcoming day. He was nervous about answering the questions he knew were coming and hated the thought of lying to his colleagues. Still, it had to be better than lying to the FBI.

Howard appeared in his office at 8:00, closing the door behind him. The conversation was entirely predictable.

"Well, did old Sid Cox stop in last night?"

"Yeah, he did."

"How long did he stay?"

"I don't know, maybe five minutes. Hell, he didn't even turn his car off."

Gary shifted in his chair, trying to act nervous, just as Cox had coached him. It wasn't hard, because he *was* nervous, although Howard didn't have a clue as to the real reason behind it. Or at least Gary hoped he didn't.

"Man, I'll really be glad when those sons of bitches are out of here," Howard said. He was bouncing nervously on the balls of his feet.

Zack Brilley, the TLP General Counsel, called shortly after Howard left. He asked the same questions that Howard had asked, and Gary gave the same answers, all the time keeping his nervousness evident. Zack offered the same encouragement. "Don't worry about it, Gary, this will all be over soon," he said. If you only knew, Gary was thinking.

About 15 minutes later, Andrew Tully called and asked if he and Gary could meet. He said he didn't want to talk on the phone, and asked Gary to come down to a makeshift office he used when he was at TLP. It was located in a dismal part of the basement. Gary took the elevator to the basement level and walked through a long window-less corridor. It reminded him of a rat's burrow. It was painted pea green, and there were pipes and ducts everywhere, their tops frosted with an inch of dirt. He entered Tully's dimly lit room, the walls covered with dirty frames containing nondescript pictures of people and plant buildings, some of them stained with watermarks. This must have been the head janitor's office once, Gary thought, and Tully just left the pictures hanging.

Tully was sitting behind his desk, hunched over and looking familiarly rumpled, the perfect caricature of the ex-gumshoe he was. He spoke softly but rapidly, like a machine gun with a silencer.

It started exactly like the conversations with Howard and Brilley. Gary was doing it by rote by now. But when Gary got to the part where he asked what he was supposed to do if the Japanese called on the OPX line, the whole dialogue changed. "What do you mean if the Japs call?" Tully asked, his voice just a little louder. "Gary, I surely don't know what the hell you're talking about."

Gary's bewilderment must not have been hard to read, because Tully's words felt like a bucket of ice water thrown in his face. "If you're talking something illegal, then you'd better not be doing it, " he said without a smile, deadly serious. What a wily son of a bitch, Gary thought.

If Gary had any thoughts before that Andrew Tully was slimy they were confirmed in that moment. The smirk on his face oozed deviousness, but the message couldn't have been clearer: Gary was on his own. It was his neck in the noose. Nobody, least of all Andrew Tully, was really on his side. But it also meant Tully was nervous about the whole situation.

"Hell, Gary in few weeks Cox'll be long gone," Tully said. He was definitely nervous. "We should be handling shit like this ourselves without the government anyway."

The whole day somehow disappeared. Gary couldn't focus on work at all. Segments of his conversation with Cox kept replaying in his mind. Every time the phone rang he thought it might be Hargiss summoning him to the sixth floor to send him packing. "They don't control the FBI," Cox had said. Gary wasn't so confident. With all his Washington connections, Hargiss might find out even if Cox didn't go directly to him. When Cox talked about his superiors, how far up the line did that go, and how far before his statements reached someone in Hargiss's vast circle of contacts?

CHAPTER 55

Sid Cox got to his desk a little late that morning. Steuben was at best a two-man office, and since the latest round of Government cutbacks, it had been reduced to one man, Cox. He felt cold, and turned the thermostat up before making a pot of coffee.

The TLP referral had come out of the Extortion Division in D.C., and handed down to the Indianapolis regional office, then forwarded to him by the Special Agent in Charge, Jim Thompson. Cox's normal course of action would be to send his report back to Washington, with a copy to Thompson, but in this case, he felt like he should send it to Indianapolis first. Thompson could sort out what needed to be done with it. After all, that's why he got the big bucks.

Cox filled out a 302 form and placed his notes along with the sheets Gary had torn off the flipchart in Mexico into a file and wrote TLP on the tab. Then he called Indianapolis and told the clerk to expect an eyes-only fax for the boss. Let's see how Big Jim reacts to this little baby, he thought as he hung up.

He faxed the report and thumbed through a few other files, but nothing interested him. Then he put the files in a cabinet and sat back down, elbows on the desk, fingers together in front of his face. In a few minutes, he had the beginnings of a plan. Its success depended on how Dr. Gary Long would react to it, but he was pretty sure he could handle that part. He thought he had built some real trust with Long as a result of their late-night, four-hour conversation. Besides, what else could Long do? He's in a box, Cox thought. On the one hand, he's already confessed to obstruction of justice; on the other, one call from me to TLP and Long's whole career is in the toilet.

He reached for a Kleenex and blew his nose. The phone rang, and when he answered it, Jim Thompson's voice jumped out at him. "Cox, what the hell kind of a hornets' nest did you get into last night? If even half of what that boy told you is true, we've got ourselves a landmark case here. It's simply incredible. Do you believe this guy?"

Cox told Thompson it all seemed to fit. "I've heard some stuff about these guys before, but William Hargiss has such a solid reputation that it's hard to believe it could really go on."

"Well, there's a problem in itself. The original case was referred to the NSA by Hargiss himself, so we've got to make sure none of this gets back to him. I think we just send back a quick report to Extortion. That'll close their files.

Then we open up a new case in the Antitrust Division. That'll keep it off anyone important's radar scope until we're well down the line. Before we do anything, though, I want to meet Long, look him in the eye and see if he's full of shit or not. Set it up."

Cox agreed to call Gary the next day and set up a meeting for the three of them.

That night, Gary and Jenna got the boys settled in for the night and went into the family room, where he replayed the conversations with Howard, Zack Brilley and Tully, and told her how hard it would be to accept what could happen if this thing blew up in his face. Jenna was supportive. "Gary, you've done the right thing, I know you have." They talked for a long time about his future at TLP, their involvement with the FBI, and where it all could ultimately lead. When they finally turned out the lights and went upstairs to bed, Jenna was still steadfast about the decision. As Gary drifted off to sleep he wished he could be as sure as she was.

Still, he slept easier that night and felt more confident the next day when he went to work. Jenna phoned him in the morning and told him Cox had called and wanted Gary to return his call from a phone somewhere other than his office. Gary went into the empty conference room next door and dialed the number.

"Gary," Cox said, "I've been going over the things we talked about with my superiors and I want to meet with you tonight and bring my boss, Jim Thompson. He's a really good guy. He sees this as a very serious case, and wants to meet and talk with you. You can treat what he says as gospel and he reports directly to Washington."

Gary wasn't sure if that was good or bad, but agreed to meet that night at 7:00 at the pool house. Cox was concerned about being watched by TLP and felt the appearance of his car in Gary's driveway might cause problems. After thinking about it for a few moments, Gary told him he would leave the garage door open so Cox could pull directly into it and close the door behind him. He found Cox's caution both unnerving and reassuring. On the one hand, it indicated the depth of their conspiracy, but on the other, it signaled that he was thinking hard about protecting him from TLP.

The blue Dodge arrived right on time, and the two FBI men got out, closed the garage door and made a beeline to the pool house where Gary was waiting for them. Cox introduced Thompson and the three men sat down at the glass-topped table. Jenna made some coffee and brought the pot and a warming plate to the pool house. Thompson began the conversation with a brief sketch of his background and credentials. Born and raised in Pennsylvania. Lehigh

University. Recruited out of college by the Bureau 25 years ago. That looked about right to Gary. Thompson appeared to be in his late 40s, with salt-and-pepper hair, just about six feet tall with a medium build. He possessed a measure of formality absent in Cox, and was dressed in a dark suit and a plain tie.

Gary gave Cox a notebook with the names and phone numbers of all the people he had talked about two nights before. Cox took them and sat down on a chaise lounge, while Thompson and Gary continued to talk over the table. Thompson started by saying earnestly, "Gary, you did a great thing here and we admire and appreciate what you've done. We've looked over your information and we see a very serious obstruction of justice case and a number of other crimes. We want to pursue them, but we're going to need some help." Gary wasn't exactly sure what he was driving at, but as he listened, he looked over at Cox, who was still furiously transferring information by hand onto a yellow legal pad.

Thompson snapped his wandering attention back when he said, "Gary we need a guy on the inside to prove these things are happening." He watched Gary intently for a reaction. "We also need to add credibility to your story by getting proof that what you told Cox is true. We need hard evidence, not just hearsay." He paused for a moment to let it all sink in.

Gary didn't respond immediately, but eventually gave voice to his thoughts. "Do you want me to work undercover for the FBI?" he asked, stammering.

"No, not at all," Thompson quickly replied. "All we need is for you to go in for a week or two and get the proof of the obstruction of justice and then we will know that all these other things that you told Cox actually happened. If they wanted you to lie, it's because they're trying to hide something and that's what we need to get proof of." Gary wasn't sure what the difference was between that and working undercover, but he didn't ask. He just listened and took it all in without saying a word. "Gary, we need you to help us out for a couple of weeks, no more than that. We have to get enough information to see whether or not we really have a case here," Thompson said.

At that point, Cox looked up and joined the conversation. "Gary, here's what we need to do," he said. "There are some key facts we gotta get on tape, the stolen technology and how Howard was the one orchestrating how to steal. Now, Gary, you need to let him do the talking, this is important. Extremely, extremely important."

Tape! They wanted him to tape Howard incriminating himself! What was the slang they used on the cop shows: wear a wire? Oh, no! Gary's face showed his dismay. Cox paused and then calmly but firmly laid out the facts of life. "Now that we're involved, we will be investigating your allegations with or without your help," he said. He paused for a moment, waiting for Gary's reaction.

Gary was numb. He was trapped like a rat on a wharf rope: a cat on one end and the ocean on the other. Well, Gary thought, at least the cat looks kind of friendly. He spoke slowly but firmly, "I'll get you what you need."

"Great, great. You've made a good decision, Gary," Cox said.

"Absolutely," Thompson added. "You can be proud of what you're doing."

"We're gonna give you a tape recorder before we leave tonight," Cox explained. "I want to go over with you how to phrase the questions."

For the next half hour, Cox and Thompson coached Gary on how to pose questions, not just to Howard, but to Andrew Tully as well. Gary was to have them confirm on tape that TLP habitually stole technology, had casual price fixing conversations with their competitors, and that he had been systematically coached on how to lie to the FBI. The key was to let the others do the talking.

On that last point Gary remembered the conversation he'd had with Tully in his dingy basement office. "Tully's already backing away. I'm not sure he'll admit to anything," he said.

Cox and Thompson exchanged curious glances. Cox cleared his throat and said, "Well, Gary, we may not get everything we want and that's okay, but let's practice how to ask the questions so we have the best chance of getting what we need."

They worked on the questions until Cox felt Gary could deliver them with ease and understood how to get his interviewees to volunteer the information. At the end Cox suggested that Gary drop Tully's name into the conversation with Howard to see if he could get him to confirm Tully's involvement. Then Cox handed him a black tape recorder the size of a Good-&-Plenty box with a microphone attached to a 12-inch cord. Gary was to slip the recorder into his inner suit jacket pocket and clip the microphone onto the top edge of the inside pocket.

Gary looked at Cox quizzically. "You mean this thing can pick up conversations from people several feet away?" Cox assured him the recorder wouldn't miss a word, instructed him on how to operate it, and inserted a fresh battery.

"We need a way to communicate," Cox said. "I don't want you using your home or office phone. Tully's ex-CIA and probably has a lot of experience with this type of equipment so I don't think those phones would be safe."

"Well you could use my answering machine," Gary suggested.

Cox thought about it. "Yeah, that'll work. I'll leave you a message with the sound of my pager turning on and then you can call me," he said, handing Gary the phone number for his office.

The final order of business for the night was signing a form that permitted Gary to record people without their knowledge. Gary also had to acknowledge that all his activity was of his own free will and he agreed to do all of the taping voluntarily. What, Gary wondered, was the meaning of the word "voluntarily" in a situation like this? What choice did he have? Some philosophers don't believe free will even exists, and at the moment, Gary could see their point.

Thompson and Cox reviewed the taping procedure several times, repeating the questions Gary was to ask and stressed in a parting shot that he was not working for the FBI, but only helping to build his credibility and get hard evidence. Somehow Gary couldn't see the distinction. He was laying his career on the line to gather information for the FBI but was technically not working for them. Cox told him it might take a couple of weeks to get the information and to call him when he had it.

Later, Gary told Jenna what he had been asked to do, and that he hoped he could do the whole thing in one day instead of taking two weeks. The sooner it was over, the better. He showed her the tape recorder and how it worked. Jenna wasn't worried and Gary felt good about that. He'd already added more than enough stress to her life.

CHAPTER 56

Gary awoke the next morning at the crack of dawn, nervously excited. He was eager to start taping and get it over with quickly. On the drive in to work, he recalled the things Thompson and Cox had told him to say: he even practiced them out loud. In the safety of the car, he turned the recorder on and off, tried to see how it looked in his pocket. By 7:15, when he got to his office, he felt fairly confident.

Howard was in his office by 8:00. Before Gary left his desk, he flipped the switch of the recorder on and made certain the microphone was clipped to his pocket flap properly. He asked Howard's secretary, Dinah, if it was okay to go in, and she nodded. Howard was seated behind his desk, absorbed in the morning TV newscast. He glanced up as Gary walked in.

"Hey, Howard, you got a minute?"

"Sure," he said looking sideways at him. "Sit your ass down."

"Haven't heard any thing from the Feds yet, have you?" Gary asked.

"Nope, not moo nor quack," he replied.

"Good...good." It was now or never, so Gary went in for the kill. "I'm sure glad I sat down with you and Tully before I went out to meet Cox so I would know what to say and what not to say."

"We wouldn't think of letting you meet him without talking with us first," Howard said without hesitation. He was reading the situation just as Gary hoped he would: a nervous employee needing reassurance.

"Can you fucking imagine what it would have been like if you hadn't been coached? It'd come out that we're trying to steal fucking technology from those geeks, and you'd have told him to tap your home phone instead of the OPX line." Howard paused, took a deep drag on his cigarette and continued. "We all gotta speak the same language," he said, stubbing out his butt.

"Yeah, you're right, Howard," Gary replied. Bells were going off in his head. Within two minutes he'd gotten everything the FBI asked for.

Howard kept on talking. "Anyway, call those Japs like I told you to, and tell them not to call your home or office. Tell 'em to cool it for a while, so we can let this thing blow over. Then we'll call 'em up and get these prices back where they oughtta be. The Feds may screw us up for a few weeks, but they'll give up when nothing happens."

Gary could hardly contain himself as he left Howard's office. This was easier than he had imagined. Howard had just handed him everything on a silver platter and Gary had hardly said a word. As he walked into his office, he gave Brad Redfoot a high five, much to Brad's surprise, and sat down at his desk. This was great stuff for the FBI, and Gary was sure they would be ecstatic.

Easy it may have been, but that didn't erase the moral dilemma in his conscience, and Gary began feeling pangs of guilt as the morning wore on. On the one hand, here were men who completely trusted him, who gave him bonuses and raises. He had to face them every day. On the other hand, they had asked him to lie and break the law, and it was apparent, from his chat with Tully, that he would be the one left twisting in the wind if it got exposed. The fact was he had made his bed; now he had to sleep in it. Gary had to prove to the Feds he was telling the truth.

Gary's pulse quickened a bit as he entered Tully's subterranean office. He hadn't worried about Howard spotting the recorder, but Tully was trained in this stuff, and he might look for something like a wire. Gary had visions of being patted down as soon as he entered.

Nonetheless, he did it, and found Tully his usual unfriendly self. "So what do you want, Gary?" he said gruffly.

"I'm kinda nervous about the FBI and when they're gonna be out of here. I've never used the lines they tapped for price fixing, but what if they've tapped some other lines without me knowing?" It wasn't hard to act nervous. Tully took the bait, hook, line and sinker.

"Listen, assume all the lines are bugged and stay calm, cool and collected. Keep your mouth shut about anything you don't want the Feds to hear."

Gary was on a roll so he decided to go for it. "Man," he said, "I'm sure glad you told me what to say before we met with the FBI. I'd have screwed it up royally without even knowing it."

Tully didn't even pause. "Yeah, Howard and I talked about it after he met with Cox and we decided you needed some coaching. I know you're not used to this stuff, but you did great, followed the script like a pro."

"Well I'm sure glad I lied about the OPX line." Gary said.

Tully just nodded in agreement, then Gary thanked him and left. Everything recorded but confirmation on the OPX line, Gary thought...too bad Cox couldn't hear Tully's head nod.

This was fantastic. The conversation had lasted only a few minutes and he got almost everything confirmed from Tully, too. He couldn't wait to call Cox.

"You're kidding me," Cox said after Gary gave him the news.

"Nope, I got it all on tape."

"Did it come out good?" he asked eagerly.

"I haven't dared play it back," Gary said. "But if the machine works as slick as you said it would, I think you're gonna like it."

"Can you meet me for lunch?" Cox sounded like he was practically foaming at the mouth.

"No, there's no way I can now. Everyone is gonna be back in the lunch room and I don't think it'd be smart to be gone now, but I can meet you after work."

"Okay, we'll meet at the Holiday Inn. I'll get a room. I'll call you and leave a room number on your answering machine but I'm not going to leave my name."

Gary had gathered all the information they wanted, caught his peers incriminating themselves, established his credibility, and set up the rendezvous with the FBI all before lunch. What they had thought might take two weeks Gary had done in a few hours. Well, isn't that just like a TLP man, Gary thought, smiling to himself at the irony.

That evening, before Gary left the office, he checked his voice mail and got the room number. Around 6:00, he pulled into the lot at the Holiday Inn, walked around the side of the building and went directly to the room. After one knock, Cox answered the door and ushered him in.

"Wait'll you hear this tape," Gary said. He was brimming with enthusiasm. He opened his briefcase and handed the recorder to Cox, who promptly removed the tape and inserted it into a small machine that looked like a miniature stereo.

The recording was astonishingly clear. When Cox heard Howard's voice tell Gary to call the Japs, he lit up like a pinball machine on tilt and practically shouted, "Bingo!" After both conversations were completely played through, Cox said, "Man, Gary, this establishes obstruction of justice and price fixing both. I need to play it for Thompson and write a report. After that I'll get back to you. This is just what we needed: hard evidence."

Jenna was waiting for Gary at the door, anxious about his day. He told her all the details of the tapings and the meeting with Cox. They wondered what the FBI would do with the tape and thought they might walk right into TLP, play the tape and read them their rights. What would happen then they couldn't imagine.

Only one piece of business remained. Cox said he would leave a pager message on Gary's voice mail within a few days so he could call back from a safe phone.

Gary had taken the test, and knew in his heart he had aced it. He had done what was right. Soon the instructor would call and confirm his grade. He felt waves of relief sweeping over him. It was over.

CHAPTER 57

About a week later, Gary picked up his phone and dialed his machine. The beeping sound told him Thompson had listened to the tapes. He went to the meeting room next to his office and called Cox, who wanted to meet at the Best Western Hotel parking lot, next to Shakey's Pizza. "We won't need a room to tie up the few loose ends I need," Cox said. "I just want you to call the Japanese and get them to confirm what you've told us about setting prices."

So, Gary thought, it wasn't quite over after all. Well, that call shouldn't be too hard. Cox wanted him to call from a pay phone with him right at Gary's side. They agreed to do it the following night, morning in the Far East.

The next morning, Gary asked Jenna if it he could drive the truck to work that day. "I'm meeting Cox in a parking lot," he explained, "and I'm nervous someone will spot the Cadillac."

At the appointed hour, Gary pulled into the Best Western parking lot and found Cox's Dodge waiting with the motor running. It had turned cold, and he could see the FBI agent bundled up, huddled behind the wheel. Gary parked the truck and walked over to Cox's car. As he approached, Cox opened the window just a crack. "Get in," he called, quickly shutting the window again.

"Gary, everything you told us about the way you were coached was confirmed on the tapes," Cox said, once Gary was in the car. "All my superiors really appreciated what you did. We just need to get confirmation from the other side of the conspiracy." Cox explained what he wanted Gary to say to Numata and Song, and what he wanted them to say about the price fixing and the meeting in Mexico.

Then, while Cox watched over his shoulder and shielded him from prying eyes at a row of four pay phones inside the motel, Gary placed a call to Sumiko Numata at Nippon Kagaka. Holding the microphone up to the ear piece as Cox had instructed him, Gary asked for Numata. "Howya' doin' Sumiko?" Gary asked in his best everything-as-usual voice.

"Ah, Dr. Long. Is all right for us to talk again?"

"Yeah, everything's cool," Gary replied, remembering that their last conversation had been the one when Gary told him not to call for a while.

For the next minute or so they talked in generalities about business and what was happening in the market place. "Prices are coming up pretty good, huh, Sumiko?" Gary asked, knowing the answer. "Remember what Howard said in

Mexico?"

"Uh, yes, I do. Mr. Hargiss promise seventy-five cents by fall. He right on target."

Bingo, Gary had all he needed – confirmation of pricing discussions. With no need to waste further time, he bade a quick goodbye and hung up.

Then Gary called Song Dian-Nuan at New World. "How do you feel about the way prices are moving?" Gary asked.

"We still going to have some problem since we not have a volume agreement," Song countered, worried about the details of the conspiracy and oblivious to the real purpose of Gary's question.

"But can you agree we have a good start after the meeting in Mexico?"

"Ah, yes. I think Howard have some good ideas. He said price would go up if we work together. He also right about volumes. Extra volume have big negative effect."

Another bingo. Albeit in broken English, Song had confirmed both things Cox was looking for. First, there was a meeting in Mexico, and second both price and volume had been discussed. Gary ended the conversation quickly and hung up.

As they walked back to his car, Gary could tell the FBI agent was pleased. He took the recorder from Gary, extracted the tape, and to Gary's surprise, handed the recorder back to him.

"I'm going to give you this recorder and three tapes. I'll need you to sign a form," Cox said.

"Why, what for?" Gary asked, stunned.

"Gary, I want you to confirm what happened with the other price fixing stuff, and more information about the hookers at Thomasville and stealing the vitamin additive technology. Don't ask it all at one time. Spread it out over several conversations, and just try to fit it in."

He opened the door to his car and motioned Gary to get in on the other side. Gary glanced over at the pickup three spaces away. He clenched his hands and tried to speak the words, "No, Sid, I'm not going to do that. I've done all I can." Desperately, he tried to say those words and then just walk away and get into the truck and drive home. But he couldn't. Dropping his head, he walked around the front of the Dodge and climbed into the passenger seat.

Cox could read the body language like a book with big type. It was motivation time. First, he started the car to get the heater going. "Gary," he began, "you're a hero, a real, live walking and breathing hero. What you're doing for the cause of justice, the courage you showed in coming forward like you did that night at your house, it's probably the greatest thing I've ever seen. It's like Whittaker Chambers exposing the spy rings back in the forties, or Bobby Kennedy going after the Mafia." Cox reached into a pocket in his coat, took out a lozenge of some kind and popped it into his mouth.

"And, Gary, the day is going to come when people will know what you've done. It's not that far away, either, I promise you. These guys at TLP, they're crooks on a massive scale. You're bringing them to justice. Without honest citizens like you, guys like me don't have a chance."

"I sure don't feel much like a hero," Gary said.

"Believe me, I know it's tough," Cox said. "But so are you. I saw that picture of those two little boys of yours, the one on the landing of the stairway. Think about them, Gary, how proud they'll be when they grow up and realize that their dad broke the biggest corporate corruption case in the history of the United States.

"Are you with me, Gary?"

Like an athlete who finds energy late in the game by knowing that it will soon be over, Gary had counted on being rid of the recorder, and the tension that went with it. Now the game was going into overtime, and Coach Cox's words had the desired effect. Gary could tell Cox was excited, and some of his enthusiasm began to rub off. The hypochondriacal FBI man, his heavy coat pulled tightly around his neck, was the very picture of the Secret Agent. He was Eliot Ness, and for the moment at least, Gary could feel a sense of excitement building.

"I'm with you," he said.

With that, Coach Cox turned from motivation to Xs and Os, telling Gary how to ask the questions. "You know, say things like, 'boy, G.T., isn't it a shame they didn't get that technology from the Japanese in Thomasville with the hookers?'"

Gary's excitement began to wear off on the drive home. It was not, after all, a movie. He was in the process of throwing away real money, a real career with a fabulously promising future. He had just made corporate vice president and was on track to riches he had never imagined. In a few years, Gary thought, I could be in William Hargiss's league, friend of senators and presidents, a major player in the international corporate community. Why was he chucking it all down the crapper? Why was he working to betray the men who had given him so much opportunity? They would be indicted, thrown in jail, their lives and careers ruined. Some of them Gary liked, others not, but none of them had ever done anything to hurt him, at least not in their own minds.

Simple morality was a sufficient answer, of course. There was right, and there was wrong. But the practical side of Gary clung to another hope: that the FBI was going to help him clean up the company, and he could get rid of all the shady dealings, keep the aggressive, no-red-tape style and make TLP both successful and honest. Gary imagined the board of directors, hugely successful men like Randolph Thad, Robert Aiken and Ian Howes, men Gary believed to be innocent of all the shenanigans that had been going on at TLP, turning to him as the savior of their reputations and hailing him for putting things right.

Was Gary back in movie script mode, or could it really come out like that? By the time he got to Wonanonly, he believed with all his heart that it could.

CHAPTER 58

Over the next few days, Gary taped several conversations with Howard and G.T., and the more he taped, the more his confidence grew.

G.T. was easy to tape. The more crooked the deed, the more he liked to brag about it, and Gary was in his office several times every day.

"You know, G.T., our contamination problem would sure have been easier to handle if we'd had another bug to use to strengthen our process."

G.T. didn't miss a beat. "You mean like the bug we hired the hookers to get for us in Thomasville? It's a damn shame that didn't work out. I don't give a shit what Howard thinks, that was a great idea."

"How did it get put together?" Gary asked.

"Ah, Tully hired somebody out of New Orleans to put it all together. Fuckin Tully knows people everywhere."

Gary and Howard spent half an hour hashing over how the prices had been doing since their meeting in Mexico. Gary told him that they had crept past the seventy-five cent level in the U.S., although they were still lower in Latin America and Asia. Howard was quick to take credit for the rise.

On a trip with G.T. to Colorado, where they were working on the purchase of a flour additive plant, Gary decided to ask about the Chemical Club incident and confirm what he had heard from Leigh Curtis about the bugged rooms. He tried to phrase the question in the most indirect way he could think of, but it still set off alarm bells with G.T.

"What do you want to know about that shit for?" he asked.

Gary tried to keep the horror he felt from appearing on his face. He shrugged and said, "Oh, it's just a rumor I keep hearing around the plant, and I wondered if it was something I could use."

G.T.'s reply was as stern as anything Gary had ever heard from him before. "You let us deal with that kind of stuff, and just stick to your end of the business."

Besides learning how far he could push his questions that day, Gary learned it was almost impossible to tape on the plane; the background noise level was so high it drowned out the conversation.

Gary's in-laws were scheduled to gather at the house for Thanksgiving dinner, and the day before, Jenna interrupted her culinary preparations to propose an idea that shocked Gary.

"Why don't you tell my folks about what's happening?" she asked.

He almost dropped the Indian corn he was hanging on the back door. "What?"

"You know, tell Mom and Dad about the FBI and everything."

"Why in the world would I want to do that?" he stammered.

"Because," she said, uneasy at his strong negative reaction, "I think it would be good for someone else to know what's going on, so if something happens to us, the true story will come out."

"Jenna, I think you're becoming paranoid."

"I am not. And what about you?" she answered. "Taking the truck to your secret meetings so no one will spot your car?"

"That's different. It's just a sensible precaution."

"It *is* sensible. And so is not talking too much on the phone. And so is telling Mom and Dad what's going on. Don't you think you can trust them?"

"It's not that," Gary protested. "I'm not sure it's wise, for them as well as us. I don't think we should put that kind of pressure on them."

Jenna thought a moment. "Why don't you at least tell Dad," she said finally. "He can handle it, and I'd just feel better knowing someone else knew the truth."

Gary still felt it was an unnecessary risk, but he agreed to let Bud Potter in on the secret.

After dinner, as the two men were watching the Cowboys while the women did dishes and the boys played video games upstairs, Gary told Bud about his involvement with the FBI and played one of the most recent tapes he had made. Bud was shocked at what passed for casual conversation at TLP. Not only did he find the salty language offensive, but as a staunch Republican and firm believer in free enterprise, he found it hard to believe the company that provided jobs for so many people could be capable of such criminal behavior.

"How in the dickens could this go on?" he asked, pacing back and forth in front of the fireplace in the family room.

"I'm not sure; I guess they've done it for a long time."

Bud was silent for a few minutes. "Well, I can't say I approve of it," he said at length, "but I can't say I think you're doing the right thing either, telling the FBI all of this stuff. It kinda seems like tattling. It just doesn't feel right, Gary." That was all he had to say. Gary started feeling like the turkey and stuffing was rotting inside him instead of being digested.

CHAPTER 59

Gary called Cox the next Monday and told him he had what Cox wanted. They agreed to meet that night, in the Holiday Inn parking lot, behind the hotel and away from the road.

It was dark when Gary drove into the lot. Cox flashed his lights and as Gary pulled alongside his car, he hopped out and got into Gary's. Gary handed him the recorder and gave him a brief summary of what he had on tape and who had said it.

Cox was clearly pleased. "Sounds like you did great," he said. "Again."

Gary went on to tell him about his close call with G.T., and explained the trouble he had with taping on the plane.

"Yeah, that could be a problem," Cox said. "I'll talk to some of the tech guys and see if they have any ideas on how to they could improve the sound quality."

Gary's mind raced for a second. Was he talking about how to improve *future* sound quality, or the sound quality of *this* tape? Surely he meant he would see about some way to remove some of the background noise on the tape he had just been given. That had to be it.

Gary took his next words as confirmation. "We're going to pull the phone bug out of your house in a few weeks," he said.

Then Cox turned on the tape recorder. "Yes!" he exclaimed several times when he heard Howard and G.T. incriminate themselves. When he got to the noisy airplane conversation, he snapped the machine off.

"I think we got things set up real nice here to get lots of evidence in this case," he said. "The way you're going, you can get them to confess everything they've ever done." It wasn't over. Shit, it wasn't over. Gary had a sinking feeling in the pit of his stomach. He waited to hear if he was going to get another assignment, but all Cox said was that he would be back in touch after Thompson had a chance to listen to the new tapes. Then he got out of the car. Gary gunned the engine and sped out of the parking space before Cox even reached his own car.

He was angry, depressed and panicked. All of a sudden, he could see his dilemma stretching on for months. Tattling, Bud Potter called it. If his own father-in-law saw Gary as the villain in the drama, what hope was there that anyone else would see him as a hero? The feeling in his stomach started to turn to real nausea, and he stopped at a drug store on the outskirts of Steuben to buy a roll of Tums. Outside the store, a Salvation Army volunteer was ringing her bell beside the familiar red kettle. Gary scowled at her and jumped back in the Cadillac. Now he felt really miserable. He always put something in the kettle. The Salvation Army was his mother's favorite charity, and the Long kids had been brought up to respect the work it did around the world. What must the woman with the bell be thinking? This man in an expensive coat, driving a Cadillac, and he wouldn't even give her a smile, much less a buck. What the hell was he becoming? He tore open the Tums and downed three of them. They didn't help at all.

How am I going to get out of this? he asked himself as he sped through the darkness. He turned on the radio in an attempt to distract his frenzied brain. It was a talk show, and the topic of the moment was that crazy doctor from Michigan, Kevorkian. Gary pulled up at the stoplight in Hardin. The Olde Coach Steak House was on his right, its windows festooned with Christmas decorations, just as they had been a year before when he and Jenna had their first date there.

Recalling that dinner only made him more depressed. It had held so much promise, and after a series of fits and starts, the promise had been fulfilled. That night, what had been on his part merely a physical attraction to a beautiful woman had crossed over into the beginnings of love with a woman who was not only beautiful, but worthy in every way he could imagine. But what were the consequences of his love? How could he justify having dragged her into the TLP cesspool? Where, exactly where, had he gone wrong?

Wrong? What *was* wrong?

"Right!" said a caller on the radio. "It's a matter of right! A person has the right to commit suicide if he chooses to!"

Well, Gary thought to himself, that would be one way to end his troubles. He was joking with himself. Joking. He knew that. He was not seriously contemplating suicide. The light turned and he started up, reaching over to turn off the radio. He didn't need to hear any more of *that* discussion. Of course, if he did die, Jenna, Justin and Mark would be well provided for, and however much she would miss him – she *would* miss him, he believed – she would also be released from the terrible burden he had placed on her. And he wouldn't have to do any more price fixing, or rat on his friends. He could do it right now, just by speeding up and steering a little to the right and ramming the car into that telephone pole. No, they weren't telephone poles, they were power line poles, the telephone wires were all underground now. Anyway, he was past that one. The next one. Too late. Maybe he could pick one out a few hundred feet farther on, or start counting them, select a number in advance and ram into it when the number came up. A nice round number, like ten. He looked in the mirror. The road was deserted. He was completely alone.

What the hell was he doing? Nearly 80, according to the speedometer. He slowed to 65. The crisis had passed, but the depression was still there. I've become suicidal, he thought. I didn't do it this time, but maybe next time I will.

I'm really not ready to call it quits on life, he thought, but I definitely need some help sorting all of this out.

Should he talk to Jenna? No, it would only frighten her even more than she already was.

He decided to talk to Sid Cox; maybe the FBI had a psychologist or a psychiatrist who routinely dealt with problems like this. Or maybe Cox knew someone on the outside. He called Cox's office number the next morning.

"Sid, I've got a real problem dealing with all this pressure," he began. "I feel like I don't know why I'm doing what I'm doing, and I feel like crap all the time. I don't think I can take much more of this. I've even thought about killing myself."

Cox considered what Gary told him for a few seconds that seemed like minutes. "Well, how would you do it?" he asked.

Gary was stunned. He wanted help dealing with his depression, not help on how to commit suicide. Well, he thought, maybe this is a technique. What was the answer to Cox's question? For some reason, he didn't want to talk about running his car into a utility pole. He looked up from the phone. The wall of the conference room was lined with photographs of significant events in TLP history. In one of them, Killer Keddy was cutting the ribbon for the then-new ag products building.

"I'd probably take something," Gary heard himself say to Sid. "Some poison. Probably" – he thought back to the million chemistry classes he had taken – "sodium cyanide, I think."

Cox seemed a little surprised that he actually had an answer. "Why would you use that?" he asked. Gary gave him a chemistry lesson. "Well, where would you get something like that?" Cox eventually asked.

"Well, we probably manufacture it right here at TLP," he said. It was all so nonchalant Gary began to shake.

Finally, Cox made at least some attempt to offer Gary a little bit of encouragement. "Well, Gary, that would be a shame because you really are going to be a hero when this is all over. I know it seems tough right now, but believe me, it'll all be worth it when this case is over. You are really doing the right thing,

Gary. Just hang in there."

"Yeah, but I need help, Sid, I need to talk to someone to sort all of this stuff out."

"Well, what kind of help do you mean?"

"You know, like a doctor."

"Well, you can forget that, so just put it out of your head. Who could we trust? You spill your guts to some shrink, and TLP'll know about it before your check clears the bank."

"Isn't there someone I could talk to inside the FBI?" Cox considered that for a moment. He was surprised with the matter-of-fact manner in which Gary talked about suicide, but he had been trained to expect it, sooner or later. Discreetly, Cox had called the Bureau's profiling unit and after he described a generic Gary, they provided him with a profile assessment. It included the possibility of a suicide discussion. Cox had been prepared for the discussion and given tips on how to handle it. The psyche guys had hit it on the head. This guy wanted to be a hero. They'd also told him the first time the subject of suicide came up, it wouldn't be serious.

"Nah," he said. "You just need to realize what the end result of all this will be, and remember it's all worth it. If your involvement with this case gets out, it'll just screw it all up. You don't want to do that, Gary. Not when you're so close to winning."

As Gary hung up, he wondered what winning would be. The satisfaction of seeing the Hargisses, G.T. and Andrew Tully in jail? He took no pleasure in that thought, except for Tully. Getting out of Steuben altogether, starting over somewhere? He thought about his old jobs at Foremost and Technochem. How drab and boring they seemed now. There was only one scenario that excited him: a cleaned-up TLP, with Dr. Gary Long in charge. Was that possible? Would men like Randolph Thad, Robert Aiken and Ian Howes turn to him in the wake of the slaughter? Or would the whole thing kill TLP entirely, force it into bankruptcy and an asset sale in which Nippon Kagaka, Foremost and the others would gobble up what was left? And even if he did ride back into Steuben on a white horse and with the board's blessing, could he or anybody else actually run the company the way he wanted to? Maybe the price fixing, political payoffs and skullduggery were essential to make an action-oriented, no-red-tape management style profitable.

No, he thought, it can't be. I have to aim for that goal. If I reach it, I'll find a way to make it work.

CHAPTER 60

Gary and Brad Redfoot were reviewing the latest customer order analysis when Buffy Carney stuck his head in. The PR maven was grinning from ear to ear. "Be sure to catch the *Wall Street Journal* in the morning, guys," he said, "cause you're both in it and I'll bet my Christmas presents you're going to like it."

"Whoa, what's this all about?" Redfoot asked.

"Well," Buffy began, pulling up a chair and draping his lanky frame over it, "it seems Mr. William C. Hargiss gave a little talk to a group of financial analysts in the Big Apple yesterday, and predicted that bio-tech was the future of TLP and credited you two by name for making it happen."

Gary had known about the meeting, and could pretty well guess what Hargiss had said. "How's our stock doing?" he asked.

"Up three quarters, and I predict we'll go up a point or more tomorrow after the story hits."

"Ah, the power of the press. They can make you or break you," Redfoot said, remembering the hot summer days when their production problems kept all three of them scurrying to tamp down stories about the disaster.

"Did Hargiss call you to flak the story?" Gary asked.

"Actually, no," Buffy answered. "One of the analysts leaked the story and the reporter called me for confirmation." Then he laughed. "Among other things, he wanted to make sure our sales manager was really named Redfoot."

They all laughed now. "I hope you didn't confirm it," Brad said. "Knowing that might drive the investors away."

"I told them you were a full-blooded Sioux whose grandfather befriended Theodore Roosevelt and that you lived in a teepee out behind the citric plant."

"Oh, mother," Redfoot roared.

"That's not politically correct," Gary said, suppressing his grin and trying to look sternly at Buffy.

"Look, compared to Howard and G.T. and most of the other execs around here, I'm the very soul of political correctness," Buffy grinned.

"Well, at least it's better than when I was working for Samuran and all my bosses kept calling me Ledfoot."

"What's all this horsing around?" Leigh Curtis asked, walking into the room with some papers for Gary to sign.

Gary told her about the article.

"Well, piddle," she said. "Anybody around here could have given them that story. The rumor as I get it is that our own Dr. Long will be the next president of TLP."

"Yeah," said Buffy. "And folks like you and Redfoot are going to ride that horse right to the top of the hill."

"We Sioux plenty good horsemen," Redfoot said.

"Horse manure," Leigh said. "You're no more Sioux than I am."

Gary looked around the room. He saw the beginnings of a team that could rebuild Tamson-Long Products from the ashes of the conflagration that was about to consume it.

The next day, Gary received a voice message from Numata. He returned the call, not knowing what to expect, and more than a little apprehensive. Numata cut the greetings short and quickly said, "I want for you to know we like to have another meeting. Could you do in January?"

"I don't know, I need to check with Howard. Hold on a minute."

"No problemo," Howard said, enthusiastically. "I don't have anything planned for the whole winter. I say they looked at our fuckin' plant, saw how big it was and have decided it's the season to talk turkey. Good for fucking them."

Gary switched back to Numata and suggested the seventh of January.

"Yes, yes," Numata said. "How you like to do in Paris?"

Howard whooped with joy when Gary told him they were going to Paris. "That sure beats the hell out of fucking Tokyo," he said.

Numata promised to fax the rest of the details, adding that he would be inviting representatives from New World and Daehan Hwa-Hak, the Korean producer, to join them as well. By the time Gary hung up, both Howard and G.T. were in his office. G.T.'s excitement was evident. "Everything is starting to come our way, huh?" he said. "We've got the plant under control again and now these assholes are ready to make a deal on price."

Gary figured the *Wall Street Journal* article hadn't hurt either, and said as much to Sid Cox when he called him with a heads-up about the scheduled meeting.

With the holiday season at hand, Gary got a brief respite from the tensions of being a double agent. There was a ton of work to do at the office, but it was real work, the kind Gary loved. The Colorado deal was nearing completion and he and G.T. had started negotiations on a joint venture with 3-C on a vitamin plant in West Virginia.

It seemed like almost every day during the season, a UPS or Federal Express truck pulled up to the house. There were cardboard boxes from his family and from Jenna's sister in California, filled with brightly wrapped presents. There were innumerable Harry and David fruit collections from TLP suppliers and clients. From TLP itself, Gary received a leather notebook, embossed with the company logo. Opened, it had a notepad on the right side, and on the left side a calculator and a digital clock with a gold map of the world. When you touched the map, the clock would show what time it was in the place you touched.

Gary planned what he was sure would be a merry Christmas for the family. He bought horses for each of them, and on Christmas morning, a large trailer with a huge red bow on the back pulled into their yard. The horses would have to go back to their stable for a while, but Gary also arranged to begin construction on a barn and paddock at their home. A mild winter was predicted, and the builder felt confident the work could be completed quickly. Christmas Day itself was warm, and Gary delighted in watching the boys, helped by a man and woman from the stables, ride around the yard with big smiles on their faces. He'd paid a big premium for the Christmas Day delivery, but it was worth it, and he figured the extra money probably helped make the stablehands' Christmas merry, too.

CHAPTER 61

Gary's flight to Paris with Howard was typical. Howard spent his time on crossword puzzles and complaining, and Gary spent his reading books. Euro Dolce, the Nippon Kagaka subsidiary, hosted the meeting at the Ritz-Carlton. They arrived in Paris about 8:00 in the morning and had no scheduled events until late that evening, so Gary took a nap. Around noon, Howard called and they met for lunch. This was Howard's first trip to Paris, so Gary showed him the sights, putting on his best tour guide attitude. It was fun to have a chance to utilize the experience Gary had gained in the years he'd lived in Europe. Later they headed back to the hotel to get ready for the meeting.

A few minutes later, Gary's phone rang. "We need to get together after the meeting tomorrow," the familiar voice of Sid Cox said. "Meet me at the American Embassy. We'll be in the next room during the meeting, so if you happen to spot someone you know in the hallway, don't act surprised."

Dinner that evening was at the hotel, in a large formal room off the main floor area. The walls were covered with impressive looking art, and the furnishings suggested the age of imperialism.

The usual faces were already present by the time Howard and Gary arrived: Sumiko Numata and Masahiko Yamasaki represented Nippon Kagaka, along with Jacques Coté; Song Dian-Nuan and Bai Ken-ren were on hand from New World. The new face was the Korean, Kim Jungwoo, President of Daehan Hwa-Hak. Kim had salt-and-pepper hair and carried an air of formality and intensity about him.

"So you Gary Long, heard lot of good things about you," Kim said. Gary returned the compliment. Daehan was a relatively new competitor in the U.S., but had been a force to be reckoned with in the Asian markets for several years. Kim had the reputation of being highly aggressive, but Gary was convinced Daehan was at a substantial disadvantage because of its cost of raw materials.

"You same Gary Long that invented seriobacterium division?" Kim asked.

"Yes," Gary replied, "I did that back in the eighties."

"Ah," Kim nodded. "We use your process."

"And I'm glad you do," Gary smiled.

The formal meetings were scheduled for 8:30 the next morning, and everyone arrived a few minutes early. At one end of the meeting room there was a large blackboard on the wall. The men spaced themselves around a large rectangular table, and Coté opened the session.

"Welcome, everybody," Cote said in English, "to this important meeting to organize an association for the artificial sweetener industry. We at Euro Dolce are delighted to have you all in Paris, and we trust you will enjoy your stay here. I know I speak for the representatives of our parent company, Nippon Kagaka, when I say that we think it is important for everybody to be a part of the association, so we are glad you are all here. I believe the best thing to do now is to turn it over to Mr. Howard Hargiss, of Tamson-Long Products."

Howard had no intention of taking over the meeting at this early point and there was an uncomfortable silence for several seconds. "Perhaps someone should review what was said at the last meeting," he said finally.

"I will do it," Numata offered. He stood up and walked to the blackboard where he wrote production capacity numbers alongside the company names. He's got the numbers exactly right, Howard thought; exactly what we put up on the flip chart in Mexico City. It told him something important; Numata completely understood what was going on. When he came to Daehan, Numata looked over at Kim and asked, "Is this number right?"

"I think so," Kim responded hesitantly after shifting his gaze between Numata and the blackboard a number of times.

He clearly hasn't been given a heads-up on what the meeting is all about, Howard thought.

When Numata wrote the usage and loss figures, all pretense of understanding by Kim fell away. "I not understand," he said.

It took almost 15 minutes for the group, variously trying four different languages, to explain what the loss represented and how it had been arrived at. Finally Numata said, "What do you think, Mr. Kim?"

Kim rocked back in his chair and then leaned forward and said, "Sorry my English so poor. I not sure I understand. I understand plant size, and usage, but what does blackboard have to do with association?"

The man may be confused, Gary thought, but he's not dumb. Poor English or no, Kim had put into words the same question Gary had been asking for months.

Numata addressed the group. "We've been thinking about that," he said. "We propose that problem is plant capacities are much larger than the current market, even though market is growing." Numata took a breath. "Therefore, we went to TLP's plant and we feel they talk a lot about their 113,000 metric tons and their big capacity. But what they don't talk about is fermenters could be used for something other than Sugere. They could be used for Sugere and they have the size, but they could be for many other products as well."

Numata paused and took a deep breath, "Our proposal is that TLP produce 45,000 tons." Then he stopped. Song Dian-Nuan was shaking his head in agreement. Howard got red in the face and slapped the leather notebook he had open in front of him closed and said, "Never. Never will TLP agree to 45,000 tons, when we built a plant three times that size. We won't even discuss it."

Song Dian-Nuan stood up and looked at Howard earnestly. "If you going to insist on full production, there is no way we can have association."

Howard snapped back, "What you mean is that TLP would be the only one at less than half capacity." All the men were sitting on the edge of their seats, the room electrified. Even Kim, who was still having difficulty following what was being said, was sitting on the edge of his seat. All eyes were riveted on Howard; no one took a breath. "I'll tell you what," Howard continued, "we can't possibly agree to 45,000 tons, but I will say we do build for the future and have some plants running at less than full capacity, but none anywhere near as low as half. We might be convinced to go below 113,000 tons if the price would go up first. That would provide the incentive to become flexible. The higher the price, the more flexibility."

No one said a word for what seemed like a minute and then as if on cue, the Asians all started talking to each other at once. It seemed to Gary that most of the conversation was in Japanese, but he couldn't be sure. Coté looked at Gary, smiled and shrugged his shoulders. The rumble of voices died down and Numata spoke. "Mr. Hargiss, we talking about what kind of price is necessary."

Howard thought for a second and then leaned forward in his chair. "Well, I will say this, it was my idea to get you guys talking on this customer trick bullshit, and that's why the price has started to inch up. To put an exact number on it, though... ."

Howard looked over at Gary. "Well, what price could it be, given the price of sugar now Gary?" Coté quickly spoke up. "Sugar has been steady at fifteen point five cents a kilo," he said.

Howard screwed up his face. "7¢ a pound," Gary said quickly. "The equivalent price for our purposes is a 1.40," he added. Sugere had 20 times the sweetening power of natural sugar, pound for pound.

"Well, my friends, we're obviously not going to go from eighty cents to a buck forty overnight. If we do, we'll all be locked in jail, but we can get somewhere in between. I guess what my proposal would be is that we go from where we are gradually over a few months to something close to a dollar. If it got close to a dollar, all I can say is we can talk to our management and see if they would be willing to budge off their hundred and thirteen ton capacity." Howard took a deep breath, leaned back in his chair and folded his arms.

"It would be premature to even discuss what an acceptable production would be, but I'd be willing to go back and discuss things," Howard finished. Gary could tell the stage was being set.

Numata and Song began to talk again in Japanese while the rest of the group looked around the room and got up to stretch their legs. Gary headed over to the pastry tray and Jacques followed him. "Now I know why Hargiss is here," the Frenchman said.

"What do you mean?" Gary responded.

"He's here to negotiate volumes and prices. He's the man who does that for all of Tamson-Long."

Gary tried to put a positive spin on the truth Coté had just spoken. "Not really, but he has lots of experience with markets and a strong business background with the company..." Gary never got to finish because Numata suddenly raised his voice to address the group.

"Mr. Hargiss, we understand you not approve 45,000 tons because of price, and we agree we should move price up toward a dollar. One thing is we must go slow or customers will wonder why a price war one day and peace with a dollar the next. Think of reaction to that. We must move up slow and try to get to one dollar by April."

Howard mused over the Japanese man's point. "In order to do that, you guys reporting on the customer tricks will be even more important now that prices are going up."

Heads nodded agreement from all sides, and Numata spoke up. "Whenever you have a problem for Mr. Kim, you should call me and we will talk to him for you," he said. Howard nodded and said, "Okay."
Lunch was served.

In the next room, a gaggle of FBI agents slapped each other on the back. One man raised both hands in the air, signaling a touchdown. The others just gaped, not quite believing what had just transpired next door. Never before had they been on the inside of a price-fixing conspiracy.

After lunch, Howard went back to his room. Gary hung back, pretending to look at some items in the gift shop. Once the elevator doors closed, he went outside and found a taxi.

A few minutes later, Howard reemerged from the elevator into the lobby, checked the gift shop to make sure Gary wasn't still there, hailed a cab of his own and pulled a crumpled piece of paper from his pocket. The driver read the address, suppressed a grin, and drove off. When they arrived at the location, Howard peered out through the window. It was a seedy neighborhood. I don't want to get stuck here, he thought. He reached into his pocket and pulled out a French phrasebook and a wad of francs. "*Attendez-moi ici,*" he said with his best Indiana accent, handing the man two 100-franc notes.

Gary arrived at the gate of the American Embassy and pushed a buzzer. He identified himself and was escorted to the fourth floor, where Cox was waiting for him with an American woman who identified herself as an FBI agent. "Hey, you did a good job, everything went fine." Cox said.

"Well, I have to get back," Gary replied. "Howard and I are going to have dinner." He was feeling pressure, wondering if Howard was already looking for him. Still, they persuaded him to undertake one more task before he left. They wanted him to call G.T.

"Hey Gary, how ya' doin'? How're the women over there?" G.T.'s voice boomed. Gary was already embarrassed and stealing glances at the female agent who was listening.

"What are you talking about G.T.? Hey, I thought you might like to hear about the meeting."

"Fuck the meeting, I want to know how the women are over there," G.T. said. The female agent began turning beet red as Gary was sure he was. "You can't be thinking about the meeting all the time. There's more to life than Sugere. I'm tired of hearing about Sugere, and Sugere prices going down. If you don't get yourself laid at least five times, then I don't want your ass back here, and you're fucking fired."

"G.T., I don't have time for this, I want to tell you about the meeting," Gary said.

"Oh don't give me that bullshit. This isn't the military. I'm not your sergeant."

Gary was determined to get him on track. "Well, they made a little progress. They proposed 45,000 tons."

"That sounds like a piece of shit to me. What does Howard think?"

"Um, Howard thinks they've got a long way to go. But he and Numata and the others did agree to try and get the price up."

"Really? Well, that's good. Let me talk to Howard."

Damn, Gary had to think fast. "Uh, he's not here right now." Gary could tell G.T. was puzzled by his voice.

"Where are you at?" he asked.

"I'm just in my hotel room." By now Gary was almost shaking, worried that G.T. might try to call right back, or have him go get Howard. "I think Howard's taking a little nap. Anyway, people are still a little unfriendly, but I think we made some progress."

"Well, they'll get there, all good things take time. But if you don't get laid then don't come home." Gary quickly ended the conversation and hurried back to the hotel.

When Howard got back to the hotel, he took his package to his room and dialed Gary's room. Where the hell is he? Howard wondered. Then he placed a call to G.T.

By the time Gary arrived, Howard was pacing around the lobby. "Where the hell have you been?" he demanded.

Gary's heart jumped up to his throat. "Ah, I was just taking a walk."

"Walking, I just saw you get your ass out of a taxi!"

"Well, I was walking and I got pretty far, so I thought I'd better take a taxi back."

"Where in the hell did you walk to, the Eiffel Tower?"

"Actually no, but it's only about thirty minutes from here."

Jeez, he was getting in deep, what if Howard had talked to G.T.?

"I called G.T. and he said you called him from your room." Oh, shit, Gary thought.

"Well, that was a while ago."

"Oh, I thought it was just a few minutes ago."

"Nah, I called him right after the meeting."

"Oh, okay. He also told me if you're not getting laid, you're not coming back anyway. You haven't been out getting laid, have you?"

Waves of relief began flooding over Gary. The subject was changed and Gary had escaped. "I think you ought to listen to G.T. and do what he says," Howard said.

"Yeah, well I'm still having a little trouble keeping up with Jenna."

"No shit! She is one hot-looking woman. How did you manage to snare that one, anyway?"

"I guess she fell for my boyish good looks."

"Not likely," Howard grinned. "Of course," he added, dropping his eyes to Gary's crotch, "you may have hidden talents."

The next morning they caught an early flight and were back in Steuben by late afternoon. Howard and Gary headed into the office, where they briefed G.T. in person. Toward the end of the discussion, G.T. got up and slapped Howard on the back. "Well, my boys, we're making progress," he said jovially. "We've got a ways to go, but we're making progress."

Howard hung behind after Gary left the room. "I bought you a belated Christmas present," he said, grinning. He opened his briefcase and handed G.T. a small bottle.

G.T. read the label. "Rohypnol?" he asked. "What the hell is that?"

"You don't know?" Howard grinned.

"Is this the stuff that grows hair?" G.T. guessed, reaching up to smooth back the waning gray wisps on his head.

"No, you fuckhead," Howard snorted. "You don't have to all the way to fucking Paris to get *that*! This stuff is seduction in a bottle. It's hard as hell to get over here. You put a few drops in some chick's drink and in a few minutes she's putty in your hands."

"Oh, yeah," G.T. said. "They call it the date-rape drug. I read about it."

"Well, now you got some," Howard said.

When he left, G.T. tossed the bottle into a desk drawer. No doubt Howard had kept some of the Rophynol for himself, and probably would use it. Howard was all libido, but G.T. was all bluster. In 27 years of marriage to Cathy, he had never once been unfaithful. He'd handled all the temptations, wormed himself out of all the difficult moments, and kept up a foul-mouthed patter that had convinced the likes of Howard Hargiss they were two of a kind.

CHAPTER 62

Dan Anthony's whine about fixing prices in his Specialty Products Division finally reached the breaking point with Howard and G.T. On Ground Hog Day, they lowered the boom and fired Anthony, giving him six months' pay as severance.

What they didn't know was that Anthony had been keeping meticulous files and had written records of all the price fixing conversations. The morning after he was fired, Anthony cornered Gary in his office. Gary flipped on the recorder in his coat pocket.

"With what I know, I could put these assholes in jail for life," Anthony said. "I'd think that would be worth more than six months' severance. At my age and with all the downsizing going on, how in hell am I going to get a another good job? I've still got kids in college."

"Well, I don't know, Anthony," Gary said. "Six months does seem a little low."

"A little?" Anthony retorted, and launched into a play-by-play of the meetings he set up, how TLP squeezed out McLaughlin Chemicals, and how he, G.T. and Howard worked for months to get the German chemical producer Petrawerk to agree to production schedules. "With what I've got, I can send them both up the river," he said bitterly.

"Well, maybe I'll talk to them and see what I can do," Gary replied.

As soon as Anthony left, Gary flipped off the tape machine and called Cox. "Great thinking," Cox said. "Make sure when you talk to Howard and G.T. you specifically say price fixing, be explicit about it, in detail and what product it was."

The next morning Gary walked into Howard's office with the recorder running. Howard had one arm so far into his fish tank stirring up the pebbles that his rolled up shirt sleeve was wet. Gary could tell when he looked up he had been deep in concentration.

"Howard, Dan Anthony is really pissed off about his severance," Gary said.

"Whadda ya mean? How long has the guy been here?"

"Well, twelve, maybe thirteen years."

"Well, shit, six months is a good severance. Fuck him, get out of here." Howard's arm was still making circles in the water.

223

"Well, he said he did a lot of things with vitamin additive products with you and G.T., you know, fixed a lot of prices. He said when he started they were at fifty cents a pound and now they are over a buck, thanks to everything he helped with on Petrawerk and the other European companies. I guess he feels like with what he knows, six months is not enough."

Howard stopped playing in the fish tank and dried his arm. "Well, talk to G.T. about it," he said. "I'm so pissed off at Anthony I'm not rational. But I'll go along with whatever G.T. wants."

Gary trundled off to G.T.'s office and began the conversation the same way, being sure to use the words "price fixing." "I talked to Howard about this just now, and he said he'd go along with whatever you wanted," he said. "I know you always said Anthony kept good notes, so I thought you might be worried about what he might do if he's really unhappy, which I can assure you he is."

"Well," G.T. said, "I got all the notes...cleared his files out the night before we let him go. Of course, he could have copies of them at home, too."

Gary nodded his agreement. "Even if he doesn't have copies, he sure knows a lot of stuff with or without paper, at least it sounded like he did."

"Hoooly shit. That son of a bitch. If there's anybody who'd go to the fuckin government, he would. I mean that fucker's unreal. Ya know, I never did like Anthony. Shit, I don't know."

He paced back and forth for a moment, then picked up the phone and dialed Howard. "It pisses me off as much as it does you," Gary heard him say, "but discretion is probably the better part of valor here. The son of a bitch can hand me my ass with what he knows, especially if he's got papers. I say we give him two years' severance." There was a short pause. "Yes, Howard, he can hand you your ass, too. Or he can hand you mine and me yours, and I sure as hell would hate to get that as a Christmas present. God only knows what kind of creepy crawlies it's got."

He turned to Gary. "What about his car, what was he driving?"

Gary thought for a second. "I think he just got a new Oldsmobile."

G.T. spoke into the phone again. "Well, then, give him the damn car. Give him two years and tell him to keep his car. That should be enough to keep him happy. Let's have Gary present that – no erase that. I'll present it to him, then let's have Gary call him afterward and see how he felt about it. That way we'll get a read if he's gone for good and we don't have to worry about him."

G.T. called Anthony as soon as Gary left. An hour later Gary called him from his office with the recorder mike held up to the phone receiver. "Hey, Dan, what's going on?"

"Shit, that worked...you going to G.T."

"What are you talking about?"

"He called me. I can't believe it. Keep your severance, have another year and a half, keep your car. You know, everything but the kitchen sink."

"Well, are you happy about it now?"

"Oh yeah, I'm definitely happy about it."

"Did you make copies of those notes?"

"Yeah, I have copies of the notes."

"Well you should get rid of them now."

"No, I'm keeping them for safety reasons."

"Well, good luck Dan, I'm glad it all worked out."

Two nights later Anthony received a visit from the FBI who replayed copies of the various tapes for him, but in a manner that made it sound like his phone had been tapped.

The next evening, the phone rang at Gary's house. Jenna answered and said, "Dan Anthony wants to talk to you." Gary picked up the receiver and the familiar voice said back, "Gary, I'd be careful with...remember all those times I told you to be careful about Howard?" Gary could hear trucks and cars behind him and was sure he was calling from a pay phone.

"Yeah, I remember. You've said that for a long time."

"Well, I'd be even more careful now. You never know if the government might get involved."

"What are you talking about?"

"Ah, I don't think there's anything in particular, but I'd just be really careful, and not get involved with those guys."

Gary smiled at the gesture Anthony was making; he was really trying to help him. But he had to keep up the act. "Well, you gotta do what you gotta do around here. You're either in or you're not."

"Yeah, well, just watch your butt, Gary," Anthony said.

CHAPTER 63

"It is time," Jenna said to Gary a few nights later, "to consummate our marriage."

They were on the couch in the family room, a fire blazing in the fireplace.

He leaned his head to the side, raised his eyebrows and peered intently into her deep, lamp-lit brown eyes, then allowing his gaze to widen and drop, following the line of her soft brown hair, which brushed against her burnt sienna sweater above her breasts. "My memory may not be the greatest," he grinned, "but I'm sure I recall an evening on the beach in St. John..."

"Not *that*," she teased, her expression playful. "Is that all you ever think about?"

"No," he replied, still smiling. "It's just the best thing I ever think about."

"Me too," she said, leaning over and drumming her fingers on his thigh. "But what I meant was that it's time to prepare our first joint tax return."

"Oh, whoopee," he said sarcastically, rolling his eyes and shaking his head.

"I know, but I've got your W-2, and my pitiful little one from Potter Realty, and a bunch of stuff from John Caldwell. You want me to send it off to the Potter family accountant?"

"Yeah, sure," he said. "Why not? Now can we talk about sex?"

"Talk, talk, talk," she pouted. "How about some action?"

He jumped up and grabbed her, one arm under her knees and the other around her shoulder, lifting her, squealing, from the couch and depositing her on the soft rug in front of the fire.

A few days later, Gary was sitting in his office when Buffy stuck his head in the door. He was carrying a stack of booklets under his arm. "Annual reports," he announced grandly, waving one of the booklets at Gary and dropping it on his desk. "Read all about the fabulous success of Tamson-Long Products in the Year of Our Lord 1992."

"Yeah, right," Gary smirked. "My division lost millions."

"Not to worry," Buffy responded, quickly and confidently, raising his hand in front of him like a traffic cop or a witness on the stand. "Remember, TLP does not, repeat not, disclose profits by division." Then he lowered his voice and leaned over to Gary. "The world will never know what a loser you really are, Long. You can count on the bookkeeping genius of our chairman and the brilliance of our fabulous public relations department to keep your secrets bottled up tighter than an Irishman on Saint Paddy's Day."

"Yeah, right," Gary said again, grinning a little in spite of himself. He picked up the annual report and tossed it in his briefcase.

CHAPTER 64

Sid Cox had been busy preparing a sort of annual report himself. He had orders from Jim Thompson to assemble the TLP case file for presentation to the prosecutors at the Justice Department. It was a key turning point, Cox knew, the first time anyone outside the small working group Thompson had carefully put together would be told anything about the case. Cox needed to have all his ducks in a row. The prosecutor would be a man named Kevin Rasmussen, and Thompson was pleased with the choice. But selling Rasmussen on their plan was critical.

"It's got to be so convincing on its face," Thompson told Cox, "that he'll accept what we're doing from the moment he reads it. If he's the least bit goosey about anything, he'll want to talk it over with someone else at Justice, and the minute he does that, all our efforts to keep this thing a secret will be blown sky high."

Cox sneezed and coughed his way through flu-inducing February, painstakingly assembling the evidence, cataloguing the tape transcripts, summarizing his findings on overhead projection charts. In a way, Rasmussen was the first jury he would face, and he needed to make a clear case for conviction. The three men met in Thompson's office in Indianapolis, and Rasmussen was clearly impressed.

"I'm sure you can understand," Thompson told him, "the need for total security here."

"No kidding," Rasmussen replied. "And speed, too. Because every extra day this thing takes, the greater the chance something will slip. And we've got a shit-load of work yet to do." Then in precise, bullet-like fashion, he rattled off the things he wanted before he would be ready to go to a grand jury. Number one on his list was to meet with Gary Long.

That same day, Gary flew to Colorado to complete the purchase of the flour additive plant. When he called for his messages, he heard an all too familiar beep of his answering machine. It took a second for its meaning to register but when it did he felt a cold sweat on his brow. He hadn't heard from Sid Cox for weeks, and it had been like heaven; now hell was calling.

He stood at the pay phone in the lobby of the Brown Palace Hotel and returned the call. "We're ratcheting this thing up a notch," Cox said. "I need to set up a meeting between you and a man named Kevin Rasmussen. He's the First Assistant U.S. Attorney for the Western District of Indiana. His involvement means that the Department of Justice has our project on its radar scope for prosecution. Jim Thompson has reviewed some of your tapes with him and he's impressed with what we've done – what you've done, really – and he'd like to discuss it with you." They agreed to meet at the Steuben Holiday Inn in two days at 6:30 pm. "I'll leave you the room number a couple of hours before the meeting," Cox finished.

Before leaving the pay phone, Gary called Jenna and told her about the meeting.

Two days later, he landed in Steuben after a miserable flight through the February snow in the Falcon 50. It was already almost 6:00, so he checked his voice mail from the car phone, got the room number and headed off to the Holiday Inn.

Gary knocked on the door, and Cox ushered him inside. Jim Thompson was sitting on the end of a bed and introduced him to a small, well-dressed, dark-haired man who was seated at a table.

"Mr. Rasumssen has an idea he'd like to present to you," Thompson said. Rasmussen invited Gary to the other chair at the table. Thompson returned to his seat on the bed. Sid Cox remained standing near the door.

"Dr. Long," Rasmussen began, "I want you to know how much I appreciate what you are doing to help Thompson and Cox. I couldn't be more impressed by the evidence you've brought in. Without question, we are going to pursue this case. We will bring indictments and we will get convictions." Gary nodded. "Everything you've told us has been borne out," Rasmussen continued. "I am convinced you have told the truth and nothing but the truth." He looked intently at Gary.

"Now, Gary, I need to ask if you've told us the whole truth. Is there anything else illegal going on that you've not told us about?"

What does he mean? Gary asked himself. He'd given them all the price-fixing information he knew about. Doubtless there were things he didn't know about, but he hadn't held anything back. He'd told them about the hookers and the bugged rooms and a bunch of other things that hadn't even interested them. All of a sudden, he thought of something. He could feel his ears getting hot, and wondered if they were visibly reddening. The bonuses!

He didn't want to delay answering any longer, but he desperately needed time to think. "Well," he said slowly, "I'm sure I don't know the whole truth about everything that may have happened over the years. Tell me what you

Whatever Rasmussen said in response, Gary didn't hear it. His mind was racing. He didn't know for sure that there was anything illegal about the bonuses. But the reason he didn't know was that he had studiously avoided trying to find out. Whether it was technically illegal or not, it was certainly a deception. In the beginning, he had assumed that since it was company policy to pay bonuses like that, it must be legal. Everybody at TLP did it. Now he knew the question of legality played no part at all in determining company policy. And "everybody" at TLP included a whole lot of people who were headed for jail.

Maybe Rasmussen already knew about the bonuses. Maybe they had ways to find out about the bank accounts in Geneva and Hong Kong. Or maybe Gary was overreacting. Maybe the question was just routine. And then there was the question of the money. With as much uncertainty as there was in his future right now, the last thing he wanted to do was jeopardize the nest egg he and his family might need. Keep quiet, he thought, keep cool.

And keep your eye on the main thing you want right now: for all this to be over. He'd done his part. If the Justice Department wanted to make a larger case, they could do it without him.

"I can't think of anything I've left out," he told Rasmussen.

"Well, that's great. Because we would like you to work with us on this case. You're a high level person, obviously going farther up in the company, so you get into a lot of things that no one else can."

Damn. One thing was for sure; they didn't want his involvement to end.

"We feel very lucky to have someone at your level. What I'd like you to do is go home and talk to your wife about working with us on an eighteen-month to two-year project. We want to follow the Sugere price fixing." He was talking faster now, and it was obvious he had a strong grasp of what was going on, and had spent time listening to the tapes Gary had made.

What kept ringing in Gary's ears were the words "eighteen months to two-years." It sounded like a prison sentence.

"Gary, would you consider something like this?" Rasmussen said finally.

Gary sat back in his chair and thought about it for a few moments before he answered. "It's a lot to ask of me," he said. "It's very difficult to work with a company and receive pay raises and be promoted while at the same time I'm taping the very men who are rewarding me. I'm not sure I can do it. I don't see how I can commit to two years. I might be willing to continue, but I'd have to be free to leave at any time."

"Gary, I think you have three choices," Rasmussen said. "You can blow us off and stay at TLP, in which case you'll be committing crimes, and we can't possibly protect you. You can wash your hands of both us and TLP and take off for parts unknown, in which case you'll be turning your back on the cause of justice, and all deals between us are off. Or you can do the right thing and work with us, do something important for your country and be the hero at the end of the day."

Gary promised them he'd think about it.

As Gary prepared to leave, Rasmussen sought to reassure him on another point. "If you stay with us on this, there's a good chance the company won't ever know what's going on. We'll do our best to make sure you are well protected," he said.

Then he reached into his briefcase and took out some papers. "Here's the immunity agreement we want you to sign," he said. "I strongly suggest you have an attorney look it over and then get with Cox so we can finalize everything."

Gary looked down at the papers and then up at Rasmussen. Over his shoulder, he could see Sid Cox, still standing by the door, and there was a look of panic on his face.

They shook hands, still seated, and Gary was overcome by a thought from left field – bullshit, you guys would hang me out to dry in a heartbeat if it played to your advantage.

"Sid has a few other administrative things to cover with you, but I look forward to having you work with us," Rasmussen said. He stood up, grabbed his coat and briefcase, and walked out the door.

The weather was starting to get nasty, and Thompson asked Cox if he needed anything else from him. Cox said, "Nah, get on home before the roads get any worse."

When he had gone, Cox looked at Gary apprehensively. "Gary," he said, "Kevin Rasmussen is an administrator. He's a good guy, but he's never been out in the field. He doesn't know the kinds of challenges we face. I can tell you now that if you show that agreement to an attorney" – he paused and picked up the immunity agreement Kevin had left on the bed – "within a day TLP is going to know. No matter what attorney you show it to, east coast or west coast, that attorney is going to know someone at TLP, or know somebody who does. TLP has long tentacles, and they're going to find out about it. Gary, I'm telling you … you cannot show that to anyone, or it'll destroy the case."

"Kevin was pretty sure I should show it someone."

Cox rolled his eyes. "He's an administrator, Gary. If you show this to anyone, then it's not covert anymore, it's overt, and you'll be right in the middle of it all. It just doesn't make any sense."

Cox was worried. This case was his ticket. Gary was acting like a nervous Nellie, and it was driving Cox nuts. He wanted to strangle Rasmussen. Goddamn it, anyway. These fucking lawyers could screw up a wet dream if you gave 'em half a chance. Here he had a senior executive ready to go, and then Rasmussen tells him to go see another fuckin' lawyer. He had to convince Gary to drop the idea. "Gary, take it home, read it yourself, you're a bright guy," he said soothingly. "If you see something in there you don't like, call me and we'll work through it."

As Gary drove home, all he could think about was the pressure. It would be like having a second job, at no pay. Eighteen months to two years, a couple of days a week if you added it all up. He was already working 60 hours a week.

Then there was the risk. Whatever else was true, the TLP leaders were smart guys. How could Gary possibly hope to deceive them for even a few months, let alone two years?

When Gary got home, Jenna and he talked about the pluses and minuses for a long time. Jenna loved their house and being able to live in her hometown, but was not at all happy with all the social obligations of a TLP executive wife. Gary liked his job, but hated the corruption. He liked cooperating with the law, but hated the process of deception and taping.

If Gary stayed at TLP and didn't cooperate with the FBI, he was setting himself up to be indicted along with crooks like Hargiss and G.T. If he left, and the indictments came through, he might be named anyway, and would have no place in the TLP that would emerge. If he left and the case collapsed, as Rasmussen had suggested it might, then Gary was – morally if not legally – an accessory to any ongoing crimes TLP might perpetrate.

It finally boiled down to a simple fact. The opportunity to do what Gary loved at TLP was huge. There was a good chance he would be able to stay through the indictments, and if the company were cleaned up, Gary would be able to take credit and continue his rise to the top of an amazing industrial machine. With guys like Buffy and Brad Redfoot, he could make it happen. Maybe he'd even bring Dan Anthony back, if Anthony didn't go to jail himself. In the end, they decided to try it, month by month.

Their decision made, Gary called Cox and agreed to meet him behind the Holiday Inn that night.

"Sid," Gary said, "I might not be able to take it, so I have to have the ability to quit any time I want to."

ability to quit any time I want to."

"That's fine, but if you stay at TLP and don't work with us, you'll be committing crimes, and they'd have to prosecute you."

"I know, but the point is that if I do this, it'll have to be on my schedule, and there will be some weeks when I won't be able to meet at all."

Cox responded, "I'm going to call what's-his-name, your attorney there at TLP...."

"Zack Brilley?" What in hell was he going to call Brilley about?

"Yeah, Brilley. I'm going to call him tomorrow and tell him I'm pulling the recorder on your OPX line, you know, give TLP the appearance that this thing is all behind them."

Gary had almost forgotten the reason Cox got involved in the case in the first place, so much had happened. It seemed years ago that the FBI man first came to his house to install the phone tap, even though it was only a few months.

Cox paused and shuffled through his briefcase, finally locating his copy of the immunity agreement. "Let's go over this thing together, and then you can sign it."

They went over each line of the agreement and spent a good five minutes on the fact that it would make Gary immune from any kind of prosecution for anything illegal he did as long as he admitted it at the time.

Gary hesitated. It was now or never. I should tell them about the overseas money, but if I do they'll never let me keep it, he thought. I'll be out in the cold with nothing to fall back on. In the end he decided to stay the course. "Which copy do you want me to sign?" he asked.

Cox sighed with relief. The worst part was over. "Sign 'em both," he said.

After Gary signed the agreement, Cox switched gears. "Look around your office for something we could put a recorder in – a folder, maybe a notebook, something you write in a lot. Look around and see what you can find. We'd like to get together tomorrow night and start training you on some equipment."

"I think I've got just the thing," Gary told him, remembering his Christmas present from the company.

Then Gary drove home and told Jenna.

"Get those bastards," she said. Gary was surprised by her uncharacteristic comment, and it gave him strength.

The next morning Gary got a call from Andrew Tully. "That FBI guy just called Zack and said they're going to pull the recorder," he said. "They'll be

Gary mumbled his thanks, but as he hung up he felt the bile rising in his throat. If you only knew, you bag of shit, he thought. If you only knew.

CHAPTER 65

"Tom's our tech guy from Indy, kinda our equivalent of 'Q,'" Cox said, as Gary entered Room 216 of the Holiday Inn.

Tom was in his 30s, skinny, with thinning brown hair. He smiled at the comparison and waved his hand toward the bed, where an assortment of equipment was laid out. "We've got a lot of stuff to show you tonight," he said.

Gary had brought the fancy TLP notebook with the map and clock. "It was my Christmas present from the company," he said, leaving it to Cox to assess the moral implications of using someone's Christmas present to destroy the giver.

Tom was fascinated by the notebook. "Hey, this is pretty neat," he said, like a kid who had been handed a new toy. "I think we can convert this pretty easily. I'll take it back to the shop and get it all fitted out."

Then Tom showed Gary a brown leather briefcase with a false compartment, inside which was a reel-to-reel tape recorder.

"Here's how it works," Tom explained. "You turn it on by touching both hasp locks at the same time like this." He closed the briefcase, and touched both hasps at the same time. When he opened it up, the reels of the tape recorder were moving.

"If you want to shut if off, you touch both of these at the same time," he continued, pointing to the hinges at each corner. "Go ahead and try it."

Gary touched both of the hinges simultaneously, and sure enough, the big reels stopped cold. Then Tom motioned to a harness lying on the bed.

"Here's the real beast," he said, smiling. "Take off your shirt."

Gary loosened his tie and began unbuttoning his shirt; Tom explained how to put on the equipment's "girdle belt," as he called it, and how it worked. "This beauty holds six hours of digitized conversation and is sensitive enough that if you fart we'll know what you had for lunch." Gary put his shirt on the bed, and placed the belt around the top of his stomach. "You put these two wires around your shoulders, then tape these two mikes to your chest with this tape, but don't forget to shave your chest or all we'll hear is you yelling when you try to take them off. I guess we'll need to fix your pants, too, so bring complete suits next time. We have to put a hole in the pocket so we can run a wire into them where we put the switch." Then he showed Gary a little switch with a white tip. "Just make sure you keep a coat on while you're wearing the belt: otherwise it's a dead giveaway," Tom finished.

"Why do I need all these different systems?" Gary asked. He had the Radio Shack recorder he had been using, the briefcase and the backpack system. There was obviously also going to be another system built into the TLP notebook. "I could go into the electronics business with all this stuff."

"Don't you dare," Cox said. "This is U.S. government property! The little recorder is mainly for phone conversations now," he continued. "The briefcase is for you to take to meetings with the other companies. The backpack we'll want you to use for some of the meetings, mainly the ones where we're videotaping. That way, if we have any problems with the audio portion of our tape, we'll have a super high-quality backup.

"When you get the notebook back, keep it on your desk at the office. If it stays there, you'll always be ready to record anything that goes on, and won't have to keep your coat on or pull out the briefcase, or anything else that would draw attention and take time."

They've invested a lot in this, Gary thought. But it still seemed like overkill.

"Well Gary, that ought to get you up and running," Cox said. "Since the recorder on your phone's coming off, those guys should really begin to open up. Start talking about another price fixing meeting when you get the opportunity."

A week later, Gary was walking by Howard's office on the way to get a cup of coffee when Howard motioned for him to come in. Gary hit the On button for the pocket recorder and walked into his office. "We need to see the Japs again, Gary," Howard said.

Gary nodded in agreement.

"Get 'em on the phone and let's figure out a place to meet," Howard instructed him.

That night Gary handed off the tape to Cox and said he would be calling everyone in the next day or so to set up a meeting. "Good, that's great," Cox responded enthusiastically. "Go ahead, but tape while you're putting it together."

The next day, Gary called Numata, who quickly agreed, and proposed meeting in Japan the following week. That didn't work for Gary, and his next three suggestions didn't work for Numata. Eventually, they settled on March 31, a month away. Gary knew the location wouldn't go over well with Howard, but decided having Howard uncomfortable wasn't such a bad thing.

When he played the tape that night at the Holiday Inn, Gary was stunned by Cox's reaction. "They wanted to meet right away, and you stalled them for a month!" Cox was practically screaming.

"Hey, I have a job to do here," Gary replied sharply. "My regular business comes first."

"Whaddya mean that comes first? I'll tell you what comes first!"

"We'll have the meeting when I have time for it on my schedule. If I did anything else, it'd be suspicious anyway."

Cox calmed down just a little, but Gary could tell he was still seething. They listened to the rest of the tape. Then Cox started in again. "I just don't understand how you couldn't get this meeting in right away," he argued.

Gary just shrugged, and started to pick up his coat. Cox's cavalier attitude was really making him angry.

There were important inter-office consequences at stake for Cox. Jim Thompson was antsy. He had gone out on a limb to keep the Extortion Division out of the case; as long as it stayed in Antitrust, Thompson felt he could count on keeping word from leaking back to William Hargiss, but if Extortion got involved again, all bets were off. From the way the original referral had come in, Thompson knew Hargiss had a direct pipeline to the NSA, and the NSA obviously had a contact in Extortion, because that's where they had sent the case.

It was a dicey matter, and Thompson had to do some fancy footwork. He lied outright, downplaying the importance of the case, keeping silent about what was going on, even hinting that they were going to close the whole investigation down altogether. It was a big gamble, and the result was that Sid Cox was on the spot like he'd never been before.

Now that Kevin Rasmussen was involved, the pressure was even greater. "You'd better keep this thing moving," Rasmussen had told Cox.

To Cox, that meant only one thing. He had to keep Gary Long moving. It was time to take control of this witness.

He got right in Gary's face. "How the hell can you just arbitrarily delay something like this that we've waited for a long time?" he roared. Then he put his arm on Gary's chest and pushed him against a wall by the doorway.

"Huh, dammit, tell me! You're holding up the entire United States Department of Justice!"

Gary was stunned but recovered enough to push Cox away and shout, "I told you I'm doing this on my own time, and I'll make my own schedule. This case is just a sideline to me; I've got to do my job first. I'm a corporate VP because of all the acquisitions I'm doing for the company, and all the joint ventures I'm putting together, and that's all legal, legitimate business. If you don't like it then you can shove it. If you don't like the way I'm performing, then you can just go get someone else. And let me tell you something else, Cox. I don't know if I'm going to continue to be your little errand boy or not, but I know one thing, and that is that right now I'm leaving."

Gary started to open the door. Cox saw red as the anger rose inside him. As Gary started opening the door, Cox swung his briefcase and hit Gary in the arm. "You don't get in touch with me, you respond when I call," he barked. Gary's arm was hurting like hell, and part of him wanted to slug it out with Cox right there, but even more he just wanted to get out of that cheesy motel. Restraining himself, he slammed the door behind him and drove home.

After Gary left, Cox sat on the bed and rubbed his face in his hands. Maybe he'd been too hard on the guy, but dammit, this wasn't kindergarten. This was the show. He knew he shouldn't have hit Gary, but he had to establish who was in control. That was one of the first things they taught you about covert operations at Quantico. Make sure the civilians working for you know you're the boss.

CHAPTER 66

On the way home, Gary called Jenna on the car phone, but she wasn't there. He was desperate. Maybe she's over at her folks' house, he thought, and drove through Wonanonly to the Potters'. Sure enough, Jenna was there with the boys, playing in the snow in the front yard. Gary hopped out of the car and gingerly took his coat off. "Look what Cox just did. Can you believe it?" he said in a whispered voice, showing her the welt on his arm, which by now was already turning into a bruise.

A shocked look crossed her face. "What are you talking about?"

He explained what had happened. "I don't know what to do," he said, putting his coat back on and slumping against the car.

Jenna thought a minute, and then suggested calling Thompson. "If I had an employee who'd behaved like that, I'd want to know," she said. "Wouldn't you?"

"Yeah," he said, "I sure would." A snowball missed him by inches and splatted against the car window. He looked up to see Justin grinning at him, ran toward him and grabbed the laughing, squealing boy around the waist, carrying him under his good arm back to the car. "I'll take the Abominable Snowman here," he called to Jenna. "You get Mark."

When they got home, Gary dialed the number for Jim Thompson and yelled to Jenna to listen on the extension. An answering service picked up and he told whoever was on duty that he needed to talk to Thompson. "Can I tell him what it's about?" the officious voice asked.

"Just tell him Gary Long called and give him my number, and tell him it's important. I think he'll want to know I called."

Within five minutes the phone rang. "Gary, what's up?" Thompson asked.

"Jim, I've got a real problem with your agent," Gary began.

He started to tell about how Cox had hit him with the briefcase, but Thompson interrupted. "I don't want to hear about it, Gary. That's something you and he are going to have to work through. I suggest you call him and talk to him about it, 'cause I'm not going to get involved in any kind of a dispute you might be having with one of my field agents."

Gary tried to get him to listen to what had happened, but Thompson wasn't about to hear any of it.

"Why wouldn't he listen?" Jenna asked.

"I don't know hon, maybe he just didn't want to get involved in what he considers an employee squabble. To be honest, I've done the same thing myself a few times."

"Gary, what are you going to do? This isn't right."

Gary considered it for a few seconds before answering. "Jeez, I don't know, I just don't know." The frustration and pressure he had been feeling overtook him, and for the first time he could remember, tears began welling up in his eyes.

Jenna was shocked when she saw Gary's face. She hadn't considered what effect all the pressure might be having on him. The reality of the seriousness of what they were involved in hit her hard for the first time. Where will all this end? she thought. She crossed the four feet separating them and held Gary tightly, feeling tears burning in her own eyes. Stroking the back of his head, she pulled him into the crook of her neck and said, "Gary, it'll all work out. I know it. We just have to be strong. We're doing this because you know what TLP wanted you to do was wrong. We couldn't live like that. We'd always be looking over our shoulder."

Gary pulled back and gazed into her now swollen eyes. "I'm sorry I've dragged you into all of this. I…I didn't mean for you to be in the middle."

"Oh, Gary, I love you. The rest doesn't matter, as long as we're together."

They had to go through with it. Regardless of how he felt about Cox, he had to finish what he started, in spite of the pain involved. It was his only way out, other than leaving, and even leaving no longer guaranteed him a safe exit. Gary held Jenna close and let her warmth thaw the icy anguish in his mind so he could sleep.

Thompson called Cox first thing in the morning, asking what in the hell had happened the night before. Cox told him most of the story, leaving out the briefcase incident.

"You gotta judge these things, Cox," Thompson said. "You gotta find the right point between being a wuss and scaring the guy off. The other thing is, the way he's acting, I'm beginning to get nervous about how much he's really on the team. What do you think? Can we really count on this guy? He can give us all the information in the world, but if he cracks up on the witness stand, TLP's lawyers will eat him alive."

"I don't know," Cox said. This was his opening to shift the discussion from the question of his own conduct to that of his informant. "I'd be lying to you if I said I'm totally comfortable with him," he continued, searching for a reason to justify his doubt. Gary was skittish, sure, but that was to be expected from someone under the pressure of a double agent experience. Double agents were almost always triple, quadruple, quintuple agents in some way or other. It was virtually impossible not to be and keep your cover. That's why the CIA used them a lot more than the FBI. The CIA didn't need to put their guys on the witness stand.

But what if, beyond his to-be-expected nervousness, Gary was really holding something back, something important? Everything he had told them had been borne out on the tapes. But what *hadn't* he told them? He'd nailed the others. But what about himself? He knew when the tape was on. What was happening when the tape was off?

"Maybe we should schedule a session with the lie detector," Cox suggested.

"That's probably a good idea. Who knows what he hasn't told us?"

"Exactly," Cox said.

"Well, apologize to him for being so hard yesterday, then find some way to get him scheduled for a polygraph this month. Let's put this worry to bed."

Gary was still angry at Cox, but thought he should at least call him about the details of the upcoming meeting in Japan. Cox immediately started apologizing, but Gary cut him short, told him to forget about it, and agreed to meet him the next morning in a parking lot.

Sitting in Cox's car, Gary took the tapes out of his briefcase and handed them to Cox as he told him the details of the Tokyo meeting. "Shoot, I'm gonna have to call the embassy to see if I can get everything set up for this," Cox said. Then he handed Gary fresh tapes to replace the ones he had given him, apologized again, and cleared his throat.

"Gary, we need to cover one other item under the agreement that we haven't taken care of yet."

"Oh?"

"Well, it's standard when we do an immunity agreement to do a polygraph test for our files."

Gary felt his face begin to flush. "What do you need that for?"

"Well, our policy is to check out our witnesses pretty carefully before we agree to immunize them against prosecution. In this case, with everything you've done for us, your background, we didn't feel like we needed to really do much in the way of checking up on you. It's just for the files, you know, making sure we've covered our bases."

Gary's mind raced furiously. If he refused to take it, they'd know something was up for sure. If he took it, he might be able to bluff his way through it. "Yeah, okay, let me know," he said.

He drove to TLP and plopped the briefcase on his desk. He took off his coat and hung it on a hook on the back of his office door. Then he sat down at his desk and stared straight ahead at the boy fishing. How he longed for a life that simple.

Leigh brought him a cup of coffee. "You okay?" she asked.

He snapped himself out of his reverie. "Yeah, I'm fine," he said, forcing a smile. Now there's a lie, right there, he thought. I'd have flunked my lie detector test already.

"Do you have those personnel sheets for me?"

"Hmm? Oh, yeah, they're right here in my briefcase." He started to open it, and then remembered there were blank tapes on top of the papers. Jesus, I can't even do something as simple as open my briefcase without thinking about it first, he thought. What a mess my life is.

"I'll...bring them out in a minute," he said.

Leigh gave an odd little shrug and went back to her desk.

When she left, Gary opened the briefcase, took out the tapes and threw them angrily into his bottom drawer. Still angry, he grabbed the personnel document and stalked out to drop it unceremoniously on Leigh's desk. Returning to his own, he looked into the still-open briefcase. There were two large white envelopes with green diamonds printed on them: they contained his Federal and state tax returns, which Jenna had signed the night before. He was supposed to sign them, enclose checks for the amounts they still owed and take them to the post office. He took them out and set them on his desk. The only thing still in the briefcase was the TLP annual report, which had been there for almost a month, unread.

Gary thumbed through the thick, glossy pages of the report, full of beautiful color photographs and snazzy graphics. Buffy was right. Nowhere in the document was there any hint that the Bio-tech division was losing money hand over fist. In fact, there was no direct mention of Bio-tech, or any other division, at all.

His eyes fell on the page where the required list showing the salaries of the ten most highly compensated executives in the corporation was printed. William, G.T. and Howard headed the list, followed by Ed Tamson, grandson of the founder and corporate treasurer. Next came Zack Brilley, followed by a

242

hotshot salesman named Ervin Danielson. The names of Tim Johnson, Roger Kincaid, the fired Dan Anthony and George Keddy rounded out the list.

Where's my name? Gary thought. He looked at the compensation numbers. Counting his bonus, he should have been way up on the list, right after Howard, in fact. And the heading clearly indicated that bonuses were included. But of course, he realized, his bonuses hadn't been paid to him. On the books, they were invoices for services from companies in Geneva and Hong Kong.

Scummy, scummy, scummy, he thought. It's wrong, it's wrong, it's wrong. But was it illegal? He still didn't know. Nothing in his contract with TLP prevented him from owning a business anywhere in the world. And if that business earned money from TLP, well, so what? But should he have paid taxes to the IRS on the money? That he still didn't know, not for sure.

He could find out, of course. A call to Jenna's accountant, a visit to the Steuben library – hell, he could probably call an 800 number and have the answer in half an hour. If he owed the taxes, he could simply send the information back to the accountant, have him refigure the taxes and pay the hundreds of thousands of dollars that would be due.

But then he remembered his upcoming lie detector test. If he knew for sure what the law was when he took the test, and if they asked him about it, he might never pass. It would probably be easier if he didn't know for sure. And anyway, until he mailed the tax returns on his desk, he certainly wasn't guilty of tax evasion.

That night Gary did in fact go to the Steuben library, but he didn't seek out information on tax law. Instead, he read up on polygraph tests. The next day Cox called and set a date for the test. Gary began practicing some of the techniques he'd learned from the book: thinking about the truth while telling a lie; thinking about a lie while telling the truth; focusing on things that made him happy or sad.

Cox called on the appointed day and gave him a room number at the Holiday Inn. By that night, Gary felt confident he could pass.

Cox stood silently in the room, sniffling, while the polygraph operator wired Gary to the machine, and explained things Gary already knew. Once the machine was set, the operator began asking the baseline questions and quickly moved into the core questions – "Have you ever stolen anything? What's your background? What do you do?" Then in succession, he asked two questions Gary had been dreading: "Have you ever cheated on your taxes?" and "Is there anything going on you haven't told us about?"

Gary thought about his name, repeating it over and over in his mind while he gave his "no" answers. Then it was over. In less than 15 minutes they had completed the test. Cox told him to wait outside for a few minutes. "Well, what do ya think?" Cox asked the technician.

"I think I can't tell much. His baseline is screwed up, and on several questions, I just couldn't get a good read. He didn't really fail, but he sure as hell didn't pass either. I'm a little suspicious of those last two answers on taxes and if he's told us everything. What I think I ought to do is send it on to Quantico; maybe they'll have a better read than I do, but I'd have to say he didn't pass."

"Shit, this is all I need. If we have to, we can do it again, but let's do it later. I've already got this guy nervous, and I need his help, because I just found out we can't tape his next meeting. We gotta have him do it himself, so the last thing I want to do is push him."

"Well, just tell him he passed. If we have to do it again, we'll just do it. No big deal."

Cox went down to the lobby to find Gary.

"Well, did I pass?"

"Yeah, looks like you passed, no problem. I'm sorry we had to put you through it all. I don't know who the hell that idiot technician is they sent down from Chicago, but he's bitching about some problems he had with his machine. Anyway, he said you definitely passed. I hope the stupid son of a bitch is able to get all the paper out of the machine okay, because if he doesn't, we may have to do it again, but there's no problem."

Waves of relief ran through Gary. His trip to the library had paid off. The other thing was, he hadn't been asked about the bonuses. That had to mean they didn't have any suspicions about them.

Gary didn't hear anything more until a couple of weeks before the meeting. Then he got a call. "Gary, I've gotta talk to you tonight." He thought Cox's voice sounded pretty nervous. "Meet me at the Comfort Inn behind McDonald's, across from the mall. I'll leave the room number on your machine.

CHAPTER 67

When he got to the hotel that evening, Gary could tell something was wrong. Cox was pacing around the room and would barely look at him. "Gary, I've just gotten some bad news," he began. "The law is that we have to tell any foreign government what we're doing when we tape people on their soil. When we did the job in Paris, it was no real problem. The French company is just a subsidiary of the Japanese company, so there was no real French interest at stake. But if we tell the Japanese government, they'll for sure tip off Nippon Kagaka. Here's the catch, though. If you as an individual were to take your own tape recorder, you're allowed to tape, but it has to be your own tape recorder and tapes, not ours. Hell, we can't even ask you to go and do it."

Gary looked closely into Cox's eyes. He can't ask me, but he is asking me, he thought. He wants me to buy a tape recorder and make tapes for them on my own. Cox's next words removed any need for guessing. "I can't really tell you what kind of machine to buy, but if I could, I'd probably tell you to buy a Radio Shack Micro 26, just like the one you've been using. And also I'd tell you to make sure you got a second package with a microphone in it, that is, if you were interested. But I'm not allowed to tell you any of that, so you know, do whatever you want. It's your call."

He may not have been allowed to tell Gary "any of that," but the message came across pretty clearly. The FBI wanted to hear what went on in the meeting. Gary sighed and told him he'd go buy the recorder, and Cox, using almost comical circumlocutions, made sure he knew how to hide it among his clothes so it wouldn't be seen by Howard at Customs, and also to make sure to put it in his checked suitcase and not carry it through the metal detectors at the airport.

Gary went across the street to the Radio Shack in the mall and made his purchase: tape recorder, microphone, tapes and several sets of batteries. Now I'm well equipped to be a spy whenever I want, he thought, laughing as he walked back to his car. Then he stopped dead in his tracks. I wish I had a tape of the conversation I just had, he thought. He got into his car and put the Radio Shack bag on the seat next to him. He started the engine and then stared at the bag. I wonder, he thought, if I could get away with taping my meetings with Sid?

On the way home, he stopped at the office and grabbed the tax returns from his desk. He'd done nothing with them, trying to decide if he ought to check on whether he was supposed to pay taxes on the bonuses. Screw the government, he thought now, signing the forms and writing out the checks. What have they done for me lately?

·

CHAPTER 68

G.T. Binghamton was sitting in his living room, reading Michael Crichton's *Rising Sun*, when Cathy came into the room, her coat on. "I have to go to the drug store and get my insulin," she said.

He looked up at her, cursing again in his mind the disease that forced her into so many compromises with everyday life. "Would you like me to go get it for you?" he offered.

"No, honey, that's fine. I'm going to pick up a few other things, too," she replied, bending down to give him a light kiss on the top of his head. He reached up and patted her on the arm.

He returned to his reading. The book's portrayal of Japanese business practices fascinated him. Maybe the author is being too hard on the Japs, he thought, but his own experience suggested otherwise. He thought about the supposedly mutual plant tours. They had shown the Nippon Kagaka team everything about TLP they could have wanted to see, and in return, they had been stonewalled at Kagaka's Samuran plant in Iowa. Howard and Gary need to read this, he thought.

The day before their flight to Tokyo, Howard stopped by Gary's office. "Come on, let's go get our marching orders from G.T.," he said.

When they were there, G.T. reached down by the side of his desk, brought up a bag and unceremoniously dumped two books onto his desk. He handed Howard and Gary each a hardbound copy and said, "This is mandatory company reading. You can't trust those fucking Japs. We need to work with them, but on the other hand, you can't trust those little cocksuckers. This book shows what they're really like, boys, so study this thing like a textbook."

"Well, this is the meeting to get the production volume set," Howard said.

"Let's not take anything less than eighty-five thousand metric tons."

Howard shook his head, "I don't think we'll ever get that."

"Well, shoot for it anyway," G.T. snapped. "Hey, what do those Japanese women look like?" he asked suddenly.

"They're ugly," Howard replied shaking his head.

"Well then, Howard, you deserve to get laid in Japan," G.T. said with a big smile. Howard gave him the bird.

"What's that, your IQ?" G.T. retaliated. Then he turned to Gary. "What's your opinion on the state of Japanese women, Gary?" All Gary could think about was how bad all of this would sound in court. He didn't want Jenna, or anyone else for that matter, to hear him participate in any of this kind of smut.

"Well, we've got a lot to do," Gary said. "I don't think we'll have any time for messing around." He wanted to get out of this conversation fast, but G.T. wasn't ready to let it go.

"Well, Gary, their eyes are slanted, we know that for sure, but your only assignment on this trip is to find out if their pussies are slanted the same way." Then he stood up. "Don't come back unless you can give me an honest answer."

"G.T., we've got too much to do on this trip for anything like that," Gary replied. "Come on Howard, let's get out of here and go to work."

"Jesus fucking Christ, Gary, there's a lot more to life than the market share of Sugere," G.T. snorted. "Well, boys, you get the prices up to a dollar thirty per pound and a volume just as fucking close to eighty-five as you can. And then find out about the Japanese pussies. If you get all that done, you can come back."

That night when Cox listened to the tape he turned to Gary with a solemn look on his face. "Gary, you've got to loosen up some. They're going to quit talking to you if you keep on this way. Go with the flow, be like they are, one of the guys. If they want to talk about pussy, you talk about it with them. Otherwise you're gonna blow this whole thing. Jeez, if I were them, I'd be asking, 'What are you doing, taping us?'"

"Yeah, I know, but when it's on tape I don't feel like talking about this kind of stuff. It's a really odd situation for me, and I feel uncomfortable," Gary protested.

"Well, find a way to get comfortable with it," Cox snapped.

When Gary got home, he talked to Jenna about the dilemma. "Imagine if Justin and Mark were to hear me talk like that," he said. "And they might. I mean, when this thing goes to trial, there's no telling what's going to get printed. Jeez, it might even be on TV."

"The way this whole thing is dragging on," she said, "they may be grown men by the time it goes to trial."

He chuckled a little, but it was hard. "Even then I'd be embarrassed to have them hear it," he said. "Not to mention you. I wouldn't want you to think I was messing around like Howard."

"Gary, Gary, Gary," she said. "I worry about a million things these days, most of all about what the pressure you're under might do to you. But one thing I don't spend one second worrying about is you being unfaithful. I trust you completely."

He looked at her closely. She was so beautiful, so desirable. He couldn't imagine ever being unfaithful to her. Still, something in her comment startled him. It was the word *trust*. G.T. and Howard trusted him, too, and he was certainly being unfaithful to them.

And then there was Sid Cox. He wasn't sure the FBI agent trusted him at all, and now he was considering subjecting him to secret taping. He hadn't told Jenna yet about having to buy his own recording equipment for the meeting in Japan, but now he did, emphasizing how Cox had used weasel words in getting him to supposedly come up with the idea on his own.

Jenna just shook her head. "I can't believe how complicated this thing is getting," she said.

Howard and Gary took the usual King Air flight to Chicago and then settled in business class for the 14-hour JAL flight to Tokyo. They sat side by side, both reading *Rising Sun*. Gary thought the flight attendant scowled at them several times, but maybe it was his imagination. When they arrived at Narita Airport, they didn't have a lot of luggage, so they cleared Customs in record time. As they stood in the taxi line, Howard began to open up. "I'm bushed," he said. "That's all we need, to find a bunch of ugly Japanese women. Whaddya think of the book?"

"I like it, but I'm not sure how realistic it is," Gary answered. "I don't think the Japanese are that duplicitous, do you?"

"Doo- what? Ah, shit, I don't trust these guys as far as I can throw 'em, especially that pigeon toed little shit Numata," Howard responded. They got into a taxi and took the two-hour ride through the heavy traffic to the Palace Hotel.

They trundled down into the basement where the hotel had a casual café. Howard had a hamburger and fries; Gary had ramen noodles and chicken. Even with such a light meal, the bill came to a little over $80.00. Howard handed Gary the bill, which he dutifully paid and then went up to his room.

CHAPTER 69

The next morning, a Nippon Kagaka employee picked them up and took them to an old four-story building, where Masahiko Yamasaki, Numata's assistant, met them and escorted them to an elevator. The building was nothing like the fancy one they had met in before, and had the appearance of an out-of-the way, little-used facility – the better to avoid suspicion.

When they got to the fourth-floor meeting room, Numata was there, along with Mr. Kim from Daehan, who had brought an assistant, a Mr. Park. Park seemed to have a good understanding of English, and Gary supposed he was there to help Kim figure out what was being said. Song Dian-Nuan and Bai Ken-ren were there from New World, and Jacques Coté from Euro Dolce. The usual suspects, Gary thought, clicking on his recorder.

"Welcome to the meeting of the International Association of Artificial Sweetener Producers," Numata began. "Let's review where we are in our discussions."

Yamasaki got up and moved to a white marker board at the front of the room. "We see," Numata continued, "that the market's improving in quite a few places." Yamasaki wrote the words "U.S." and "Europe". Then on the other side he wrote down "Asia" and "Latin America". "Here we are doing really bad: we need to get control of our people here," Numata said.

Gary understood what was behind the concerns of the Japanese. TLP was using its own in-house people to market in Asia and Latin America, but the others were using distributors. The gaps that Yamasaki's numbers were exposing were precisely the reason TLP had been prepared to pay people like Peter Rhyner and Dink Maccabee big bonuses to buy out their independent distributorships and put them on the TLP payroll. When an independent distributor had excess inventory, he would discount the price of his stocks of sweetener, and the price would drop.

"I think the reason Europe is doing so well is because the Japanese aren't involved," Howard said. Jacques laughed but was cut short by a glare from Numata. There were no Asian smiles. Numata sat back down and said, "Big problem is volumes. People sell more than market has room for, which forces market down."

Howard said, "My thoughts exactly. I've been saying that from the first day we met. You can never keep prices up consistently unless you have the volumes worked out worldwide."

Kim and Park began to talk in Korean. Numata and Yamasaki began to talk in Japanese. Song and Bai began to talk in Chinese. Coté grinned and looked around the room with overstated gestures. "Can we perhaps say a few words in French?" he asked Gary, mischievously. "I feel left out."

"*Merde*," Gary said, chuckling. Coté chuckled, too.

Then the Asians began speaking to one another in Japanese. The conversation seemed a little heated, but Gary wasn't sure if they were disagreeing, or merely trying to communicate with each other in a common language. Finally all the conversation stopped.

Numata looked at Howard and Gary. "We agree with you, but volume problem is not us but TLP. You want too much. We will now propose volumes for everyone. Masahito, go to board please." Yamasaki complied and picked up a marker.

"We propose TLP produce forty-five thousand tons."

Howard slammed his notebook shut. "You told us that in Paris three months ago, and we told you then it would never fly. If you are going to keep insisting on such an unreasonable number, we might as well leave now. There's no reason for us to stay here. There is no way in hell we will ever agree to 45 thousand tons when we have 113 thousand tons of capacity sitting back in Steuben, By- God, Indiana!" Howard's voice got louder as he progressed. The word Indiana came out almost as a shout. Numata paused for a minute and Howard shoved himself back from the table and buttoned his coat. Gary looked at his watch and calculated that he only had another ten minutes left on the current tape.

"I am sorry to hear that, Mr. Hargiss, but we have been thirty years in the bio-tech business and you TLP have just started. You are trying to move too fast." Then he gave Howard a look that translated into English quite well. It said... you're a piece of annoying shit. "We will make new proposal for you. Do you mind leaving room?" Howard and Gary nodded assent and walked out of the room, closing the door behind them.

"I thought they'd come back with a low number," Howard said. "But I didn't dream it would be the same thing we shot down in Paris. G.T. is gonna hit the roof. We're wasting our time here." He lit a cigarette and paced back and forth for a moment. "Well, let's wait till we get back in there to see what they have to say. If it's not something that's worth taking back, we'll see how they feel about sixty cents a pound for the next ten years."

He took a long drag on the cigarette and leaned against the wall. Gary hurried off to the bathroom to change tapes.

A few minutes after he had rejoined Howard, Numata came to the door and said, "You come back in now." Gary felt like he had just been to the principal's office. Numata affected a beaming smile as the two Americans took their seats. "We thought about your proposal, and now instead of forty-five, we prepared to offer you fifty-four thousand tons."

Howard smiled back. "What did you do, just reverse the numbers?" he said sarcastically. Up on the board they had Nippon Kagaka at 73, New World at 53, Daehan at 28, and TLP at 54. Gary added the numbers in his head: 208,000 tons. They know what they're doing, he thought; that's right on the button for current world usage. Howard kept talking. "We'll go out for another fifteen minutes and you guys come up with another ten thousand tons," he concluded. By Howard and Gary's calculations, each 10,000 tons came out to 20 million dollars in profits.

Numata would have none of it. "This is the last offer," he said. "If you do not accept, then the price war will continue." It had been less than five minutes since they had walked back in the door, but Howard began to move to a more conciliatory tone. "We're thinking closer to eighty-five," he said. "Obviously we can't make a final decision here. We work for G.T. Binghamton, and he has to make that decision. We'll be back in touch, but I can't imagine we will ever accept 54 thousand tons."

The the meeting continued with discussios on a series of smaller matters. When it finally ended, Gary headed back to the bathroom to change tapes again. As they walked to the limousine, Howard said, "You sure go the bathroom a lot. Are you okay?" Gary wasn't sure what his face looked like, so he gazed down at the steps and said, "Yeah, I've been drinking a lot of water since we got over here."

They stepped into the limo and Gary started quizzing Howard about what he thought G.T.'s reaction would be. "You think G.T. will agree to numbers like this?" he asked.

"Nah, but you've gotta admit they went up nine thousand tons quick. Right there gives us some room." He took a drag on his cigarette. "We'll never get eighty or eighty-five, but I'll bet we get over seventy." The driver turned around at a stop light and said, "No smoke please, no smoke." Howard pretended he didn't understand. "I'll be glad to get out of this damn place," he said.

When they arrived at the airport, Gary realized he had to get to a restroom and put his recorder into his bag to be checked before he went through the metal detectors. Howard wanted to go immediately to the ticket counter, but Gary said, "I need to go to the john first."

"You just went to the fucking john. What the hell is wrong with you?"

Gary affected a sheepish grin. "Now it's Number Two," he said.

"Well, fuck it, give me your bag and I'll get in line while you go take your shit."

"No, I'll keep it," Gary said, making a grab for the bag just as Howard's hand reached out for it. Gary beat him by a split second, and Howard gave Gary a dirty look.

Gary went to the bathroom, locked himself in a stall and pulled the recorder and microphone out of his coat, then put them inside some dirty underwear like Cox had taught him, and headed back out to rejoin Howard. "I hope I never come back. A country like this trying to compete in the world market and they have a restroom worse than a fucking truck stop," he snorted. Howard seemed to appreciate the sentiment.

On the long flight to Chicago, Gary reflected on all the plans he'd made in case he got caught. He decided to tell Howard he wanted to tape the meeting so that they could listen to what they were saying over and over again, and maybe even get someone to interpret what the others said in Japanese during their asides.

When they got to O'Hare, Gary flew through Customs, called Cox from a pay phone and told him what he had. It was about 8:30 in the morning. Cox asked if he could meet him behind the Pizza Hut on the north side of Steuben as soon as Gary landed in the King Air. The weather was poor, and the flight to Steuben promised to be bumpy and uncomfortable. Gary was dead tired; the only thing he really wanted was a shower and some sleep. He decided to risk Cox's wrath and told him he was going straight home from the airport. They could meet the next morning early. To his surprise, Cox didn't yell at him for delaying the operation. "Hey, look," the FBI man said, "you don't have to give me the tapes at all." That statement seemed rather pointless. Gary had just risked a lot by taping them, he wasn't about to throw them away.

"Did you make a deal?" Jenna asked Gary when he got home.

"Nah, it's still a long way off. We're closer, I guess."

"Oh," she said, trying to conceal her disappointment. All the while he was gone, she had been thinking about the situation they were in. She desperately wanted it all to be over as soon as possible. How much tape does the FBI need? she had wondered. Thinking about it some more, she decided that they were waiting for the deal to be struck. Once it was, they would have what they wanted, and Gary's ordeal would soon be over.

Gary went to the bathroom to shower, shave and brush his teeth. When he emerged, he felt a lot better, but he was still exhausted. Jenna was waiting for him in their bedroom.

"I've been thinking about something," she said. She told him her idea that the end to their agonies would come only when the price-fixing deal was finally cut. "In these meetings, it seems to me like you ought to press real hard to bring things to a conclusion," she said, hoping he wouldn't be offended by her implied criticism.

"I usually don't say much at all," he admitted. "I just back up Howard with technical information, that sort of thing. "Besides," he added, "I don't want to incriminate myself."

"But you've got immunity," she said.

"That's true," he said. She was right, of course. He wasn't sure he had any ideas that would step up the pace of the negotiations, but if he could think of something, it would certainly help the cause of getting the whole taping nightmare over with.

"You want to listen to the tapes?" he asked her, suddenly.

"Right now?"

"Sure."

"But you're so tired."

They could have been talking about sex, he thought. "Yeah, but I feel a lot better now that I'm cleaned up," he said. Then he had an idea. "I think I'll make a copy for us to keep," he said.

"You know," he added, "you're a pretty smart chickie. There probably are some ways I could be more forceful in advancing the agenda."

The compliment seemed to please her. "Well," she said, "I don't know anything about big business negotiations, but in real estate, you know, we sort of try to move things along as quickly as possible, so we can get the house sold."

They went down to the family room and played the tapes, making a copy as they did. When they got to the part where the volumes were being discussed, Gary said, "There. Right there."

"What?" Jenna asked.

"I could have said something right there," Gary said. He didn't want to stop the tape, since they were making a copy, but he rummaged around in a cabinet and found a note pad and started jotting down some numbers. Jenna glanced over at him, but kept her attention on the tape.

After a few minutes, Gary looked up with a satisfied smile. "They were giving themselves just about seventy-three percent of their capacity," he said. "Each of the other companies. But at 54 thousand, TLP would only be at about forty-eight percent of our capacity. I could have brought that up and it might have had some impact."

Jenna grinned at him.

When the tapes were finished, he went to bed and slept until after the kids came home from school. That night he put his personal taping equipment back in the closet and got out the FBI stuff to use the next day.

CHAPTER 70

At 6:30 the next morning, Gary met Cox and handed over the tapes from Japan. "Here's a little present for you," he said, somewhat sarcastically. "Something I didn't have to do, but I did anyway."

When he got to the office, it was only about 7:30, but Howard was already waiting for him. "Time to go tell G.T. about our little meeting," he said.

"Well, boys," G.T. greeted them. "It's a good sign you being back and all. Remember I said you couldn't come back unless you found out which way that slit ran, vertical or horizontal."

"Or diagonal," Gary said, trying to be one of the guys. "You really wanted to know if it was slanted, like their eyes."

"Whatever," G.T. said.

"Howard, I think you know the answer better than I do," Gary said.

Howard said in a mocking voice, "Oh, Gary, we didn't have time for that!" Then he changed his tone to disgust. "Besides, those women are ugly. I wouldn't want to be in their pussies no matter what shape they are."

G.T. screwed up his face. "That's disappointing. I expected an answer from you guys."

"Why don't you rent a Japanese porno flick?" Howard said. "Then you'll have your answer."

"We did have a good meeting though," Gary said, trying to move onto another subject.

G.T. looked at him and smiled. "Doogie Howser here wants to get back to business."

Gary started off. "Well, we have a long way to go, but we are making some progress."

Howard interrupted him. "First they offered to let us have forty-five thousand tons."

G.T. whistled. "Jesus Christ, why did you even bother to go? I thought we already rejected that in Paris!"

"Yeah, well, wait a minute G.T., there's more to this. We were asked to leave the room for fifteen minutes and when we came back in it was up to fifty-four."

G.T. smiled, "Well boys, why didn't you leave the room again and get sixty-four?"

"Nah, that's the highest they would go, and there wasn't anything else said at the meeting that shows they have any flexibility either."

"What do you think we will realistically get out of this? Do you think we can ever get it up above eighty?"

"Nah, we won't ever get there now, but it really doesn't make any difference since the market's growing each year. Realistically I could see us getting to seventy or seventy-five and that's what we should work for."

"That's about right," Gary said, pulling out the notes he had made at home the previous afternoon. "They were giving each other about seventy-three percent of their capacity, and us forty-eight. Now, current usage is about 208,000 tons – that's what their number is based on, and it's about right. Using the numbers they put up in Mexico, industry capacity is 327,000 tons. That means the market right now is running just about sixty-three percent of capacity. For us, that would be a little over seventy-one thousand tons. So I think we could get that if we hang tough."

G.T. swung his feet off the desk. "Doogie's been doing his homework," he said. "But goddamn it, we've got a plant that's designed for 113 thousand tons and we still got construction going on. We should stop it now if that's all we're going to get."

Howard turned to face G.T. "But the market is growing so fast, we'll need it in five years. We'll grow into it."

G.T. nodded in agreement. "Yeah, you're right. We did the same thing on cellulose."

"G.T., there's for sure more room. The fact that they went from forty-five to fifty-four in a few minutes proves it," Howard said.

G.T. glanced over at Gary, "Whadda ya think, Doogie?"

"Well, I agree with Howard, eighty will be too hard to get right now. If we get up to seventy-one, we'll be at eighty-five within a couple of years."

G.T. stared at Gary, then said, "Well, we ain't there yet, and fifty-four don't cut it. Go back and tell 'em no deal. Then, let's put some teeth in our proposal. Let's drop our price a nickel a pound."

"G.T., the prices are already low. We've been trying to get it up to a dollar five, but it's stuck under ninety right now because of volume pressures," Gary said.

"I don't give a rat's ass. The best cure for low prices is lower prices. Get 'em down." And with that G.T. dismissed them.

Gary went back to his office and called Brad Redfoot into his office. "Phone the regional vice presidents," he said. "Tell them to drop the price of

Sugere a nickel."

"I thought we were trying to drive the prices over a dollar," Redfoot said. "What are we doing dropping a nickel?"

"Well, there's things going on, I can tell you that," Gary explained. "This is just politics, and G.T. wants to make a point to the competition."

"All right, we'll do it," Redfoot said.

At home that evening, Gary got a call from Masahiko Yamasaki. "Our guys at Heartland said you dropped prices a nickel a pound," Yamasaki said. "What is going on?"

Gary took the cue. "Well, Howard and I talked to G.T., and he didn't like what you guys proposed. There's no way he'll accept fifty-four thousand tons, so we're going after the bigger volume this way."

"Wow, I'm surprised. I can't believe it. I thought we trying to get prices up."

"Well, we were going to call Mr. Numata tomorrow afternoon, but you can tell him for us. We're dropping a nickel and it may go even lower than that."

Yamasaki sighed and responded, "Are we wasting our time having these meetings?"

"Well it looks like it," Gary said. "We have all this capacity and fifty-four just ain't gonna fly. We'll just have to see."

"They'll talk," Howard said when Gary relayed his conversation with Yamasaki. "That nickel a pound will get their attention. If that doesn't do it, then another twenty cents will. I hope we don't have to go that low, but sometimes you have to lose money to make it."

That night Gary spent three hours with Cox going over all the tapes and explaining to him what they meant. Even Cox was impressed with the boldness TLP demonstrated by cutting its price.

Two days later, Gary was eating in the executive lunchroom with Brad, Buffy and Roger Kincaid, the accountant. Zack Brilley, TLP's General Counsel, walked in and patted Kincaid on the back.

"Hey, Rog," he said. "What's the quarter going to look like?"

Kincaid turned around and looked at Brilley for a second. "Well, William hasn't had a chance to review the numbers yet, so I don't know," he said.

"One thing's for sure, after he makes up his mind what the quarter's going to look like, what it is, it is."

"We'll pull money out of our ass if we have to, huh Roger?" Gary asked.

Kincaid started to respond, but Buffy cut him short. "Why do we even work here anyway? You'll just pull the money from the Caymans if we're short."

"Like I said guys, what it is, it is," Kincaid repeated.

That night Gary told Cox about the way the quarterly earnings we're derived. "Ah, don't worry about that stuff. We've got enough with what were working on to keep us busy," Cox said.

A few days later the division managers were all in for a lunch and tried adding up their earnings figures from the various divisions. Even with everyone present from each of the divisions, they came up almost $30 million short of the announced earnings. Because Cox had passed on any further interest, Gary didn't bother to record the conversation. But he couldn't get it out of his mind. What kind of a game was Hargiss playing? And what did Buffy mean, "pull money out of the Caymans"?

When I'm running this place, he thought, renewing his fantasy about how the FBI investigation would end, I'll run everything on the up and up.

CHAPTER 71

William C. Hargiss sat alone in the study of his home overlooking the Wabash River a few miles southwest of Steuben. It was almost 9:00, at which time Virginia would come into the room with his evening Manhattan, and they would talk for a half hour or so. Then he would return to the stack of papers on his desk.

He often worked at home like this, and one night every quarter in particular, he would work well past midnight until he had all the numbers just where he wanted them. He got up from his desk and looked out across the tops of the trees sloping down to the riverbank, a quarter mile below him. The air was crystal clear, and an almost full moon glimmered above the landscape. Across the water, he could see the lights of three little river towns, strung out from northeast to southwest.

In those towns, he thought, people are at home, enjoying their evening, or not: doing the dishes, arguing with their children, dozing in front of the television set. Somewhere, one of them might be struggling to balance a checkbook. Hargiss was made of the same flesh and blood they were, but his life was very different. The checkbook he was going to balance tonight was unique in all the world.

On one side of the ledger were the books of one of the largest corporations in the world. That part the people in the villages could comprehend, even if the complexity of it all might baffle them. In the end, that part of his checkbook task was the same as theirs; only the numbers were bigger.

On the other side of the ledger, the secret side, the numbers were written in invisible ink. Only he could read them, and keeping the secrets they told was his real job.

Old Jim Carney had first introduced him to the shadow world of national security. Carney had been OSS during World War II, and after the war had continued to provide very special services to the United States government. In 1962, he had suffered a mild heart attack, and, fearing for his life, had selected Hargiss to carry on in his stead. In fact, Carney had lived almost another 30 years, but by then, the scope of Hargiss's secret activities dwarfed anything the old man had ever imagined.

It suited the Government well that William Hargiss take over Tamson-Long Products. Without the credit line which was thus made possible, it could never have happened. With it, the fix was in and the deal assured. He brought G.T. Binghamton along with him to make sure all the pipes fit, and proceeded to build an industrial giant that could support the clandestine operations his country counted on him to manage, operations neither G.T. nor anyone else at TLP knew anything about.

In the shadow world, a man would wait in the night on a barren plateau in Afghanistan, listening for the sounds of an approaching helicopter which would bring him 200 M-1 rifles and a million rounds of ammunition. The man wouldn't ever really know who had sent the helicopter. That was part of the secret. But Hargiss would know, because he would pay for it.

In the shadow world, a man in Colombia would one day find he had a new buyer for his product, and another man in Miami would find he had a new supplier. Neither of them would ever know who the middleman was, but William Hargiss would know, and the profits generated would go to Geneva or Georgetown to await the next call for M-1s in Kandahar or grenade launchers in Matagalpa.

Or, maybe it would go to line the pockets of a politician in Paris or Pretoria. It might even finance a business or build a school. It might be responsible for a computer in the basement of a building in Warsaw, or a fax machine in Kiev.

The money came from many sources. Some was drug money. Some was siphoned out of oil tanks in Kuwait. A lot of it, now more than ever, was dug out of the ground in Sierra Leone, where a woman would use tools supplied to her by a man wearing a black headband and carrying a rifle to turn a yard-high mound of gravel and very possibly find a diamond. The diamond would find its torturous way through the bush and across the border into Liberia, spend a few days in a safe in the Firestone compound near the airport, and then go on to Antwerp into the safekeeping of a gem cutter whose profits went into accounts with names like Interoceanic and Tracinda, to be withdrawn at the discretion of William Hargiss. The smallest part of the cost was the rough diamond. The largest part was keeping Sierra Leone in turmoil. But the gross was hundreds of millions of dollars a year, and you could buy a lot of West African mayhem with that, and still have plenty left over.

Still, the system did not work well enough for Hargiss.

Ever since the day his own brother had almost blown the system sky high, Hargiss had searched for a better way to finance the shadow world, and when he had finally come up with it, and sold the idea to Washington, he moved the whole operation to the next level. And helped win the Cold War in the process.

The drug, oil and diamond money was still there, but the new source dwarfed them all. At least it had until he had gambled a billion dollars on biochemistry. Now, the excess profits of TLP were being drained off by losses in the new division. He had to find a way to turn it around.

In the process of building his empire, William Hargiss had become an old man, and unlike Jim Carney, he had not provided for a successor. His plan had been to divide the ledger book, giving Howard the TLP side. He had long known that Howard could not be trusted with the other side. A person with his lack of self-control might be fine as a CEO, a senator, even a president. But to give him the responsibility Hargiss bore was unthinkable. Nor could G.T. handle the job. For all his skills as an engineer, G.T. could never get along in the shadow world. Howard couldn't control his nose or his pecker, and G.T. couldn't control his mouth.

So now he was counting on young Gary Long. Was this the vessel that could carry the water? It would soon be time to find out for sure.

"So deep in thought, my darling?" Virginia said, entering the walnut-paneled study with his drink and a glass of wine for herself.

He turned his gaze from landscape to portrait, and looked at the woman with whom he had shared so much. Still beautiful after all these years, he thought.

She handed him the cone-shaped glass and they walked together to the couch against the far wall. "How was your day?" he asked her.

"Very nice," she said. "I handed out the scholarships at South Steuben High. Two lovely young black girls, a white boy and another boy who looked sort of Middle Eastern."

"And tomorrow is your bridge group?"

"Yes."

"Well, it's that time again. I'll be gone before you get up, so I'll leave you a little note. Make sure Madeleine Caldwell gets the number right."

"She does pretty well."

"Yes, she does."

At quarter to one in the morning, Hargiss finally had everything where he wanted it. He wrote a few lines on a yellow pad, tore the page off and put it on the kitchen counter. Then he went to bed.

In the course of the next day's bridge game, Virginia let a few things drop in the conversation. Madeleine Caldwell made mental notes of them all, and called her husband from the car on her way home. John Caldwell immediately phoned the senior analyst at the home office of his brokerage firm in New York. Two days later, the analyst would predict the quarterly earnings of Tamson-Long Products. He would be one penny per share under the actual amount announced later in the week, and both his prediction and the subsequent announcement would nudge TLP stock up. The difference would add half a million dollars to the net worth of William and Virginia Hargiss.

CHAPTER 72

While Mrs. Hargiss was playing bridge, Admiral Jonathan Decatur read a brief note from a friend in the Extortion Division of the Federal Bureau of Investigation. They were closing their books on the investigation of Tamson-Long Products. There had been no developments for six months; the investigation was at a dead end.

Decatur placed a quick call and read the note to Hargiss. Hargiss already knew that the phone tap had been removed, but confirmation that the investigation was officially closed came as a welcome relief to him nonetheless. He'd made a stupid mistake in getting it started, and Decatur had made a stupid mistake in getting the FBI involved. But in the end, it had come to nothing.

After hanging up with Decatur, Hargiss sat back in his chair for a few minutes. Then he picked up the phone and called G.T. "I want to get together with you, Howard and Gary," he said.

Half an hour later, the four men sat in Hargiss's office.

"The FBI is out of our hair," Hargiss began, "and it's time to get the deal done on Sugere."

"God knows we've been trying," Howard said. "These things take time."

"Well, we're running out of time. I put the quarterlies together last night, and let me tell you, it was a struggle. The day is going to come when the board is going to get real nervous. *Real* nervous." In truth, he wasn't really worried about the board. He could always handle them. But he'd had to squeeze the other side of the ledger hard this time. He had another quarter, two at the most, before something would have to give.

"What's the sticking point?" he asked.

"Volume," G.T. said. "They're only willing to give us fifty-four thousand metric tons at this point, and we need between eighty and eighty-five in my opinion. These guys," he waved at Howard and Gary, "think they can get it up to seventy, maybe seventy-five..."

Howard started to say something, but Hargiss cut him off. "Gary," he said, "how do we get this thing done?"

Gary swallowed hard. The tape was running. Part of him wanted to shrug and say something like they just had to keep working at it. Part of him wanted to impress Hargiss. Part of him wanted to follow Jenna's advice and move the deal to closure as fast as he could. Cox would like that, too. But still another part of him worried about becoming, on tape, a prime mover in advancing a crime. To heck with it, he thought, I've got immunity.

"There are three things I think might help," he began. "First, we need to remember that about ten percent of the Sugere we're selling is in liquid form. That's being counted at full weight in the volume discussions, which gives us a real advantage, since it's mostly water. The big users of liquid Sugere are the soft drink manufacturers, which means we ought to be able to increase the share with some aggressive marketing, because the U.S. dominates soft drinks and that's to our advantage. The more we can do that, the lower volume we can accept from Nippon Kagaka and the others.

"Second, the real key is market growth. The world market has gone up about twenty thousand tons since we started, and it hasn't topped out yet. That means the key is the alpha." He paused a moment to look at William and make sure he understood the term "alpha", the annual growth in the market. Satisfied he didn't need to define it, he continued. "I think it might be a whole lot easier to get the others to agree to concessions to us on the alpha than on the starting volume."

"Why?" Howard asked, puzzled.

"Because I think they're lying about their capacity. They thought *we* were, but now they know we're not, because they came here and saw what we have. They didn't reciprocate by showing us their plant because they can't afford to let us see their real capacity. They could give us the full alpha for several years and still be at the same percent of capacity we would be at."

He paused again, and looked at the others. They seemed impressed.

"What's the third thing?" Hargiss asked.

"You," Gary said. "My guess is that your personal intervention into the negotiations would have a dramatic effect on the Asians. They are very respectful of authority and seniority."

"I don't know," Howard said. "We've always protected Dad in these kind of discussions."

"True," Gary countered. "But don't think for a minute they don't understand our organization chart. William C. Hargiss is a legend. They'll be in awe of him."

"I'm glad somebody understands our organization chart," G.T. snorted.

"Well, boys, I'll do whatever you think best," Hargiss said. "I just want the volumes set and the deal done. Let's keep the liquid product thing in our back pocket, but make it part of your mental calculations. Push hard to get the full alpha. If I can be useful by being at the meeting, I'll be there. If not, it's no problem. If I'm going to attend a meeting, though, it has to be here in Steuben," he added.

Howard felt he needed to make a substantive contribution to the meeting. "I think it's really important," he said, "that the next meeting be their idea. If we call them and request it, it'll look like we're bleeding the most, and we'll lose the advantage. We've got to let them call us."

"Then we've got to keep up the pressure on the price," G.T. said. "It's the only way to get them to blink."

That night, Gary copied the tape, and met Cox early the next morning. "I've finally got the big fish for you," he said, handing Cox the original tape.

CHAPTER 73

Jimmy T didn't really know much about the man with the glasses and the scraggly beard, but he knew he was tougher and smarter than he looked. He had met the man twice. The first time, they sat on one of the hard benches in the visitors room and the man made his proposal, which Jimmy T had accepted on the spot. The second time, on the same bench, the man handed him the most impressive parole pleading Jimmy T had ever seen, and he knew something about parole pleadings. Jimmy T signed the document, no questions asked.

Now, as he walked blinking through the bright sunlight to the man's car parked outside the Indiana State Penitentiary, he figured it was safe to ask a question. "What sort of work will I be doing for you, Mr. Tully?" he asked.

"Oh, this and that," Tully replied. They got into the car. "The first thing is, I need an audio system rewired."

That was good. Jimmy T knew audio.

They drove through the gates and onto the highway. "It's in a sort-of hotel," Tully said. "At the Steuben Club. The original system was put in years ago. It's out of date and all fucked up. I want you to pull it out and put in a whole new system."

"Can do," Jimmy said.

They drove for several minutes in silence. "How come you decided to help me?" Jimmy T asked.

Never mind," Tully replied. "Let's just say an old customer thought you deserved a break."

"You were never a customer," Jimmy said. He always remembered his customers' faces.

"No," Tully said. "Not me. Never mind who it was. It's not important." He told Jimmy he could stay right there at the Steuben Club while he was working on the job. "Just remember," he added a moment later. "This is a top secret job."

"I figured it was," Jimmy T replied.

CHAPTER 74

The Asian producers matched TLP's nickel price drop, and TLP dropped another nickel the same day. In a matter of weeks, the price had plummeted to 65¢ a pound.

That put the pressure on G.T. to maximize production efficiency, and he took to the task like a duck to water. He spent countless hours in the plant, meeting with engineers, vetting ideas, coming up with good ones himself. The plant reached all-time efficiency highs in both quality and yield.

Sugere operations were still losing two million dollars a month, but that was only half of what it had been when the price was a dollar, because of the efficiency gained on production.

Finally, Nippon Kagaka blinked. Gary was out in the plant when the call came late one afternoon. Leigh Curtis tracked him down. A quick calculation told him it was about 6:00 in the morning in Tokyo. He raced back to his office and returned the call.

"The other members of the Association," Numata began, "feel it time for another meeting." Gary read volumes into the wording. It was probably exactly right. Numata had no doubt been badgered by Song and Kim, whose bottom lines must be hemorrhaging in the wake of the price drops.

"We would be happy to meet," Gary said. "And I believe it's our turn to act as host."

Numata proposed the May 27, and Gary said he would check it out and confirm the next day.

By noon the next day, it was all arranged. G.T. and Howard were higher than kites, and Hargiss seemed pleased as well. That night, Gary called Numata from home. After confirming the date, he dropped the bombshell. "Mr. Binghamton will join us in the meeting," he said, matter of factly, "and Mr. William Hargiss as well."

There was a moment of silence on the line. "If Mr. William Hargiss to be present," Numata said, "then I will attempt to bring Mr. Sadaaki Hamanaka to meeting also." Interesting, Gary thought, remembering Hamanaka's brief presence in the room the first time he and Howard had gone to Japan. Hamanaka is their CEO. The stakes are definitely getting higher.

"That would be wonderful," he said. "It would be a great honor for us to host Mr. Hamanaka in Steuben. Sumiko," he added, "as you know, Steuben is not a major city. We would like to put all the participants up at the Chemical Club here, which I assure you is much nicer than any of the commercial hotels in our area. It won't compare with the splendor of the Palace in Tokyo, of course, but it is the best we have to offer."

"Thank you, that would be very nice," Numata replied.

The next morning, Gary told G.T. about his conversation with Numata. "Good, good, GOOD," G.T. said. "See, I told you. The best cure for low prices is lower prices. A lot of people in the industry don't understand that, but the best way to end a price war is to have a bigger price war, because somebody is going cry uncle."

Then Gary headed over to Howard's office and told him the news. His reaction was the same as G.T.'s. "You've just got to be patient," he reiterated. "Let them break down first."

"Yeah," Gary replied, "it's like G.T. says: the best cure for low prices is lower prices."

Howard's lips curled in a rare smile. "You're learning, Gary" he said.

If anyone was happier than Howard at the news of the upcoming meeting, it was Sid Cox.

When Gary played the tapes for Cox that night at the Best Western, the agent rubbed his hands together in glee, and roared with laughter when he heard Howard's comments. Then he began to plan the best way to capture the meeting on tape.

"We need to get into corporate in advance and check it out," Cox said. Gary thought for a minute and suggested he could sign them in as customers.

In the early afternoon of the Friday before the meeting, a day Gary knew Howard and G.T. were in St. Louis, he again drove into the Best Western parking lot, where two technicians jumped in the car. They had on business suits and were carrying briefcases. One of them was Tom, the engineer who had instructed Gary about the recording equipment. Gary took them back to the plant and signed them in as buyers for Royal Crown Cola. They followed Gary to his office, talking in hushed tones and pointing as they tagged along. While they scoured his office for any signs of surveillance equipment, Gary casually walked out to the outer office.

"Leigh," he said, "I need you to run an errand for me."

"Sure," she said. "What is it?"

He went through a carefully rehearsed speech. He'd left some papers at home, on the kitchen counter. Jenna wasn't there or he'd have had her bring them in. He told Leigh he really hated to trouble her, but he needed the papers.

"It's no problem," Leigh said. "Since you've got guests, I'll call upstairs and have someone come down to watch the phone while I'm gone."

"No, no," he said quickly. Too quickly, he wondered? "Just let the answering machine get it."

"Well, all right. If you're sure."

"I'm sure."

"You want me to bring some coffee for your meeting?"

"No, no, we don't need any."

She had a puzzled look on her face.

"I asked," he said, shrugging his shoulders. "They declined. Maybe they only drink R.C.," he added, forcing a grin.

Leigh cocked her head quizzically, but decided to give up. She reached into her desk drawer, took out her purse and left. Gary exhaled for what seemed like the first time in minutes. Man, this was nervewracking. How many more times was he going to have to make excuses before the day was over? What if he messed up and made someone really suspicious?

"The room's clean," Tom told him when he went back into his office.

He led them down the hall to G.T.'s office. "Joyce," he said to G.T.'s secretary, "I know G.T.'s out of town, but I need to take a quick look at his production notebook." He quickly introduced his guests, and ducked into the office. He picked up the notebook and began to chatter away as if he were talking to the men. To his relief, Joyce kept typing and didn't follow them into the office. While Gary talked, Tom and his companion searched the office, again looking for a hidden camera or microphone. After a long couple of minutes, Tom nodded and Gary returned the book to its place.

"Thanks," he said to Joyce as they left.

"Yes, thank you very much," Tom said, with a smile and a nod. Then they went to Howard's office. There was no one around except the fish. Gary stood guard at the door while the technicians repeated the search process.

When they finished, they followed Gary to the conference room where the meeting with the Asian producers would be held. Gary got out the slide equipment, and pretended to give a presentation. Tom stood on the conference table and began to lift up panels in the drop ceiling. Gary looked back at the glass door that led into the kitchen. Suddenly, he saw movement behind the door.

"Get down!" he whispered, spitting out the words. Tom jumped to the floor. A face materialized behind the glass. It was Brad Redfoot. Gary didn't think he had seen Tom jump, but he couldn't be sure.

Gary quickly got up from his seat and moved over to open the door. "Can I ask you something?" Redfoot asked. He looked upset.

"Sure," Gary answered, stepping into the kitchen. Behind him, the two men started talking and looking through some papers. "What's up?"

"I ran into Leigh in the hallway a few minutes ago, and she said you were meeting with some buyers from Royal Crown," Redfoot said testily. "I thought I was the sales manager for Bio-tech."

"Jeez, I hope you are," Gary said. "I sure as heck don't want the job." Come on, mind, he thought. Click in, click in.

There was just the slightest pause. "Look," Gary said. "I'm sorry I didn't call you, but be grateful for small favors. This meeting is nothing but a pain in the butt and nothing's going to come of it." Then he almost made a mistake. Royal Crown was out of Atlanta, he was thinking, and he almost said that he was just doing the meeting as a favor for Dink Maccabbee. But what if Brad said something to Dink? He stopped his mouth in the nick of time. "I don't know how I got roped into this," he said, "but since I'm wasting my time, you need to be talking to some real prospects." That wasn't very good, but it was the best he could do.

"Okay, okay," Redfoot said. "But I still should have been told."

"You're absolutely right, Brad. I'm sorry," Gary said. He watched Redfoot stalk out of the room, shaking his head. Another bullet dodged, but just barely. How in the devil was he going to get through this day? He glanced at his watch. How long did they have before Leigh would return? Try as he might, he couldn't seem to focus his mind on the simple arithmetic. What difference does it make? he thought, finally. We just have to get this done as quickly as possible.

Everyone was jumpy, and it showed. The men hurriedly assembled their radio equipment, got on a walkie talkie and started talking to a van they had driving on the street in front of TLP. For the next 40 minutes, they kept asking, "Can you hear the signal now?" The unfamiliar voice on the other end of the team kept saying, "Not yet." They kept moving antenna positions while Gary gave his slide presentation, over and over. Finally they gave up, packed their bags and left the room.

As they reached the hallway, Leigh Curtis stepped out of the elevator. "Ah," she said, "did you gentlemen have a good meeting?"

"Oh, yes," Tom grinned, good-naturedly. "It was very informative. We learned a lot."

"We're going to take a little tour; I'll be right back," Gary said, noticing the file folder under Leigh's arm. "Just put that on my desk. And, thank you," he called over his shoulder.

There was one job left, and they took the elevator to the sixth floor. There was an electric breaker box behind a panel in the executive dining room, and for some reason Gary didn't understand, the men needed to get into it. It was the trickiest part of the whole operation. There were security personnel roaming the hallways at all times; they weren't a problem anywhere else, but this was different, because Gary had no logical reason whatever for being in that room at that time.

He had prepared carefully, following Cox's instructions, getting the rounds of the security people down so he would know what time they would come through the area. Gary and the two bogus Sugere buyers waited in the sixth-floor elevator lobby for the guard to come by. Once he had left, they would have just under 15 minutes to get the job done. On the wall of the lobby, there were photos of TLP facilities around the world, and Gary made a pretense of showing them to his guests. Presently, he heard someone coming down the hall, and moved to one side so he could see who it was at the first opportunity.

When the man came into view, Gary felt his stomach turn. It was a security man, all right, but not one of the uniformed watchmen he had expected. It was Andrew Tully. Of all the people he didn't want to encounter that day, Tully was at the top of the list.

"Gar," he said, "just the man I'm looking for. In fact, I was just heading to your office."

What do you want? Gary's mind screamed. Get the hell out of here! Why do they even let slugs like you on the sixth floor? Get back in your hole in the basement where you belong! "Look, I've got some people here," he heard himself say. "Can't it wait until later?"

Over Tully's shoulder, he saw the security guard walk by. Damn, damn, damn. If they didn't hurry, they'd have to wait another 15 minutes. Tom looked at his watch.

"Nah, this won't take a minute," Tully said. "I just wanted to let you know..." Tully eyed the other men, suspiciously. "...that the, ah, gentlemen who are coming in next week, you know, the ones from overseas, well, I'm all ready for them at the, ah, you know, the Club."

"That's great, that's great," Gary said. He was so eager to get Tully out of there that he actually reached over and pressed the elevator button in hopes of speeding up the process. The elevator must have been waiting right on that floor, because the door slid open immediately.

Tully scowled at Gary. "Be sure and let me know if there are any changes in the drill," he said, stepping on the elevator. "You know, like any new faces I'm not expecting."

The door closed and he was gone. Gary collapsed against the wall. "Come on," Tom urged him, "we've still got time if we hurry."

They slipped into the dining room, where the other man took the panel off the breaker box and busied himself with the wiring. Tom counted off the minutes. Ten, nine, eight.... It was like a rocket launch, Gary thought, only it feels like it's my intestinal system that's being launched. When Tom got to two, the other man started putting the box back on, and on one, they walked out into the empty hall.

They were back in the elevator lobby when Tom suddenly said, "Damn, I forgot something underneath your credenza!" They went back to Gary's office, greeted Leigh and closed the door. Tom found the item, a wand of some kind he had used when checking the office for bugs.

As they left the TLP grounds past Guard Shack Number Three, Gary said goodnight to the guard on duty. Recognizing him, the man said, "Hey, good night Dr. Long. We've had an entertaining afternoon here. Some nut keeps driving back and forth in a van."

Gary looked over at Tom and said, "Gee, I wonder what that's all about?" Then he gunned the engine and made their escape onto the street.

They drove back to the Best Western and went to a room, where Cox was waiting for them. Cox and Tom immediately began to discuss tactics, while Gary, still shaking from nerves, sat on the bed with his head in his hands. He looked through his fingers at the other men. They didn't seem upset by the day's events at all.

After a few minutes, Cox said, "We couldn't get a good signal, Gary. We're going to have to use the backpack on you and the briefcase recorder. You'll have to get here early in the morning to put it on."

Gary was still shaking when he got home. Mark ran to him and hugged him around the waist. Gary tried his best to pull himself out of his self-absorption and respond with his usual enthusiasm. But it was hard. Mark wanted to show him a new game he had learned on the computer. Gary looked plaintively at Jenna across the room.

"Daddy's extra tired tonight," she said. "Let's let him relax for a few minutes."

Relax. Fat chance. He'd just had the most nerve-wracking day of this whole nerve-wracking experience, and at the end of it, he'd been told the day of the meeting would be even worse. Instead of being able to concentrate on the meeting and rely on the FBI to handle the taping, he was going to be strapped up like a mountain climber. Every move he made would have to be carefully done to make sure he didn't reveal the equipment.

"The boys have already eaten," Jenna said. "I've fixed some of the pork barbeque." It was one of his favorites, but tonight the mere thought of it put his stomach in an uproar. In the end, he wound up eating some leftover tomato soup and crackers. Then he made a desultory attempt to show interest in Mark's computer game. Justin kept interrupting his brother's explanations of how it worked, and Gary found himself snapping at the older boy.

"Let *him* show me," he barked, instantly regretting it.

Then he went upstairs and lay down on the bed. Jenna got the boys tucked in for the night and tiptoed into the bedroom, not wanting to wake him if he was asleep. He wasn't, and so she came over to the bed and lay down beside him while he recounted the events of the day.

"The meeting is Thursday," he said. "If I can just get through that..."

"Do you think the deal will get done at this meeting?"

"Yeah, I do. With Hargiss there, and Hamanaka, there should be a lot of momentum to make it happen."

"I hope so," she murmured. "Then maybe this nightmare will be over."

"It'd better be," he said, stroking her hair. "I don't think I can take any more."

That night, he had a crazy, disjointed dream in which he was at the Chemical Club taping Howard while Tully was taping him and the FBI was taping Tully and the Japanese were taping everyone.

CHAPTER 75

On Monday morning, Gary was at his desk, deep in preparation for the Thursday meeting. He had told Leigh to hold his calls, but she knocked on the door and came in when he beckoned.

"I thought you might want to take this call," she said. "It's a Mr. Park, from Korea. He says it's very important."

Park? That was Kim Jungwoo's assistant, from Daehan. Why would he be calling? It couldn't be a customer trick call. Park never called him for that, had never called him at all. "I'll take it," he said, waiting for Leigh to leave the room before he picked up.

"Dr. Long," Park began, "I am calling from Chicago. I would like to meet with you before the meeting on Thursday."

What is this all about? Gary wondered. It would never do to have Park wandering around TLP while everyone was preparing for the meeting. If he and Gary were to get together, it meant Gary would have to meet him somewhere else.

Gary told him he thought it would be okay, but he needed to talk to Howard first. He also needed to talk to Cox.

Howard enthusiastically approved the idea, even though he was as puzzled as Gary as to what Park could want. Then Gary called Cox. "We can set it up in Chicago," Cox said. "Let's do it Wednesday afternoon."

"No way," Gary said. Wednesday is definitely out. I'll be up to my ass here trying to get ready for Thursday. It has to be tomorrow morning. That's the only time I can squeeze in."

Cox started to argue, but Gary cut him off. "You jumped all over me when I put off the trip to Japan," he said. "You said you were in a hurry. Now you don't like it when I move too fast. Deal with it. The meeting's tomorrow morning."

"You're getting to be a fucking pain in the ass," Cox said.

"Are you going to hit me with your briefcase again?" Gary snapped.

"I apologized for that," Cox said coldly, "but don't provoke me or I might." Then he backed off his anger. "All right, set it up for the Marriott Hotel on Rush Street," he said.

When Gary hung up, he realized he had forgotten to turn his recorder off between his calls to Howard and Cox. That night, he carefully put the tape in a cabinet in the family room, where he was building a library of the copies he was making.

The next morning, Gary flew to Chicago and met Cox and Tom at the hotel an hour before the meeting time. They took him up to the room they had set up and showed him the layout.

The room had two chairs and a table with a lamp between them. Tom told Gary to have Park sit in the seat on the left as he was facing the chairs because that's where the camera was set up. The plan was for Gary to meet Park in the lobby and bring him up to the room.

"We don't want you to talk business on the way up," Cox said. "Save it for the camera."

Gary found Park in the lobby and made small talk in the elevator on the way up. When they entered the room, the door didn't close immediately, and when Gary turned to pull it shut, Park quickly crossed the room and started to sit in the wrong chair. Turning from the door, Gary instantly realized what was happening. He bounded across the room and literally grabbed the chair out from under him as he started to sit down, catching the confused Korean before he landed on the floor. In the process he nearly knocked the lamp off the table, catching it just before it fell. It was like a third-rate sitcom. "No, no, Mr. Park, you should sit over there," Gary panted, pointing to the other chair.

Park looked perplexed. "This one's no good, it's broken. It's better you sit on this other chair," Gary babbled. Park un-rumpled his suit from the near fall and sat down in the proper chair.

"Now then, what do you have in mind?" Gary asked, straightening the lamp.

Park cleared his throat and began, "With the meeting coming up with Mr. Hargiss and Mr. Hamanaka," he began. Then he paused, as if trying to choose the English words carefully, "I can't tell you enough that you TLP need to be more flexible. Even though your plant capacity is 113,000 metric tons, and we've offered you the chance to produce fifty-four, they realize you won't go along with that, but they're not going to agree to 113,000. It is very important that Mr. Hargiss comes to a level with Mr. Hamanaka that both can agree to, because if not, the deal will never get done."

The point of Park's trip was now clear to Gary, at least in part. Daehan Hwa-Hak would be represented at the meeting by Kim Jungwoo. With his poor English and low status as the smallest of the four producers, Kim would have no real opportunity to influence the negotiation. But the entire future of Daehan depended on its outcome. The low prices were killing them; they couldn't hold out much longer. Perhaps Kim had decided on his own to send the message, or perhaps he and Numata had put it together jointly. Either way, Park's mission was to serve as an early warning device. Park could have said the same thing over the phone from Seoul, but by going to the expense and trouble of sending him all the way to Chicago, Kim or Numata or both of them underscored the importance of the point, and made it perfectly clear that this would be the last chance.

When the meeting was over, Gary escorted Park to the lobby, and watched as the Korean got into a taxicab and drove away. Then he headed back to the eighth floor and knocked on the door of the room next to the one where he and Park had met.

When Gary walked into the room, it looked like a recording studio: wires were running everywhere, hooked up to all kinds of tape machines and control panels. Three men and a woman were in the room, gathering up the equipment. They looked like they'd just been fired.

"It's a fucking disaster," Cox snarled. "When you grabbed for the chair, you hit the lamp and knocked the microphone out. We didn't get a goddamn bit of audio. All we've got is a silent movie of some idiot Korean sitting in a chair with his lips flapping. Why in hell did you have to do that?" he asked angrily.

"I'm sorry," Gary said. "He was going to sit in the wrong chair."

"Well, you should have stopped him before he got to the wrong fucking chair," Cox replied in a whiny, sarcastic tone.

"It wouldn't have happened if we'd had time to set the room up right," the woman said. She seemed a little embarrassed by Cox's tirade, and probably thought she was helping Gary. But her remarks only set Cox off again.

"Fucking A," he said. "And we'd have had time if you'd set the meeting for tomorrow, like I told you to."

Gary was so furious he just stalked out of the room and caught a taxicab to Meigs Field, where the King Air was waiting for him. He didn't even bother to tell Cox he'd taped the whole conversation with Park on his pocket recorder. But he did resolve to tape the meeting in Steuben for himself, too If the FBI's fancy equipment failed on that day too, he couldn't afford to lose the taped record of the event he was sure would be the climax to his whole ordeal.

CHAPTER 76

On Thursday morning, Gary arrived at the Best Western at 6:00. He had awakened from a fitful sleep at about 4:30 and wandered around the house until it was time to leave. Cox and Tom greeted him and began to shave his chest and back while they chatted with him. The whole process took about an hour, and Gary listened to his final instructions from Cox. "Make sure if you leave the room you take the briefcase with you. You can't leave it behind or that tape will be useless to us." The law was clear on that point: at least one of the people being recorded had to know it was happening.

There was a note on Gary's desk when he got there. It was from Howard. "Come to my office as soon as you get in," it read.

As he neared Howard's office, he spotted Andrew Tully heading in the same direction, escorting a strikingly beautiful Oriental woman. He paused at the door, and as he suspected, Tully and the woman had the same destination.

Howard and G.T. were waiting for them. Both of them got big eyes at the sight of the woman.

"Guys, this is Koken Saburo," Tully said. "International actress. Fluent in Japanese, Chinese, Korean and a dozen other languages you don't care about."

As soon as he heard the woman's name, Gary almost laughed out loud. "You're Japanese?" he asked her, smiling.

"Yes, I am," she said, sweetly. "I was born and raised in Osaka, but I live in Los Angeles now."

"How wonderful," he said, still straining to hold back the urge to chuckle. So much for Howard's bigoted blanket condemnation of Japanese women.

Howard and G.T. recovered their composure, and the group sat down.

"We'll have a full written English transcript of the tapes by tomorrow," Tully said. "But you wanted a summary before the meeting. Koken, tell them what you learned from the tapes."

Koken opened a small notebook and began to speak. "There is not too much," she said. "Mr. Kim made one phone call to San Francisco, to a Mr. Park. They talked about the meeting in very general terms. Mr. Park said he had done everything he could with Dr. Long, whom he found quite non-committal and a little strange."

"That's an understatement," G.T. snorted.

Koken blushed.

"Please, go on," Howard said.

"Mr. Kim said he certainly hoped a deal would get done, because things were really getting desperate. Mr. Park asked him what number he would accept, and Mr. Kim said he would have to accept whatever he could get. He hoped it would not be less than twenty-five. I'm sorry," she said, blushing again, "I do not know twenty-five what."

"That's all right," Gary said. "We know what he meant."

"From Mr. Song and Mr. Bai," Koken continued, "I have nothing, really. Mr. Bai came to Mr. Song's room and asked him if he wanted to talk, and Mr. Bai said 'Yes,' and then they went outside."

"That figures," Tully said. "A Chinaman would assume every room he's in is bugged."

"When they got back to their rooms, Mr. Song went straight to bed. Mr. Bai watched a movie."

"*Prison Love Doll*," Tully said, consulting some papers, "starring Wendy Whoppers. Perhaps he was boning up on American penal institutions."

Howard and G.T. hooted; even Gary broke into a broad grin. Koken was really blushing now.

"Tell me, Koken," G.T. asked, still chortling, "did you hear any unusual sounds on the tape during the movie?"

"No, I'm afraid not, " she said, smiling herself. "I don't think the equipment...that is, the *recording* equipment, is that sensitive."

The men hooted again, and Howard said, "Damn it, Tully, get more sensitive equipment in that place!"

Tully shook his head. "There *is* no more sensitive equipment," he said proudly. "I had the whole damn system upgraded just for this event."

"How about the two Japanese men?" Gary asked.

"Mr. Numata and Mr. Hamanaka met for about half an hour in Mr. Hamanaka's room. They discussed many numbers, and seemed to be using a calculator a lot. At the end, one of them said 'We can give them another nine then,' and the other one said, 'Yes, because there's ten points in the '93 total over '92, but don't mention it because they may not think of it.' Does that make sense to you?"

"Oh, yes," G.T. said. "It makes lots of sense."

As Tully escorted the lovely Miss Saburo down the hall, Howard and G.T. hung in the doorway.

"I don't care which way her slit is slanted," G.T. said. " I wouldn't kick her out of bed."

"I'd suck the slack in her pantyhose," Howard added, "just for the smell."

CHAPTER 77

At 10:15, the receptionist called to say that Gary's visitors had arrived. He shook hands with Numata, who reintroduced him to Mr. Hamanaka. Neither one was overly friendly. He escorted them to the conference room where Howard and G.T. joined them. Numata eyed G.T. suspiciously. Hamanaka looked G.T. squarely in the face as if sizing him up and said, "I am glad to meet you, Mr. G.T. We have been looking forward to this day."

"My father will be right with us," Howard said, dealing ashtrays out like cards on the table.

Leigh Curtis entered the room, escorting Song Dian-Nuan, Bai Ken-ren and Kim Jungwoo. There were bows and handshakes. Then William Hargiss walked in.

Gary introduced Hargiss to the other men, praising each of them in turn for his significant contribution to the industry. He had rehearsed these lines carefully, after reading their biographies and company press releases. Bai's introduction was slightly shorter than Kim's, which was slightly shorter than Song's and Numata's. Hamanaka's was the longest and most flowery.

"Mr. Hargiss," Hamanaka said, "we are extremely pleased that you could work us into your very busy schedule so that we could come."

"The pleasure is all mine," Hargiss answered, graciously. "Please be seated."

He strode to the head of the table, as the others took their places in the purple chairs. "I want you all to know," he began, "how much we at Tamson-Long value good relationships with our competitors in the many product areas in which we operate. Our company has been in business since 1925, and I have been its chairman and CEO since 1965. Mr. Binghamton has been our President since 1969, and my son, Mr. Howard Hargiss, has worked alongside us since he joined the firm in 1978. Dr. Gary Long joined us three years ago, when we made a billion-dollar commitment to enter the field of biochemistry. Under his leadership, and Mr. Binghamton's, we built the largest artificial sweetener plant in the world, which I understand some of you have had the opportunity to see."

He paused and looked around the room. Everyone was sitting quietly, in respectful attention. "As I said," he continued, "we value good relationships with our competitors, and that is why we have so earnestly sought to create an association of artificial sweetener producers.

"We have a motto here. Not for public consumption, mind you, but something each of us in this room believes in fervently: 'The competitor is our friend. The customer is our enemy.'"

He looked around the room, passing over each face quickly until he got to Hamanaka. "Mr. Hamanaka," he said. "Perhaps you would like to say a few words."

Hamanaka rose from his chair as Hargiss sat down. He and William are of an age, Gary thought, the only ones in the room who remember Pearl Harbor. They were grown men by the time the atomic bomb had dropped on Hiroshima. The whole Cold War had come and gone between then and now, and America and Japan had learned to deal with one another across conference tables instead of island battlefields. Had the hatred these two men must once have felt for the other's race subsided? Or had it simply moved to a new battlefield, less deadly, but just as intense? Howard hated the Japanese because he found their food and women unpalatable, at least until that morning. G.T. disliked them because of a novel he had read. But Hargiss must have had friends killed in the Pacific Theater. And Hamanaka had lived through the humiliation of defeat, seen his sacred Emperor bow down to General MacArthur. What hatreds lingered in their minds? And how would it affect what was going to happen today?

"Our companies," Hamanaka began, giving a small wave of his frail hand to include Song and Kim, "have been talking for almost a year now about an association. We all want it to happen. We all want to work together on an agreement that will allow the prices and volumes of our sweetener products to achieve mutually beneficial levels."

He turned to face Hargiss directly. "There is, I believe, only one, how do you say, stumbling block. And that is the unwillingness of Tamson-Long to accept a volume consistent with the world market demand and fair to the other companies. You say the customer is your enemy, and I understand the sense in which you mean that. But if you truly believe the competitor is your friend, then you must not insist on a market share that is unfair. That is no way to treat one's friends."

Everyone was impressed by the eloquence of Hamanaka's remarks. There was silence as each man wondered who would attempt to follow them. Only Gary was thinking something entirely different: that Hamanaka had just convicted himself of criminal price fixing.

Finally, it was G.T. who broke the silence. "What must be borne in mind," he began, "is that Tamson-Long is a unique company. Even though we're a public company, under Mr. Hargiss's leadership we're run like a private company. William, Howard and I make almost all the important corporate decisions. We don't allow ourselves to be hamstrung by our board of directors, our attorneys or anyone else. As a result, we move more quickly than any other large corporation in the world. We do things in a big way. That is our corporate culture, and it must be preserved. To do otherwise would be to rip the soul out of each of us, and everything we have built over the past thirty years."

Howard looked at G.T. with astonishment. He had given a whole speech without a single swear word, not even a grunt. Howard had known G.T. all his life. Never had he heard him talk like that.

Hamanaka looked down at the table and tapped his fingers together. "Well, in our company we are more structured. We have a lot more bureaucracy and don't make decisions as quickly. We are a more traditional company."

"We respect that," William Hargiss said. "Truly, we do. But G.T. is right. We know only one way to do business, and that is full speed ahead. We have invested heavily in our Sugere operations. We built as big a plant as we did so that even if our entry into the market resulted in lower prices, we could still make money. We are very satisfied with our Sugere business today and we can go long-term with it the way it is today."

"As a result of a streamlining effort we have just completed," G.T. added, unable to resist patting himself on the back, even if the Asians wouldn't understand, "we're now estimating our costs at under fifty cents a pound."

That was an overstatement, and Gary could sense the wheels turning inside their guests' heads as they looked at each other and attempted to convert the pounds to kilos. Would they believe it?

Howard, sensing the Asians were on the ropes, moved in to hit them again. "Yep, we're very satisfied with the Sugere market," he said. "If there's a way to expand the market, we'd be glad to do it, but we'll be happy as clams if the price stays right where it is."

The men began talking back and forth to one another, trying to decide what to say next, or perhaps simply trying to translate Howard's colloquialism. After a moment, Numata cleared his throat. "Perhaps so, Mr. Hargiss, but with higher price you would be happier than even more clams."

Howard smiled. "Yeah, I guess I would be," he said. "Gary," he continued, "what are the prices now?"

Gary had been as quiet as a mouse in a corner, his briefcase-recorder on the table in front of him. He pursed his lips and said, "Mmm, mid sixties, low seventies in some regions."

"Obviously," G.T. said, following up, "if it's a dollar, or ten dollars a pound, the higher the better. But we have to look at what's realistic and what volume we can sell. I'm personally familiar with the proposal you gave to us in January when Gary and Howard went to Japan. We can never live with something like that. We've got way too much invested in this business and we have a big advantage in raw material costs. As a result, we're committed to take our advantage to the market place. We are confident we can win in the long run."

"But as friends," Hargiss said, looking squarely at Hamanaka, "we will be more than happy to end the price war before any of you goes under. If there is a reasonable proposal on the table," he added.

Gary stole a look at Kim. He would be the first to go under; that was the meaning of Park's trip to Chicago. Kim sat rigid as a statue. He's literally scared stiff, Gary thought. Song Dian-Nuan and Bai Ken-ren didn't look much better. Their situation was different. Their factories produced whatever the government in Beijing told them to produce. But they would suffer great loss of face if they were told to pull the plug on their sweetener operations.

As for Nippon Kagaka, it could probably ride out the storm, picking up a share of the business left behind when the other two folded. But in the process, the cost would be astronomical.

Beads of perspiration showed on Hamanaka's forehead as he conversed quietly with Numata.

"We would still be interested in pursuing an association and working together on sweetener prices in the marketplace," he said eventually. "We can be more flexible on volumes. We are truly interested in pursuing this.

"Mr. Song? Mr. Kim?" Hamanaka said, turning to face the two, who were seated at the far end of the table. "Do you wish to proceed?" Then he said something in Japanese, which Gary presumed was a translation of his question. Song Dian-Nuan responded in Japanese, and Kim Jungwoo nodded eagerly, his rigid body relaxing just a little.

"Well," Howard said, not waiting for Hamanaka to confirm the obvious decision. "What do you think we can accomplish today? We've been Mickey-Mousing around for more than a year and it doesn't seem like we're making any progress. The real question is, what can we accomplish today?"

Numata picked up the gauntlet. "First, we think the 113,000 metric tons that TLP is pushing for is too much. We realize your plant is that size, but you made a mistake and built it too fast."

G.T. said, "Well," and stood up. He moved to a flip chart on an easel before continuing, "In order to understand that a little bit more, let's review where we are." He wrote all the companies' names on the left side of the sheet.

He then marked off three columns to the right of each name. He headed the columns "Capacity," "Tokyo," and "Final." He smiled a little as he wrote the last word. The implication was clear: TLP expected a final agreement today. Before the men left the room, that column would be filled in.

"As I recall from Howard's and Gary's report from the meeting in Mexico City," he then said, "the capacities were like this." He spoke each number as he wrote it down: "Nipon Kagaka – 100; New World – 74; Daehan – 40; TLP – 113." Does anybody disagree with these numbers?"

He paused and looked around the room. Bai Ken-ren said something to Kim Jungwoo, who nodded. No one objected to the numbers.

"Now, Mr. Numata," he said. "would you please give me the volumes you proposed in Tokyo?"

Numata squirmed. He was being asked to give numbers that had already been rejected, and he knew that as soon as he finished he was going to get a lecture from G.T. or Howard or William or all of them together. But there was no help for it.

Slowly, he said the numbers as G.T. wrote them down: "Nippon Kagaka – 73; New World – 53; Daehan – 28; TLP – 54."

G.T. stepped back from the flip chart. He put his hand to his chin and pretended to study the numbers as if he were looking at them for the first time. "Howard," he said, "does this all jibe with your memory?"

Howard snickered. "Yeah," he said, "that's what they said after we had to go out and wait in the hall."

Hamanaka gave Numata a puzzled look. Numata's report to him had not included that little detail, and it sounded like bad form to Hamanaka. If Numata had made Howard and Gary lose face by forcing them to leave the room, that was not smart negotiating or proper etiquette.

William leaned back in his chair. This is going very nicely, he thought.

G.T. wrote the word "Total" below the company names. Then, without any pretense that he had to do the addition, he wrote the numbers below each of the two columns: "327", "208".

Numata dropped his eyes and swallowed. He knew what was coming next.

"Gary," G.T. said, "what percent is two hundred eight of three twenty seven?"

"Sixty-three point six," Gary replied.

"Isn't that interesting?" G.T. mused. "Let's just see how that overall percentage compares with the individual percentages for each company.

Wouldn't that be interesting?"

On the chart next to Nippon Kagaka, he wrote "73%". "I can do that one in my head," he said. "Gary, what are the other percentages?"

Gary looked down at the yellow pad in front of him. Slowly, he read out the numbers. "New World – 72%. Daehan – 70%. TLP..." He paused for emphasis. "48%."

G.T. wrote each number beside the company name. He put the cap back on the marker and dropped it onto the little shelf on the easel. Then he stepped back to his place at the table and sat down.

"And you wonder," he said, "why we won't accept that deal."

Hamanaka spoke next, addressing himself to William Hargiss. "This meeting would not be taking place," he said, "if we were not prepared to adjust our proposal. But we do feel that the percentage granted to TLP should be lower than the others because you are new to the business, whereas we others have been in business for many years. We are prepared to offer you sixty-three thousand tons."

"Mr. Hamanaka," Hargiss began, "I know how important seniority is in your countries. As an old man myself, I often wish it were more highly honored here. But in this matter, it is not possible to consider that factor. TLP is the lowest cost producer. We're the only vertically integrated sweetener producer in the world. We have all the key components in-house – the media, the electricity, the steam from our co-gen plant. We can be profitable at lower prices than you can. That is simply the reality of the situation. TLP should have a larger, not a smaller, share of the market."

"Just take the media," G.T. said. "The stuff you pay for, we used to throw into the river as waste."

Hargiss took the floor again. "I believe you have two choices. You can continue to try to compete with us at low prices, at which we will be marginally profitable and you will be ruined. Or you can agree to a reasonable volume for us, in which case we will all make a lot of money. If you choose the first option, then our enemies, the customers, will be the winners and we will all be the losers, you Asian manufacturers most of all. If you choose the second option, then we friends here at this table will be the winners."

Hamanaka turned to Numata and they began talking earnestly, jotting down numbers on their pads. Gary craned his neck to see if he could understand what they were discussing, but he couldn't make anything out.

I think the time is right, he thought, to give them a little help.

"Excuse me," he said, standing in his place. "But it may be helpful at this point to consider the market size. In the Mexico, Paris and Tokyo meetings, and so far today, we have all been basing our calculations on a total market size of 208,000 tons, which is the 1992 figure. But the market is increasing, thanks principally to what we at TLP are doing through our promotional and sales efforts. I feel confident we can look forward to a 5% increase for 1993, which means we can deal from a base of 218,000 tons. That adds ten thousand tons to the total we can divide up." They had already been counting on that, Gary knew from Tully's tapes, but since they hadn't mentioned it, they were stuck. They had already committed to increasing TLP's share.

"Thank you, Dr. Long," Numata said sourly. He and Hamanaka resumed their private discussion. Presently, Numata looked over at Song Dian-Nuan and said something in Japanese. Song nodded. Then he spoke to Kim and the Korean nodded.

Numata stepped up to the flip chart and, referring to the yellow pad in his hand, wrote numbers in the column G.T. had headed "Final." Smart, Hargiss thought. By putting them on the sheet instead of just announcing them, they were signaling a final offer, not just a negotiating point. When Numata had finished writing, he stepped back and let everyone examine the numbers.

Nippon Kagaka – 70
New World – 50
Daehan – 26
TLP – 72

Howard suppressed a smile. He knew there would be an agreement today. Now it was just a question of how much more they could get. It was time to play the alpha card.

"Unless I am mistaken," he said. "We are still below the average as regards percent of capacity. But because we are all friends here, we could overlook that, if..." He paused and looked around the room, "...if we could get the full alpha for the next twelve months."

At that point the meeting broke down, with private conversations in three languages creating a hubbub Gary knew would yield nothing of value to the FBI. Hargiss got up from his chair and motioned Gary to a corner.

"Go over the liquid situation for me once more," he said.

"On a dry matter basis, we're selling a little over six thousand tons," Gary said softly.

"And that's an advantage over the others?"

"Absolutely. Daehan and New World are not in liquid sweetener at all, and as best I can calculate, Nippon Kagaka is doing less than a thousand tons.

Brad believes we can increase liquid as a share of our total production, too," he added.

"So our seventy-two thousand tons is really more like seventy-eight."

"Not bad, huh?"

"Not bad at all. Let's see how much of the alpha Howard can get."

"Remember," Gary said. "Alpha from now on may not be five percent because we'll be dealing with much higher prices."

Hargiss nodded.

When he returned to his seat, Hamanaka spoke. "The full alpha is too high," he said. "If it is five percent, it would put TLP way above their share of capacity. Nonetheless, we do not want to be unfriendly, even though we have already given much in this meeting. We propose that TLP get half of the 1994 alpha, and we others will divide the other half."

"No," Howard said. "That's not enough...." He started to amplify his point, but his father cut him off.

"Actually," he said, speaking directly to Hamanaka, "I think that is a fair offer. I would propose, however, that we get the first half. That is, we would get the first two and a half points of increase, and you all would get everything above that. If the alpha is greater than 5%, you would come out better that way."

Gary did some quick figuring in his head. The two and a half points was almost five and a half thousand tons. That plus the liquid factor put their total volume allotment at eighty-three and a half, right where G.T. wanted it in the first place.

"There is risk for us," Hamanaka said. "but I will agree, if Mr. Song and Mr. Kim agree."

Kim nodded. Song said something in Japanese to Hamanaka. They're discussing how to split their share of the alpha, Gary thought. Then Song cleared his throat and said, "I agree."

William Hargiss and Sadaaki Hamanaka stood up. Hamanaka bowed, and Hargiss returned the custom. Then they shook hands. Gary reached across the table and shook hands with Numata, and immediately everyone was shaking hands and bowing.

Eventually, the room quieted, and Song Dian-Nuan spoke up. "Now that we have agreed," he said, "how we going to monitor? How we going to make sure everyone sells this amount and no more?"

Howard stood up. "What we do with vitamins is we've got monthly sheets," he began. Since he didn't have a copy, he drew one on a fresh sheed of the flip chart. After he finished, he talked about how it worked and concluded, "This is really something we don't have to decide here. It should be decided at another meeting, by the people that will be handling the details. But I recommend that we call the numbers in each month. Why don't we call them in to you, Sumiko?"

Sumiko looked a little pale. He did not see himself as a clerk. "Maybe you should call them in to my assistant, Masahiko Yamasaki," he suggested.

"Fine, we will call them in to Masahiko. Then the next day after the end of the month Masahiko puts them on a sheet starting what, let's say July first, and he sends the sheets to everybody. If after four or five months it looks like one is selling too much and another too little, you start adjusting. One sells less and lets the other catch up. At the end of the year, if someone is really out of whack, say four or five thousand tons off, the one who sold too much has to buy from the one who sold too little."

"If everybody really does what he's supposed to, it should never happen. But that would be hypothetically what would happen," Howard finished.

"But," Song Dian-Nuan objected, "we are concerned about how can you trust numbers people report? Someone may report five thousand tons, but who to know if number is correct?"

It was the obvious question, and Howard had an answer. "What we do in citric is we have an auditor, a Swiss company that goes through the exact numbers in everybody's books. You know, to confirm what you said was what you really sold. We could do something like that."

He waited for a reaction and then plunged ahead. "The problem is that then you would have an outside auditor coming in."

Numata agreed that it would be a problem for them, too. Howard continued, "The Swiss auditor was demanded by the European Citric Acid Manufacturers Association, which is the group dealing on prices for citric additives. We went along, but I think it's cleaner not to have an outside auditor unless we have to, because it does raise some eyebrows within the company. Another thing we could do is use our own auditors, and have them write a separate report on how much sweetener was sold, and every company could do the same: that way there's not so many red flags popping up."

A quick round of discussion followed with everyone agreeing.

"Well, gentlemen," William said finally, "we have accomplished a great deal. I do believe, however, that we are somewhat late for lunch. We have an excellent menu planned for you upstairs, and then you will all have plenty of time to make your airport connections."

Amid much bowing and handshaking, the men gathered their papers and began moving out of the room, G.T. leading the way to the elevators. Gary hung back, and so did Hargiss.

"Gary," the old man said with great sincerity, almost fatherly, "I know you have had some misgivings about our practice of price and volume negotiation. But I am convinced that regardless of what the law says, this sort of price fixing is a good thing. I've put together half a dozen of these deals now and this one has the most potential of all. This will be huge, Gary, for all of us, in ways I hope you will come to understand more and more as time goes on."

"It was a very successful meeting," Gary said sincerely. In ways *you* will come to understand more and more as time goes on, he thought, his eyes falling to the briefcase in front of him.

After the luncheon, Gary, G.T. and Howard gathered in Howard's office, grinning like hyenas. William stuck his head in the door. "Good job, boys," he said.

How odd all this is, Gary thought. I am part of a team that has just scored a huge victory. Everyone is overjoyed. So am I, but for very different reasons. It's bizarre.

G.T. produced a bottle of French champagne, and poured it out into three plastic cups. "To Sugere," he toasted, and they all raised their glasses.

At that moment, part of Gary wished price fixing were legal, and he could really feel like a member of the team. But the rest of him just wanted to get out of there, get out of the office, meet Cox and Tom at the Holiday Inn and get the oppressive backpack off. He hoped to hell he never had to put it back on.

This has to be it, he thought, as he drove to the motel. Everyone from the very top on down is completely and thoroughly incriminated by this tape. The end game is in sight.

CHAPTER 78

Tom unwired Gary from the backpack while Cox listened to the tape from the machine. When Cox heard Hargiss's opening remarks, he gave out a low whistle. When he heard Hamanaka say the words "prices and volumes," he absolutely whooped. "Gotcha, you Japanese crook," he exclaimed, clapping his hands together. Tom looked at Gary and grinned.

The cumbersome backpack off, Gary redressed himself. It felt good to be rid of the dead weight of the machine, and, from Cox's reaction to the tape, his confidence that his days of taping might actually be over grew. He left his jacket off and stretched out on one of the two double beds, feeling the tension of the past several days draining from his body. Cox sat at the table, hunched over the recorder, listening intently. Whenever he heard someone make an incriminating remark, he would clench his fist and raise it into the air, exclaiming, "All right!" or "Yes!"

This is the real victory celebration, Gary thought. William, Howard and G.T. all believe they won the game today, but they didn't have a clue this game even existed. He looked at Cox, whose joy could not have been more obvious. No matter what problems I've had with this guy, Gary thought, they were probably just the inevitable result of the psychological pressure cooker we've both been in. He was prepared to concede that Cox was not a bad person. He was just doing his job. And for all the anguish Gary had suffered, it had paid off. Gary had done the work, solved the equation, hit the...

"Home run!" Cox almost shouted when he heard Hargiss explain Hamanaka's two choices. "You're going to jail, you price-fixing son of a bitch."

Cox stopped the tape and turned to face Gary. "Gary, this is the stuff," he said. "This is what it takes for us to get the resources we need to make this a real ball buster."

He stood up and reached into his pocket, pulling out a handful of change. "Tom," he said. "I need a Coke. Get one for yourself. Gary, you want one?"

"Sure," Gary said.

Tom returned with the cans. They popped the tops, and Cox raised his in the air. "We win!" he cried.

"Are we ready to go to the grand jury?" Gary asked.

Cox took a swallow of his Coke.

"Nah," he said. "We've got a lot to do yet."

Gary's heart sank. "What do you mean?" he asked, hoping the "we" didn't include him.

"Two things," Cox said. "We need some videotape. We need to have something to show the grand jury, so they can see the faces, see how cold and calculating these guys are. The other thing is, we need to have evidence that the deal is actually being implemented. I want to show it in operation for at least a year."

Another year! Another year of being a furtive rat. Tears started to well in Gary's eyes, and he fought to keep them back.

"What are you going to do?" he snapped, his voice rising in anger, "strap a camera to my head for a year, turn me into a Gary cam?"

Cox and Tom looked at each other and shook their heads with condescending grins.

"Nah," Tom said, "that doesn't work."

"Are there going to be meetings?" Cox asked. "You know, meetings to monitor how things are going on the agreement?"

"Listen to the rest of the tape," Gary answered sourly. "Yeah, there'll be meetings. Probably quarterly."

"Terrific. Try to get them in the U.S., at, like, hotels or someplace. Then we can wire the room for video, like we did Tuesday in Chicago. Only this time, don't fuck it up and knock over the equipment."

As he drove home, Gary felt more depressed than he could ever remember. Twice he reached for the car phone to call Jenna, but he was afraid he would break into tears at the sound of her voice. She had counted on this meeting at least as much as he had. She had helped him devise the strategy that had clinched the agreement. He almost couldn't bear to tell her that in spite of their brilliant plan, they were trapped into another year of anguish. At any moment, he could commit the slip that would plunge them into disaster. He could blow his cover, get caught with his tape recorder running. The FBI could learn about the bonuses and withdraw his immunity. So many bad things could happen, and even if they didn't, he wasn't sure he could keep his sanity with all the pressure.

He watched the light poles slide by. Don't go there, he told himself. Don't let the depression control you. He willed himself away from morbid ideas by focusing his mind on Jenna. By the time he pulled into the driveway, he had gotten a semblance of control over himself.

The boys were helping feed the horses with Donnie Bradford, the stable hand Gary had hired. Jenna was waiting for him in the kitchen. "Well," she said, "how did it go?"

He took a deep breath and forced a smile. "I've got good news and bad news," he said.

I will be strong, she said to herself. I will not fail him. She didn't know what the bad news was, but she could guess. At least there was good news, too. She went to the refrigerator and poured them both a glass of lemonade. "Just start from the beginning and tell me about the whole day."

They sat down at the breakfast table and he started talking. He told her about getting his body shaved so the backpack tape wouldn't rip out his chest hair. She laughed with him when he told her about Koken Samuro. He went through the meeting, detail by detail, and recounted the champagne celebration in Howard's office.

When he finally got to the part where he was driving away from TLP, she knew her sad guess about the bad news was right. There was nothing left that could go wrong except his meeting with the FBI. When he told her it was going to be another year, she tried to hold back the tears, but she didn't quite succeed. Within seconds, they were both crying. He got up from the table and turned away from her. She got up and came around the table to stand behind him. She reached her arms around his waist and pressed her face to his back, staining his shirt with her tears. After a few minutes, she released him and walked across the kitchen. She tore some paper towels from the roll, and then tore what she had in half. She dried her eyes with one half and handed him the other.

She looked out the window. The boys were still in the stable. "I've got some good news," she said softly.

"What's that?" he asked, wadding the paper towel in his hands.

She reached over to the counter and held up a manila envelope. "It's from Bobby."

"Is it the release?" he asked, eagerly. If there was anything that could distract him from his depression, it would be for her first husband to have finally signed the consent agreement that would allow him to adopt Justin and Mark.

"Signed, sealed and notarized," she said, smiling just a little. His enthusiasm at the news pleased her immensely. "Even a little conciliatory note."

"Oh, darling, that's fantastic," he said. In a flash, he realized what he really wanted. More than all the money in the bank, more than the chance to reform TLP, more than the satisfaction of helping put crooks in jail, he wanted this family.

"Where are Justin and Mark?" he asked.

"In the stable, with Donnie."

"Let's go," he almost shouted, heading for the door. On the porch, he grabbed his wife by the hand and they ran together across the yard to the stable.

CHAPTER 79

Dr. Walter Harrison's business card simply said "Psychologist" and listed an address and a phone number in Chicago. In fact, he worked for the profiling department of the FBI. He helped agents throughout the Midwest with their own problems; he helped them figure out what the bad guys were thinking; he helped them get what they wanted out of witnesses.

The morning after the price fixing meeting, Sid Cox called Harrison. Without mentioning any names of people or companies, they spent almost an hour talking about Gary Long. Later that same day, Harrison called him back.

"Mr. Cox," he said, "you've got a guy here who needs to please. He wants to feel like he's doing something that's important and that he's important to you. Have you got a picture of his family?"

"Um, I may, yeah, he sent me a Christmas card with a family picture," Cox responded.

"Good, that'll work just fine. Put that picture in your wallet. Look for an appropriate moment to show it to him. Tell him you think of him as family. Make him feel like you're his friend, more than just a co-worker. He'll begin to think of you as a friend, not a handler."

"Any thoughts on his suicide and depression talk?"

"Well, if he's talking about it, there's probably not much of a chance he'll do it. Just try to be his friend, talk to him about it, reason with him. I'm pretty confident you can get through this without incident."

On Tuesday, Cox had an opportunity to put Dr. Harrison's idea to the test. He and Gary met after work at the Comfort Inn, and Cox had a long list of tasks for Gary. He wanted the flip charts from the meeting. He wanted copies of all the production sheets from the citric acid and vitamin additive price fixing operations, and the Sugere production sheet as soon as it was done. He wanted Gary to lure Howard into a conversation about price fixing and why they did it; if other companies behaved like TLP. He wanted to make sure Gary understood how the price and volume monitoring meetings had to be set up in order for the FBI to videotape them.

Gary began the meeting feeling really good. He was at his desk early, meeting with Brad Redfoot to get the price increase strategy in motion. Then he ducked out at noon to meet with Jenna and Will Barron, the lawyer handling the adoption case. That meeting went well; Barron was confident the boys would be his within a few weeks.

But the longer Cox talked, the worse Gary began to feel. Cox was doing his best to be friendly in the way he presented his agenda, but to Gary, it was still just a list of orders. He found himself saying, "yes, sir" several times, and wondering why he, a PhD with a distinguished business resume, on track to be the president of a major corporation, felt he had to call this rumpled gumshoe "sir."

Finally, he just blurted out, "I'm going to see a doctor regardless of this case or not."

Cox's antennae went up. Be his friend, he thought. Be his friend. "Why, Gary? Tell me why."

Gary stood up and looked out the hotel window. The room faced the street, across which was the mall, and Gary's eyes focused on the Radio Shack sign. It's time, he thought, and with a much-practiced air of nonchalance, he put his hand in his pocket and turned the recorder on.

"Because I'm worried about my sanity," he said, turning to face Cox. "Please tell me I can do it. Please tell me I can consult a psychologist to help me deal with all this pressure."

"No, you can't," Cox said, "because I'm really worried about what will happen to you if you do. I just don't see how you can do it without running a huge risk of blowing everything away, everything you've worked so hard on since you and Jenna first talked to me." That was good, he thought, bringing Jenna into it. "If you go to a doctor, just like I told you with a lawyer, like I said back in November, William Hargiss will find out. You don't know how hard we've worked to protect you all these months."

"But you've got to have people in the FBI who could help me."

Yeah, we do, Cox thought, but I can't trust them, either. He thought about how guarded he had been in describing the case to Dr. Harrison. William Hargiss *was* amazingly well connected. He couldn't afford a misstep now. "Gary, I'm sorry," he said, "there's nobody."

"I just don't know if I can go on," Gary said.

Cox looked at the crestfallen face of his witness. "You know, Gary," he said. "I'm your friend. I care about you. But I have to answer to people on up the line. If you bail out now, you'll get prosecuted. I'd never forgive myself if I let you do that. Your best salvation is to get the evidence as quickly as you can and then walk away clean."

"I don't believe you," Gary said. "All you care about is this stupid case. You don't give a damn if I live or die."

Cox couldn't have had a better line delivered from a Hollywood script. He reached in his back pocket, took out his wallet and opened it up to the cellophane picture section where a trimmed Christmas picture of Gary, Jenna, Justin and Mark was inserted on top of Cox's Blockbuster card.

"Gary, that's not true, I think of you guys like family. I really want all this to work out."

Gary stared at the wallet and then back at Cox. It was hard to argue any more, so he just let it drop, got up, mumbled goodbye and headed for home.

The next night, Gary found his opportunity to talk to Howard. Gary had stayed late to finish working on his board report. As he stuffed the report into his briefcase, Howard appeared in the doorway. "Hey, Doogie, late night, huh?"

"Yeah, I'm trying to get the board report finished. You?"

"Nah, I've got that shit done. I'm hanging out here waiting for a call from Keddy. He's down in St. Louis meeting with some other folks that make some stupid herbicide."

Gary felt for the switch in his pocket and turned it on. "Umm, does Killer have some things working like us, or is he close to getting a deal on something?"

"Well, it looks like it might be positive. We're already working with 'em on another product, so it shouldn't take too much to get an agreement."

Gary let the conversation drop for a minute while he thought about the best way to get the information Cox wanted. "Do you ever feel bad about fixing prices?"

A deep furrow appeared on Howard's face. "Do I what?.... Jeez, you sound like a character on *Mr. Rogers Neighborhood*. What the fuck are you talking about?"

Gary struggled to recover. "Well, you know, it seems like we do this in an awful lot of areas. It is against the law isn't it?"

"Well Doogie, let me explain something to you. First of all, how many people work in your plants now?"

Gary thought for a minute. "Um, let's see, I guess around three hundred fifty."

"Well, those three hundred and fifty people didn't have a job in this company two years ago, because all the product was being made by one of our overseas competitors. Why don't you ask them how they feel about price fixing?"

Gary listened attentively while Howard gathered steam.

"If you think for one minute those fuckin' Chinks haven't been working together on sweetener prices for the last ten years, you're outta your frigging mind. Take a look at what's happened to the price over the previous years before we entered the market. We did. That's one of the reasons we talked to you in the first place – we knew the market was rigged. Let's take a look at who's been hurt by our entry into the market. Is it the consumers? Well, we know the fucking answer to that one, don't we, Doogie?

"Two years ago they'd never paid less than a dollar for artificial sweetener since the product was first introduced fifteen years ago, now they're paying seventy-five cents, only a little more than half what they were paying when we started to ramp up production. I guess they haven't been hurt. How about the U.S. Government? Well, they're collecting taxes on three hundred and fifty employees that probably weren't working before we hired them. They're also getting a lower balance of trade deficit since we're exporting, and we've put four hundred million dollars into the local economy buying supplies and paying workers to build our plants. Now we're paying real estate taxes on that plant to the local schools. The state's getting all of that fucking unemployment tax we have to pay, plus we've imported about forty people here with high incomes.

"You know what, it may be against the law, but if it is, it's a stupid fucking law. No one in his right mind could argue with what we've done. Besides, we're not price fixing, just trying to come to terms with our competitors on the volumes we can produce." Howard smirked.

"If it's such a good thing, why isn't everyone in the country doing it?"

"Because they're idiots. Look, we've got to recover the money we spent to built this plant. We're not trying to make a killing at this, only a fair return. If everyone did it, we'd have the strongest fucking country in the world. Right now the Japs are taking over first place, and I guess maybe they do a little price fixing," Howard said in a mocking voice.

"So does everyone we approach in all of our product lines go along?"

"Eventually, the smart ones do. Some don't, you know, mostly big companies, but a lot of the small ones eventually have to or else they'll get driven out of business. McLaughlin was pretty big, and they wouldn't play ball, and now they're out of business."

"Well, I can see that the consumers have had it pretty good up till now, but what happens when we get the volumes established?"

"Then they pay the market price, a fair price that lets us recoup our sunk capital costs. The price probably won't ever get above a buck fifty. That's where it was headed when we stepped in. The only people that suffer are those slanty-eyed little Orientals. Fuck them, anyway."

Gary thought Howard's rationale was pretty interesting. He took the tape home, made his copy and put it into the cabinet in the family room. The next morning, he met Cox in his car in the Ramada parking lot. He handed the original tape to Cox. As Cox listened, a frown began to grow on his face. When it was finished, he looked out the window of the car. "Gary, you've got to get rid of that tape. Take it home and put it in the garbage, throw it out of the car, burn it up, I don't care, but get rid of it."

Gary was astounded; nothing said in the tape had contradicted anything he had told Cox. Why did he want him to get rid of any tapes? Gary decided to ask him that exact question.

"Because it doesn't help the case," he said. "If that tape exists, then eventually TLP's lawyers will get it, and they'll use it in front of the jury to show they're not really bad guys, they're trying to provide jobs for people and pump money into the economy. Once I have it, I've got to send it to Thompson, and he's got to send it to Rasmussen, and then it's part of the case. Believe me, it's a whole lot easier to get rid of it now, when only you and I know about it."

"But if saying that helps them, won't they just put Howard on the stand and have him say those things anyway?" Gary asked.

"Maybe they will, and maybe they won't, but even if they do, it won't have nearly the impact after the fact. The jury will think they're just trying to justify their actions. But if they can show that this stuff was their motivation all along, when they weren't even in any trouble, that'll carry a lot more weight. A lot more.

"We've got to win this case, Gary. That's the only way you get to take over TLP and run it right, and the only way I get the hell out of Steuben, and get rid of these stupid, petty nigger drug crimes that take up most of my time. I know what's important, so please work with me on this."

Gary shrugged his shoulders, said "Okay," and took the tape back from Cox's outstretched hand. As he drove toward Wonanonly, he clicked his pocket recorder onto replay just to make sure he had gotten everything Cox had said on tape. When he got home, he put both Howard's tape and Cox's in the cabinet. Taping the FBI is no harder than taping anyone else, he thought. It's an insurance policy. For all he knew Cox could get bought off and some of the key tapes would disappear, leaving him in a mess. Taping his conversations with Cox would be his guarantee that the FBI took care of him. If not, he would release the tapes himself.

He definitely wasn't going to take any chances from here on out. He'd tape everything and everybody and then sort out what was important and what wasn't later. He also decided he had become so busy that he would no longer allow himself to be at Cox's beck and call. Cox was going to have to work on his schedule. If he could get what he needed or wanted without too much of a hassle, then he would gladly do so, but the days of playing gofer were over.

I can get through the year this way, he thought, and for the first time in a long time, he felt like he was in charge of this life again.

CHAPTER 80

When he walked out of Jim Thompson's office in Indianapolis a few days later, Sid Cox was on top of the world. The tapes of the price-fixing agreement were a big hit with Thompson and Rasmussen, and finally won Thompson over on a point Cox had been arguing for months. Thompson was sending another man to Steuben, to take over the routine work of the office, freeing up Cox to spend virtually full time on the TLP case.

Rasmussen was confident that once he had some videotape and evidence that the price-fixing agreement was actually being implemented, he could win the case. "As I see it now," he had said, "we'll win huge fines from both TLP and Nippon Kagaka, and we'll convict Hamanaka, Numata, both Hargisses, Binghamton, and probably that guy Keddy and the one they fired, Anthony."

"What about New World and Daehan?" Thompson had asked.

"I don't think we'll go after them," Rasmussen had said. "Dealing with the Chinese is too sticky to be worth it, and I'm not sure I can ever prove the Korean guy understood enough of what was being said to convict him."

"Then the whole case depends on how Long holds up on the witness stand," Thompson had said. "Sid, what's your judgment?"

"What can they do to him?" Cox had asked. "Everything he'll testify to will be on tape."

"All the same," Rasmussen had responded, "they'll try hard to discredit him, and people who rat on their friends are notoriously unsympathetic. Besides, we've got an inconclusive polygraph on the guy."

"Well, let's at least take care of that," Thompson had replied. "Sid, schedule him for a retest."

Cox said he would, and asked for a different technician this time. He didn't relish having to coax Gary into repeating the test, but that was a minor downer compared to the victory he had won in getting an assistant.

I was right all along, he said to himself. It was a beautiful June day in Indianapolis. Maybe, he thought, I can be someplace warm by winter. No, it wouldn't go that fast. The next winter, maybe.

Gary and Brad Redfoot were reviewing the Sugere sales reports. Since the agreement, they had raised prices a dime, and Gary had been concerned that sales might tail off as the price went up.

Brad didn't think so. "The word is starting to get out on the street," he said, "that prices are going to go up for the next six months to a year. That expectation will keep the buyers anxious to keep their inventories up, because they'll know that each order will likely be at a higher price."

"Well, we need to make sure we don't hit a stone wall at some point," Gary said.

"I don't think we'll have much of a problem unless we get over at least a buck twenty," Redfoot said. "As long as sugar is at seven cents, that means we're a bargain up to a buck forty, and the margins for sugar are low enough, they can't drop much. Unless Nippon Kagaka doesn't follow our price lead, I think we'll be safe."

"They'll follow our lead," Gary said. "Count on it."

He instructed Brad to put together a chart showing price point increases for the next twelve months. "Top it out at a buck fifteen," he said. "Then I'll show it to Howard and G.T. and if they buy it, we'll have a plan."

"Done deal," said Brad.

Leigh Curtis walked in. "You need to get out of here," she said to Gary.

He looked at his watch. "Hey, I sure do," he exclaimed, standing up and stuffing papers into his briefcase.

"What's up?" Brad asked.

"He's got a date in court," Leigh said, smiling. "He's about to become a father."

CHAPTER 81

The Steuben County courthouse was old. There were grooves in the marble floor, worn by a hundred years of foot traffic. Judges, juries, petitioners, witnesses, criminals, victims, people seeking marriage licenses and divorces, virtually everyone who had lived in the county since before the beginning of the century had trod there at least once.

Gary, Jenna, Justin and Mark arrived 15 minutes before their hearing. They found the specified room and sat down on a wooden bench in the hallway. People were scurrying about, but they didn't see Will Barron, their lawyer, anywhere.

"He won't forget, will he?" Jenna asked.

Gary reassured her. There was a statue in the center of the building, from which walnut-paneled hallways radiated in all four directions. The boys wanted to go look at the statue.

"Who is it?" Gary asked Jenna.

"Steuben, of course," she said.

"Field Marshall Baron Friedrich von Steuben," Justin read on the plaque in front of the heroic statue of a severe-looking man in an 18th Century military uniform.

"Hero of the Revo..." Mark began.

"Revo-*lutionary*," Justin coached him.

"Revolutionary War," Mark finished.

"Very good, boys," Gary said.

"What did he do," Mark asked, "to become a hero?"

"Well," Jenna began, "when the American colonies were fighting to become a free and independent country, he came from Germany to help. We didn't have very many men who knew about military things, and he was a real expert, and he was very important in getting our army shaped up so we could win the war."

"You mean, he wasn't even an American, but he was in our army?" Justin asked.

"That's right," Jenna said. "America owes a lot to foreigners – men like Steuben, and all the immigrants who've come here over the years."

"But I thought the Germans were against us in wars," Justin said.

"Well, they have been in some wars," Gary said. "But sometimes they've been on our side."

"I guess it's hard to know who your friends are sometimes," Mark said.

No kidding, Gary thought. "Do you know whose statue we have in the courthouse down in Madison?" he asked. "Where I grew up and where Grandma and Grandpa Long live?"

"No, who?" Justin asked.

"Why, Madison of course. James Madison, fourth President of the United States and father of the Constitution."

"What's the Constitution?" Mark asked.

"Well," Gary answered, "it's the supreme law of America. It set up our whole government and the freedoms we have."

"Oh," Mark said. He squinted his eyes, and the others knew he was thinking about something, trying to figure it out. Gary thought he might be struggling with the meaning of the Constitution, or government, or freedoms, maybe foreigners or immigrants.

In a moment, Mark formulated his question. "Did Madison and Steuben know each other?" he asked.

Gary smiled. "I can't say for sure," he said. "But I wouldn't be surprised."

"I think it would be neat to have a statue, and a whole town named after you," Justin said.

"Well, here's the happy family," a voice behind them boomed, and they turned to find Barron walking toward them. "Is everyone ready to face the judge?" he asked.

"Here come de judge," Justin chanted.

"Shhh," Jenna said, laughing.

The hearing couldn't have been more cut and dried. Barron presented the consent agreement to the Honorable Judge Miriam S. Czernowski, who studied the papers for a few moments. Then she peered over the bench and asked, "Is Mr. Robert Sholes represented by counsel here?"

Barron waited a few seconds, and then replied, "I believe there is a waiver of attorney in the documents you have before you."

The judge thumbed through the brief. "Yes, I see it," she said. Then she turned some more pages. "Is the Department of Children and Family Services present?" she asked.

"We are, Your Honor," replied a thin woman, rising from her seat at the end of the first row of chairs. Neither Gary nor Jenna had noticed her, but Jenna remembered the telephone conversation she had had with the woman.

"I see by these findings that you consider Dr. Long to be a fit father for these boys," the judge said. "Is that reading accurate on my part?"

"It is," the woman replied.

"Dr. Long," the judge said, "is it true that you are a vice-president of Tamson-Long Products, Incorporated, that on the fifteenth of June, nineteen ninety-two, you were legally married to Jenna Potter Sholes, and that since that time you and she have lived as husband and wife, that Justin and Mark Sholes, her children by a previous marriage, have lived with you, that you have provided for their support during the ensuing time and functioned as a *de facto* father for the boys, and that you now desire to become their legal father?"

"That is all true," Gary said.

"Mrs. Long, is it your representation that Dr. Long has the qualities to make a good father for your sons?"

"It is," Jenna answered. "A very good father."

"Justin," Judge Czernowski asked, peering over her glasses at him, "do you agree with that?"

"Oh, yeah," Justin said. "He bought us horses and everything."

"I see," she said, affecting a stern look. "And you, Mark, what do you think about him?"

"He's neat," Mark said. "He knows all about the Constitution and everything."

Judge Czernowski couldn't quite stifle a smile, but she regained her dignity, rattled off a paragraph of legalese and asked Barron if it was acceptable to his clients.

"It is, Your Honor," Barron replied.

"Then by the power vested in me by the laws of the State of Indiana and the County of Steuben," she said in a loud voice, "I hereby grant the petition for adoption and change of name. Henceforward, Dr. Gary Long of Route One, Wonanonly, Indiana, husband of Jenna Long, is the legal father of Justin Long and Mark Long.

"I wish you all a most happy future together with your horses and your continued study of the Constitution," she added, lowering her voice. Then she banged her gavel and it was over.

CHAPTER 82

"Well, what should we do to celebrate?" Gary asked as they walked past the statue of Baron von Steuben and out of the courthouse.

"Let's go play miniature golf!" Justin exclaimed.

"Miniature golf?" Jenna asked in amazement. "Where did you get that idea?"

"Wouldn't it be fun?" Justin cried.

"Yeah, miniature golf!" Mark agreed.

"Where *did* he get that idea?" Gary asked Jenna. "I don't even know where there's a course."

"I've seen one somewhere," she replied. "Let me think."

"It's out on the Lafayette Road", Justin said. "Coby's dad takes him there all the time."

"I'm not sure that's a very good recommendation," Jenna grinned at a quizzical Gary. "Coby's Dad's kind of strange."

"How bad can it be?" Gary chuckled. "It's a miniature golf course." They piled into the car, laughing and kidding one another.

"We're a bit overdressed," Jenna said as they started up. "Maybe we should go home and change first."

"No, it'll be fine," Justin cried. "I just need to take off this stupid necktie."

"It's in the opposite direction," Gary said, "and it may rain later. Anyway," he chuckled, "I just need to take off this stupid necktie."

"Okay, but let's stop somewhere where I can find something to wear on my feet instead of these high heels. Stupid high heels," she added, turning to grin at Justin.

The golf course was new, fancier than they expected. It was called "Wonders of the World." Because it was the middle of the week, the course was virtually empty of customers, and the odd little hunchbacked ticket taker was half asleep when Gary approached his booth. Still, he smiled a gap-toothed smile at the boys. "Welcome to the Wonders of the World!" he said, doing his best imitation of Igor, the mad scientist's assistant. "Be very, very careful."

The first hole was called Niagara. The ball was putted into a stream of water that fell over a cliff and through an angled grate to be pumped back up again. The grate stopped the ball, causing it to bounce out somewhere in the vicinity of the hole. The whole thing seemed like a very creative idea to Gary, except that part of the water ran off to the side and formed a small pool in which mechanical crocodiles lurked, rising above the water from time to time to snap menacingly.

"I don't think they have crocodiles in Buffalo, do they?" Gary asked Jenna.

There were man-made as well as natural wonders at Wonders of the World. The third hole was the Great Pyramid, where the ball was putted right into the pyramid, and then the player entered too, adults stooping to walk through a small doorway into a gloomy interior, where a holographic mummy stared down from above.

"I'm beginning to understand why Coby's Dad likes this place," Jenna said, shivering in her cheap new drug-store tennis shoes as they walked back outside and turned toward the fourth hole.

"Was that cool or what?" Justin asked.

The light changed suddenly, and Gary felt a breeze on his face and looked up to see that a front of clouds had intercepted the sun. "Think it'll rain before we're through?" Jenna asked.

"If it does, we can find shelter in the Great Pyramid," Gary answered.

"Not on your life," Jenna said.

At Mt. Vesuvius, there were audio effects, with explosions and people screaming. At Henry Ford's Factory, the ball was putted onto a conveyor belt, which might then drop it off in any number of places, including back at the player's feet. It happened to Gary, and when he looked up, exasperated, he saw the gnome-like attendant smiling at him from across the Grand Canyon.

Gary and Jenna were both feeling somewhat unnerved by the time they reached the final hole, the Tower of Babel, but the rain had held off so far and the boys were still enjoying themselves. Justin shot first. The idea was to put into a tunnel under the four-sided, stepped structure, which rose about eight feet high. On the steps were engraved the words

> Our country.
> May she always be in the right
> But our country.
> Right or wrong.

Justin, who had already made several lucky shots, put his ball straight in the tunnel, and they heard a whirring noise. In a moment, they saw the ball come out the top of the tower and fall down the back side. They heard it bounce down the steps. Gary walked around to the right and saw the ball land on the green, which was slightly saucered so as to channel the ball into the hole. The others clambered around the other side to look, and Justin was whooping and jumping up and down. Gary looked back and contemplated the tower. A ball might come down any of the four sides. To the left or right, the player would have to shoot around the tower to get the hole. Back down the front meant starting over, putting back into the mousehole-like opening at the bottom. There was a one-in-four chance of hitting the jackpot.

Then Gary saw the writing on the steps on the right side. It was in Japanese. He couldn't read it, but when he got to the back side, he had only to see the French words on the top step, "*Notre pays*," to get the point. This was, after all, the Tower of Babel.

Each nation, with its own language, all wanting to be, and believing they were, in the right. Whether the fourth side was in Spanish, German, Arabic or some other tongue, it was sure to be the same quotation.

"The guy who designed this place was not your average miniature golf course architect," he said to Jenna.

"Oh, no, definitely not," said the attendant from close behind him.

Gary didn't turn, just arched his eyebrows. Jenna flashed a nervous smile at the man. "Gary," she said, "I was trying to think, what is the name for the shape of the Tower of Babel?"

"It's called a ziggurat," the strange man answered.

Mark had just walked up. "Sugar rat?" he asked, looking up at the man with quizzical eyes.

CHAPTER 83

Doing Caesar's Gaul one better, Gary's life was divided into four parts. There was the legitimate business of building his division at TLP. He exulted in the task of managing an ever-growing enterprise. His staff loved working for him, his colleagues respected him and his customers were happy with the products he sold to them. Best of all, the summer production problems that plagued the Sugere operations were minor by comparison with previous years. The bug was clearly getting stronger.

The second enjoyable part of his life, and it was the most enjoyable, was his family. He had a beautiful and loving wife, two sons who were becoming more of a delight to him every day, and a home that was classy and comfortable and replete with the amenities due a highly prosperous executive. Even his extended family brought him happiness. His parents, brothers and sister made frequent trips to Wonanonly, especially in the summer, when the pool and horses made their visits a virtual vacation.

"I can't believe how Bert, Mary Lou and the girls idolize you," Jenna teased Gary after a visit by his brother's family. "Kim and Kandy just dote on you – 'Uncle Gary this and Uncle Gary that' – and Mary Lou and Bert are about as bad. Is that the homage rich uncles get in southern Indiana?"

Gary was embarrassed. "I don't think it's that," he said. "I've helped Bert out from time to time, and I think he's appreciative. That's all."

Jenna's sister from California visited, too, and the first night she was there, as Gary and Jenna snuggled into bed, he asked about Rachel's first impressions.

Jenna giggled. "I'm not going to tell you," she said.

"Why not?"

"Cause you'd get a big head."

"Oh, you don't like my big head?" he teased, tickling her bare bottom under the shortie nightgown she was wearing.

"Stop it!"

"Then tell me what she said."

"She said I won the lottery."

Jenna's mother clearly thought the world of Gary, and even his father-in-law seemed able to put aside the misgivings he had about Gary's involvement with the FBI. He never mentioned their Thanksgiving conversation on the subject, and Gary decided Bud had repressed the memory.

The other two parts of Gary's life were not pleasant. As a criminal price fixer, he spent a share of each day that summer setting up the details of what was coming to be called the "Steuben Agreement," as well as dealing with the ongoing customer trick calls. The final part, where he played the role of secret informant for the FBI, was a roller-coaster of emotions. Sometimes, his taping seemed so routine he almost forgot about the implications of it all. But at other times, the sense of his being a tattle-telling rat crept over him and sent him into the throes of depression. Sometimes, his meetings with Cox were almost enjoyable, as they exulted together in a successful taping. Other times, Cox's constant need to be in charge of everything drove Gary to distraction.

"Gary, remember when I said we might have to take another polygraph because the paper screwed up the first time?" Cox asked one morning at a routine tape handoff.

"Yeah."

"Well, we need to set up a time to do it again."

Gary considered the request. It was probably better to get it done sooner rather than later. "Uh, I guess I can do it next Monday," he said.

That weekend, Gary revisited the library and checked out the books on polygraph tests; by Monday night he was convinced he was ready to go. The technician was new, but the questions were pretty much the same. Again, Gary concentrated on giving truthful answers while he lied about the tax questions and if there was anything he hadn't told them.

After Gary left the room, the technician delivered the verdict to Cox. "I think the son of a bitch is lying to us about taxes and the full disclosure question, but I'm not sure. I can't get a clear reading, but I've got a gut feeling he's not telling the truth."

"Whadda ya mean, gut feeling?" Cox exploded. "This is supposed to be science, goddamn it. Don't tell me what you feel, what do you know?"

"Jeez, don't yell at my ass. I'm telling you right here that I think he's lying. I can't prove it, and the machine isn't giving me a clear signal, but it's enough of one to tell me he's not telling the truth."

Cox pondered the meaning of what he had just learned.

"I tell you what Sid, if I were you I'd sit my informant down and have a long talk with him. Make sure you cover your ass on this one."

Cox stepped outside to talk to Gary. "Hey, thanks for coming over," he said. "I'll let you know if we need anything else." To Gary, it sounded like he'd passed with flying colors.

After Gary left, Cox called Jim Thompson and told him what the technician had said.

"Well," Thompson said, "maybe it's not important. Maybe the income tax thing is something minor from his past, you know, just enough to make the results squirrelly, without really being very important. Maybe that's why it doesn't show clear one way or the other.

"As for the part about not telling us everything, that's more worrisome. Maybe he's trying to protect somebody in the company, somebody he really likes, maybe a woman."

"Well, hell," Cox said, "he's fingered the top three people in the company, and two other division presidents. If he's protecting somebody, it can't be anybody really important."

"That's true," Thompson replied. "Still, it's worrisome."

"You want me to talk to Dr. Harrison again, see if he can suggest a way to get it out of him?"

"Oh, God no. You'd have to give Harrison a lot more information than I'm willing to part with. That shrink talks to everybody in the Chicago office."

"Well, I guess we just charge ahead, then," Cox said.

At their next meeting, Cox instructed Gary to quit taping the customer trick calls. "We've got enough of them to establish what we need to," he barked, "so stop taping those damn things. We just have to sort 'em all out and it's taking too damn much time." He paused and consulted his notes. "The other thing is," he began again, "are you absolutely sure you've told us everything about TLP? Are we missing something that we should be investigating anywhere?"

Pangs of guilt struck in Gary's stomach. "No. Why do you ask?"

"Um, well, we just want to make sure we get everything there is to get on tape."

"If I think of anything, I'll let you know," Gary said, leaving a little wiggle room for himself.

CHAPTER 84

The first quarterly association meeting on volumes and prices was set for the tenth of September in Chicago. The annual convention of the International Chemical Manufacturers Association was being held that week at McCormick Place, and all the companies would be in town, so it was a logical venue.

Gary spent the week before the meeting making sure all the numbers were in order. The price of Sugere had climbed to 95¢ a pound, and was tracking right on Brad Redfoot's graph. At that price, Sugere sales were adding almost four million a month to the TLP bottom line.

William Hargiss had finessed the second quarter report with no problem, and was actually looking forward to writing the third quarter report. The overall economy was strong, sales were up across the board and the biggest drain on TLP profits had turned around. He was confident that in the third quarter he would be able to move some money from the company side of his ledger to the shadow side, for the first time in more than a year.

Two nights before the Chicago meeting, the FBI spent hours coaching Gary on what role he was to take, and how the operation would go from their side. The morning of the meeting, Gary got up at 4:00 and met the technician at the Holiday Inn, where he was fitted with the backpack for the second time. Gary went straight from there to the Steuben airport, where Howard met him at the TLP hangar. Zack Brilley also hitched a ride, to attend the convention. He would go directly to McCormick Place, while Gary and Howard would head for the Chicago Hilton where they were staying, and where the price-fixing meeting would be held. G.T. was already at the convention, and had agreed to sit in on the meeting, at Gary's urging. Cox wanted G.T. on the videotape.

"We need your big, ugly kisser for this one more meeting," Gary told G.T.," smiling inwardly at the aptness of his metaphor. "After that, you can leave everything to Howard and me."

Landing at Meigs Field, on the Chicago lakefront, was always an adventure. The single, short runway ran parallel to the lake, which meant there was inevitably a crosswind. As the plane dipped and bobbed on its approach, Brilley leaned over to Howard and said, "Whenever I come in here, I always figure there are two choices. We're either going to land on the planetarium or in the parking lot. The runway is out of the question. I always hope for the parking

312

lot."

Nonetheless, they made it to the runway. As soon as they were on the ground Gary flipped the record switch on. A late summer heat wave had engulfed Chicago for a week, and when the co-pilot opened the door to the plane, a blast of hot, humid air hit them in the face. As Gary stepped out of the plane, Brilley said, "Good luck at your price-fixing meeting, boys."

"I'm just glad we're not meeting outdoors in this heat," Howard replied.

Walking toward the terminal, Gary decided to head to the men's room.

"You and your fucking weak bladder," Howard snapped. "Hurry up, for Christ's sake. I'll find a cab."

The morning sun had already softened the black asphalt tarmac, and Gary could feel the heat through the soles of his shoes. By the time he reached the terminal, Gary was so hot he felt like he was roasting, and he took his coat off while he peed, forgetting about the large hump on his back. While he was standing there, a man came in and stood behind Gary, fixing his hair in the mirror.

"Hey, what you got on there, buddy?" the guy asked. Gary had to think quickly.

"Oh, I have to wear a brace for my back," he explained.

"Yeah, right," the man retorted, and headed out the door. When Gary found Howard, he was just getting into the taxi, and Gary joined him in the back seat. He almost died when he recognized the cab driver as the man who had been in the bathroom. The cabbie never said a word, but Gary's heart didn't stop pounding until they reached the hotel. He gave the man a tip equal to the bill.

They entered the Hilton through the revolving doors and went up the marble staircase to the lobby level. Right after they checked in, Gary spotted the female FBI agent who had helped with the abortive taping of his meeting with Park Soo-hee. Howard spotted her, too. For the Park taping, she had been dressed in loose-fitting work clothes, but here, the better to mingle with the upscale crowd in the Hilton, she had on a smart-looking blouse and a short skirt.

"Look at that broad!" Howard drooled. "Wouldn't you like to fuck her? She is unreal." He was right in ways he couldn't imagine, but Gary avoided the issue, knowing she might soon be listening to everything they said.

"I wonder if Sumiko is here yet." Gary said.

"Fuck Sumiko, look at that broad, she's got legs like peanut butter!"

"Howard, come on, we gotta find the meeting room," Gary pleaded.

"Jesus Christ, Gary, what the hell's wrong with you?" Howard growled and returned to the subject of the incredible beauty of the FBI agent. Gary was surprised Howard didn't go up to her and try to pick her up on the spot.

"We're supposed to be in Room 4-L," Gary said. "I assume that's on the fourth floor." Howard allowed himself to be guided to the elevator, but he kept looking over his shoulder at the woman.

When they got to the room, Jacques Coté was there, along with Song Dian-Nuan and Kim Jungwoo. There was a table with coffee and soft drinks, and a waiter who looked suspiciously like an FBI agent to Gary was setting out bagels and sweet rolls. Gary set his briefcase on the conference table in the middle of the room. The waiter finished his work and nodded at Gary as he exited the room. Immediately, the door opened again, and G.T. strode in. Gary introduced him to Coté, and they struck up a conversation about French wines. Numata and Yamasaki walked in a few moments later.

"Well," G.T. boomed, "it looks like the gang's all here. Let's get this circle jerk started."

They took seats at the table, and since TLP was hosting the meeting, Gary got things started. "Welcome to the quarterly meeting of the International Artificial Sweetener Producers Association," he said. "We are delighted to have all of you in Chicago."

He picked up a small stack of papers, and handed them to Song Dian-Nuan, who was seated beside him. "Here are copies of the agenda for today. I hope it meets with your approval." Song dutifully took an agenda and passed the stack around the table.

Howard snorted. The agenda, as everyone in the room knew, was as phony as a three-dollar bill. It was simply a paper trail ruse, so that in case anyone ever questioned what these men were doing meeting together, they would have a ready answer, and documentation to back it up.

That formality over with, Gary called on Numata to give the production report.

"First let me say," Numata began, "and I think I speak for everyone here, how delighted we are with what has happened to sweetener prices since meeting in Steuben last May. They are, as you all know, back in one-dollar range, very good news. Good things happen when friends agree.

"Masahiko," he continued, nodding at Yamasaki, who was sitting beside him, "has prepared detailed analysis of sales volume figures." Yamasaki got up and walked around the table, handing each man a copy of his report.

"We begin tracking June first," Numata continued, "and figures are complete through August thrity-first. So we have three full months to look at.

"Now," he continued, "on basis of volumes in Steuben Agreement,

314

quarterly quota for Nippon Kagaka is seventeen point five thousand metric tons. For Xin Chieh Fa Xueh, it is twelve point five thousand metric tons.

"What the hell is Zin Cheese whatever-the-hell-he-said?" G.T. asked Gary.

"It's Chinese for New World," Gary answered. "Or rather, New World is English for it."

"Well, Zin Cheese is a better name for them. I think that's what I'll call them from now on."

"For Daehan Hwa-Hak, Numata continued, number is six point five thousand metric tons, and for Tamson-Long, it is eighteen thousand metric tons."

He turned the page, and continued. "According to the papers you submit at end of each month, actual sales volumes for three month period are: Nippon Kagaka, seventeen point five thousand metric tons." He paused and allowed himself a satisfied smile, as if bragging that his company had hit its quota on the nose. "For Xin Chieh Fa Xeuh," he continued, "thirteen thousand metric tons. For Daehan Hwa-Hak, six point seven thousand metric tons, and for Tamson-Long, eighteen point two thousand metric tons.

"It would seem," he concluded, "that the market has been slightly stronger than we anticipated, and that everyone except Nippon Kagaka has exceeded its quota."

"I suggest you fire your marketing director," G.T. said, bringing a ripple of laughter from the group. "And hire the guy from Zin Cheese.

"Actually," he continued, "it strikes me that this thing is working very well. Everyone is within a few tons of his quota, and that shows that we are all abiding by the spirit of the Steuben Agreement. Howard," he said next, looking to his left where Howard was busy skimming through the rest of Yamasaki's memo, "do you have any suggestions at this point?"

"Shit," Howard said, "these numbers are so close to perfect, it's amazing. With citric, it took us almost a year to get the balances to come out this close. What we need to do is to let it ride for another few months and see where we are. Then if we need to make adjustments, we can make them.

"These things typically bounce around some, month by month. For example," he picked up Yamasaki's report, "if we had had this meeting last month, and only had data through July, Nippon Kagaka would actually be a couple of points over its quota, and we would be under."

Well, Gary thought, the FBI ought to be happy. They've got Numata, Howard and G.T. all making incriminating statements, and Yamasaki's written report will make a fine piece of evidence.

Song Dian-Nuan started to talk about his favorite subject, the auditing procedures. Gary wasn't paying much attention, but suddenly, something happened which brought him to the highest state of panic he had ever known in his life.

His briefcase started ticking like a time bomb. He looked up at the group, who were arguing with Song about something or other, but he knew that as soon as the hubbub slacked for a moment, they would hear the noise. There seemed to be no escape.

He got up and walked over to the bagel table, carrying the briefcase with him. He set it on the table and pulled the Velcro straps which exposed the tape machine. It was a huge risk, but he had to see if he could figure out what the hell was going on.

The false top had Velcro on every side but the bottom, and as Gary pulled on the base, it sounded like a hundred firecrackers going off, at least in his ears. His thoughts flipped to what the FBI agents in the next room were thinking. He still couldn't see what was making the clicking noise, so he just started tapping on stuff in time with the tapping noise the machine was making. His mind was racing. He thought about taking it out of the room, but remembered he couldn't leave or it would ruin the whole meeting, from an evidence standpoint. The FBI had to have one person in there at all times who consented to the taping; they had drilled that into him over and over.

Gary finally decided to just shut the damn thing off. He slapped the false top back into place and closed it up, getting ready to touch the hasps. Then the noise stopped, just like that.

Seconds later, the men stopped talking and G.T. turned to him. "Gary, does that sound all right to you?" he asked.

Gary didn't have the slightest idea what G.T. was referring to. He picked up a bagel. "I'm sorry," he said. "I was distracted. Does *what* sound all right to me?"

"Get your fucking nose out of the cream cheese and pay attention," Howard snapped, but with a smile, so the Asians wouldn't think he was really mad at Gary.

Gary never did know what G.T.'s question was.

"Come on, Doogie, let's catch a cab," G.T. said after the meeting.

"You guys go on ahead. I've got a few calls to make. I'll be along in a few minutes."

"All right," Howard responded, as he and G.T. started down the hall.

"But if I see Miss Peanut Butter Legs again, I'm kidnapping her, skipping the piss ant convention and spending the rest of the week fucking her brains out upstairs."

He didn't see her, of course, but Gary did, as soon as the others had gone. He walked into the room next door to find the woman, along with Cox and four other men, including their waiter, busying themselves packing up video equipment.

"Fantastic job," Cox said. "We got some great video and everybody said just the right things.

"But, Gary," he asked, "what in hell were you doing with the briefcase?"

CHAPTER 85

At the Hargiss family Christmas dinner, William pulled Howard aside and into the library off of the main dining area. "Son, it looks like things are moving ahead in Bio-tech. Is the volume agreement holding?"

Howard was sure his father already knew the answer. G.T. told the old man everything. Howard wanted that kind of relationship with his father, but G.T. had supplanted him. "Yeah, it looks like everyone is pretty much adhering to the agreements by the way the price is moving up," he said without emotion.

William put his arm on Howard's shoulder. "I can't tell you how glad I am to see this thing finally working out. This is the first time I think the goddamn board was really beginning to question me. Thanks for all your efforts. In fact, that's the reason I wanted to talk to you."

Howard stared silently at his father.

"I've pretty much gotten the consensus of the board to make you the vice chairman. We'll make it official at the next annual meeting, but I think it's a done deal."

Howard shook his head and smiled. "Dad, I don't know what to say."

"'Thanks' would be appropriate. The board's been on my ass to get a succession plan in place. I think they're sold on the idea of you taking over my slot and Gary taking over G.T.'s slot. Gary's gonna have to be involved in a lot more of the operations than he has been. You okay with that?"

His father was asking his advice, what the hell had come over him? "Well, he's done a great job on the association. He's come a long way, but he's more goody-goody than Tully thought."

"Humm, well, maybe we should give him another hooking bonus. Make it a big one this time, you know a couple million, in one sum. We've got to make sure he's under control. If he's going to end up second in command, we've got a lot to teach him, and you, over the next couple of years."

Then he stopped and stared at Howard. "Don't fuck this up. I've worked a long time to get this in place. I don't want to have to bare-ass lie in front of a hundred shareowners to explain why you're qualified to be the heir apparent. Concentrate on coming up to speed and meeting the key people. I know you know a lot of them, but they need to begin seeing you in a new light."

"Thanks, Dad. I'm kind of shocked by all this."

"Let's go eat. Not a word of this to anybody for now, and especially not to Long. We need to make sure he's gonna be a real team player. I'll talk to G.T. about his bonus."

Howard went to bed that night with an upset stomach from gorging himself with too much standing rib roast, and too many conflicting thoughts about his father.

CHAPTER 86

Gary confided to Ralph Sori on New Year's Eve that by the end of the following year, bio-tech products would count for a third of the $560 million in profits that TLP would report. Of that number, $120 million would come from Sugere alone. By the first of January, Sugere prices had climbed to $1.15 per pound.

On a snowy January seventh, Gary called Masahito Yamasaki from the Holiday Inn with Cox in the room. TLP's volume was just slightly below target and Masahito told Gary he was the first to call. "As soon as I get rest of numbers I will send settlement sheet," Masahito said.

A week later, Masahito, true to his word, faxed Gary the settlement sheet. Everyone was within a point of target. Gary showed the numbers to Howard and G.T., got their comments on tape, and handed the tape and a copy of the sheet over to Sid Cox.

"It's Nippon Kagaka's turn to host the next review meeting," Gary told Cox. "Numata wants it in Japan."

"Ah, shit, you can't do it over there Gary; we can't tape there, remember? Get it somewhere in the U.S.," Cox whined.

"Sid, I'll try, but they've been over here so much, it's really our turn to go over there."

"Well, how about Hawaii? That's in the middle. Find some reason to set it there and we'll take care of finding the hotel."

Numata eventually agreed, and Howard was so enthusiastic he volunteered to go along just for the chance to play a little golf.

TLP was making a lot of money, and when Buffy arrived in his office with the new annual reports, he recalled the visit from the previous year. "What a difference a year makes," he grinned. "Now I bet you wish we'd report earnings by division."

"Yeah," Gary said. "But thanks to you guys in public relations, the world will never know what a winner I really am."

In truth, though the annual report would never show it, Gary calculated that Bio-tech had contributed over 80 million to the bottom line of the corporation. Whatever the details, the strong overall earnings caught many Wall Street analysts off guard and drove the price of TLP stock up almost two points.

CHAPTER 87

When Howard and Gary arrived at the hotel on the secluded Makaha shore of Oahu, Gary was instantly embarrassed. Every meeting that had been held up to this point had been hosted at a four or five-star posh hotel. This place looked like a dump and had bamboo furniture scattered around the lobby. By prearrangement, Gary went to Cox's room after checking in.

"Sid, this place is shabby; these guys aren't used to staying at places like this," Gary complained.

Cox didn't appreciate Gary's criticism of his abilities as a travel agent. "Deal with it," he barked. "I need a key to your room since it's next to the conference room. When you come back from dinner, don't be surprised if your room looks a little different."

The next morning, Gary ran through the drill, checking each piece of equipment to make sure it was working. For some reason the briefcase wouldn't turn on. He tried everything, all the buttons and latches, but it still wouldn't work. Everyone was now in the conference room next door, and he needed to be there, too. Quick-step, he walked past it to the next room and knocked. Cox answered, opening the door just enough for Gary to see his face. Gary whispered, "The briefcase doesn't work. I've got to get to that room, you've got it wired anyway, and this thing was just a safety net."

Cox opened the door a few more inches and took the briefcase from him. Gary headed next door to the meeting, where he took stock of the seating arrangement. The room was pitifully small and Gary ended up taking a seat next to Howard on a couch. Jacques Coté, Song Dian-Nuan and Kim Jungwoo sat around a tiny conference table, and Sumiko Numata sat on a chair in the corner.

"Good thing Mr. G.T. not here," Song said. "We have to hang him from ceiling."

Just then someone knocked on the door.

Numata jumped up and said with feigned horror, "Oh, my God, it must be FBI! We caught, we dead meat, let's all give up." Everyone started laughing and whooping it up. Coté opened the door and Sid Cox walked in.

"Is there a Mr. Gary Long here?" he asked.

"That's the guy," Numata said pointing at Gary. "You take him."

Cox tried to suppress a grin. "Did you leave a briefcase in the lobby, sir?"

"I sure did," Gary replied, feigning embarrassment.

"Well, we found credit cards with your name on them and wanted to make sure you got your briefcase. Everything seems to be in order."

Gary understood what he meant by "everything seems to be in order". Cox was telling him the briefcase was ready to go.

A couple of minutes after the meeting was called to order, the phone rang. Since Gary was the closest, he answered it. Cox was on the other end of the line. "Hey," he said as soon as he knew it was Gary, "we can't see a fucking thing, there's something in front of the video. I know you can't say much, but act like we're bringing more juice or water and move whatever's in front of that lamp on the side table. Get whatever it is the fuck outta the way."

Kim's briefcase was in front of the lamp. Nonchalantly, Gary moved it and said, "They wanted to know if we need more juice."

"Tell them hell no," Howard said. "What we want is more room."

Numata returned to business. "Now, first thing to do is go over reports." He passed out the fourth quarter numbers. Then he collected everyone's sales numbers for the month of January.

"It look like everybody right on," Song said, scrutinizing the papers. "If numbers accurate."

Howard looked up. "I'm sure everyone's numbers are accurate," he said, "and it looks to me like you guys have got the hang of this thing. And, Mr. Song," he continued, "I wouldn't think anyone whose bottom line has improved as much as yours has since May would have any complaints."

"No complaints," Song said, "no complaints."

Numata drew a breath and, avoiding looking directly at Howard, asked, "Everything look good right now, but what will happen if sometime we don't hit volume, go over it, by a lot maybe?"

Without skipping a beat Howard replied, "Have you ever seen the movie *The Godfather*?" and then looked Numata straight in the eye.

"I hear about it but I have not seen it," Numata replied.

"I tell you what, in *The Godfather*, Corleone, the Don, if you don't do what you say you're gonna do, he has a big, tough guy take your hand like this, and take a big knife and he goes like this and you have one less finger. So if your volume is consistently too high, you're going to look like this." And he held up his hand with one finger hidden. "And if your volume is still too high, you're gonna look like this." And he held up his hand with two fingers down. "And if your volume is still too high, you're gonna look like this." And he held up a fist with no visible fingers.

Numata was dumbfounded. He thought Howard was just joking, but he wasn't sure.

After a few seconds that seemed like minutes, Numata got back on course and said, "Well you can see we must stick to volumes we agreed to." Nobody grinned or laughed; the mood was deadly serious. In the back of his mind, Gary was chuckling, knowing the FBI was listening. But whatever problems Howard had caused for himself on that front, from the standpoint of association policy, he had won.

Coté started talking about prices, quickly demonstrating that he was the best versed of anyone in the room on the world markets. "Right now prices world wide are averaging a dollar sixteen, when less than a year ago they were averaging a little over sixty cents, so we've really come a long way. In fact we are moving nicely to a dollar forty." The entire mood of the meeting shifted. For the next few minutes everyone was in complete agreement.

As the meeting started to close, Numata gave everyone a fake agenda and they left for lunch on the terrace, and a round of golf. The second review meeting had been a success, and everyone looked forward to the next meeting, which they scheduled for Bangkok in May.

"You had a hell of a month, Gary," G.T. said a few days later.

Gary took a quick look at the numbers. The bottom line for his division was over ten million dollars for the month of January.

"What do you think you'll be able to do for the rest of the quarter?"

Gary looked again at the numbers, and then up at G.T. "Well, Sugere is a buck sixteen, we may be able to push it up to a buck twenty by the end of this month. If that happens we might turn another million or two to the bottom line."

"Well, then, I think it's about time for another payment to Dr. Long," G.T. said. Here we go again, Gary thought, an almost unbearable mixture of pride, anger, fright and embarrassment churning inside his head. But there was nothing to do for the moment but go along. "What do you want me to put it in for?" he asked.

"Well, let's see… I'm not going to give you a full month's divisional earnings; I'll give you a fourth. Go ahead and write it up."

Gary wrote up the contract for a fictitious company he named AOP, which sounded like ALP, a company they had done some business with. G.T. signed it without comment and Gary didn't get any feedback this time from Kincaid either. He set it up with a banker in Switzerland, and that was that.

Jenna hadn't asked him about the bonus money since Gary had first told her about it, and he didn't see the need for bringing her up to date with the latest addition to the coffers. The less she knew about it, the better for her, he thought.

Still, it left him with a nagging feeling, knowing that there was something he was hiding from her. Even though he had never, even yet, specifically researched the subject, he knew in his heart he was supposed to be paying taxes on the bonus money, in spite of the fact that G.T. had told him specifically that he didn't have to, and was not to do so.

The reason G.T. didn't want him to pay taxes on it, he figured, was because it would run the risk of exposing that nobody else was paying. Would it, really? Gary didn't know. I think I may show it this year, he said to himself, reaching over to the calculator on his desk and multiplying two pint five million by 38%. It would cost him almost a million dollars. Still, if G.T. had given him only a million and a half dollar bonus, instead of two and a half, would he have been any less pleased? He figured he wouldn't. The other question was, if he reported this one, would that trigger something at the IRS that would expose the earlier bonuses? He didn't know the answer to that one, but there was a way out of that, too, he figured. He could file amended reports. There would be huge interest and penalties to pay, and the whole thing would cost him a fortune, but at least he'd have one less worry on his mind. He decided to study the question carefully and see what the best plan would be, and he felt good about his decision. No matter how much it cost, he'd still have a nice nest egg left to provide for his family if everything came a-cropper, and that was his main concern – that and knowing he would be clear of any wrongdoing in the eyes of the law.

Of course, he had plenty of time. He didn't have to file anything with the IRS on the new bonus until a year from April.

CHAPTER 88

The second week of March rolled around and the profit margins were going like gangbusters. One evening, Gary drove to the Hampton Inn to make a tape drop to Cox. As he walked toward his car after the meeting, he looked up and saw Howard waving at him and smiling as he drove by on his way home in Stevens Glen. As soon as Howard was out of sight, Gary went back up to the room where Cox was sorting out the tapes.

"Sid," he said, "we've got a problem. Howard just drove by and waved...at me. He's gonna give me the third degree tomorrow about what I was doing here. The only logical explanation is that I have some visitors in town, but I don't, and he'll go over the visitor log and see that." Gary was starting to panic; the more he thought about it, the more indefensible his position became.

Cox was unfazed. "Fuck him. You know, hearing all these tapes, these guys have more affairs going on than we can keep track of. If they get on you, just say, 'Hey, bud, it's my personal business and not yours and then laugh. He's gonna guess that you just got laid. Let him guess."

When Gary told Jenna about it that night, she immediately understood the implications of the problem, and that the rumor mill in all probability would start up. Who knew how the gaggle of TLP geese at the country club would feed on this juicy tidbit of gossip? She'd heard them tear apart other less fortunate women whose husbands had found an occasional blonde, and the thought of being the subject of a gossip feeding frenzy made her ill. Still, she somehow felt responsible for getting Gary into this mess, so she'd have to take her lumps. But she hated it.

The next morning Gary was sitting at his desk when Howard walked up to the door. "Doogie!" he exclaimed. "Guess what happened to me last night. I'm on my way home, and I drive by the Hampton about a quarter after nine, and as I drive by, I look over and what do I see but Gary, and it seems like he's just a-smiling. What's going on, you got some visitors coming in today? Yeah, that must be it. What time are your visitors coming by today, Doogie? I sure do want to meet them. Why didn't you pick them up before you came in to work today? Ah, I know, you're letting them sleep in a little while. When will they be here, 'cause I sure do want to meet 'em."

"You know there aren't any visitors," Gary said. Then he went into his rehearsed lines. "Howard," he said, "you know, everyone around here seems to have someone they can spend a little time with to release pressure and I tell you what, I feel like it's something I'd just rather not discuss."

Howard beamed, "Ahh, I figured there's something going on there. Gary Long's getting laid and, let's see, who do I think it could be? Someone on this floor? Well, let me guess." Then he started naming names. As Howard was rambling off a few prospects, G.T. entered the office.

"G.T., I've got something to tell you," Howard said grinning. "Wow, have I got something to tell you about our friend Mr. Long here. I was driving into town to get a loaf of bread last night about nine-fifteen and out comes Smiley here from the Hampton Inn. Just as happy as he can be, strolling out of the Hampton Inn, so I just said to myself, 'Well he's got some guests in today'. So I come down to introduce myself to his nice guests, but there's no guests here, G.T. None. Look, you see any? And here this guy was, walking out of the Hampton last night, smilin' like a Cheshire cat. But he's got no guests here and I'm worried about that. I think we need to go pick up his guests."

Anything Gary did from that point on just added fuel to the fire. They were convinced they finally had cornered him in a compromising situation.

I hope both you guys get sent up the river for a long, long time, Gary thought.

CHAPTER 89

Admiral Decatur carefully replaced each document in its appropriate folder: three folders containing enough dynamite to destroy a presidency.

The quest had started two years before when a certain notorious Chinese businessman-spy they had been trailing for months booked a flight to Washington, and led the amazed operatives following him directly from Dulles Airport to the White House, where he produced an invitation to that evening's State Dinner and marched in the door.

From that point on, Decatur started paying attention to a lot of things, and the file he built made him furious everey time he thought about it. "This guy is the fucking Manchurian Candidate," he whispered to himself.

It was necessary to conduct this investigation off line. The Director could not be a part of it, or even know about it. Decatur liked this Director. He was a competent man. But he was still a Presidential appointee, and thus, not to be trusted with material which made the President out to be under the substantial influence of a foreign government.

Decatur almost couldn't believe what they'd come up with: policy favors for campaign cash. If they hadn't strung up that other little Chink, the one with the suitcase full of money, they'd never have figured it all out. They'd trailed the man from Beijing to Djakarta to San Francisco. There he had rented, of all things, a Geo Metro, and begun driving across country. They picked him up at a rest stop on I-80, somewhere in Utah, and after 20 hours of interrogation, faced with imaginary but to his mind very real terrors at the hands of his American captors, he'd given up the first link, and provided some tantalizing hints to the rest of the plan.

CHAPTER 90

Sid Cox and Jim Thompson spent a Monday afternoon reviewing the evidence in the TLP case. "Looks like we've got enough to put this to bed," Thompson told him. "Why don't you tell Gary to cool it? I don't think we should do anything else that might compromise him."

The next evening, Cox told Gary to quit taping anything unless it was really extraordinary. Gary could tell that they were close to getting all of the stuff they needed. Cox didn't dwell on it, but it began to register in the back of Gary's mind that things could soon change.

On an otherwise lazy Thursday in late March, Leigh Curtis interrupted Gary's efforts to prepare for a staff meeting. "John Caldwell is on the phone, says he's sure you'll want to talk to him."

Caldwell had begun taking care of more and more of Gary's business, not only buying and selling stocks, but exercising Gary's by now voluminous TLP stock options as well. Gary couldn't recall any business hanging between them, but he took the call.

"Hey, John, what's up?"

"What's up? Jeez, have you read Gruber's report on TLP this quarter?"

Betty Gruber was an analyst for Salton-Jones, a brokerage firm in Michigan, and a favorite of Hargiss's.

"Nah, haven't seen it, what's it say?"

"Jeez, she's published a forty-page report on TLP, and in the section on management, she discussed the transition of the management team from Hargiss and G.T. to Howard and Gary. Looks like things are moving along pretty well for you, you son of a bitch. Why didn't you tell me this was happening? Congratulations!"

Gary breathed deeply in a state of shock and simply mumbled, "Thanks."

Betty Gruber was the first to publish what Gary had been hearing privately from G.T. and Hargiss for the past 18 months. He called down to the library and asked for a copy of the report. It went into great depth on how Howard would be the inside guy, handling production and pricing details, while Gary would be the outside guy, working with all the joint ventures and Wall Street.

G.T. had often told Gary to expect this move. Gary had taped it a number of times, because he wanted the FBI to know he was seen as a future leader at TLP. Hargiss was about ready to phase out, and G.T. said he would be ready to hand over the reins in a couple of years.

Gary began to see himself as destined to become the top man in a giant enterprise. Of course, there were things even Betty Gruber didn't know.

CHAPTER 91

Sid Cox didn't object very much to having the next quarterly meeting in Thailand. "It doesn't really matter," he told Gary. "We've pretty much got what we need, and we're about ready to spring the trap."

That news filled Gary with a mixture of joy and anxiety: joy because he had so desperately wanted the end to come for so long, and anxiety because he knew the closing scenes of the drama would be the most difficult of all. Moreover, he was still unsure about how it would come out.

For several months, he had been going out of his way to impress Ian Howes, Randolph Thad and Robert Aiken. They were the board members he would need to succeed in his plan to resurrect TLP after the crash. He thought he'd scored points, but there was no way to know if it would be enough.

How would G.T. and Howard react? Forget that, how would William react? That was what really mattered. Gary just didn't know.

Song, Bai, Numata, Yamasaki, Kim and Park were at the meeting at the Ritz Hotel in Bangkok, and they were all in a festive mood. The price of artificial sweetener had stabilized at $1.23 and the market had enjoyed just over five percent growth. The volume reports showed all parties abiding by the agreement, and they were all flush with profits. Gary didn't pay too much attention to what was being said. He took a few notes, but all he could think about was the end game.

As he looked around the table, he knew all the men at the meeting would be going down when the case blew open, and it made it hard to sit there and listen while they laughed it up. Gary bade them all good-bye knowing that if he ever saw any of them again, it would not be pleasant.

When the meeting was over, he exited quickly and caught a taxi to a restaurant, where he had a meeting scheduled with Armand Pomerleau, TLP's talented top man in Europe. Gary had originally planned to go home the long way, and meet Pomerleau in Paris. But once he learned from Cox that the end of the price-fixing game was at hand, he was eager to get back to Steuben.

Still, the meeting was important and he had persuaded Pomerleau to make the flight to Bangkok. Pomerleau was doing an excellent job as head of TLP's Eurpoean operations, and there were plans on the drawing board to build a new Bacitracin plant near Prague. The Czech officials were eager to make it happen, and Gary needed to review the plans and blueprints.

Armand was waiting for him, and they spent the evening together. The work that had been done was top-notch, and Gary had only a few suggestions to make. "Are we ready to announce this?" he asked the Frenchman.

"The Czech government wants to send its top two industrial development men to Steuben first," Armand said.

"Why?" Gary asked.

Pomerleau grinned. "Well, when I asked them that, all I got back was some, how do you say, gobbledygook, but I think there are two reasons. One, they would love to take a vacation in America, and two, that way they can come back and make it look like they put the deal together themselves."

"Well, all right," Gary said. "Work out a date with them and G.T. Then have Leigh check it against my schedule."

After dinner, Gary headed to his room. Getting on the elevator he was surprised to see a very drunk Sumiko Numata swaying in the elevator holding on to a very young Thai woman. To Gary, Numata had always seemed like a very conservative, straight arrow kind of person. This was highly out of character.

"Sumiko, who's your lady friend?" Gary said winking at him.

"Uhhhh, this my sister Helen." Sumiko was in his fifties, and the girl couldn't have been more than 19, if that.

"Prolific father you got there, Sumiko," Gary commented, trying not to grin, as he stepped off the elevator.

The next morning Gary saw Numata at the breakfast table. "It was really nice meeting your sister last night," he said.

"Oh, ho, what you talking about? Just forget it, no big deal."

"Oh yeah, I'll forget about it. I won't bring it up at the next meeting."

The incident made it easier for Gary to reconcile being responsible for Numata's impending downfall. He had had some qualms about entrapping the distinguished Japanese executive, who, he often thought, was probably simply acting in a way that was customary among big business in his culture. It was good to know the man had shortcomings, too. Of course, he thought then, taking a little nocturnal pleasure was probably part of Japanese big business culture as well.

Gary headed back to his room, packed his bags and left for the airport and home.

During the return flight, Gary couldn't stop thinking about the changes that were coming in his life, and by the time he landed, he was sick with worry. After turning in the tapes of the Bangkok meeting, he told Cox his concerns.

"Ah, don't worry about it," Cox said. "We'll take care of you, you'll see."

"Yeah, but will people know it's me? Can I stay anonymous until the indictments?"

"Gary, it'll all work out, and it's almost here. We're going to try the case in Chicago, because we think we'll get a better grand jury there than in Indiana. Kevin Rasmussen's already looking for an apartment to live in while it's all going on. I'll have to have you go up there to give your testimony before the grand jury, so pick out some time to do it."

Gary dutifully and somberly selected a few dates that would work and forwarded them to Cox. Cox called back and said the prosecutors had selected three days, one a week over a three-week period.

"Three whole days?" Gary asked. How in heck could he manage to be out of communication all that time?

"Yeah," Cox said. "Only the last one will actually be in front of the grand jury. The others will be preparation meetings. The Chicago people need to be brought up to speed on everything."

Three days before the first meeting in Chicago, Rasmussen and Gary met in Steuben to go over his testimony. "You'll want to bring your lawyer up to speed on all of this," Rasmussen said.

"I don't have an attorney. Sid told me it wouldn't be the best thing to do," Gary said.

Rasmussen's mouth fell open. "I thought I told you to get one," he said.

"Yeah, you did," Gary responded, "but Sid vetoed the idea."

Rasmussen shook his head and resumed his review of Gary's testimony.

CHAPTER 92

During the entire time Gary had worked at TLP, he had never left town without someone knowing where he was. And since she began working for him, that someone was Leigh Curtis. As he prepared for his testimony, he was at a loss as to how to cover his tracks. He couldn't have his cell phone going off during a hearing. He would have to turn it off. He could probably explain that away by saying that it had accidentally been turned off and he hadn't realized it. But no matter what excuse he gave for being in Chicago, there was virtually no chance that someone wouldn't want to reach him. So if he invented a cover story, it would be blown as soon as someone tried to reach him wherever he said he was going to be. If he simply disappeared for the day, half the executive office would be pestering Leigh and Jenna to find him. He could just imagine G.T. yelling at Leigh. "What the hell do you mean you don't know where he is? Find the son of a bitch!" Her instinct at that point would be to call Jenna, and what would she say? If Jenna said she didn't know, they wouldn't believe her, because if she really didn't know, she would be in a panic and would assist them in calling out the state police and anybody else she could think of to look for him. If she made up an excuse, say, perhaps that his mother had taken sick and he had driven to Madison, then they would descend on Madison and disprove that. Tully would be on the case in no time.

On the other hand, if he had Jenna disappear for the day, the problems were even worse. She would have to take the boys out of school or they were likely to be called, and when they said they didn't know where either of their parents was, red flags would go up all over the place. Then someone would probably call the Potters, and who knew what Bud might tell them, given what he knew about Gary's activities and how he felt about them.

He would have to have help, or his cover would be blown. Cox would have a fit if he ever found out, but Gary decided he had to tell Leigh what was going on. The day before his testimony, he told her he was taking her to lunch. This was not a conversation he wanted to have in the office.

The trouble was, he didn't really want to have it in a restaurant, either. Someone might overhear them. No matter where they went in Steuben, there was risk.

The first thing he said to her as they drove out the TLP gate was, "Leigh, this is going to be a lousy lunch. We're going to get some McDonald's hamburgers and eat them in the car." Then he drove past the two McDonald's closest to TLP and pulled into the drive-in lane of one on the far side of town, near the river. "What do you want?" he asked as they stopped in front of the menu board.

"So many fabulous choices, I hardly know what to choose," she responded. They got Quarter Pounders and fries, and Gary drove to a secluded river overlook, where he parked the car.

"Leigh," he began, as they unwrapped their meals, "I'm going to Chicago tomorrow and I'll tell you what, I'm not going to give you the number where I can be reached." Leigh's face registered a little shock. "Leigh, I trust you completely, but for more than two years, I've kept a secret from you. Now I'm going to tell you, and I'm sorry to have to do it, because it's going to put a lot of pressure on you, but I need your help. Tomorrow will be the first day of several over the next few weeks when I'm going to need you to cover for me – if you're willing."

Leigh couldn't have been more confused. Her first thought was that he had found another job. But that couldn't have been going on for years. She thought maybe he was having an affair, maybe he was planning to leave Jenna, but that didn't make any sense, either. She stared at him, blank-faced, the hamburger untouched on its wrapper on her lap.

"There's a lot of things going on at TLP that shouldn't be. You know that, some of it anyway. But it's much, much worse than you have any idea. The other thing you don't know is that for the past two and a half years now, I've been working with the FBI, making tapes on Howard, G.T., William, everybody. I'm a mole, Leigh, and I've helped the FBI build a case that will send them to jail."

"Oh, my God, Gary!" she said, staring wide-eyed at him.

"Tomorrow, the whole thing comes to a head, at least sort of. I'm going to be with the Justice Department prosecutors all day, preparing testimony for the grand jury."

Leigh's mind was racing, and Gary paused to let it all sink in.

"Have you always been a mole?" she asked. "I mean did you come to TLP in the first place to do this?"

"No," he said, firmly. "I came here to build a biochemistry division for the company. What happened is that there came a point where I had three choices. I either became part of their criminal conspiracy, or I quit, or I went to the authorities. I chose to go to the authorities."

"Does Jenna know about it?"

"Yes. She's the only one." He saw no need to tell her about his father-in-law.

"What is it all about?"

"The big thing is price fixing. All the meetings with Nippon Kagaka and the others, they've all been about setting up an illegal price fixing scheme on Sugere. And it's going on in other divisions, too, with other products and other competitors."

"Oh, my word," she said. "I can't believe this. Gary, I can't believe...I can't believe you had the courage to do it. I mean, you've taken your life in your hands. Those guys are brutal and scary. A man like Andrew Tully, he wouldn't hesitate to kill you, especially if Hargiss told him to do it."

"Well, I don't think that's going to happen now," Gary said. "I think the danger of that has passed. If I'd been caught a year ago, maybe, but once tomorrow is over with, they wouldn't dare."

"Maybe not," she said, her voice choking with emotion, "but they're ruthless and powerful men. They won't give up easily."

"I know," he said, choking up a little himself, "but I've got the law on my side, and if I can win this thing, then my goal is to take over the company and run it right, with the help of people like you and Brad and Buffy. If that doesn't work, I'll go somewhere else and start over."

"What do you want me to do?" she asked.

"Tomorrow, you have to stall anyone who wants to get hold of me. There will be some breaks when I'll be able to get to a phone. I'll call you then for my messages. I want to avoid having to return calls if at all possible, so try to hand off anything you can to Brad or whoever."

They spent another 20 minutes figuring out how to handle all the contingencies they could think of. She's going to be okay, Gary thought. She's scared stiff, but she's going to be okay.

"Hey," he said finally, "I paid good money for these hamburgers and they're getting cold."

The next morning, he and Jenna got up early. "You seem calm," she said over coffee.

"Focused," he said, giving a little gesture with his fist. "That's the in-word these days. I'm focused."

"We're in the home stretch now, aren't we?"

"Yes, we are. It's going to be tough and mean and no fun at all for a while. We may come out on top, or we may lose everything. In a way, I almost don't care any more – you know why? Because they can't take you away from me," he continued, answering his own question. "Or Justin and Mark. We may be ruined financially, and have to live in a cheap apartment in some slum somewhere, but as long as we're together, I'll have no regrets.

"Would you?" he added.

"Gary, I'm so proud of you..." she said.

"No," he interrupted her. "I'm proud of *you*. You pushed me to go to the FBI, and you were right. And now I understand why, I mean from my own selfish standpoint. Because if I'd gone on at TLP and become part of their conspiracy, even if they – we – never got caught, it would have been an issue between you and me, and it would have driven us apart, and sooner or later, you'd have had enough and I'd have lost you. I could never bear to lose you."

He stood up, walked behind her chair and began rubbing her shoulders. She leaned her head back against his stomach. They stayed like that for a minute or more, wordlessly. Then he bent over and kissed her on the top of the head. He poured some coffee in a travel cup, grabbed two doughnuts out of the breadbox, wrapped them in a paper towel, took his briefcase in his other hand, and walked out the door.

She followed him onto the porch. The air was springtime soft. She watched him intently as he put the cup and doughnuts on the top of the car, opened the back door, and tossed the briefcase onto the seat. Then he took off his suit jacket, reached into the side pocket for his keys and hung the jacket on the hook by the window. He turned and looked at her, keys in hand.

"I love you, Jenna," he called across the lawn.

"I love you, Gary," she called back.

He opened the front door and started to get in. "Don't forget the coffee," she called. With a sheepish grin, he stood back up, retrieved the coffee and doughnuts and got back into the car.

CHAPTER 93

The meeting was held in a solid, glass-walled room on South LaSalle Street. They treated Gary very well and went over the transcripts of the tapes he had made. Cox was there, along with Thompson and Rasmussen. There were also two people Gary didn't know. One was a pudgy woman in her mid-50s. She had reddish, dyed hair and wore an expensive-looking business suit.

"Gary, this is Susan Henry," Rasmussen said. "She is the First Assistant U.S. Attorney here in Chicago. Since we will be trying the case here in the Northern District of Illinois, she will have overall charge of everything.

"This," he continued, turning to the other person, a lanky, rawboned man in his 30s with wild blond hair," is Alex Bremerton, also with the U.S. Attorney's office here. He will be doing much of the actual prosecution work when the trial begins. I have been placed on temporary assignment here to oversee the strategy and planning. That way, we keep the number of people who know what is going on down to a minimum. That's important, especially for the next 60 days or so."

When they got to work, Rasmussen did most of the talking. As Gary listened, memories of the past two years began flooding back into his mind. Some things he had almost forgotten about were suddenly in front of him again. Tapes he had thought inconsequential when he made them now took on new importance. At times, he almost felt like it wasn't he they were discussing, that he was an outsider looking in, or a ghost hovering over his own body. Occasionally, he had trouble matching dates with events. It seemed so long ago, could it have been only last year?

When they broke for lunch, Gary hustled to a telephone and called Leigh.

"I'm alone," she said. "How are you doing?"

"So far, so good," he answered.

"Well, it's been reasonably quiet here." She went through the calls he had gotten, and what she did with them. He gave her some instructions on a couple of the messages. There were none he absolutely had to return himself. Then he called Jenna to tell her everything was going well. He was hungry, having had nothing to eat all day except the doughnuts at about 5:00 a.m., but when he hung up from talking to Jenna, he realized he had no time left to get lunch. He bought two packages of cheese crackers from a newsstand in the lobby of the building and went back to the meeting room.

At the end of the day, Cox told Gary he would not be present for the subsequent meetings. Gary grabbed a sandwich, retrieved his car from the parking lot, called Leigh to get updated and headed back to Steuben. It hadn't been so bad, he thought. Another hurdle passed. One less to go.

The next Wednesday, he went through the same drill. This time, Bremerton asked most of the questions. When he got into his car for the drive back and called Leigh, she was frantic. "I've been holding Howard off for two hours," she told Gary. "He says he's got to talk to you."

Gary called him from the car and resolved Howard's crisis. "Where the hell are you?" Howard asked him.

"In my car."

"Well, where have you been all day?"

"I'll be home tonight," Gary answered, avoiding the question. "You want me to call when I get there?"

"Nah, I'll see you in the morning," Howard grumbled.

A week later, on Thursday, Gary was scheduled to report to the Federal Building on Dearborn Street where the grand jury was empaneled.

Gary's role was simple, answer questions with a yes or a no for the most part. They played videos of the various meetings and some selected clips from the audiotapes. Then they brought out transcripts to review in detail. At lunchtime, Gary headed across the street to a Chinese restaurant, calling Leigh from his cell phone while he waited for his order. Everything was under control, she reported. What a trouper she is, he thought. There's no way I could have pulled this off without her.

After lunch, it was more of the same – more tapes, more questions, more simple answers. Then it was all over.

A week later, Cox called and said he needed a date in the near future when Howard, William, G.T. and Gary would all be in town. "We want to talk to everyone the same night, and it'll look weird if you aren't investigated along with the others. We're going to come at night and go to people's homes. But when we talk to you it'll be a ruse."

Gary thought about it. "I'll talk to all the secretaries and try to plan some meeting that I need all of those guys at. Everybody travels a lot, so I don't know if I can pull it off, but I'll try. "What time frame are you looking at?"

"We'd like to try for sometime this month," Cox answered. "Other than that, it's up to you. The key is to have everyone in town at the same time." June was already almost a week old. When Gary hung up, he felt the nausea beginning to build, and his palms were sweating.

Over the next four days, he came up with a plan. Armand Pomerleau had scheduled the visit of the Czech officials to Steuben on June 24th. Howard and G.T. were lined up to be present, and Gary invented a reason to have Killer Keddy put the meeting on his schedule, too. That left only William, and a quick call to his secretary revealed that he planned to be in town.

"It would be really nice," Gary told her, "if he could spare a few minutes to say hello to these guys," he told her. "They're pretty high up in the Czech Republic government." She didn't think it would be a problem, and Gary told Cox the 24th would be D-Day.

"Perfect," Cox said.

"It's up to you now," Gary told him. "I think I've even got William Hargiss here."

"Actually," Cox said, "and you probably should know this, we've decided not to hit Hargiss on the night of the raid."

"Why not?" Gary asked. He'd gone to some trouble to make sure Hargiss was around.

"We want to give him a day or so to think about it," Cox responded. "We want to see what he'll do. Maybe he'll call some of his important friends, and we'd like to know who they are."

"Yeah," Gary replied, "but in the meantime, I'm hung out to dry. If he figures out it was me, there's no telling what he'll do."

"Don't worry about it," Cox said. "Our guys aren't going to leave any hints at all that this is an inside job. We figure everybody's first suspicions will fall on the Japanese. We may even drop a little disinformation in that direction.

"Remember," he added. "We're not going to arrest anybody on the twenty-fourth. We're just going to serve notice that we're on their tail and gather evidence. We'll target you just like the others, so all you have to do the next day is pretend to be as scared shitless as they all will be.

"And keep your tape recorder running," he added.

CHAPTER 94

The days leading up to the raid were pure hell. Gary was barely touching his meals, and Jenna was sure he had lost weight. He didn't want to make love, and many nights she awoke in the wee hours to find him gone from their bed. The first time, she went downstairs and found him in the family room, stretched out on the couch under an afghan her mother had made. The television was on.

She found a little space beside him and stroked his hair. "Come on up to bed," she said.

"I've been tossing and turning," he told her. "I didn't want to wake you."

He let her lead him upstairs that night, but there were others when he stayed downstairs all night, and was gone when she awoke in the morning.

His nerves were a wreck, and hers weren't much better. Gary still found time to be with Justin and Mark, but his attention span was short. They had opened the pool as usual on the first weekend in May, but it was now mid-June and he had yet to get his toes wet. Mostly, he just wanted to be alone. As the day of reckoning drew near, it was becoming increasingly hard for him to think about bringing his colleagues down. They had given him pay raises, bonuses, pats on the back, and wanted him to lead the company into the next millennium.

One Saturday, they couldn't find their cat, a calico named Smokey. All day they searched, to no avail, and when Jenna put the boys to bed, she prepared them for the worst, but late the next afternoon, Justin came rushing into the house. Jenna was in the living room, reading. "We found Smokey," Justin cried. "She's hurt."

Jenna called to Gary, and they all ran to the stable. Mark and Donnie Bradford were keeping vigil over the cat, who had hidden herself behind some bales of hay and was licking a wounded leg. They found a box, put Smokey in it, and drove to the veterinarian.

Dr. Burns lived out in the country south of town. He examined Smokey carefully. "She's going to be all right," he told them. "I'd say she got in a fight with something, a dog maybe, or a raccoon, something bigger and stronger than she is."

"If she was hurt, why did she hide? Why didn't she come and let us help her?" Justin asked.

"When an animal is wounded, it wants to be alone," Dr. Burns told him. "The fact that you were able to find her at all means she decided she was going to live."

They left Smokey with the vet for observation overnight. As they drove home, Jenna couldn't stop thinking about what Dr. Burns had said. *Gary is like a wounded animal*, she thought. *That's why he just wants to be by himself.*

When he didn't want to be by himself, Gary talked with Jenna, who felt bad for the families involved. She liked Cathy Binghamton a lot, and worried about young Tommy. The Keddys had a retarded son they had dutifully cared for over many years. Through Madeleine Caldwell, she had met Virginia Hargiss, too. What sort of an impact would all this have on that gracious lady? Did she even have an inkling about the evil her husband and son presided over?

Jenna could well imagine what torture awaited the families of the men involved. She expressed her thoughts to Gary, and it made him feel even worse. Before it had all been James Bond, now it was real life. Now it was happening, and people, even innocent people, were going to suffer.

Two days before the trap was set to be sprung, Gary reviewed his plans to take over the company after the fall. He understood that there would be enormous publicity about what would surely become known as the TLP Scandal. If he were going to come out of this a hero, it meant he needed to control that publicity, right from the start. He decided to let one more person in on the truth: Buffy Carney.

Buffy agreed to come to Gary's house the next night, and they met in the pool house. It was just after 8:00, and the sun was still bright in the long June day.

"It all started here, right in this room, and the climax will come in just about twenty-four hours," Gary told Buffy, who listened intently, betraying no emotion as Gary detailed the story from start to finish.

When Gary explained his plan to take over the company, Buffy whistled.

"When the dust has settled, I want you and Brad and me to be in charge," Gary told him. "Brad doesn't know anything yet," he added, "but I need you to be my spin doctor."

Now that Gary had spilled his guts, Buffy was trying to decide whether or not to reciprocate. There were things he knew that Gary had no clue about. Should he tell him, should he reveal all the snippets of Carney family lore about the old days when William Hargiss and his grandfather had been on the front lines of Cold War era espionage? Buffy had no direct knowledge of what Hargiss had been up to in recent years, but he was sure in his mind the secret world still existed.

Cautiously, he framed a question. "I can see Howard, G.T. and the others going down," he began, "but do you really think they can get William?"

"The FBI is confident they can," Gary answered. "I've tried every way I can think of to tell them how powerful he is, but all I can say to you is that they think they've got him."

Maybe, Buffy thought to himself, they don't need Hargiss anymore, what with the Cold War over and all. Otherwise, it was hard to believe the FBI could get the case this far without bells going off all over Washington. He decided to play it close to the vest.

"I think," he said, his face brightening, "your plan sounds like fun. Count me in."

Fun? Gary didn't think anything about it was going to be fun. Not for a long time. Right now, he felt like a dead man walking.

Still, he was glad to have Buffy on board. "I think the three key guys," he said, "are Randolph Thad, Robert Aiken, and Ian Howes. They're the board members with real independent stature. I've been brown-nosing them for a year now, even longer than that, really. I just hope it pays off."

"Forget Aiken," Buffy cautioned. "He'll be completely on the other side. His law firm will represent TLP throughout the trial, which means he'll be shoulder deep in trying to destroy you as a witness and in every other way."

Gary hadn't thought about that. It was disappointing news, but good to know now, before he had gone any farther.

"With the other two," Buffy added, "you've got a chance."

On the morning of the 24th, Gary got up at 5:30 and went to work, preparing for the Czech meeting. At noon, he left for the airport to pick up the dignitaries. Jiri Svoboda was a tall, distinguished, gray-haired man in his 60s, who spoke no English. He did know some French, and Gary was able to communicate with him a little. Ludek Mruzek was younger, stout, and had a round face beneath a shock of coal-black hair. His English, although heavily accented, was excellent. Both were pleasant, smiling men, and Gary liked them instantly. They were a welcome distraction. Buffy called twice to make sure everything was still on.

At 4:30, Gary turned the Czechs over to Leigh, who took them to their rooms at the Chemical Club to freshen up before their dinner at the Country Club a few miles away. By 5:00, the distraction no longer available to occupy his mind, Gary was a nervous wreck. The end of the road was here. At 6:00, he called the lone Steuben taxicab company and gave some very explicit instructions. Then he left for the Country Club.

The plan was for G.T. and Gary to meet for drinks at 6:30. Leigh would drive the Czechs to the Country Club and then go home. As far as anyone else understood, Gary would drive them back to their rooms at the Chemical Club. Gary, of course, knew he wouldn't be able to do that. As soon as he got to the Country Club, he spied the taxi waiting in the driveway.

He walked over to the driver and spoke to him through the open window. He handed the man a $50 bill, considerably more than the confused driver had expected to make for the evening. Then he went back inside and waited for G.T. and the Czechs.

"I hope to hell this won't take too long," G.T. told him when he arrived. "I've got to catch a plane at the crack of dawn for a meeting in Cleveland."

Suppressing the urge to make a wisecrack, Gary reassured him.

Then the Czechs arrived, and three of the four men enjoyed their cocktails, Gary trying his best to maintain an air of normality and pay attention to the conversation. How he and Armand Pomerleau would ever resurrect the project in the Czech Republic, he had no idea; either they would come up with something or not. It would have to wait. At 7:15, Gary suggested they go upstairs for dinner.

They were just preparing to order when two men approached the table and identified themselves as FBI agents. They asked to speak to G.T. and Gary separately and privately. G.T. looked at the agents with dumb incomprehension, and Gary tried to imitate his confusion. Gary held back just a little, and watched G.T.'s broad back start to move across the room. Quietly, he spoke to the startled Mruzek. "Something has come up," he said. "Please enjoy your dinner. There is a taxi in the driveway, which will take you back to your hotel whenever you are ready. Everything has been paid for." As the FBI agent led him away in the opposite direction from the one G.T. and his agent had taken, Gary heard his two guests talking excitedly in Czech.

"What is happening?" the uncomprehending Svoboda asked Mruzek.

"Truly, I do not know," Mruzek said. "It seems almost like the old days back home."

When the interviews were over, the agents disappeared and G.T. and Gary met back in the bar. They went to a quiet corner, shooed the waiter away and quickly compared notes.

"We've got to get to Howard," G.T. said. "Let's meet at his place."

"Do you think he got a visit, too?" Gary asked, feigning incredulity at the whole event.

"Who knows?" G.T. said, his eyes wild with terror. "Who the fuck knows what the hell is going on?"

I do, Gary thought as they rushed from the bar, got into their separate cars and headed off into the night.

Howard met them at the door of his odd, contemporary-design home with drink in hand. "Interesting night, huh?" Howard said. That answered one question.

They started to tell their story, but Howard cut them short. "I don't trust any of you guys, why don't you tell it to Zack Brilley," he said. Then with a wave, he dismissed them and slammed the door, leaving G.T. and Gary to stare at each other until the light on the porch went off.

Howard locked the door and gulped the vestiges of the drink he'd made just five minutes before. Somewhere, they had a fucking rat in the operation. Nothing else could explain the kind of information the FBI claimed they had, and nothing else could explain the videotape of the meeting in Hawaii they showed him on some kind of portable video player. That's when he slammed the door in their faces and told them unless they had a warrant they'd better get the fuck off his property.

Less than ten minutes later, Gary and G.T. had shown up. Well at least they were all in this thing together. Fuckin' slant eyes. They'd probably set this whole thing up, he thought. Dad will be so pissed off he'll breathe fire. Jesus, he thought, maybe they grabbed him, too. He picked up the telephone.

"Dad, we've had a little trouble over here."

"What's up, Howard?" William said, curtly. No, Howard thought, he doesn't know anything.

"I've had a visit from the FBI."

"What!" All pretense of gruffness in William's voice yielded to genuine surprise.

"Yeah, they showed me a video of a meeting we had in Hawaii with the fuckin' Japs and then said they needed to talk to me for several hours about price fixing. I told them unless they had a warrant to get the fuck off the property and they left. Ten minutes later, Gary and G.T. showed up. I guess they'd had the same kind of thing happen too."

"Is this some kind of a bad joke?"

"Dad, I'm a little scared."

"Don't say another word over the phone. Get your ass over here right now."

"What's the matter?" Virginia Hargiss asked her husband.

"I don't know," he said. "That was Howard. There may be some serious trouble. Do me a favor and make some coffee. Then trundle off to bed. It may be a long night."

"Is Howard in trouble?" she asked, walking to the kitchen to start the coffee. Her only child had more than once had gotten himself into scrapes that had required the use of his father's influence.

Hargiss knew what she was thinking. He only wished Howard had been busted for drugs, or beating up one of his whores, or anything but this. Fixing that sort of thing was child's play. "No, no," he reassured Virginia. "It's not that. It's business."

Five minutes later, G.T. rang the buzzer at the gate at the end of William Hargiss's driveway.

"Who is it?" Hargiss spoke into the intercom, expecting to hear Howard's voice.

"It's G.T., William; we've got problems."

"So I've heard," he said, his anxiety jumping another notch. He pushed the buzzer to open the gates, and met G.T. at the door.

G.T. started babbling immediately, but William held up his hand and led him to the kitchen, where they sat down at the breakfast bar. "Get your wits about you," William said. "Howard is on his way over." The coffee maker finished its cycle and let out a sigh and a burble.

G.T. started his story.

"Wait a minute," William said when G.T. talked about the videotape he had been shown. "It was a meeting in Chicago?" G.T. nodded. William was sure Howard had said the tape he had been played was from a meeting in Hawaii. That meant the FBI had more than one tape. Jesus Christ, he thought, what if they taped the meeting I was at in Steuben?

"What the hell are we going to do, William?" G.T. whined when he finished. Hargiss got up and began pacing. This was clearly not part of the game plan. Was this a double cross by the NSA? Did they want to extract more from him than they already had?

No, more likely this wasn't even on the NSA radar screen, he thought, retrieving some cups from the cupboard and pouring coffee for them both. Maybe this was something initiated by a competitor. That had to be it; the NSA would never stand for this type of thing going on. They had more to lose than he did. Well then, the first order of business was a call to Jonathan Decatur. Just then Howard arrived.

Howard looked at G.T. first, and then turned to his father. "What the fuck is he doing here?" Howard said pointing at G.T.

"Howard, for Christ's sake come to your senses. He's part of the family. I can tell you one thing for certain, we can trust G.T.," Hargiss said.

"Yeah, well, I don't trust anyone. Did you guys set me up for all of this?"

"Howard, your mouth is running before you engage your brain. Shut the hell up and sit down while I make a call."

He dialed the all-hours number for Admiral Decatur.

The phone rang, he punched in his code and heard the phone click several times before the line was connected. "Jon, this is Bill, we've got a situation here."

"Bill, you gotta believe the agency didn't know this was going on," Decatur pleaded after listening to the story. "I need to get the Director in the loop and see if we can get this thing shut down before it goes any farther. I'll call you first thing in the morning." Then the line went dead.

Decatur's mind was whirling. What the hell had happened? In the back of his mind, he thought he knew. He had gotten the FBI interested in TLP two years ago, when Hargiss had been concerned about industrial espionage by Nippon Kagaka. Then Hargiss had wanted the whole investigation shut down, and Decatur's contacts assured him it had been. Somehow, that information must have been wrong, he realized. The FBI must have continued working, which meant they'd been at it for years. He picked up the phone and dialed the Director at his home. Once they had the line secured, Decatur filled him in. "What do you think is going on?" Decatur asked.

"They didn't come by to see Hargiss?"

"No, sir. Not yet, anyway."

"Well then, they don't have the full story, or they'd have hit him immediately, to see if he'd cave. I need to try to sort out what's happened. You need to get out there and begin talking to the agent in charge to find out what he knows and how this whole thing came together. You get your ass on the fucking jet right now, and be there before the sun rises. Then report to me as soon as you have any information. If I have to, I'll call that bitch over in Justice tomorrow and see if I can straighten everything out."

CHAPTER 95

After leaving Howard's, Gary drove to the Holiday Inn to meet with the FBI. He took the elevator to the top floor, where two agents were standing. "This floor's closed off for the evening," one of them said.

Gary gave him his name and told him Sid Cox was expecting him. "Ah," the man said. "You're Dr. Long. Right this way."

He led Gary to the suite at the end of the hall. There were several agents in the room, and they felt pretty good about the evening's activities. Others milled in and out.

"Get Crowley in here," Cox barked, and a few minutes later a balding man came into the room.

"What did you mean, earlier, when you said Mrs. Curtis seemed to have advance knowledge?" he asked Crowley, sharply.

"When I showed her my badge, she said she'd been expecting me," Crowley answered.

"I confided in Leigh Curtis a month ago," Gary spoke up. "I had to, or I'd never have pulled off all those trips to Chicago to meet with the prosecutors and the grand jury."

He could tell that Cox was really upset.

"Why in hell did you do that?" Cox yelled at him. "She's a fucking material witness! She could have blown the whole thing! You should never have done that without talking to me first."

Gary was worn out and on edge. "If I would have told you, you would have said no. I had to have her help to make sure I could be gone that long without getting caught."

"Who the hell else have you tipped off?" Cox demanded, and Gary told him that the only other person who knew was Buffy. Buffy had not been a target of the raid, and his name didn't ring a bell with Cox.

"He's one of my best friends, and he's as interested in the company being clean as I am," Gary explained. After another outburst, Cox finally dropped the subject and moved on.

"We need you to tape some reactions tomorrow if you feel safe, like them telling you to destroy documents, or anything else you think would be obstruction of justice. I want to put these guys under lock and key for a long time. We haven't talked to William Hargiss yet, but we're going serve him tomorrow morning. That's when the fireworks will really begin," Cox said, smiling.

While Gary was on his way home, Buffy called him on the car phone and was higher than a kite when Gary told him the raid had come off smoothly. As soon as he hung up, the phone rang again. It was Brad Redfoot. "Jesus Christ, I've been trying for an hour to catch you," Brad said. "Do you know about the FBI?"

Gary assured him he knew, and told him he had been questioned as well. "Don't worry," he said. "You're clean. I've got a hunch this is all going to turn out just fine."

Jenna was waiting in bed for him, and they talked until they fell into a fitful, exhausted sleep.

CHAPTER 96

At his home in Indianapolis, Jim Thompson was already out of the shower when the doorbell rang at 6:45 the next morning. He wrapped a towel around himself and opened the door, surprised to find an older man dressed in a suit standing there. Looking beyond the man, Thompson saw two men in a waiting Lincoln by the curb.

"Jim Thompson?" the gray haired man asked in a soft voice that carried both congeniality and an air of seriousness. Thompson nodded. "Jonathan Decatur, NSA."

My God, Thompson thought. It *was* Decatur. He'd seen his picture before in several publications. What the hell was this all about? He didn't have to wait long for his answer.

"Tell me all about the TLP case."

"Well, I really should clear with Justice since the investigation has moved to overt."

"I think I have the necessary security clearances, Mr. Thompson."

Thompson stumbled for words while he thought about what he should do. "Uh, Admiral, this case started in your agency, you've probably got the original files."

Decatur's mind raced. His first and worst thoughts had been correct. But how in hell had that little matter exploded into this? "I'd like to take a look at the 302s. Do you still have copies of all of them at your office?"

Thompson thought for a second. "Yes, we have the originals."

"Good. I'll let you get dressed, then I'll have my car follow us to the office, that is if you don't mind me riding with you." Decatur wanted to make sure Thompson didn't make any calls yet.

"Uh, yeah, sure. That'll be okay."

Gary left home at 6:30, spotted Donnie Bradford having his morning coffee and gossip with the men at Steven's Auto Repair in Wonanonly, and made his way on to Steuben and TLP. He noticed Howard's and William's cars in the garage. He wondered where G.T.'s Mercedes was, and then remembered that G.T. was in Cleveland.

He won't be worth a tinker's dam in that meeting, Gary thought.

He checked his pocket recorder, just to make sure it was working. He flipped the familiar black switch on the microphone and looked inside his coat pocket to make sure the little red light had come on. Then he turned it off again. Everything was working, including his stomach. Where was the switch to turn it off? It felt like a volcano ready to explode.

There was a swarm of people in front of Howard's office and around his secretary's desk. Gary spotted Killer Keddy and Roger Kincaid among the group.

His own office was a mess; the FBI had gone through it with a fine-tooth comb. No doubt they had taken dozens of files, but it was impossible to tell, given the rat's nest they had left.

He rearranged enough papers so he could get some space to work on the desk and tried to tell himself this day was all to the good, just something to be endured in order to bring the much longer nightmare to an end. But he knew it was just a hope. He needed to collect his thoughts; the ride to work had not been long enough to pull everything together. But he wouldn't be granted the time he needed. Keddy walked through the door. "Did you have any unusual visitors last night?" he asked.

"Yeah, I did," Gary replied seriously, reaching for the switch. "The FBI came to see me at the Country Club when I was with G.T."

"Me, too," Keddy said. "Matter of fact, about everyone I've talked with this morning got a visit."

Gary asked, "What did they have to say to you?"

"They asked me all kinds of things about price fixing and collusion with our competitors. I didn't even let them in the door. I told them to get the hell out of there. They asked the questions and I didn't respond. I acted as if I didn't even know what they were talking about. This doesn't look good, does it? I'll bet 'ol G.T. is shitting bricks right now."

"Nah, it doesn't look good," Gary responded. "They asked me the same kind of questions."

"This investigation didn't start last night," Keddy said with a thoughtful look on his face. "They knew too much for it to be starting then."

"Yeah, from what I heard last night, it's probably been going on for a long time."

Keddy whistled and said, "Holy shit, I gotta get back to work."

Gary turned off the recorder. He still needed to clear his head, so he went for a cup of coffee in the Xerox room and headed back toward his office. On the way back, he spotted Tim Johnson, the head of the commodity division, and his top assistant, Steve Allison, sitting in Johnson's office. Normally, he had little to do with either of them, but there was nothing normal about this day. Gary turned the recorder back on and walked in. Johnson had just started saying that his interview hadn't lasted long. "I told them I trade oils so I didn't know very much about Sugere."

Allison spoke up, "They asked me about Howard and what kind of guy he is, was he nicknamed the 'Price Fixer,' and then they asked me about G.T., and you," he said, pointing to Gary. "They also asked me if I knew about the vitamin C bug being stolen from Allied and a citric bug from Universal, and about some hookers in Thomasville that were planted to steal the Sugere bug. I told them I didn't know anything. Obviously someone blabbed a whole bunch of shit to the FBI," Allison concluded. Gary left Johnson's office and walked back to his own.

Leigh was sitting at her desk in front of Gary's office when he got back. Gary said hello and nodded to her as he slipped back into his office. Within seconds she was in his office.

"I got visited by the FBI last night," she said.

"What did they ask you?" Gary responded.

"They asked me if I knew about some prostitutes Tully hired, which I didn't, and the bugging of the Chemical Club, which I told them I did know something about and even told them the names of the others who were involved in that. You didn't tell me they were investigating that," Leigh concluded breathlessly.

Killer Keddy hadn't let the agents in the door. Tim Johnson had stonewalled. But Leigh had been forthright and honest, and told them what she knew. It was a nice continuum, from conspiracy to honesty. Gary wondered where he was on it.

"Yeah, they'll probably talk to all of them," Gary said. Leigh stopped for a second, then said, "Good...Gary, be careful. I'm very worried about you." She turned on her heels and walked out with a tense look on her face.

It was almost 8:00, and Gary's phone buzzed. It was the receptionist in the lobby. "Gary, your visitors are here." His mind jerked from one kind of reality to another. Had the Czechs come back? No, it wasn't them, it was a group of industry leaders from Pennsylvania who had come to visit TLP and hear about some of the fabulous new ways they were using petroleum byproducts in production. Gary had scheduled the meeting months before, and completely forgotten about it in all the excitement.

Gary gave presentations like these in the same conference room where the Steuben Agreement had been made. He rescued his slide set from the office mess, asked the receptionist to take the guests to the conference room, called Billie Mitchell to join him, and headed there himself.

He somehow stumbled through the slide show and fielded a few questions before sending them with Mitchell to take a tour of the plant.

"Bring them back here for lunch," he instructed Mitchell. "I'll join you then." That gave him time for a few phone calls.

He desperately wanted to call Armand Pomerleau in Paris, to bring him up to date on the situation with the Czech politicians. Armand had worked for months to put that deal together, and he deserved to know that Gary had probably killed it, but when Gary walked back into his office, he was staggered by the number of phone messages. The first he returned was from Zack Brilley.

"Gary," the company attorney began, "let me bring you up to speed with what we're doing. We're flying in legal counsel to meet with everyone who had his office cleaned out by the Feds. TLP will provide the attorneys. That's part of each man's personal contract with the company."

"My personal attorney, paid for by TLP," Gary reiterated, just to be sure.

"That's right," Brilley confirmed. Gary was to meet with his attorney at 6:00 p.m. at a local law office. G.T. and Killer Keddy were also going to be meeting at the same office. Howard's meeting was to be in Chicago, Brilley said.

"Are the lawyers all from one firm?" Gary asked.

"Yeah," Brilley responded. "Bob Aiken's sending them in from various offices of his firm around the country. Why do you ask?"

"Oh, just curious," Gary said.

By the time he got off the phone he was sweating bullets. He looked through the rest of the messages and started to return more calls. Only two were from people not on the TLP payroll, and Gary decided to return them last.

All the internal calls were from people asking about what they should do and how he was. Most of the callers were from various division offices and were trying to get a handle on what had really happened, since the rumor mill was now cranking at full tilt. One was from a TLP distributor in Venezuela. TLP had become a giant, worldwide version of Steven's Auto Repair.

One of the calls from outside the company was from John Caldwell.

Caldwell's clients owned tens of thousands of shares of TLP stock, and when his wife told him that morning about a phone conversation she had just had with Virginia Hargiss, all his antennae shot straight up. He tried to reach Gary and several of his other friends at TLP, but no one would return his calls. Finally, he even called Ralph Sori in Chicago.

When he told Gary he had called Sori, it explained the other non-TLP call Gary had in his stack of messages; it was from Ralph. John's call was Gary's first indication that anything had leaked outside TLP. Gary told Caldwell there was trouble, but he couldn't really say anything else. Then he called Ralph and told him the same thing.

As soon as he hung up from talking to Gary, Ralph called Caldwell. "What's TLP selling at this morning?" he asked. Caldwell told him it was unchanged from the day before. "Sell all my shares, right this instant," Ralph told him.

John Caldwell sold a lot of TLP stock that day, virtually every share he had discretionary authority over, including his own.

Gary checked his watch. It was a little after noon. He had to look in on the tour group.

For the Pennsylvanians that day, TLP was a technological marvel. They examined its virtually endless array of pipes and vats, the computer-driven flow monitors, the tanks filled with media and bug, unconcernedly chomping away, making Sugere. The group glimpsed an exciting economic organism, robust and strong, without ever for a moment suspecting the cancer in its belly.

CHAPTER 97

Things in Indianapolis weren't moving well at all. The more 302s Decatur looked at, the more concern he had. This wasn't a fly-by-night operation. More than 50 agents had been used in the case, and it had already been in front of a grand jury. On top of that, they had tapes, more than 1,200 of them, at least ten of which were very damaging to William Hargiss. Hargiss was scheduled to receive a visit at 11:00 that morning, and by 10:45, Decatur knew there was nothing he could do to prevent it. The only good news was that the sole crime they were focusing on was price fixing, but it was clear he had to move fast to prevent the case from mushrooming.

It was going to have to be handled at a very high level.

At precisely 11:00, two FBI agents arrived at the TLP gate and requested a meeting with William Hargiss. The confused gatekeeper phoned Hargiss's secretary who quickly located Hargiss. After a deep breath, Hargiss told her to send them onto the lot, and that he'd meet them at the front desk.

It had been a long time since the ladies of the reception area had seen William Hargiss come down to greet a guest. When he arrived, they quickly found things to do, keeping their eyes off him.

Within a minute of his arrival, two gentlemen came through the doors. Hargiss greeted them, and escorted them to the sixth floor. If the events of the previous 18 hours hadn't been enough to set tongues wagging, this certainly was. Within ten minutes, the word was on the street: William Hargiss had real trouble on his hands.

The two agents played five clips that featured Hargiss, including his speech at the Steuben Agreement meeting. They told him he was the subject of an FBI investigation, and asked if he had any information to offer. As expected, he shook his head, said his lawyer would be in touch and asked them to leave. Their arrival had the desired effect, and as they left they noticed the stares cast in their direction. They felt a great deal of satisfaction.

Before they reached the gate, an enraged William Hargiss was on the phone to Washington. Told Decatur was out, he asked for the Director, and within two minutes had him on the phone.

"I just want you to know, Director, I've got a lot of secrets to tell, things a lot of people won't understand, and won't like. If I have to, I'll tell the whole story, and right now I'm so mad, I think just for fun I'll let a few crumbs drop. If you don't get this goddamn mess cleaned up pronto, I'll rip open your political life and shit on your future. Do you understand?"

The Director, who was not pleased with the news he'd been given ten minutes earlier by Decatur, understood all too well. "Mr. Hargiss, I'm making the necessary phone calls now to make this thing go away," he said. "It's not going to be quick 'cause it's so damn messy, but it will go away. Do you understand me?"

Hargiss understood and hung up the phone without saying anything else for emphasis. As soon as the Director heard the empty line he clicked the receiver and placed a call to the Attorney General, the woman he often called the "Dreaded Dyke." How he hated politics.

CHAPTER 98

Politics, on the other hand, was mother's milk to Adrian McWhorter. For 30 years, he had worked at the Rose Law Firm in Little Rock, helping politicians cover their legal bee-hinds, as he so often put it.

In the process, he'd become the number one fixer in the state of Arkansas. He'd only had one big failure in all that time. He'd tried every trick in the book to keep Governor Winthrop Rockefeller from closing down the illegal gambling operations in Hot Springs in 1967, but to no avail. The problem with having a Rockefeller as governor was that he couldn't be bought. He was the only governor McWhorter had ever known, or ever would know, who couldn't be bought.

It was at that time that he first met young Bill Clinton. Part of the strategy for saving the gambling operations was to stir up the local population to protest the impending shutdown. They didn't need much encouragement. The whole economy of the town depended on the tourist dollars the casinos brought in, and the fact that it was all criminal didn't count for beans with the locals. Everybody from the insurance agent to the guy pumping gas on Malvern Road knew his or her personal prosperity depended on those casinos.

Clinton was in college then, and he showed up in McWhorter's office as a volunteer, offering to work on getting petitions signed to stop the shutdown. And what a job he did. Within three weeks, he was virtually running the whole public protest operation.

When, a decade later, Clinton decided to run for office, McWhorter signed up immediately, and the two had been close ever since, to their immense mutual benefit.

Now, McWhorter was Deputy Attorney General of the United States, and anybody who was anybody in Washington knew that this rumpled, paunchy Arkansan was the man to see if you needed something done or undone in the Justice Department.

He had just had a call from his de facto boss, the Attorney General. The matter they discussed seemed important. There were supposedly national security concerns at stake. Adrian McWhorter didn't give a fig about national security, but the name she mentioned triggered something in his mind. He hunched over his computer and opened a file only he knew was there. He scanned the list of names. Yep, there he is, he said to himself. The record showed that William C. Hargiss, of Steuben, Indiana had been responsible for pumping more than $600,000 into the right places since 1992.

"Well," he said out loud, though there was no one to hear him. "I guess this case *is* important."

CHAPTER 99

When Gary got back to his office after his lunch with the Pennsylvania tour group, Buffy called. "You want me to start something?" he asked.

"No," Gary said. "It's got to break from outside first. Just be ready to jump when it does."

Dan Anthony called. Since his firing, Gary had almost forgotten about him. Now he remembered that Anthony had been the first person at TLP who ever spoke the words "price fixing" to him. "I think we're all fried," Anthony said.

"You get a visit from the Feds?" Gary asked.

"Yeah. See you in Leavenworth," Anthony responded sourly.

Brad Redfoot came into the office, wearing a face like a basset hound. Gary tried to talk to him about ordinary business, but Brad's mind was elsewhere.

"I'm going to call a headhunter," Brad said. "I've got to get out of here."

"Don't do that yet," Gary advised him. "Just sit tight for a little while. This thing may still come out good for us."

"You've got to be kidding," Brad said. "Your ass is in a sling, and mine may be, too. I put together that price chart and a bunch of other stuff."

Gary tried to reassure him. Somehow, he had to keep Brad going, and he knew for a fact that Redfoot was not a target of the investigation.

If I know any facts at all, he thought.

CHAPTER 100

Admiral Decatur returned Hargiss's call from the Gulfstream 500 on his way back to Washington. The 302s painted a clear picture of what had happened, but he had to be careful at this stage about what he told Hargiss. He desperately wanted to reveal who the mole was, but if he did that, Justice would throw a hissy fit, and any chance of his striking a deal with them would be lost. The wrong combination of words could make it impossible to extract TLP from this situation. Besides, he reasoned, if he knew William Hargiss, he'd find the truth soon enough on his own.

"Bill, going secure."

"Secure here."

"The Director has already talked to Justice. They had no idea of your and TLP's importance to this country. We have to walk a pretty fine line with this or it could all blow up in our face."

"It's already blown up in mine. I got a visit this morning that wasn't too damn pleasant. I'm madder than a boiled owl right now, and I'm telling you, Jon...."

"I know, I know. Please, give us a day or two to sort this out. The press is going to have a short term field day; there isn't anything we can do about that, except limit the damage and begin working on paying back the source. I'm sure a lot more things will be clear in a couple of days."

"You'd better hope so."

Then the line went dead. Decatur knew Hargiss was really steamed, but there wasn't much he could do about it. He sighed, and phoned the Director again, filling him in on more details from the 302s, and his conversation with Hargiss.

Hargiss hadn't meant to hang up on Decatur, but his hand was so unsteady he had clicked the phone off accidentally. Get it together, old boy, he thought.

He picked up the phone again and told his secretary to ring Buffy Carney and have him come up to the sixth floor.

"I guess you know what's going on," Hargiss said as Buffy walked in the door.

"Well, I know a whole bunch of people got raided last night, and I know it's about price fixing and some other stuff, and I know the investigation's been going on for two years," Buffy replied. "Other than that, I don't know a lot, except everybody and his dog around here is getting loony."

"Two years!" Hargiss said, sharply. "Who told you that?"

Buffy gulped. He'd just screwed up, big time. There'd been lots of speculation, but the only person who had told him about the two years was Gary, two nights before in the pool house.

"Well, I guess I don't know that part for sure," he stammered. "That's just sort of the consensus guess around the office."

"Well, you're going to need to stay close to me for the next few days," Hargiss said. "The press will be all over this like flies on a cow patty, and we're going to need serious damage control."

"I'm at the ready," Buffy said, breathing a sigh of relief when Hargiss dismissed him.

The next call Hargiss made was to Zack Brilley. "Have you got a list of everyone the FBI came down on last night?" he asked.

"Yeah, I think it's complete," Brilley answered. "You want to see it?"

"No," Hargiss said. "What I want you to do is look through it and figure out who the highest ranking person in the company is who's not on it."

A few minutes later, Brilley called back. "It's not always easy to tell who's above whom on our organization chart," he told Hargiss, chuckling, "but as near as I can figure the answer to your question is Buford Carney."

Later in the afternoon, G.T. returned from his trip to Cleveland. It must have been an interesting plane ride, Gary thought as he walked over to G.T.'s office.

"G.T.," Gary said, "this is the pits, isn't it?"

"Yeah, yeah, we'll deal with things as they come," G.T. said. "We'll have attorneys and they'll tell us what to do." His words were matter of fact, but his face had a worried look to it.

On his way back to his office, Gary ran into Zack Brilley, who pulled him aside and said, "Watch what you say to Buffy."

What the heck did that mean? Gary wondered as he stuffed pink telephone slips into his briefcase and left to go to the appointment at the attorney's office.

CHAPTER 101

The First of America Building was in downtown Steuben and housed several law offices. The one Gary wanted, Hirsch, Danza and Cobb, was on the fourth floor. Gary was a few minutes early.

Gary rang a doorbell beside the office door and Louie Cobb himself let him in. "Your attorney will be right with you," Louie said. "They're in a meeting right now."

G.T. was already sitting in a chair and Killer Keddy walked in shortly after Gary. The three of them sat silently and waited. Some minutes later the attorneys broke up their meeting and came into the room. Louie Cobb introduced Gary to John McCloud and said everyone would be meeting separately with his counsel.

Gary's meeting with McCloud was in Louie's personal office and, as he sat down, he noticed several pictures of the short, pudgy Louie playing golf with various TLP executives. McCloud shut the door, sat down and asked Gary to talk about his background.

That done, McCloud returned the favor. He said he had worked for the Department of Justice for several years and then had gone to Mitchell, Aiken and Forrest, where he specialized in "trouble" or criminal law. He worked in the San Francisco office, and had flown all day to get to Steuben. After taking it all in, Gary asked him to make it clear who he really represented. He told Gary that the company would be paying him, but that he would be representing Gary personally. Gary still wouldn't let it go, Rasmussen had drilled him on this one.

Finally McCloud had enough. "Look, I know all about the relationship between clients and attorneys. I don't represent the company, I don't represent the shareholders, I represent Gary Long and I will only do what is in the best interest of Gary Long."

Gary decided to trust him. "You're going to find this story interesting," he began. He told the whole story of his relationship with the FBI. He talked about price fixing, stolen technology and his own exposure. After listening intently and asking questions for an hour and a half, McCloud stood up and said, "These guys are dead meat. What are you going to do?"

Gary told him he would be cooperating with the government and that he was going to so advise the company. Then McCloud said, "If that's the case, I'm not sure I can represent you."

"Why not?" Gary asked him.

"Like I said before," McCloud answered, "I specialize in trouble, and you're not in trouble. You'll have the Government on your side. What do you need me for?"

"Even the Government told me to have an attorney," Gary replied. He was shocked. He had just opened up completely to this man, telling more than any one other person except himself knew. Now the man was walking out on him. A mist began closing in over Gary's eyes. What the hell had he just spent three hours for? This guy was backpedaling so fast that if the wall hadn't been behind him he would have been out on the street by now.

After a few seconds of silence, Gary cleared his throat and, his voice shaking, asked, "What should I do?"

"Well," McCloud replied, "I can give you some names of people if you'll call me in the morning. You need someone to protect you from the company, not the Government. I protect people from the Government. Another thing," he continued, "is that I am an employee of Mitchell, Aiken and Forrest, and it would be a conflict of interest if I worked for you now that I know your interests are at odds with those of TLP. I am definitely not the right guy to represent you."

Gary was terrified. McCloud had left no wiggle room, so it seemed pointless to try to get him to change his mind. "Tell me one thing," he said, standing up and looking down at the seated McCloud, "is everything I've just told you covered by attorney-client privilege?"

"Absolutely," McCloud said.

"And no one else will hear it?"

"No one."

"Not even Zack Brilley? Not even Robert Aiken?"

"Gary, I understand your concern," McCloud said. "I don't know what else I can tell you except that everything you have said in this meeting is strictly confidential between us, and that's how it's going to stay."

Gary couldn't ask for more than that. As they got up to walk out, McCloud asked Gary how he was going to handle it with Brilley, and Gary said he would tell him that he was going to cooperate with the government as of that night. Rasmussen had been clear on that point. Gary had to tell TLP that much, and no more. Not a hint that he had cooperated earlier.

Brilley was shoveling a pizza into his face in the kitchen lounge area. Gary asked him if they could talk for a minute and he agreed. They went back into another corner office on the opposite side of the reception room and Gary said, "Zack, I've gotta tell you something."

With a tremendous lump in his throat Gary continued, "I met with my attorney for the past three hours, as you know, and the main thing I want to say is that I am going to be cooperating with the government."

Brilley looked shocked. "Have you thought it through, Gary?" he asked.

"Yeah, I have," Gary replied. "I've really thought it through. I was just doing things I was told to do and I was not a decision maker in any of it. Therefore I have made the decision to help the FBI."

The disappointment in Zack's face was evident. "Well," he said, "you've gotta do what you've gotta do." He couldn't think of anything else to say.

Then Gary walked out of the office and got on the elevator. When he got to the ground floor, G.T. was also just getting off another elevator. "Hi," Gary said.

"We shouldn't talk about anything," G.T. replied. Then he changed his mind. "Is the guy you met with going to represent you?" he asked.

"G.T.," Gary responded, "I'm going to be cooperating with the Government."

"What?!"

"I'm going to be cooperating with the Government."

G.T. quickly took a step back as though he didn't want to be so close to Gary. "We shouldn't talk any more," he mumbled, and then added pointlessly, "see ya later."

Gary's departure left McCloud swimming in a sea of disbelief. Nobody believed this case was about a mole inside TLP; the whole focus of the discussions had been to determine which competitor had been feeding information to the Feds. This put an end to that speculation, but what could he do about it? Should he recuse himself from the whole case, given what he now knew? He was trying to figure it all out, when a shout from the conference room soon put an end to his mental gymnastics.

"Get your ass in here now, McCloud."

He covered the 40 or so feet to the conference room in five leaping strides. When he came through the door, Robert Aiken and Zack Brilley stood up. Louie Cobb stayed in his seat.

"What the fuck did you tell Long?"

"Ah, well..."

"You'd better clarify what went on in that room right now," Aiken said, in a voice much louder than conversational pitch.

"Well, I'm really under privilege here," McCloud said quietly, hoping to deflect the storm.

"You're really talking about your job here," Aiken said without skipping a beat.

McCloud let that one sink in. He looked at Aiken's face for some kind of smile or something to indicate the threat wasn't real, but all he found was a face chiseled in stone.

"You think about this for a second. I've gotta take a piss, but by the time I come back, you'd better find some way to overcome your new-found interest in ethics," Aiken said, leaving the room.

McCloud thought through the dangers of telling what he knew, and quickly searched for ways to mitigate the damages. Long before he'd reached a satisfactory answer, Aiken re-entered the room.

"Well boy, what's it going to be? I can tell you it's a long walk back to San Francisco from Steuben-Fucking-Indiana. But I'm a reasonable man. For right now, you don't have to say a word. Just listen to my questions and if you can find it in your ability to occasionally nod when I hit upon something that's interesting, I'd appreciate it. I think our friends here will back me up in saying you'll be well taken care of if you know anything of value here."

McCloud stared at Aiken, not sure if he'd really heard the offer he thought he'd heard, but Aiken didn't give him a chance to consider much.

"Did you advise Long to cooperate with the government?

McCloud found his head moving from side to side, almost involuntarily.

"Did he tell you the name of the mole?"

He nodded yes.

"Good, good. Now let me see, how can I do this...is it someone from one of the Asian companies involved in the price fixing?"

The headshake said no.

"Is it someone who works for TLP?"

McCloud paused, gulped, and slowly nodded yes.

"Shit, fucking shit, piss ass, goddamn, cunt-sucking shit!" Brilley exclaimed.

"Is the name Buford Carney?"

This time McCloud's head moved from side to side.

That was the only name inside the company that had even been a little bit suspected. That left, oh no, it couldn't be, but he had to ask. "Is it someone who was here tonight?"

McCloud closed his eyes and nodded yes.

"Is it Gary Long himself?" Aiken asked, holding his breath.

McCloud nodded, this time squeezing his eyes tightly shut, feeling the bile in his gut beginning to head for the exit ramp.

"Jesus Lord Almighty," Louie Cobb said in a whisper. Gasps came from the rest of the men.

McCloud ran from the room holding a hand over his mouth.

The drama in the room equaled the best movie any of them had ever watched, and they fell into complete silence, exhausted from the tension.

"Houston, we have a problem," Aiken said finally. "We'd better get Hargiss down here now."

On the way home, Gary wanted to call Jenna, but if he had worried before that his phone might be tapped, he was paranoid on the subject now. So he drove in silence.

As soon as he got home, they went for a walk in the rose grotto. Gary tried to hold back the choking feeling he had in his throat as he went through the story. "This is starting off to be a big mess," he said. "All we can do is hope this guy McCloud doesn't say anything."

He looked up to see headlights pulling into their driveway. It was Buffy. Gary was glad to see him, among other reasons because he wanted to tell him what Zack Brilley had said in the hall, and see if Buffy could think of any reason he would be under suspicion.

Buffy blanched when he heard what Gary said. He didn't dare tell him about his little slip in William Hargiss's office. "I don't know," he said, "but everyone's been really cold to me all day."

"I think," Gary said, "they suspect you of being a mole for the FBI."

"Well, there's one thing that would be worse," Buffy said. "If they suspected *you*."

"After my meeting tonight, they know I'm going to be cooperating with the government from now on. But there's no reason to suspect I already have been," he said. "For the time being, that's a critical distinction."

After Buffy left, Gary and Jenna talked some more and then collapsed in bed. About midnight, the OPX line from TLP rang. Gary had only ever received a handful of calls on the line, and never at this time of night. The ring, very different from that of the regular phone, startled him, but he shook off his surprise and sleepiness and answered the phone. It was Robert Aiken.

"We've been thinking," Aiken said, "and we feel it's best if you don't show up at the office tomorrow."

"Why, have I been fired?" Gary asked.

"No, no, it's just that we understand that you didn't use the counsel that we arranged, and we feel that the best way for you to spend your time is on getting counsel," he replied. "TLP will pay for it, of course, but, really, spend some time finding an attorney."

All of a sudden, Brilley was on the line as well. "Gary, I've got some recommendations for you," he said. Although he had no intention of using anyone they would recommend, Gary thanked them, hung up and went back to bed.

William Hargiss didn't have the luxury of sleep that night. News of the raid had leaked out, and the story was the lead item on the local evening news. Tomorrow it would hit the national press. Somehow he had to find a way to weather the approaching storm.

He'd spent the past four hours talking with every board member personally, reassuring them that the problem was short-term only, caused by a jealous competitor and sure to be over in a few weeks. When the call came from Aiken, it delivered a blow that nearly caused him to fall over.

Within 15 minutes he was sitting at the table with Louie Cobb, Aiken and Brilley. "We need something to discredit this kid with," Aiken said. "He was your golden-haired boy William, I hope you've got some way to insulate us from him."

Hargiss reacted immediately. "He isn't my boy, he's the answer you and Randolph and the others wanted me to find to the succession problem. We should have never gone outside for this. But there may be a way to discredit him. I'll tell you for sure in the morning."

When he got home, Hargiss called G.T. and asked him to come over. Even at two in the morning, G.T. didn't even mumble a complaint. "Yeah, I'll be right there," he said.

Twenty minutes later, Hargiss buzzed G.T. in. "Tell me about the bonuses you paid Long; what companies were they through?"

G.T. thought for a minute. "I told him to use bogus companies, or sound-alike companies."

Hargiss exhaled a sigh of relief. "That, my friend, is the best news you could have given me. Pull his AFEs first thing in the morning, and have the accountants go over his expense reports with a fine-tooth comb. Anything that looks odd, pull it and check it out. Also, you need to get Tully in here first thing. I suspect we're going to be seeing a lot of him over the next few weeks. Long was a mole for the Feds."

"No shit!"

"Yeah, and we need to cloud up and rain all over his fucking parade as fast as we can. Coordinate everything with me, and with Zack. Not everyone knows about the bonuses, remember, so be discreet. And make sure you get Tully in the office tomorrow morning first thing."

CHAPTER 102

Gary woke up at the usual time the next morning and called Sid Cox. He told him about the reactions around the office to the raid, and about his meeting with McCloud. Then he told him about the call from Aiken and Brilley, advising him not to return to work. Cox thought about it for a second and then encouraged him to return to the office as early as possible.

Gary thought it was odd how small details intrude into big doings. That day was the birthday of one of the secretaries in his division, and Gary was supposed to provide the birthday cake. As he debated whether or not to go to the office, it was that which tipped the scales. The cake, which Jenna had picked up the day before at the bakery, sat on the kitchen counter. "Happy Birthday, Kerry," it said in green gel on the white frosting.

When he pulled in the parking lot at 9:00, hours past his usual arrival time, Gary noticed a security guard run over to a phone. He locked his car and headed up the elevator. He put the cake on a table and turned to go into his office when Doug Marshall, an assistant to Zack Brilley, walked into the room and stood in the doorway. Doug had been a good friend, but the set of his jaw was pretty unfriendly. Gary could see Leigh behind him with an anxious look on her face.

"Gary, I think you were told you weren't supposed to be here today," he said.

"I was also told that you can't keep me out."

"That's true Gary, but you have two options. You can leave, or you can work with me sitting in your office all day long."

After a couple of minutes Gary realized there was no way he could work that way, so he decided to leave. He drove to the FBI office; no need to avoid it now

Thompson and Rasmussen were there, deep in conversation. They acknowledged Gary's presence, but not much more. Gary Picked up the phone and called Jenna.

"Buffy just called," she told him. "He said it was very important."

Gary called Buffy back on his direct line and heard the news he had dreaded.

"Gary, what are you doing?" Buffy asked.

"I was kicked out about 9:00 and they told me not to come back."

"Well, I can tell you why. William Hargiss was just in here and he told me he knew who caused all the problems – you."

"You're telling me that William knows I was the mole?" Gary asked, raising his voice so the others could hear what he was saying. Eyes blazing, he moved his gaze to each of the men in turn as he talked.

"Yes," Buffy answered. "That's what I'm saying. William was enraged. He kept saying he was going to make you wish you'd never been born. 'We're going to make his life miserable,' he kept saying."

"Thanks you, Buffy, I'll be in touch," Gary mumbled.

It was time for Gary to vent. "Look what you guys got me into!" he shouted. "You said this was all going to be good, that I'd be a hero. I don't see any of this as good at all."

Cox started to say something, but Gary wasn't about to let them off the ropes yet. He started yelling at the top of his lungs. "This has been a rotten waste of time. You got all the evidence you wanted, but what did I get? I'm a walking time bomb, and the three of you are totally responsible."

He walked over to Cox, and stood toe to toe. "If I bring out some of the stuff you did, you're gonna be in worse shape than they are," he said in a menacing whisper.

A brief look of panic crossed Cox's face, but he controlled it. "Calm down Gary, don't start bringing that stuff up. We're here to help you, were going to get through all of this," he said.

Then Gary walked over to a wall where they had a chart of strategy of what they were doing next and when. "Don't look at that wall Gary, it's confidential," Cox said quickly.

"I don't give a crap about that wall," Gary snorted. "I told you everything that's on that wall anyway. This case came from me and only me. You didn't have a clue about it until me. So don't tell me not to look at that wall. Every single piece of evidence you got I gave to you."

The room went quiet for a second, and then Cox spoke softly. "Well," he said, "you're right about that. We really appreciate it and that's why were going to do anything we can for you." The quiet continued for a few moments.

Kevin Rasmussen broke it. "What about your plan, Gary, your plan to take over TLP and run it right? You can still do that. Nothing's changed."

"The hell it hasn't," Gary said. "I needed time, time to make my case to the board before Hargiss got to them. Now that's down the toilet. Hell, I even thought I could get Robert Aiken on my side, and now he's leading the lynch mob. This is a mess. I'd never recommend that anybody do this. Look at this schedule." Gary showed him his appointment book. "I've got things I need to be doing instead of sitting around here."

"With what we just heard," Cox said soothingly, "the first thing you need to do is get an attorney. Do something productive instead of getting angry."

They were right. Gary now knew he should have had one two years ago, but that apparently hadn't crossed Cox's mind until he heard that Hargiss knew Gary was the mole. "Yeah, you're right. I don't know who I should call though, because there isn't anybody local who can handle this kind of stuff."

Then Rasmussen spoke up. "Let me make a phone call, see if I can come up with some names," he offered.

Gary nodded assent, and Rasmussen placed a call. "He'll get back to me in an hour," he said.

The next hour wasn't very pleasant for anyone in the room. Gary continued to rail at them for causing the world to crumble down around him. They continued to try to reassure him.

"Gary, it'll work out. If the company fires you, you can sue them for more than you'll make in a lifetime," Jim Thompson said.

That was small comfort to Gary. "I want to work, to do things," he said.

Thompson continued trying to calm Gary. He said that he had come to feel like he was one of Gary's good friends and he always carried a picture of him and his family with him. He opened his briefcase, fumbled through some things in the small pockets and took out the Christmas card with the Long family picture on it.

Sid Cox's head sunk onto his desk as Gary went berserk. "Everything you creeps do is just a trick!" he yelled. "What the hell is that? Page six of the agent's manual? Or do we have here the biggest fucking coincidence since the Big Goddamn Bang! "Tell him, Sid!" Gary shouted menacingly at the crestfallen FBI agent.

Thompson finally realized what Gary was talking about, and tried to think of something to say. He was saved by the bell. The phone rang, and Rasmussen grabbed it.

The prosecutor talked for a few minutes, taking notes. "Thanks for your help, Ted," he said into the phone. "This guy has been really, really helpful to us and he needs the best.

"That was my contact about the attorneys," he said to Gary after he hung up. "Ted Asturian is an Assistant U.S. Attorney in Chicago. He's number two there, after Susan Henry. "Here's the name he recommends, Keith Parr. I know him a little. He's real good." He handed the paper to Gary.

Gary got home about 2:30 and told Jenna the bad news; they both agreed that he should call Parr, and Gary immediately rang the number in Chicago. After Gary told the secretary who he was, a confident voice came on the line. "Hey, I was expecting you," Parr began. "It's good to meet you over the phone."

Obviously, someone had already called him about the case. Gary only hoped it was Rasmussen or Asturian. "I'd love to meet with you. Can you get in here this afternoon?"

Gary explained they lived almost four hours away, and set a time for the next afternoon for the meeting. Parr enthusiastically endorsed Gary's idea that Jenna be present, too.

That night Gary got a call from Leigh Curtis.

"I can't tell you how upset I was at the way Doug Marshall treated you this morning," she said. She was almost sobbing.

"It's all right," Gary tried to reassure her. "It's just temporary. I'll be back, and we'll clean up the mess and live happily after." He didn't think he'd convinced her, and knew he wasn't convinced himself.

"Anyway," she continued, "there's something else I need to tell you." Then she said something that shocked Gary more than everything he'd heard that day. "G.T. was upstairs on the accounting floor telling Roger Kincaid to pull some invoices. He said they were going after you for embezzlement. The way I heard it, Roger threw a fit and said it was just going to open a can of worms they wouldn't be able to close, but G.T. said they'd deal with it."

"What are you talking about?" Gary stammered.

"I don't know Gary, I can't imagine. But he just acted like he knew some invoices that he could get you on."

Gary said thanks and hung up. They were going after the bonus money. Of course G.T. would know all the invoice numbers, he probably kept them somewhere in a drawer, but surely he wouldn't expose the whole bonus system just to get me, Gary thought. He tossed and turned all night wondering what they had in mind.

The next day Gary and Jenna met with Parr in his office in the Wrigley Building. The attorney proved to be a handsome man in his mid-40s. He stood about six-foot one, and had wavy black hair. They spent a couple of hours giving him the details of the story. Parr held a yellow legal pad in his hands and wrote on it constantly as Gary and Jenna talked.

"The final thing is, I got a call last night and I found out they're going after me for embezzlement," Gary said.

"What's that about?" Parr asked, and Gary spent another half hour telling him about the bonus system and how it worked.

"How much did you get?"

"A little over a million," Gary said. Well, he thought to himself, it isn't actually a lie. Four million is a little over a million.

Jenna screwed up her face. She thought she knew why he had low-balled the number. He was just too embarrassed to tell this man he had just met how much there really was.

"Who else got bonuses?" Parr asked. Gary gave him a rundown as well as he knew it.

Parr looked up from his notes. "I don't think you have anything to worry about," he said.

"Really?" Gary asked. For the first time in two weeks, he felt a ray of sunshine.

"Yeah, those guys are mad and upset. They're talking like they're going to do something, but there's no way if they're in their right minds they could do something like that when they're getting bonuses, too. It's going to come right back at them. My bet is they don't pursue it."

He looked down at his notes again. "You said the FBI doesn't know about the bonus system?"

"Not from me, and I'm pretty sure not from anyone else, either."

"Well, don't tell them now."

He flipped back through the yellow pad again. He must have taken 20 pages of notes. "Gary, I definitely want to represent you on this," he said finally. "I have a lot of respect for the Justice Department and Ted Asturian. I've known him for twenty-five years. "Why don't you two talk it over for a few minutes, while I visit the little boy's room," he said, rising from his chair. Then he stopped. "That's pretty rude of me," he added, grinning sheepishly. "Would either of you like to use the facilities?"

They both thought that would be a good idea, and Parr retrieved a key to the ladies room from his secretary's desk. "Left for you, right for us," he told Jenna when they were out in the hall. Then he and Gary headed off together.

"One more thing, Gary," Parr said when they reached the deserted men's room. "Would you consider just severing your employment with TLP right now?"

Gary thought about it for a moment and told him he really hoped it could work for him to stay. "I'm doing so much important work and I'd really rather not try to sever anything now," Gary said. It's about time for me to talk to Ian Howes and Randolph Thad, he thought.

When they returned to the outer office, they waited for Jenna. Then Gary and Jenna went into Parr's private office. He shut the door behind them. "Let me know when you've decided," he said.

They didn't take long. They both felt comfortable with him. He seemed to know his stuff. And perhaps most of all, if they didn't hire him, they'd have to tell their story all over again to someone else.

They opened the door. Parr was reading some papers, standing at his secretary's desk. He quickly put them down and joined Jenna and Gary in his office.

"We'd like you to represent me," Gary said.

"Great," Parr said, grinning. "I think we'll work well together."

Outside, Gary and Jenna gazed for a few minutes at the Chicago River and talked about how nice it felt to have things in good hands.

"Hey," Gary said suddenly. "Why don't we call Ralph and Becky and see if they can have dinner with us? It doesn't matter what time we get home. The boys are staying with your folks."

"But won't you get tired, driving so late?" Jenna asked.

"Nah, I'll be fine. And remember, now that I'm unemployed, I can sleep late in the morning."

Gary called Ralph Sori at his office, and held on the line while Ralph checked with Becky. "This is a terrific surprise," he said when he got back on the line. "I can get off early, so I'll dash home, pick up what's-her-name, and meet you guys at Gibson's Steak House on Rush Street at six-thirty.   "I   do their PR, so we'll get a good table and the best food. Wait till you see their desserts."

Gary felt hungry for the first time in months. It was a pleasant summer afternoon, with a cooling breeze off the lake, so he and Jenna strolled up Michigan Avenue to kill time and enjoy themselves. They looked into several of the upscale shops, and spent almost an hour in the De Graaf art gallery, where Jenna admired some paintings by John Carsman. Gary tried to remember which ones she liked best. If he could, he'd get her one for her birthday in October. Last year, he'd gotten her a Range Rover, and she loved the fancy, sporty vehicle; still, it was a masculine, mechanical sort of gift. This year, something more cultural would be nice, he thought.

They retrieved their car from the garage and drove to Rush Street. Gary pointed out the Marriott Hotel, where he had met with Park. He wondered what his Asian colleagues were thinking. By now, they surely had heard the news.

Dinner was fun. The noisy, crowded restaurant gave Ralph, Becky and their friends the royal treatment, the manager himself coming to their table. After they had been served their thick, juicy steaks, Ralph finally broached the subject he had been dying to ask about.

"What in heck is going on at TLP?" he asked.

Gary gave him a brief account. "I'm the mole," he told them. "I started the whole thing." Ralph and Becky were flabbergasted, but very supportive. Few people had more reason to hate TLP than they did. They immediately launched into a recollection of their anger at G.T. over his reaction to their marriage, and what it had cost them. Then it was Gary and Jenna's turn to be supportive. When Gary looked down at his plate, he couldn't believe he had eaten everything on it. He was still hungry.

"Don't worry," Ralph chuckled. "What this place is really known for is their incredible dessert menu.

"Lucy," he called to the miniskirted waitress, "bring us some cake."

As he began to delve into the huge mound of cake on his plate, Gary turned to Ralph. "That story you told me once about Hargiss's brother," he said. "Do you really believe it?"

"All I know is that Carrie claimed it was gospel," Ralph answered. "She claimed she overheard G.T. and Tully discussing it."

That piece of additional information gave the whole story a lot more credibility in Gary's mind. He still wasn't sure he believed it, but now it sounded plausible.

When they finished dinner, Ralph and Becky wanted them to go for drinks in one of the bars that lined Rush Street, but Jenna objected. "We've got a four-hour drive ahead of us," she said.

"We'll take a rain check," Gary promised.

CHAPTER 103

It was raining and mid-morning in Shanghai at that very moment. General Su Wen-lie waited by the door of his personal jet at the airport. Quickly, a soldier with an umbrella appeared and shielded the General from the elements, walking awkwardly beside him to the waiting limousine.

The limousine whisked the General through the crowded streets of the city. Finally, they arrived at the factory gate. Above the gate, Chinese characters spelled out the name of the company that existed behind it: Xin Shi Chieh Fa Xueh Gung Sze, the New World Chemical Corporation.

The General snorted. What was happening to his country? he wondered. A corporation! What would Chairman Mao have thought? But Mao was long dead, and the new rulers had decreed that here, in Shanghai, an experiment would be tried: a tiny beachhead of capitalism in the People's Republic. It wasn't real capitalism, of course. Any Westerner could understand that. If the Westerner were a pessimist, he would see the whole thing as a sham perpetrated by the masters in the Forbidden City. If he were an optimist, he would see it as a crack in the heretofore impenetrable great wall of Communism in the world's largest nation.

Whatever they really were, a few companies like the New World Chemical Corporation had been allowed to exist.

The General's car proceeded through the gate, and stopped in front of the main building. The General waited for the driver to open the door, and marched to the building, disdaining the rain, which in any event had slackened to a misty drizzle.

Once inside, the General strode past the shocked office workers without a word. He mounted the stairs to the second floor and marched into the office at the end of the hall.

Song Dian-Nuan literally jumped from his chair at the sight of his visitor. "General Su!" he exclaimed.

"Honorable Corporation Chairman Song," the General said with a practiced air of authority, "news reached me last night from the United States that has important consequences for you."

"What can that be?" Song asked, stunned and confused.

"The business arrangements you have concluded with the Tamson-Long Company have come to the attention of the American authorities," the General said. "As a result, I have made a decision. You are to cease production of artificial sweetener immediately," he continued, "and devise a plan to convert the machinery being used to make another product. Within thirty days, you will report to me that it has been done."

"But, General," Song stammered.

"Honorable Corporate Chairman," Su said sharply. "You are completely aware of the reason it was decided to begin operations in biochemistry."

"Yes, of course."

"The artificial sweetener operations are merely a screen to cover our experiments in biological products which may be useful to the People's Army."

"Yes, yes, of course, but..."

"The actions of the American government against Tamson-Long will bring worldwide attention to artificial sweeteners. This is not acceptable, as it means that our operations could come under international scrutiny. Therefore, as of this moment, you are no longer to make the product.

"Do you understand your orders?"

"I understand, General Su."

"Then I shall expect to hear from you within thirty days that all is complete. If the matter is not resolved to my satisfaction at that time, it will be necessary to transfer you to another position. We have considerable need for men of your talent in Qinghai."

Song gasped. Qinghai! The end of the world. The farthest and most backward outpost of the vast People's Republic! His family would live like peasants, without any hint of the modern conveniences they enjoyed in prosperous Shanghai.

He drew himself up to his full height. "It will be done, General," he said, every nerve in his body locked onto the task of filling his voice with confidence.

CHAPTER 104

Far away in Steuben, Indiana, William Hargiss began to feel he was making headway. He'd been worried that the bonus system was part of the investigation, but it did not seem to be, which meant Long had not told the FBI about it. The dumb kid had made a fatal, greedy error. Hargiss made a mental note to himself to revise the whole bonus operation as soon as it was safe.

The next few days were hell, as Gary continued to hear from people inside TLP that they were going to go after him on the bonus payments. G.T.'s secretary, Joyce, called him on Sunday and confirmed that TLP was moving full steam ahead on the embezzlement charges. "They're not worried about anything," she said. "G.T. said they've got stuff on you that's going to make you a lousy witness." Gary tried to pry more out of her, but she either didn't know or was being coy.

On July 19, Parr met with Brilley and Aiken, and then called Gary. "TLP doesn't want you anywhere around the office," he said. "They're willing to continue to pay you with all your benefits, but there's no way they want you in at work." Then he paused. "They also want to meet with you and see what you taped. They want to know if it was just price-fixing stuff, or if you had tape on the bonuses. I told them I didn't know, and that you were prohibited from talking to them by your contract with the government."

Gary began to feel a little woozy. "I'm telling you," Parr said, "they're trying to find out if you did tape them on the bonuses because it looks to me like they may try to use it against you if you didn't. I still think they're crazy if they do, but that's where they are."

That same day, William Hargiss convened a meeting in his office with Tully, G.T. and Howard. "Tully here's got a few interesting things for us to discuss," he began. "Go ahead, Tully."

Tully shuffled through some papers in front of him. "I spent a few days knocking around the books. I count a hundred and seven overseas bonuses paid out altogether. The paperwork looks good on most of them, but there are a handful where either the contracts or AFEs are missing. You guys are pretty fortunate you've all gotten your bonuses overseas through legitimate companies. I figure those companies will be scared shitless to blow the whistle on anything they've done with you, 'cause you'll pull the plug on the business you're doing with 'em. Gary's bonuses, on the other hand, as you know, were paid to phony companies. G. T., how in the fuck did it happen that you had Gary do that?"

"Ah, he didn't really know anyone yet that I thought we could trust. Everyone else is tied in because of the price fixing," G.T. answered

"Damn lucky break for us. I think you guys can really hang this little cocksucker out to dry."

"Considering you brought him in here in the first place, Tully, you're damn sure on the hook to get us out of this mess," Hargiss said.

"Well, what are we waiting for? Let's get moving on this," Howard said.

"You've gotta do this thing right," Tully said. "We need to plan for this a little bit, make sure it looks like we just stumbled onto it. You'd better get that rich little peckerhead Buffy in on this."

Hargiss considered it. He still wasn't sure he trusted Buffy, but he went back over it in his mind, and decided he had been too hasty in suspecting Buffy. There were two factors in his suspicion. One was that Buffy was the highest-ranking person the FBI had not talked to. That didn't count for beans any more, because they had obviously phonied up the whole deal. Why else would they have talked to Long? The second factor was Buffy's comment about the two years. Maybe he was just repeating scuttlebutt. All manner of speculation was running around the office that day. Still, he had looked like a deer in the headlights when Hargiss had called him on it. "Yeah," he said, "but we'd better not tell him much. I'm still not a hundred percent sure he's not in with Long on the whole thing."

"Call him in here, let's see if he knows where his bread's buttered," G.T. said.

Hargiss summoned Buffy. "Buffy," he said, his eyes intent on the young man's face, "we're going to execute a strategy to discredit Gary Long. I'd like you to head it up."

Buffy stood frozen for a second. "What do you mean, Mr. Hargiss?" he asked.

"Well, we've found a few irregularities with some of the things Gary worked on, and we'd like you to work on the strategy to get the word out."

"What kinds of irregularities are you talking about?"

"Well, we've found some money that Gary had overseas."

Buffy's mind had been working a mile a minute. "You mean, like money he embezzled?" he asked.

"Yeah," Howard snorted. "Like he was robbing us blind."

"Wow," Buffy said. What he said next was carefully calculated, and entirely invented. He took a couple of steps backward, and leaned against the door jamb. "That can be a tough road to go. I remember once when my grandfather tried to nail an employee on embezzlement, and before it was all over, half the damn company was in trouble."

Hargiss stared at the young man. Thoughts of his relationship with old Jim Carney flooded into his mind. He had almost forgotten that this lanky kid was Jim's grandson. He looked at Buffy closely. He was taller than Jim, and Hargiss had not known Jim at Buffy's age, but the family resemblance was unmistakable.

"Who the fuck cares?" Howard said.

"Buffy," Hargiss said. "How much do you know about your grandfather's business?"

Buffy could feel the temperature of his forehead lowering. He was pretty sure his subtle message to Hargiss had gotten through. "Well, some things," he said. This was now a conversation between him and William, a conspiracy between them against Howard and G.T. "I mean, he talked some about the business, and about a lot of things he did overseas..."

"Who the fuck *cares*?" Howard repeated.

"I do know one thing," Buffy continued after the interruption. "He really wanted me to come to work here, because he said that you, Mr. Hargiss" – his eyes were intent on William's face – "he said that you were the only man in the world who was his equal, and that if I worked for you, I would learn things no other person could teach me."

"Who the fuck fucking cares?" Howard shouted.

"I do, Howard," Hargiss said, quietly but firmly. "Buffy," he continued, "I understand. Now you have to understand the importance of this project to discredit Gary Long. Everything I've worked for, everything your grandfather worked for, is riding on it. I want you to make it happen. Will you do it?"

"Give me all the details," Buffy said. "Everything you've got, and I'll get started on it."

As Buffy walked back to his office, he knew that he had preserved all his options. Now he just had to figure out his priorities.

Tully joined him in his office a few minutes after he got there, and they went over the specifics of Gary's bonus arrangement. When he left, Buffy realized that he was the only person in the world who knew everything that was going on. He decided to share a little of it with Gary.

Gary started going crazy with worry after Buffy's call. Until that point, he had held himself at bay because of Parr's conviction that they would never use the bonus deal against him. But according to what Buffy revealed, Parr was wrong. His bonuses were different because they had been paid to phony companies, whereas the others hadn't. That was news to Gary, and it made an enormous difference. Gary decided to call Zack Brilley to see if he couldn't smooth things out. Over the next two days he left several messages for Zack, saying he wanted to meet with him and Robert Aiken. He called Aiken as well. Finally he got through to Brilley.

"Gary, this is kind of an odd thing for you to want to talk like this," Brilley said. "You have a lawyer now, and lawyers just don't call another lawyer's client. Maybe I'll have Aiken call you."

Within five minutes, Robert Aiken called. "What do you want Gary?" he asked.

"I'd like to meet with you."

"What about?"

"There's a lot of things in this case…I've heard from people inside what you're doing, that you're going after me. But there's a lot of things that happened in this case you'd be surprised about that I had nothing to do with. There are things it would be definitely valuable for you to know."

Aiken was silent for a second. "Well, I'd sure like to meet with you," he said. "How about tomorrow at the TLP hangar at one o'clock?" Gary agreed and hung up.

An hour later Gary got one of the nastiest phone calls he had ever gotten in his life. "What in the fuck are you trying to do?" Keith Parr demanded.

"What are you talking about?"

"You have a meeting with Robert Aiken tomorrow."

"Who told you that?"

"Aiken just called me." And then he was off. For several minutes he berated Gary for going behind his back. "Gary, you can't go rogue on me like this," he finished

Gary had had enough. "You know as well as I do this is a serious issue where they're headed," he began. "I've got a lot of stuff that would be useful to them about what Sid Cox did in this case and you know it. That's the purpose of this meeting – for me to be able to tell all that because I think it could head off the whole direction of where they're going."

"We've got to do this in the courtroom: you don't do it by meeting with these guys alone," Parr replied, still steaming. "I'm not going to represent somebody whose going rogue, so you're either with me or you're not."

Gary thought for a few seconds before saying, "I'm with you."

"Good," Parr replied. "I'll call Aiken and let him know it's all off. Don't ever go behind my back again."

On the 26th, Gary got a call in the stables from Buffy. "Gary," he said. "I just got off the phone with Alan Bishop, he's a *Wall Street Journal* reporter, and he's here in town. He knows you're the mole and he wants to see you. He asked me where you lived and I didn't want to give him exact directions but I told him a good fifteen minutes south of here. He's going to find out where you live and he's going to be at your house. I was just going out when he showed up here and I was real open with him."

I'm not ready for this, Gary thought. Bishop might be there at any minute. He decided to stay in the stables. He picked up the phone and pressed the intercom button. When Jenna answered, he gave her the instructions.

I'm now reduced to hiding in a horse barn, he thought. This isn't a James Bond movie after all. It's a cheap, stupid, Grade B Western.

Bishop arrived 20 minutes later and talked to Jenna on the porch. She told him Gary wasn't there, but he continued to plead with her for an interview, saying that Buffy had told him Gary was someone he should talk to. Finally, he gave up and left his number, saying he would be in town all week, and begging her to have Gary call him.

Later that day, Gary and Jenna talked for a long time, seated at an umbrella table by the pool while Justin and Mark splashed in the water. For the first time, Jenna began to really understand about the bonus system, and the trouble they might be in because of it.

"The number one stupidest thing I've done in this whole thing," Gary confessed, "was not telling the FBI about the bonuses in the first place. Then it could have been part of the immunity agreement and we'd be home free."

"Why didn't you tell them?" she asked.

Gary tried to reconstruct his frame of mind at the time he had signed the immunity agreement. "You know," he said finally, "you know how some people like to flaunt their wealth. Fancy clothes, Rolex watches, big cars, extravagant homes..."

"And you don't?" she asked. "You've got all those things, except the Rolex," she added, looking over the pool to the stables, "I mean if this house isn't extravagant, I don't know one that is."

He grinned, a little sheepishly. "I know," he said. "But I only bought it to get a date with you.

"Besides," he continued, "and this was always very much in my mind, this house may be extravagant, but it's way out in the middle of nowhere, on a back road that only goes to a bunch of corn fields, so it's not like I'm showing off with it."

"I don't really think you're a show-off," Jenna said. "Far from it. But are you saying you didn't tell the FBI about the bonuses because you were embarrassed to tell them you had so much money?"

"That was part of it. I didn't even tell you until we were on our honeymoon."

Thoughts of the afternoon on the beach on St. John flooded into her mind, and she blushed to recall her brazenness. "What was the rest of it?" she asked.

"Well, I don't know. I guess it all seemed so remote from what their investigation was all about. And at the time, I really was still deluding myself that there was nothing illegal about it."

"The bottom line," Jenna said, "is that what's done is done, and what we have to do now is figure out where to go from here."

"I think," Gary said, "that our problem is that we're only playing defense right now. We need to get on the offensive somehow."

"Have you given up on your big picture plan?" she asked. "You know, taking over TLP when all the dust has settled?"

When he mentioned going on the offensive, Gary had been thinking about going after Cox and the FBI for their indiscretions, which he had on tape in the family room. Jenna's words reminded him of the even bigger picture, the main chance. "This embezzlement thing has put a crimp in the plan," he said slowly, "but I'm not ready to give up quite yet."

CHAPTER 105

Ian Howes was alone in the study of his country home in the Cotswolds. Just before the doorbell rang, he had been reading a letter from Cecily. Cecily was his only daughter, and since the death of Mrs. Howes, his only immediate family.

How often he had wished she would present him with grandchildren, and now, finally, at age 30 and James almost 40, it was going to happen. Of course, she and James would have to return home, to England, and that would be good, too. Sierra Leone was no place for an Englishwoman to have a baby.

They had lived all over the world, James and Cecily, these past eight years. James was an exceptionally bright young man, and his employer, Barclays Bank, used him as a troubleshooter. Ottawa during the Quebec secession scare, Hong Kong with the announcement of the end of the mandate, Colombo when Sri Lanka was threatened by the Tamil rebellion, and now Freetown, Sierra Leone.

Ian remembered Sierra Leone at the time of its independence, in the early '60s. In all of sub-Saharan Africa, he had considered it the country most likely to succeed. The British had left it with a superior infrastructure: a fine railroad, good highways, the best university in West Africa, and an educated elite that seemed quite capable of managing the whole. It had beautiful mountains, spectacular beaches, and of course, all those minerals, especially the diamonds.

But things had gone badly, sadly wrong. Alternating corrupt governments and civil war had destroyed everything. At the moment, it was war. Well-armed rebels, an army of mostly teenagers kept high on drugs, roamed the countryside. It was a very dangerous place.

So the news that Cecily was pregnant was doubly good, and he read with a wave of relief that she and James would be back in London within the month.

He looked up from the letter toward the door. Odd, he thought. Who can that be? He heard Mary, the only servant he kept, move to answer it, her skirts swishing. He could hear her talking to a man at the door, and a moment later, she appeared in the study and handed him a business card.

My, he thought, examining the card, this is odd. "Show the gentleman in," he instructed Mary.

"I'm Clarence Pettigrew," the man said, "MI-6."

He was a small, dapper man, wearing a vested suit and a bow tie. The principal feature of his face was a sizable black moustache.

"Yes, yes," Howes answered, standing to greet the visitor. "I'm pleased to meet you, Mr. Pettigrew. How may I help you?"

"Really," Pettigrew said, "I hope I can help you, or at least provide you with some information that may be useful to you."

What in the world? Howes thought. "Well, go on," he said.

"Well, sir, it has to do with your association with the American firm Tamson-Long Products, Incorporated."

"Yes?" There was trouble at TLP. He knew that already. William Hargiss had called him a week ago. But why was MI-6 involved?

"As a member of the board of directors of that company, you should – or rather, the Department feels that you might wish to – be aware at this time of certain information in our files regarding the company's Chairman, Mr. William C. Hargiss."

"At this time? Why at this time, particularly?"

"Well, sir, it would appear that certain activities of the company – of which you have always been, we have no doubt, entirely unaware, and entirely innocent of any complicity in – certain activities of the company have run afoul of the American Government."

"Yes," Howes said. "You are quite right in that. I have been so advised by Mr. Hargiss. But surely none of this is of concern to British Intelligence?"

"Well, sir, that is very true, except...except the Department feels that as this matter develops, it may create rather a mess inside the American Government. A jurisdictional dispute, I should say, in which one agency of the Government seeks to prosecute Mr. Hargiss, while at the same time, another seeks to protect him."

Howes sat down in his chair and furrowed his brow. "Mr. Hargiss has many friends in American politics," he said, "and no doubt a certain influence, but I still don't see what concern this is of Her Majesty's Government."

Pettigrew reached into the leather satchel he was carrying and extracted a manila envelope. "If it were just American politics that was involved, you would be absolutely correct," he said, "but I'm afraid it goes quite beyond that. It's all in this report, sir, and I can tell you that it involves international matters of great sensitivity." He handed the envelope to Howes.

Howes set the envelope carefully on his desk. "Well, then," he said, "I shall read the report with great interest." He looked down at Pettigrew's business card. "If I should have any questions once I have read it, may I call you?"

"Yes, of course," Pettigrew answered, giving a little bow of his head. "But I suggest you adopt an alias if you call. It wouldn't do for a receptionist to know that the former Prime Minister was calling a simple bureaucrat such as myself, now would it?"

"Shall I be Mr. Smith then, or Mr. Jones?"

"Mr. Smith would be fine."

"Thank you, Mr. Pettigrew. I shall read this report with great interest."

As soon as the little man left, Howes opened the envelope and read every word of the report. The more he read, the more his blood began to boil.

He was still fuming the next day when Mary told him he had a telephone call from a Dr. Gary Long, in America.

"I'm calling you," Gary said, "to discuss the future of TLP." Howes listened intently as Gary detailed his remarkable story. "Let me assure you," he heard Gary say, "that at all times, my actions have been completely focused on what is best for the future of the company."

"And what do you wish me to do?" Howes asked.

"I believe that William and Howard Hargiss, as well as G.T. Binghamton and others will be convicted. That leaves the question of who will run the company, build it back up from whatever the damage turns out to be, and run it in a first-class, above board and well-managed way. With integrity. Integrity, Mr. Prime Minister, that's what I believe I have that the others do not. I also believe that I have demonstrated the skill to manage the company in an efficient and profitable manner. What I really hope is that you will use your position on the board to assist me in cleaning up the scandal and rebuilding TLP."

"I see," Howes responded, "and I'm impressed. Have you discussed this with any other members of the board?"

"No, sir," Gary said. "I feel that you are the most important, and the most independent of the Hargiss influence. That's why I called you first."

"Well," Howes said, "I am inclined to be supportive of your plan. Perhaps I could call Bob Aiken and some of the others on the board and sound out their views."

"Thank you," Gary said. "Thank you very much. Only I wouldn't suggest you call Robert Aiken. His firm will be representing TLP in the case, and he's completely compromised in all of this."

"I see," Howes responded. "That's too bad. That's a big blow." It really is, he thought. Aiken was the board member he knew best, and handled all of his own legal business in the U.S. "Well," he continued after some thought, "let me call Randolph Thad then, and see what he thinks."

Gary had placed the call from the Potter Realty Company. Bud was out showing a house. Jenna had promised to settle the charges with her father when the bill came in. Now, Gary placed one more call, to Alan Bishop's hotel room in Steuben.

Gary met the reporter in the stables and he showed Gary everything he had. Gary was amazed at the details he knew. He showed Gary copies of the subpoenas for all the various cases as well as lots of detail on the price fixing case. He kept asking Gary to just confirm what he had already heard. Gary did, and Bishop left.

On Thursday, July 28, the story broke nationwide that Gary was the mole. All in all, it was pretty positive for him. He called his parents and said they should get a copy of the *Journal*, and that he would talk to them later about it. Up to that point they had no idea of what was going on.

Gary was on his way to Chicago to meet with Parr when he called home. Jenna said they were getting a ton of calls. Reporters had already begun circling outside their house, and people were just stopping in the road and looking. Gary had talked to Buffy earlier in the morning, and Ralph Sori called from Boston, where he was on business: the story was big news there.

Gary met with Parr, who had begun negotiating a seven-million-dollar severance package with TLP that would have ended the shooting between them, costing either party a million dollars every time they said something negative about the other. "Brilley and Aiken wanted to talk it over and they'll get back to me on it."

By the time Gary got home, he had received several threatening phone calls, and the traffic in front of the house was continuous. The *Wall Street Journal* might view him as the hero in the case, but in the local news, he was a rat. And almost nobody in Steuben County read the *Wall Street Journal*.

Jenna called Cox the next morning after somebody walked up onto the lawn and yelled threats. "Sid, there's a mess down here," she cried. "We have threats on the phone and people are trespassing on our property. Don't you think there is some way we could get some security?"

"Well, we haven't announced a case yet, so there's no way I could put somebody down there," Cox answered.

"What do you mean, it's not a case?" she asked, amazed. "Gary's been working with you guys for years!"

"Yeah, I know, but it hasn't officially been announced yet, and until they're ready to announce it, my hands are tied," he told her.

Jenna yelled at Cox for another five minutes and then realizing she was getting nowhere, hung up. It was a disaster outside. At times during the next day, Gary counted 15 cars lined up on the road in front of their house. People were getting out of their cars and snapping pictures.

"So much for our country seclusion in the middle of nowhere," Jenna said, shaking her head.

All Gary wanted to do was hide.

Parr submitted a final proposal for the severance agreement. Gary expected a counteroffer, but within a day or so he got an anonymous call from someone who claimed to know about the proposal. The man said there was no way TLP would ever accept it. "The way they're going to fight this case is by discrediting you, Gary. They can't do anything that would tie their hands in that regard." The voice was disguised, but Gary thought it was Doug Marshall, the TLP lawyer who had barred his way to the office the morning after they found out he was the mole.

CHAPTER 106

Adrian McWhorter looked intently into the face of the distinguished-looking man across the table from him.

"Mr. McWhorter, thanks for taking time out of your schedule to meet with me," the man said.

"It's not a problem, Admiral. The Department of Justice is always concerned when problems of national security are at stake. I must say," he added in his deep Arkansas drawl, "that I feel a sense of the cloak and dagger, meeting in a place like this."

They were in a restaurant called Rip's Country Inn, somewhere in Maryland. The dining room featured low lighting, and the booths were designed to look like horse stalls. Each of them was labeled with the name of a famous Thoroughbred. The walls between them were high, and hearing a conversation from one to another was virtually impossible. They were seated in the "Spectacular Bid" booth.

"Well," Admiral Decatur said, "it's about halfway between Washington and my office in Fort Meade, so I thought it would be equally inconvenient for both of us."

A waitress appeared, and took their drink orders.

"As you know," Decatur began again, "this is all about your case against Tamson-Long."

"Yes," McWhorter said. "I've looked through the files."

"The Agency is anxious," Decatur continued, "that no harm from this should come to William Hargiss. Our hope would be that you in Justice could find a way to drop the whole matter."

"That, I am afraid, is impossible. The prestige of the Department is at stake. Fifty FBI agents and half a dozen prosecutors have been involved in the case. The publicity is enormous, as I'm sure you know. We can't just shut down cold turkey now."

The waitress returned, and McWhorter took a long drink of his bourbon and water. "Especially with what promises to be a very difficult congressional election coming up," he added, smiling.

"I'll be frank with you," Decatur said. "William Hargiss is one of our most important resources. We can't afford to lose him. Moreover," he continued, sipping his Scotch, welcoming the cold ice against his lips, "if he were to get angry at you and me, and go public with things he knows, it would cause acute embarrassment to both the intelligence community and the Administration. And, as you point out, there is an election coming up."

McWhorter stroked his fat chin. "Mr. Hargiss has been very good to the Democratic Party," he said. "With what he's got invested, I don't believe he would want to harm the President."

Decatur saw an opportunity and seized it. He bent over the table and, in a menacingly harsh whisper, said, "Mr. Hargiss has been very good to *both* parties, sir. From where he sits now, he doesn't give a damn whether your President wins, loses or drowns in the stink of his scandals."

McWhorter leaned back. "I suppose," he said, stirring his drink with his finger, "that a man in his position would be principally concerned about looking out for Number One." The news that Hargiss was a political switch-hitter came as a surprise to him. I should have checked that, he thought. Bill would have checked that.

"You're damned right he would be. And he is."

"I don't know, Admiral, this is the highest profile case for our Antitrust Division in almost forty years. It could turn into hundreds of millions of dollars in fines. Besides," he added, leaning forward, "I hear you've been out doing a little investigation on your own."

Now it was Decatur's turn to be surprised. "What are you talking about?"

McWhorter put the glass to his lips, recalling the scant but telling details he had gleaned from a seemingly isolated incident in Utah months before. The trail was difficult to follow, but he thought he knew where it led. If he was right, it ought to give him the upper hand in this discussion. "We hear you've been doing a little campaign finance research in China. I can tell you the President would not be happy about such extracurricular activities." He studied the Admiral's face for a reaction.

Damn, Decatur thought. How did he get hold of that? "Well, it's NSA's job to make sure our government isn't for sale," he said.

"Really." So, I was right, McWhorter thought.

The look McWhorter gave didn't offer Decatur any clues. What did he know, and how far was he willing to press it?

"Admiral, I'm going to have to think about these things for a couple of days. We may be able to spare Mr. Hargiss personally, but I can tell you one thing, somebody's going to have to go to jail."

That wasn't what Decatur had hoped for, but at least McWhorter was receptive to thinking about it. "Thank you, Mr. McWhorter; I appreciate your consideration on this highly sensitive matter. When should I expect to hear from you?"

"One week. I'll call you in one week."

"That'll be fine."

CHAPTER 107

Randolph Thad sat in his office in Atlanta. For him, the TLP scandal had been one enormous headache. His multiple cable TV news channels had hesitated before reporting on the affair, given the boss's presence on the board of the corporation. But they had to report something, or compromise any sense of journalistic integrity. No one had asked him what to do, nor would he have expected it. He rarely got involved in news decisions. His editors had been carefully selected. They had an excellent sense of the point of view he wished them to take, and by and large, it was their own point of view.

The call he received that morning from Ian Howes was troubling. It was clear that Howes had lost all confidence in William Hargiss. It wasn't just the price-fixing scandal, either. Howes had been explicit on that point. But Howes had refused to answer Thad's repeated requests to say what else was bothering him. "We have an Official Secrets Act in Britain." He had said that three times. What in tarnation did it mean?

What Howes had been explicit about was that the top management of TLP should be cleaned out and Gary Long given the reins of the company, that Long was the only person with the knowledge, skill and integrity to get the job done. "You're probably right," Thad told him, "but there's no way in hell there are enough votes on the Board to make it happen."

Howes pressed him to help fight the good fight anyway, if for no other reason than to clear their own names. Thad told him he'd think about it.

Now he had, and he had reached the conclusion that he couldn't help Howes. He couldn't afford to. But neither could he afford to be associated with criminal price fixing. However much he and William Hargiss had shared, there were limits.

In his mind, that left only one option. Now he just had to figure out the best way to tell Ian Howes he wasn't going to help him, and William Hargiss that he was resigning from the board.

CHAPTER 108

"At least you still have some friends left at TLP," Keith Parr told Gary on the phone.

"Well, that's good to know," Gary replied.

"I just got a call from someone – a man, I think, but the voice was disguised. Anyway, the person claimed to work for TLP security, and said he or she had something interesting to fax me. Wanted my fax number. So I gave it to him, or her, and a few minutes later I got the fax. It was sent, by the way, from the Steuben Holiday Inn. It's a copy of a letter that apparently went out from the personnel office a week ago, and it reads in its entirety, 'Please do not allow Gary Long enter the gates as of today, July 25, 1994, because he has been terminated.'"

"Well," Gary said. "I guess we don't have to wonder about that any more."

"There's a handwritten note below the letter which reads: 'Mr. Parr. The D.O.P.' – I guess that means Director of Personnel – 'put this out after W. H. reamed his ass for asking if he needed to do anything about G.L.'s benefits. W.H. said G.L. didn't have any benefits, and wasn't with the company any more. Said he had enough information to blow his ass out of the water.'"

"Well, like you say, at least somebody there still likes me, but I guess it isn't 'W.H.,'" Gary said.

"Yeah, somebody who bothered to get my name, go to the Holiday Inn and spend the money for a long-distance phone call."

That afternoon, Gary sat on his pool deck, looking at the sky. The calls from people at the office, wanting to know about some problem or another, had stopped coming in.

He took some consolation from the call he received from Ian Howes. Ian was prepared to go to the mat, and it was good to know that a man like that believed in him. But Howes had also told him the cause looked hopeless, and that Randolph Thad had resigned from the board.

The main chance was slipping away fast, and so was the easy exit; there was no way TLP would sign the severance agreement.

If the takeover bid wasn't going to work, and the golden parachute failed to open, he had only one offensive move left: the possibility of screwing over the FBI.

He looked toward the house, and his eyes fell on the two windows in the family room. He could see them clearly, framed on the left by a large sycamore tree and on the right by the maples that guarded the rose grotto. Inside that room, he thought, I have tapes that would cost Sid Cox and Jim Thompson their jobs. Maybe the tapes would also allow him to gain the upper hand. He couldn't quite figure out the ideal way to use them, but they represented the only trump card he had left.

He looked back toward the road. A car approached, slowed as it reached the house, and stopped. He saw a man get out of the passenger side door, away from him, and heave an object over the car, across the road and onto his lawn. Then the man got back in and the driver sped away.

Gary walked across the lawn and retrieved the object. It was a small piece of cinder block to which a note had been tied with baling twine. Gary took it into the garage and untied the note. "Nice house for a rat fink," it read. "Make good firewood."

He had to think seriously about security. He and his family were completely vulnerable, out here on the prairie. The FBI wouldn't help, and he didn't really want them around anyway. Jenna had called the Steuben County Sheriff's Department, but they were clearly in G.T.'s pocket and had made a dozen excuses as to why they couldn't do more than have a patrol car drive by once or twice a day.

He went inside to talk to Jenna. They sat in the kitchen and made some decisions. For the time being, they would spend their nights at the Potters. They would hire a watchman to guard the house while they were gone. What more could they do?

I almost hope they do burn the house down, Gary thought. At least that might get me some sympathy. Then he remembered the tapes in the family room. He had to get them out of there.

He thought about it for a long time, and then called Ralph Sori. Ralph agreed to take the tapes for safekeeping, and Gary bundled them up in seven shoeboxes. Jenna drove all the way to Lafayette and sent them via UPS, because Gary didn't even trust the UPS people in Steuben not to tell someone.

CHAPTER 109

Susan Henry was adamant. "I will not drop this case, McWhorter," she said firmly. "If you and your political friends have problems, then you have problems, but if you push me, I'll not only resign, I'll call a press conference so big they'll have to hold it in Soldier Field."

"I hear you loud and clear," McWhorter responded. "Let's see if we can find any common ground. What, short of prosecuting William Hargiss, will you settle for?"

"I'll call you back," she said.

She summoned Kevin Rasmussen and Alex Bremerton, and the three of them spent the next hour arguing about what they should do.

"I think we should stick to our guns," Rasmussen argued. "I'll be more than willing to submit my resignation and stand up right beside you at the press conference. William Hargiss is the biggest skunk in the whole stinking forest, and it'd be a crime to let him go."

"Kevin," Bremerton said. "I feel as strongly as you do. But the problem is that we're not going to get Hargiss."

"What do you mean?" Rasmussen wanted to know. "We've got him dead to rights."

"Yes," Bremerton replied. "And McWhorter's got us dead to rights. He's not going to budge on Hargiss. There's no way. What that means is that if we all resign – and I'm willing to do it if that's what you decide, Susan – if we all resign, then McWhorter will fill our places with people who will do his bidding and Hargiss walks anyway. Susan's threat is a big one, and a brave one, but I know Adrian McWhorter. I came up against him when I was working for the RTA, trying to clean up the savings and loan mess. You may have heard of the Madison Savings and Loan case. Little Rock? Whitewater? I was there, and I can tell you this: if Adrian McWhorter wants William Hargiss to get off, he'll get off, no matter what stink we cause."

"If Alex is right," Susan said, "then we ought to be glad McWhorter's giving us any kind of a deal at all. Let's try and figure out a fallback position."

Rasmussen was still steaming, but he was out of arguments.

Adrian McWhorter called Admiral Decatur on the third of August. "Admiral, it looks like a nice day to get together. How about meeting me on the steps of the Lincoln Memorial at two o'clock?"

Decatur quickly agreed.

Tourists crowded the great marble stairway leading up from the reflecting pool to the columns that guarded the melancholy-looking seated figure of the Great Emancipator, but Decatur and McWhorter found a quiet spot off to the side.

"I meant to ask you at our first meeting," McWhorter began, whether you happen to be a descendent of the famous Admiral Stephen Decatur, hammer of the Barbary Pirates and author of the unforgettable words, "our country, right or wrong.'"

Decatur smiled. How like a southern politician to begin even the most serious meeting with some friendly conversation. "Unfortunately, no," he replied. But reading about him did kindle my first interest in a naval career."

"I see," McWhorter replied. "Well, in any event, since our subject matter for the day is so unsavory, I thought the least we could do was get some fresh air out of it."

"A good idea. It's unusually pleasant for Washington this time of year."

"Yes, well, the A.G. wanted me to pass this message on to you. If the company'll pay a huge fine, say around a hundred million, and cooperate with us in getting a few of the other companies they've been cutting deals with all these years, we won't prosecute TLP as a corporation. The individuals are another story. We won't go after William Hargiss, but we feel like if we don't prosecute a few people from TLP, we'll never be able to defend ourselves if we get called on the carpet for our handling of this case. It's looking more and more like the Republicans are going to be in control of Congress after the elections, so we have to watch our step. That son of a bitch Harry Pelt from Maine would be Chairman of the Judiciary Committee, and he'd like nothing better than to find something to fry our ass with. Oh, and I checked. Hargiss has never given him a dime."

"Who do you want to go after?" Decatur asked.

"I think we shouldn't go into that right yet. I promise that Hargiss senior won't get drug into this, but here's the deal. You turn over all the documents and files your agency has developed on our President's campaign dollars from China, and we'll lock up all the tapes that have Hargiss's voice on 'em, and any reference to him in the 302s. We'll just make him disappear."

"How soon do you need to know if this'll work?"

"Two weeks. After that, we'll just let all the chips fall where they may."

"Fair enough. I'll be in touch before the eighteenth."

Hargiss didn't take the news well. "What the hell do you mean someone goes to jail," he yelled into the phone at Decatur. "The only people on tape are my son and my most trusted assistant."

"Don't forget Long."

"Yeah, well, that son of a bitch is gonna rue the day he was ever born. We're gonna play smear the queer with his life."

"What have you got?"

Hargiss told him about his ability to explode the bonus system in Gary's face. "We can make it look like this little piss-ant stole millions," he said.

"Give it your best shot. Anything you can do in the next two weeks to weaken their case will only make it easier to negotiate with Justice," Decatur said.

Keith Parr called Gary on a hot, sultry August evening. "Gary," he said, "they've quit talking to me. Brilley isn't returning any of my calls, and neither are Robert Aiken or that slimy weasel Louie Cobb. I don't know what they're thinking. Do you have any insight?"

"Everything I hear from inside the company says that they're going to attack me and say I stole those bonuses that were given to me," Gary told him. His gut was churning. "I just got a call from Alan Bishop, the reporter for *The Wall Street Journal*, and he told me that TLP was planning their attack and they had a big press wave heading straight for me, based on me being an embezzler. I'm trying to find Buffy to see what he knows."

CHAPTER 110

Buffy was having a hard time juggling all the balls he was handling. Over and over, he kept reminding himself that the goal was to keep all his options open, but it was getting harder and harder. His plan had been to keep a precarious balance among all the reporters clamoring for stories about the scandal. Some, like Alan Bishop, he steered to Gary. Others got the TLP side. But Hargiss wanted a major assault on Gary, a coordinated blitz that would brand Gary a crook in the public's mind. Buffy knew he either had to do it or not do it, and whichever choice he made, an option was going to close.

Eventually, he came up with the best compromise he could think of. He wasn't proud of it, but at least maybe he could save a little face. He called Hargiss.

"I think I need some big time help," he said. "We want to really control the national news, and good as I am, I can't do that all by myself here in Steuben. I want to bring in some real pros."

"You do whatever you have to," Hargiss said.

"Well, they'll be expensive."

"I don't care what it costs, I just want Gary Long's head on a platter."

As soon as Hargiss hung up, Buffy called an old friend in New York.

All day, he had ducked Gary's calls. Finally, from home, he called back.

"Bishop tells me there's a big story coming down about me being an embezzler," Gary said.

"I wish it wasn't true," Buffy said. "But the problem is, it's out of my hands. Hargiss has decided to turn the job over to a big New York PR firm, and they're coordinating everything from now on. I'll still do what I can to steer some reporters to the truth, but I can't stop Hargiss now."

God, he felt miserable.

"I do have some good news for you," Buffy said. "*Fortune* magazine wants to do a feature on you. I think it could come out really positive. You want the guy's number?"

Gary and Keith Parr met the *Fortune* reporter two days later at a hotel in Indianapolis. There was also a photographer present, and he took photos during the interview. The reporter was astounded at everything that had gone on and assured Gary the story would run in the next issue.

The next morning, Sid Cox came to Gary's house to pick up the taping equipment. As he gathered up the bugged briefcase and the other items, Gary thought about how long he had looked forward to the day he could rid himself of the stuff. Miserable as he was, at least this goal had finally been reached, and Gary could feel a little satisfaction as he helped Cox load the stuff into the Dodge. With the equipment loaded, the two men stood beside the car. Independently, their minds both flashed back to the night Cox first drove it into that yard. "Old pal," Cox said, "we've been through a lot together. I know it hasn't all been pleasant for you, but I want you to know I still think you did the right thing, and I still believe it'll turn out well for you.

"Whenever you start thinking about how bad things are," he continued, "think about what could have happened if you'd gone along with their scheme. A year, two years, five years later, someone else would have come on the scene, and played the part of Gary Long, and then you'd be right where Howard and G.T. are today. And they are going to jail, Gary. They are going."

Gary felt a sudden pang of nostalgia. Whatever problems there had been, he and Cox had shared a lot; they'd been a team for a long time. He screwed up his courage and decided to risk the wrath of Keith Parr. "There's one thing you don't know," he said, "so I'm telling you now. There was a bonus system at TLP where people made hundreds of thousands and some people got millions of dollars."

"What are you talking about?" Cox demanded.

"Well, they paid people bonuses which went through real or phony companies overseas. Everybody who was anybody at TLP got them. Now I'm hearing that TLP's going to try and claim I embezzled mine. That's bullshit, and I don't know how they can get away with it, since everyone did it, but the word I keep getting is that they're going to use it big time in this case."

"How much money did you get?"

Gary wouldn't tell him, hinting that it was in the hundreds of thousands. "Anyway," he added, "I'm sure it's going to hit the press in a few days, and I thought you ought to hear it from me."

"So that explains the lie detector tests," Cox said.

"What do you mean?"

"I mean, you never did really pass the lie detector tests. Both times they were screwed up, didn't give clear readings. The technicians just threw up their hands. Now I know why you didn't pass, but the question is, how did you keep from failing?"

Gary thought better of talking about reading up on how to beat polygraph tests. "Well," he said, "then you lied when you told me I passed."

"Oh, screw it," Cox said.

"Do you think the bonus thing will hurt your case?"

"Well, it's something we'll have to get through," Cox said. "But why didn't you tell us about it?"

"I just didn't see it as an issue," Gary replied. "They've been doing it for twenty years or more; it's just the way they do business."

Cox called Jim Thompson before he hit the traffic light in Wonanonly, and by the time he reached the edge of the town his orders were to head directly for Indianapolis.

By 6:00 that evening, it was clear to Thompson that they had a disaster on their hands. All efforts began shifting to damage control and contact was made with the TLP lawyers, who confirmed they had an ongoing internal investigation.

The next day was Saturday, and Gary called Keith Parr at his home to confess his canary session with Cox. He expected an outburst similar to the one he got when he tried to set up the meeting with Brilley, but Parr was relatively calm. "You shouldn't have done it, Gary, not without talking to me first, but the truth is, it doesn't make a lot of difference."

"Well, I figured the press was going to break the story pretty soon anyway."

Parr knew the truth of that. He'd just gotten a call from a reporter from *The New York Times*. They were planning to run the story in their Sunday editions the next day. He'd also heard from Kevin Rasmussen that morning.

"Anyway," he told Gary, "I already knew you spilled your guts about the bonuses. The Justice Department is really ticked off at you. The whole thing could have been handled better, but they were going to get ticked off sooner or later anyway. But for heaven's sake, don't talk to them on your own again. They are not your friends. Think about all they've done to you. From now on, you only talk to them with me in the room. Which, by the way, will be Monday at nine in my office. I assume you can be there."

"I'll be there," Gary said, glumly.

He spent the rest of the day with his family. They rode the horses, and then cooled off in the pool. They drove to Hardin and had lunch at the Dairy Queen. They came home and hit the pool again, Gary tossing Mark into the air and laughing with the rest of them as he splashed down into the sparkling water. Then he and the boys donned baseball gloves and played a game of three-way catch, while Jenna fixed dinner.

"Can we stay here tonight?" Justin asked at dinner.

"Yeah, sure," Gary said. "But tomorrow night, and all next week, we'll have to stay at Grandmom's." Once the *Times* story ran, things were likely to be worse than ever, he knew.

After the exhilaration of the day, Gary felt the old depression returning in the evening. He sat at the desk where he had worked so many evenings, and started writing letters to people he liked. He wrote one to John Caldwell, telling him about all of his finances, in explicit detail. He wrote one to Leigh Curtis, and one to Dan Anthony. He wrote one to Dink Maccabbee in Atlanta, to Peter Rhyner in Mexico City and to Ian Howes in England. The one that took the most time was the letter to his father. He got out his insurance files, and wrote down all the policy numbers. When he put the policies back in the file, he noticed a group of appeals from various charities he'd never bothered to respond to, but never thrown out, either. He took them out and wrote checks to each of them. Then he wrote several more checks, to local people he knew were struggling financially.

By then it was almost eleven-thirty, and he went up to bed. Jenna was reading a novel. On the cover, Gary could see a woman in a low-cut red dress. Jenna's hand covered most of the title, but he could make out the word "Passion."

"Pretty trashy stuff you're reading," he said.

"I've got my reasons," she smiled. "I thought you'd never come up."

They made love with wild abandon, rolling over and over one another on the big bed.

The next morning, they went to church at the Wonanonly Christian Church, where Jenna, Justin and Mark had been baptized. Jenna and the boys had been more or less regulars there for years, and Gary attended when he could. But this was his first appearance since before the raid.

The sermon was from John 11, the raising of Lazarus, which the pastor worked into a message of hope.

There was no place in Wonanonly where *The New York Times* was sold, and Gary couldn't bear the thought of going into Steuben to buy one. When they got home, he found a copy of the article on his fax machine, with a cover from Keith Parr. Gary read the article with a sense of deepening gloom.

On Monday, August 8, the headlines in all the papers screamed that Gary was accused of embezzling millions. When he arrived at Parr's office in Chicago, they had a copy of the *Steuben Daily News* open on a table with the headline: "Long Embezzled Three Million Dollars from TLP." Parr greeted Gary and introduced him to everyone there. People from Justice and the FBI were packed into the room. Jim Thompson started by stating that any deals Gary may have had with the FBI were off.

Then it was Cox's turn. He wanted to know when Gary had gotten his first payment, the whole sequence. Gary explained that each one had been approved, trying to relate who had told him to do this or that, but all Cox kept saying was, "It doesn't matter. I want to talk about you. We have plenty of time to get the other people who're involved."

Parr defended Gary. "They gave him the money," he said. "Wouldn't you take it?"

Cox shook his head defiantly. "No I wouldn't. It's illegal. A crook's a crook."

So, Sid thinks of me as a crook, Gary thought. Oh, what the hell. He laid out the whole scenario, everything he knew, holding back nothing. He had ceased to worry about the fallout. Finally it was over.

After the agents and prosecutors left the office, Gary said to Parr, "I'm in a big mess huh?"

"Well," he said, "you're in a mess, but it's not insurmountable. We can work through it. We've got a lot of things in our favor."

CHAPTER 111

Jenna and her father were alone at the Potter house. They were not very happy with each other.

"You have sold your soul to the devil," Bud Potter said to her in the sharpest tone she had ever heard from him. "You have disgraced the family for a swimming pool and a bunch of horses. You have reduced your mother to tears."

"I won't listen to this!" she screamed. "Why do you think the worst? You believe a bunch of crooks at TLP, and their fancy PR men! Well, I don't! I believe my husband!"

"Your husband," Bud hissed, "is a tattle-telling little rat, and the biggest crook this side of Chicago!"

"I don't have to listen to this!" she screamed again. She turned her back on him, ran up the stairs, and shut herself up in her room. She flung herself on the bed and lay there, sobbing. It was a scene from her childhood. How many times had she done this as a child, frantic with girlish anxiety over some long-forgotten scolding?

Her own children weren't having a good day, either. Mrs. Potter had taken them to a Pony League baseball game. Justin was on the team. He was just old enough for the league, and had showed enough promise to be a starter, though only marginally. He could hit pretty well, but his defensive skills were shaky, and, as a result, the coach put him in right field. There were very few left-handed hitters in the league, and thus few balls were hit to right field. It was the safest place for Justin, the coach thought, although next year, if he improved a little, they'd make him into a first baseman.

The ball field behind the Wonanonly school had only a small, four row grandstand on the first base side. On the third base side, there were no seats at all, and many people would park there, watching the game from their cars.

Mrs. Potter parked the car. "Run along, boys," she said. "I don't trust these old bones to be comfortable in the stands, so I'll watch from here."

Justin, in his uniform, trotted over to join his fellow players, and Mark headed for the grandstand.

The coach watched as Justin ran across the infield. He had hoped the boy wouldn't show up this day, but there he was. The third baseman, a boy named Billy, whose father worked at TLP, looked at Justin with a surly grin, and then turned to the coach. "I ain't playin' with the son of no crook," he growled to the coach.

"Now, calm down, Billy," the coach said. Then he took Justin away from the others. "Billy's a snot," he said to Justin. "All the same, I'm not going to start you today. I just think it'd be best for everyone."

Things weren't going any better for Mark. He had some change in his pocket, so he walked behind the grandstand, where the 4-H Club sold refreshments from a long table. He asked for a Sunny Delight, and pulled the coins out of his pocket. Just then, a group of girls Justin's age walked up.

"Where'd you get that money, Mark?" one of them said, her mouth curling into a sinister grin. "Your daddy steal it from TLP?"

"Markie's father's a cro-ok," another girl sang, and they all took up the tune. "Ya-na-na-na-na-na."

"He is not!" Mark shouted, enraged. He swung out at them, scattering his money on the ground. The girls moved closer, taunting him. One of them shoved him and he shoved back. In a flash, he fell to the ground. The first girl kicked him, hard, in the shoulder.

"Hey, stop that!" the teenaged 4-H boy behind the table cried, and the girls ran away.

Tears welled into Mark's eyes, partly from the humiliation, and partly from the pain in his shoulder.

The boy came around from behind the table and started picking up Mark's money. "You still want your Sunny D?" he asked.

Mark burst out crying and ran away. He reached the school parking lot and hid behind a school bus, trying to pull himself together. He stopped crying, dried his eyes, sniffed his nose hard a few times, and felt his shoulder. It hurt a lot. He walked out from behind the bus and took a circuitous route to the third base side of the field, staying as far away from everything as he could. He saw the two coaches exchanging lineups with the umpire at home plate. The game was about to start.

He approached his grandmother's car from behind, and opened the passenger door, startling her. "Oh, there you are, Mark," she said. "I was looking, but I couldn't see you in the stands."

"I want to go home," he said.

She looked at his swollen eyes and surmised something of what had happened. "Of course," she said. "I'll take you home now and then come back for your brother."

Seated by himself at the end of the bench, Justin saw the car pull away as his replacement trotted out to right field.

Mrs. Potter pulled the car into the driveway and let Mark out. "Run tell your mother you're home," she told him. "I'd best get back to the school or Justin will wonder what's going on."

Then she noticed her husband's car in the driveway. "I wonder what he's doing home at this hour," she said, checking her watch. It was 4:30.

CHAPTER 112

Phil McLaughlin checked his watch at the same time. He was in Indianapolis, at a meeting on a joint venture between Foremost and Eli Lilly. The meeting was running long and Phil knew he was going to miss his plane back to Newark; he would have to spend the night in Indianapolis.

Since taking over Gary Long's old job, Phil had worked his methodical way up in the esteem of the Foremost executives. He knew he wasn't the sharpshooter Long was, but he wasn't dumb either, and over time, he had established himself. It wasn't like being CEO of your own company, but it was still a pretty good job, and he had managed to recover from the humiliation and financial loss of the TLP buyout. He'd moved his family to Bernardsville and rebuilt his life.

There was a short pause in the proceedings, and one of the Lilly execs tossed a copy of the Indianapolis *Star* on the table. "Can you believe this TLP shit?" he asked McLaughlin.

McLaughlin glanced at the headline. Gary Long was accused of embezzling millions from TLP. "I don't know if this is true or not," he said, "but if it is, the guy's a hero in my book."

When the meeting finally broke up, McLaughlin called the Hilton and took a room for the night. He ordered dinner from room service and tried to watch a ball game, but his mind kept drifting back to Gary Long and TLP. He read the newspaper story twice and made up his mind: TLP was screwing Long over. He was sure of it.

Long must really be feeling like crap, he thought, remembering how he himself had felt the day William Hargiss had squeezed his heritage from him.

He wished there were something he could do to help Gary. Nothing occurred to him immediately, nothing except moral support. The more he thought about it though, moral support didn't seem inconsequential.

The porter arrived with his dinner, and made a show of setting it all up on the portable table, removing the plates with their stainless steel covers from their compartment under the table and arranging them artfully.

McLaughlin tipped the man and sat down to eat. He decided to call Gary as soon as he had finished, just to let him know that someone else understood and sympathized. Then he changed his mind. He didn't know the phone number, and even if he could get it, it might be tapped. There had been references in the papers to tapped phones. TLP wouldn't hesitate to do it.

According to one article, Long lived in the town of Wonanonly, just south of Steuben. McLaughlin got the rental car map and found the town. An hour, max, from Indianapolis. He'd drive there in the morning and offer what encouragement he could in person. Maybe Gary could tell him some other way he could help.

Gary had left Chicago a little after 1:00, and was approaching the exit for Steuben. From there, it was about 45 minutes to Wonanonly. On the drive home, Gary completely repressed all thoughts about his case. He remembered a few other letters he wanted to write, one to G.T., asking him to tell everyone the truth, and one to Alan Bishop at *The Wall Street Journal*, telling him to dig deep and find all the rottenness. I'll do them tonight, he thought.

CHAPTER 113

Mark didn't want to talk to anybody, so he didn't even tell his mother he was home. There was a big canvas swing, almost like a couch, suspended on chains from the ceiling of the front porch. Mark lay down on it and felt the tears coming again. He rolled over and buried his head in the soft, flowered cushion. In a few minutes, he was asleep.

In her room, Jenna recovered a little from her anger. She sat for a long time in the rocking chair facing the window that looked over the back yard. She opened the window, hoping to smell the fragrance of the large fir tree just outside. As a girl, she had loved to do that. Then, the top of the tree was just above the height of the window, but now it was several feet higher. After a few minutes, she heard a car in the driveway, and decided that her father had left. Or maybe it was Gary.

She looked at her watch, the beautiful one Gary had given her the first Christmas they had known each other. Four-thirty. Probably too early for Gary to be back, definitely too early for the boys to be home from the game. It must have been her father, leaving. She looked at the watch again, not for the time, but for the watch itself. It seemed to symbolize all her joy and her trouble. It was bought in love, but paid for with tainted money. She took it off and laid it on her dresser. Then she saw her face in the mirror. He fell in love with that face the first time he saw it, she thought. And he does love me. He will always love me. I will be there for him.

She picked up the watch, put it back on her wrist and went downstairs.

As soon as she reached the first floor, she realized that her father was still there. He was in the kitchen. She started to go back upstairs, but decided against it. Maybe he's cooled down, she thought.

She stepped into the room, with its smart, bright wallpaper and louvered windows, slanted half open. Bud was seated at the table, a half-empty bottle of Michelob in front of him. The newspapers were spread across the table. Bud looked up at her, and she knew instantly that the anger was still there. He started in again, talking quietly now, but firmly. For more than half an hour they argued, both of them feeling their anger growing.

Louder and louder their voices got, and finally they awakened the sleeping Mark, on the swing just outside the louvered windows. He rubbed his eyes and turned over on the cushion.

"Yes, I mean divorce!" he heard his grandfather shout.

"Divorce? Divorce?" Jenna screamed. "I'll tell you when I'll divorce him!" She paused, trying to come up with a sufficiently strong euphemism for *never*.

Mark never heard her complete the thought. At that moment, he saw Gary's car pull into the driveway. He bolted from the swing and ran across the yard, falling into Gary's arms, sobbing.

"Hey, little buddy," Gary said, soothingly. "What's the matter?"

Mark looked up at him through his tears. "I just heard Mommy and Granddad talking, and Mommy said she was going to divorce you," he cried.

Gary held him tightly.

"Daddy, don't let it happen!"

"Mark, oh, Mark," he said. "I promise you it won't happen. But you've got to help me. Can you help me?"

"I'll do anything," Mark sobbed.

"Okay, you have to be real brave now. Do Mommy and Granddad know you heard them?"

"I don't think so," Mark said, turning to look back at the house to see if they had come out.

"That's good. That's good," Gary said. "Now, son, I don't want you to tell them what you heard, or that you told me. Can you do that?"

"Yes," he said, sniffling.

"If you do, I promise you there won't be a divorce."

"Okay."

Gary grabbed the boy tighter, holding him close. "Hey," he said. "What's this bump on your shoulder?"

Mark told him what had happened at the ballpark.

"You've had a pretty bad day, haven't you?" Gary said.

"The worst," Mark said.

Gary dried the boy's eyes and led him toward the house. "Remember what I said," he cautioned, and Mark nodded.

Given their loud conversation, neither Jenna nor Bud heard anything from outside until Gary opened the door. He entered slowly, trying to make as much noise as possible, to warn them of his approach. Thus alerted, they immediately stopped talking, but Gary could tell by looking at them that Mark had told the truth.

"Mark, what are *you* doing here?" Jenna cried when she saw him. "And what's the matter with you? You've been crying!"

"Mark's had a bad day," Gary said. "I think some mean girls beat him up at the ball park."

In a few moments, they all had the story pretty well sorted out, and then Justin and Mrs. Potter arrived to fill in their side of it. Bud gathered up the newspaper and kept silent the whole time. All he could think of was that his grandchildren were being abused, and it was all Gary's fault.

A little later, Gary took Jenna aside. "Things in Chicago went pretty well," he told her. "But I've got a lot of work to do. I'm going over to the house, and it's going to take me until real late, so I'll probably stay there all night. You and the boys stay here."

"But I want to be with you," she argued.

"Not tonight. The boys need you, after what they've been through. I am so sorry," he added, "that I've caused all this to happen."

He drove home, stopping to fill the car with gas, and wrote the letters to G.T. and Alan Bishop, as well as one to Brad Redfoot. Then he wrote one to each of the boys, telling them to always believe in God and tell the truth. Finally, he wrote a letter to Jenna. He told her how much he loved her, and what a wonderful wife she was. He recalled half a dozen special moments they had shared, and wrote that the happiest day of his life was the day he adopted Justin and Mark. He wrote a long apology for all the trouble he had caused her, her parents and all the people he loved most.

When he finished, he put all the letters in the stack with the ones he had written on Saturday. He began looking through his desk for stamps, and finally found a single one. Shuffling through the letters, he pulled out the one to Bishop at *The Wall Street Journal*. He put the stamp on it and took the letter out to the mailbox. The others he left on the desk.

Then he went to bed and slept soundly.

The next morning, he got up early. He picked up the envelopes and walked outside. He got in the car, and set the letters on the seat beside him. He pulled into the garage, and pressed the remote to close the garage door. He got out of the car, listening to the soft hum of the engine, and then reentered it, sitting in the back seat.

After a few minutes, he started beating the doors of the car, railing at Cox, cursing TLP and yelling at what this whole mess had done to him.

He sat back and loosened his tie. The evil spirits that had first come in with the bribe Gary had been handed had done their work. First he could see the spirits off in the distance, then like a prairie thunderstorm he could hear the thunder, and then the winds picked up. Now came the rain. Gary could see the whole thing build in stages as he started to lose consciousness.

Woozy, he glanced to his right, and saw something half-hidden beneath a seat belt. It was a cassette tape, left there sometime, who knew when? "Goddamn tapes," he muttered, and reached to swat it with his hand. The motion carried his whole body over, and he collapsed on the seat, the cassette beneath him, and slipped into unconsciousness.

CHAPTER 114

Donnie Bradford had always loved animals. When he was a kid, he wanted to be a veterinarian. But that meant going to veterinary school, and school and Donnie just didn't get along very well.

When he got a chance to work for Gary Long, tending the horses, he jumped at it.

He lived in a shack near Hardin, kept his old Chevy running, and figured he had it made.

Sometimes he helped Jenna with the gardening, but his real love was the horses. He ran the stables as efficiently as G.T. Binghamton ever ran a chemical factory. Gary and Jenna were thoroughly pleased with the job he did.

At 6:30 Tuesday morning, the phone rang at the Potter house. Bud, who had missed most of the previous day at work, had already left for the real estate office. Everyone else was still asleep, and Jenna sprang out of bed to answer the call.

"Hello, Mrs. Long?"

It was Donnie. He sounded panicked.

"Donnie, what's the matter?"

The stable hand was sobbing into the phone. "Ma'am, I came out to the garage and I found Mr. Long in the car."

"What? What do you mean?"

"I mean, he's sick or something. I'm scared, Mrs. Long. You need to get here real quick."

Jenna dropped the phone, and ran and woke her mother. "Something's happened to Gary," she cried.

"Jenna, what do you mean? Is he hurt?"

"I don't know anything, except Donnie said he'd found him in the car. I've got to get there and find out. Donnie's hysterical. I don't know if Gary's alive or dead, if someone broke in and attacked him...." She was running down the upstairs hall to find a cover-up of some sort. "God, Mother, maybe he tried to commit suicide."

"Oh, dear," said Mrs. Potter.

"Stay with the boys. I'll call when I know anything," Jenna yelled, running out the door.

It took about two minutes to travel the distance to the house. As she pulled into the driveway, she saw the garage door open and Gary in a heap in the front of the garage. Donnie was on his knees throwing up.

With the Range Rover still rolling, Jenna shut off the ignition, threw open the door and was out of the vehicle in a flash. Fixing her focus first on Gary, she straightened him up and felt for a pulse. She saw Gary's eyes flutter and realized he was alive; then she grabbed Donnie by the arm.

"What happened, Donnie?"

"I don't know, Mrs. Long. I'm sorry, I don't know what happened."

"How did you find him?"

"I came in early because I was going to run some errands when the stores opened, and when I got out of the truck I could hear a motor running in the garage. I opened the door and the smoke was so thick it made me sick. I saw Dr. Long right away, and pulled him out, and then I called you."

Jenna had to think quickly. If she called the paramedics, it'd be all over town in five minutes. No, the best choice was to call the family physician. He would at least keep his mouth shut. She went into the garage and called Dr. Warren's house. Dr. Warren answered, and she explained the situation, and the need for secrecy. He quickly agreed to come right over and told her to get Gary up and walking if it was at all possible.

Jenna enlisted Donnie's help and together they got Gary on his feet. Within seconds, Gary began to throw up violently, restarting Donnie's vomiting, too. Jenna managed to get Gary to take a few halting steps.

Dr. Warren pulled into the driveway and grabbed a black satchel as he stepped out of his car. He hurried to Gary, noted the redness of his skin and examined his eyes, pulse and lungs. In less than a minute, he turned to Jenna and said, "Carbon monoxide, without a doubt. And a darned close call, too. How long has he been out of the garage?" Jenna looked at Donnie, and Donnie looked at his watch.

"Well I got here about six twenty-five or so, and I pulled him right out, so maybe twenty minutes all told," Donnie said.

"Hmm," Dr. Warren mused. "Well, the good news is if he's alive now, he'll probably survive a trip to Indianapolis, which is where he needs to go. I can call Methodist Hospital, and we can get him checked in there under an assumed name. You get him cleaned up and into some comfortable clothes. Walk him around a little first, make sure he's done vomiting, or he'll redecorate the inside of your car. I'll call you in a little while with the information you'll need to get him admitted. And for what it's worth, I'm sorry." He held his arms in front of his face, hands down and flapped his wrists. "Get him walking again, keep him moving."

The Cadillac was still purring away in the garage. "Donnie," Dr. Warren barked, "go shut that car off!"

Donnie was sitting on the ground, his head in his hands, his overalls covered with puke. "I ain't going in there again," he said, looking up in wild-eyed terror at the doctor. "I ain't. I ain't."

"Oh, all right," Dr. Warren said, "I'll do it." He trotted into the garage and shut the car off. As he ran back to his own car, he called to Jenna, "There's a bunch of letters in the car. I'll bet anything they're suicide notes. I'll call you in a few minutes," he yelled, starting his car.

Jenna nodded and began walking Gary around. He threw up several more times, until there was nothing left to come up.

Jenna's mother arrived. "I sent Bud home to watch the boys," she said. "They're still asleep."

"Give me back my life!" Gary screamed at the top of his lungs over and over. "Give me back my life, God, please give me back my life." Suddenly, he crumpled to the ground, sobbing.

Jenna walked him into the house. Mrs. Potter kept pacing back and forth, making a tsk-tsking sound and shaking her head. When Jenna got Gary into the house, she undressed him, got him into the shower and began packing a bag. By the time Gary stepped haltingly out of the shower, she had clothes for both of them packed and was dressed for the trip to Indianapolis. Gary got dressed with her help and followed her down the stairs into the kitchen like a puppy dog, hanging his head. Donnie was nowhere to be seen.

"I'll come with you if you'd like, Jenna," Mrs. Potter said.

"No, it's best if you stay here and take care of the kids." The phone rang and Dr. Warren gave her instructions for getting Gary checked into the Methodist Hospital psychology ward.

Jenna kissed her mother goodbye, Mrs. Potter mouthing a nearly silent, "I'm sorry" into her ear, and headed to the Range Rover with Gary in tow. A few minutes into the trip, Jenna decided she needed to tell Keith Parr what had happened. She fumbled in her purse for her little book of phone numbers, almost losing control of the car in the process. Gary sat dumbly in the passenger seat, looking away from her at the light poles flashing by.

Parr was immediately sympathetic, said he'd make the necessary calls to the Justice Department, and promised to not tell TLP where Gary was headed. Then Jenna hung up and tried to understand this latest turn of events.

Donnie was trying to get his wits back in the only way he knew. He fed each of the horses, and began to clean out the stalls, relishing the smell of the barn, reassuring in its earthiness, so different from the noxious stink of the garage that morning. He finished the job and spread a layer of fresh straw in the stalls. Smokey the cat sidled up to him and rubbed against his leg, and he bent to stroke her soft fur.

Then he walked to the door of the stable and looked back to admire his work. Carefully closing the door behind him, he walked back to the yard, avoiding looking at the garage. He got into his Chevy and drove off to Steven's Auto Repair for a cup of coffee.

An hour later, William Hargiss placed a call to Admiral Decatur.

"Jon, you probably haven't heard the news, but the government's star witness has just attempted suicide. Maybe you need to call your friend at the A.G.'s office. I'd say the price of justice has just gone down substantially."

Decatur considered the tone in Hargiss's voice. It was almost jubilant. "I'm not sure what he'll say, Bill, but it's sure worth a call."

Hargiss called Tully next. "Get down to Wonanonly and see what's going on," he instructed.

"I'd better send Jimmy T," Tully said. "It'd be safer."

When Jimmy T drove up in front of the Long house, the mailman was just pulling away. Jimmy T drove past the house, slowly. There didn't seem to be any sign of life. He could see the open garage door, and a Cadillac parked inside. He turned his car around and drove back, entering the driveway this time. He stayed in the car for a few minutes, waiting to see if anyone would show himself. When no one did, he got out and walked into the garage. He almost stepped in some vomit on the way, and when he got into the garage, he could still smell, faintly, the fumes from the exhaust. Yep, he thought, he tried to do it with carbon monoxide.

He tried the door to the Cadillac, and found it was unlocked. Peering in, he saw the stack of letters on the seat. Looking out of the garage again to make sure no one was there, he scooped up the letters and began riffling through them. He could see nothing else in the garage, so he went out and put the letters in his car, leaving the Cadillac door open in his haste.

He stood in the driveway, trying to decide if it was safe to approach the house. Then he saw a car coming down the road from town. It was an old Chevrolet, and it drove into the yard.

"Who're you?" Donnie Bradford asked him.

"Who are *you*?" Jimmy T asked back, nervously fingering the bill of his White Sox cap.

"I'm Donnie. I take care of the horses."

"I'm Fred," Jimmy T lied. "I'm a friend of Dr. Long's."

"I ain't never seen you before."

"Where'd they take Dr. Long?" Jimmy asked.

Something told Donnie not to answer. Something about this man didn't smell good. "You better leave," he said.

He's right, Jimmy T thought. "Yeah, okay," he said.

Donnie decided to leave, too. He couldn't bear to be there any more. He got into the Chevy and drove home, spending the rest of the day watching television, trying to forget.

"About a mile and a half that way," the man in front of Steven's Auto Repair was instructing Phil McLaughlin. "Big fancy place on your left. Be a jog to the left about a mile out." He knew the directions well, had given them out dozens of times in the past year.

McLaughlin found the house easily, and drove into the yard. In the garage, he saw a car with its door open. Thinking that perhaps Gary was there, he approached the garage. "Dr. Long?" he called out. There was no answer. When he closed the car door, he saw an audiocassette tape on the floor next to the car. Gary – or someone, he thought – must have dropped it. Probably while getting some stuff to take into the house. It must have been just a little while ago, what with the car door open. He thought he would take the tape to the house, picked it up and walked to the front door, absently putting the tape in his jacket pocket as he rang the doorbell. A breeze rustled the leaves of the large sycamore tree to his right. He rang again. A horse whinnied from the barn. He rang a third time. A calico cat eyed him from a chaise lounge on the porch. Something is very strange, McLaughlin thought. He gave up, walked back to his car, drove to Indianapolis and caught his plane to Newark.

CHAPTER 115

Decatur called McWhorter as soon as he hung up from talking to Hargiss. After a few rings, McWhorter's thick southern accent greeted him.

"I think it's time for another meeting," Decatur said.

"I could take a stroll to the Lincoln Memorial again, even though it's a lot hotter today than it was last time."

"I'll be there in an hour."

As Decatur sat in the back of the Lincoln, speeding down the Baltimore-Washington Parkway, he reviewed the cards he had in his hand. He had the China files to offer them. He hated to give that one up, but there was no choice. He had the embezzlement charges against Gary Long. That was bound to give Justice some pause as to how good their case was. Long's suicide attempt only added to their problem; TLP's lawyers would use it to buttress their claim of guilt on Long's part, and to attack him as mentally unstable, not credible as a witness. He wondered if McWhorter knew about the suicide attempt yet; it would be nice to spring it on him. Then there was William Hargiss himself. The Administration would not want to turn him into an enemy. He knew too much about too many things. The China files, Long's liabilities as a witness, and the Hargiss threat. Three of a kind, but how high were they? He'd know in a few minutes.

"I presume you have come to accept my proposal," McWhorter greeted him. He was coatless, his tie loosened, his ample paunch hanging over his belt.

"Not exactly. It seems to me that a number of things have changed. I thought perhaps you might want to revise your offer. It'd be a shame to walk away from the trial without a conviction."

"The only thing that's changed is a lot of allegations by Long against the company and the company against Long. We don't know who's telling the truth, but we'll get to the bottom of it. Regardless, it doesn't change what we have on tape."

"Well," Decatur replied, "that may be true. But Gary Long is still your star witness, and at this moment, he's in the hospital, recovering from an attempted suicide."

McWhorter decided it was time to wipe some of the sweat from his head, and extracted a handkerchief from his pocket. This suicide thing was news to him. He wondered if Susan Henry knew about it. The bitch probably wouldn't call him even if she did. Nonetheless, this development was bound to set her pretrial planning back, probably for weeks. "I wouldn't be out here in this hot sun at all today if it weren't for the fact that you have something I want," he said. "You see, Admiral, for me, this matter isn't about the TLP case at all. I just want your China investigation shut down and zipped up. In return, I'm willing to let our good friend William Hargiss remain a free man. But beyond that, I'm standing pat. The Hargiss pup and his buddy Binghamton get prosecuted. Probably a couple of other guys, lower down the totem pole. We'll take a hundred million dollar fine from TLP, and we'll get a bunch more from their Japanese co-conspirators.

"I will, however, give you another three weeks to convince your buddy Hargiss that this is in his best interest."

"I'm grateful for the extension," Decatur said, "but just remember, if my buddy Hargiss gets his dander up and decides to go public with everything he knows, it will be very embarrassing to you, me, the intelligence community, and the Administration."

"If that fella opens his yap, he better close it real quick. Because if I hear one word out of him that I don't like, I'll move so fast his second word will come out in Leavenworth. You just make sure he understands what's at stake for him in this."

Decatur watched the big man amble off past the Reflecting Pool. Then he turned and walked in the other direction to his car. Some extra time, he thought. That's all I got out of this. Well, I'd better use it as judiciously as possible.

He had to find some kind of an edge, an angle, something he could use as leverage and make Justice want to just drop this whole thing. He needed a fourth card. Decatur picked up the car phone and called a meeting of his top advisors as soon as he got back to Ft. Meade.

Their solutions were practical, get as many operatives with their ears to the ground as possible, get the phones tapped, check the garbage, coordinate with TLP, squeeze anyone you could get your arms around, and see what popped loose. Before they had left Decatur's office, the wheels had been set in motion. NSA's ability to move without court authority made everything a whole lot easier.

Decatur placed a call to Hargiss who put him in contact with Andrew Tully.

Tully, it appeared to Decatur, had already been a very busy man. Not only did he know what credit cards Long held, but who picked up his garbage and what days pickups were made. He also had his mobile phone numbers, codes and phone numbers for his in-laws, where, he said, Long and his wife had been spending a lot of nights.

"You want a list of his favorite charities?" Tully asked, fingering the envelopes Jimmy T had picked up in the garage. Tully had read all the letters, chuckled at the one to G.T., and found nothing of particular interest in any of them. Sob stories, he said to himself. The guy's cracked up. He took the letters, envelopes and checks and ran them through his shredder.

Decatur had all the information transcribed and passed it on to the members of his team. "As you know," he told the assembled group, "we are prohibited from taping or listening to domestic calls we intercept, but since we don't have any of the equipment in stock to identify those types of calls, you'll have to listen to all of them and decide what we can use and what we can't." His instructions were fully tongue in cheek; the men understood their assignment perfectly.

By 5:00 that night, the phones at Gary's house, the Potters' house, and Keith Parr's house and office had all been tapped. For good measure, they tapped Kevin Rasmussen, Susan Henry and Alex Bremerton. Then there was nothing to do but listen and wait, and hope to hell they learned something useful in less than two weeks. If there even *was* anything useful.

CHAPTER 116

Ian Howes boarded the Concorde at Heathrow, bound for Washington's Dulles Airport. When the news of Gary Long's attempted suicide had reached him, he had pretty much given up on trying to promote Long as the man to take over TLP. But that didn't mean he didn't still have a score to settle with William Hargiss.

Hargiss had called him two days before. He was calling all the directors, he said, to make sure they were aware of the serious trouble Gary Long was in – how his attempted suicide indicated his clear guilt of the embezzlement charge, and how, in any event, the case was a lock. "The man set up phony companies overseas and had invoices for millions paid to them," Hargiss told each of the directors. "And as for these incriminating tapes he supposedly made, I'm not sure they even exist, and if they do, I believe they'll turn out to be some sort of electronic trick. You know, with computer technology these days, they can do anything."

"I don't much care about any of that," Howes replied, careful not to telegraph the extent of his anger, "but, William, I do need to meet with you, face to face you understand, and talk to you about something very important."

Howes offered to fly to the U.S. for the meeting, and it was set for the airport Hilton in Chicago.

While he waited to change planes at Dulles, Howes picked up a copy of *The Wall Street Journal*, and was surprised to find a remarkable article under Alan Bishop's byline. Bishop claimed to have possession of a suicide note in Gary Long's handwriting. Far from confessing his guilt of embezzlement, the article said, Long's note maintained that the money he had gotten overseas was merely part of a long-standing TLP policy with its top executives, all of whom received such payments. Long was going to kill himself, the article continued, not because of anything having to do with TLP at all, but rather because he had learned that his wife was planning to divorce him.

Howes looked at the television monitor above him: "The Airport News Network." How amazing modern communications is, he thought. In the story being covered, an audio technician was talking about how it was possible to phony up a tape recording so that almost no one could tell.

Perhaps Hargiss is right about Long using electronic tricks then, Howes thought. Then he realized what the interview really meant. Hargiss's PR operation was softening up the public to believe his lies about Gary Long. The thoroughness of the operation amazed him.

No sooner had William Hargiss arrived at the suite for his meeting with Howes than the phone rang. "Glad you got there," Buffy said. "Have you had a chance to read *The Wall Street Journal* this morning? Hargiss hadn't, so Buffy read it to him.

"We just don't have anything going at the *Journal*, do we?" Hargiss asked.

"The problem is that their reporter got to Gary before our operation geared up. I think he likes Gary, and Gary likes him, and that's why he sent him the suicide letter."

"Well, I guess there's nothing much we can do about it," Hargiss said. "Just see to it that his attitude doesn't spread."

"I think we're fine everywhere else," Buffy said. "I can tell you that the *Fortune* article would have been a lot worse if I hadn't found out about it and plugged some holes. It was just so-so, but it would have been totally his side. One thing I'm really pleased with is the electronically-altered tape stuff. We've got pieces on that everywhere. I found the professor down at North Carolina State who developed the technology, and he and the equipment manufacturers are loving the publicity they're getting."

"Good," Hargiss said. "I want everyone in the country to understand that technology. Especially everyone in the jury pool in Chicago. Now," he added, "what about the divorce thing? You think his wife's really going to leave him?"

"It's hard for me to believe," Buffy said, "but I suppose it's possible."

"Well, have Tully check it out. Oh, and by the way," Hargiss added, suddenly remembering something, "while you're talking to Tully, have him brief you on another matter. Tell him I said to bring you up to speed on the Korean kid. Then figure out a way to make a splash with the story he'll lay out for you."

"The Korean kid?" Buffy asked. Was this something to do with Daehan Hwa Hak?

"Yeah, there's a little bastard running around Seoul whose daddy is Gary Long."

"No shit!" Buffy exclaimed.

"No shit," Hargiss confirmed. "Tully's got all the details, DNA tests and everything."

There was a knock on the door, and Hargiss quickly ended the call.

Ian Howes was loaded for bear. "Let's skip the preliminaries," he responded when Hargiss began by asking how his flight had been.

"Okay, Ian, what's on your mind?"

"One of the loveliest pieces of territory in the United Kingdom," Howes began, "is a tiny island south of Cuba called Grand Cayman."

"I've been there," Hargiss said, suddenly apprehensive. "A wonderful beach."

"Yes. But for all the tourists who flock to that beach and all the expensive condos and the cruise ships, the real basis of the economy of Grand Cayman Island, the reason it's the most prosperous place in the Caribbean, is its banking industry."

"So I understand."

"And in one of those banks, Barclays to be exact, there is an account whose average daily balance runs close to half a billion dollars. The account is in the name of a phony bank in Niue, out in the Pacific Ocean, which is owned by a phony trust in the Bahamas, which is in turn controlled by a phony company called Interoceanic, which is one hundred percent owned by William C. Hargiss. Am I not correct?"

"Perhaps."

"You have used Interoceanic to cook the books of TLP since 1977, haven't you, William?"

"You seem to have all the facts," Hargiss replied. "Why don't you tell me?"

"Why don't I tell the Securities and Exchange Commission instead? I think they'd be very interested to learn how the balance sheets of TLP are calculated."

Hargiss sat silently, his anger mounting. Finally, he spoke. "Your son-in-law works for Barclays, doesn't he? Is that how you've gotten your information? Because if it is, he's in serious trouble for breach of confidence."

Howes eyed him for a moment, and then picked up the briefcase he had dropped on a chair. He extracted a manila envelope, the same one Pettigrew had given him, and waved it in front of Hargiss's face. "Here it all is," he said. "And no, it does not come from James. I haven't even discussed it with him. Unlike yourself, I do not break the rules to accomplish my goals. James is an international troubleshooter for Barclays, it's true. But he and Cecily are currently in Sierra Leone.

"No, William, this report comes from a source that knows much more than anybody at Barclays ever could. This comes from MI-6."

British Intelligence, Hargiss thought. This could be more serious than I imagined.

"It's replete with detail, William. The wars you've fought, the drug money you've laundered, the secret arms deals you've financed, from Sri Lanka to Central America."

Not to mention Sierra Leone, Hargiss thought, an idea forming in the back of his mind.

"It stinks to high heaven," Howes continued, his voice rising. "It goes against everything I stood for as Prime Minister and throughout my whole career in government. I'm not against intelligence, but the sort of shady deals and trouble-making you are engaged in has no place in a civilized world. The purpose of this meeting is for me to put you on notice that I intend to blow your bloody Interoceanic empire sky-high."

"That would be most unfortunate," Hargiss said. "It would put in jeopardy the lives of dozens of good people throughout the world."

"That may be," Howes shot back, "but the continued operation of your criminal activities will kill many more, again and again, innocent people who just happen to get in the way of somebody with one of your weapons, kids right here in America who get hooked on the drugs your people sell to them in order to fill the coffers of Interoceanic. No, Hargiss, my conscience is clear on that score."

"Some lives are more important than others," Hargiss said. "But the main thing here is that what's past can't be undone." He stood up and paced back and forth in front of Howes. "Ian," he said, after a few moments, "you've got me by the short hairs. But the truth is I'm getting too old for the espionage game. If your real concern is to stop the operation, would you be willing to keep the past buried where it is? Would you, if I were to close down Interoceanic and withdraw myself entirely from the operations that trouble you so?"

Howes had half of what he wanted. "Only if you also resign from TLP," he said. "I want you out of the company, and out of every sort of international skullduggery. You must withdraw from it all. If you do, I will permit you a quiet retirement and you will go to your grave with your secrets intact. And, by the by," he added, tapping the manila envelope, "I believe I have the resources to monitor your compliance."

"A fair offer," Hargiss said. "I'll give you my answer in three days."

Howes closed the briefcase, and handed the envelope to Hargiss. "For your reading enjoyment," he said. "It is not the only copy, of course."

"Of course," Hargiss said as he watched Howes turn his back and leave the room. Three days, he thought. That should be enough.

CHAPTER 117

Bud Potter sat in the real estate office, reading *The Wall Street Journal*. He didn't normally read it, but prompted by a call from John Caldwell, he'd managed to find a copy at the Wonanonly drug store. So Gary believed Jenna was going to divorce him. No one knew better than Bud Potter that she had no intention of doing so. Why would Gary have thought otherwise? He tried to reconstruct the afternoon before the suicide attempt in his mind. He and Jenna had argued. Then she shut herself up in her room. When she came back down, they argued some more. Then Gary and Mark came in the door.

He picked up the phone and called his wife. "What time did you bring Mark home from the ball game that day?" he asked her.

She thought for a moment. "It was four-thirty," she said. "Exactly. I checked my watch when I saw your car in the driveway, because I was surprised you were home. Why?"

"Oh, nothing. I was just curious," he said. Four-thirty? That was at least a half hour before Mark and Gary came in the door. Where had Mark been all that time?

He hung up the phone and put his head in his hands. He was pretty sure he knew what had happened, and if he was right, it meant that he himself was directly responsible for Gary's decision to kill himself. He felt ashamed.

It was more than a week before Gary would talk, even to Jenna. In all that time, the only thing the NSA learned from the phone taps was where he was. They put an operative in the hospital, but each day the man reported that there was no news. The patient was recovering, his wife was with him every day, and the bug in the room revealed nothing of substance.

Decatur was worried. The clock was ticking toward McWhorter's deadline, and if he didn't come up with another card for his hand, his chances of keeping Hargiss happy, and Howard and G.T. out of jail, were somewhere between slim and none.

The prosecutors in Chicago were spending their time reworking their case, from top to bottom. They had to make it work without help from Gary Long, that was clear.

For Keith Parr, the delay was welcome. He had to figure out a defense for Gary, and for the moment at least, he had to do it without Gary's help. He could try an insanity plea. The suicide attempt would buttress that, and Gary had talked a lot about the intense pressure he felt throughout the ordeal of the taping. But proving insanity throughout the whole two and a half years was next to impossible. The straightforward defense was that, whatever he had done, Gary was only following orders, and was not a decision maker. That would be a tough road, too. A plea bargain was the obvious answer, but what could he use for leverage?

William Hargiss wasn't worrying about the case right now. The day after his meeting with Howes, he flew to Philadelphia and met privately with a tough-looking, round-faced black man. The carrot-and-stick offer Hargiss made was more than acceptable, and by the time William was back in Steuben, the other man was on a Sabena jet en route to Brussels, where he overnighted and caught a plane the next morning for Freetown, Sierra Leone. He took the ferry across the bay from the airport into the steamy town, where the rainy season was in full swing. He met with a few people and then placed a call to the United States. "It's set," he told Hargiss.

A little after midnight, the phone rang at the Hargiss residence. Hargiss was in the study, waiting for it.

"You win," Ian Howes said. "Tell your disgusting Captain Mosquito, or whatever his name is, to release Cecily."

"Now, didn't I tell you?" Hargiss replied. "Some lives are more important than others."

CHAPTER 118

You would think, Adrian McWhorter said to himself, that a man who lives in a beaten-up old trailer and doesn't own a decent pair of shoes would be more respectful to the Deputy Attorney General of the United States.

The man in question was Goochie Mudge, and he had been surprised to hear McWhorter's voice on the phone. "Well, A-rin, shee-it, how're they hangin' fer ya?" he had responded.

"Goochie," Adrian said, "I'm doin' well, doin' well. Haven't seen you for a long time."

"Tha's right. Been years."

"Goochie, do you remember the last time we were together?"

"Hee-ooo, I'd guess! Pretty exciting day, warn't it? Mena Airport. We almost got our asses shot off that night, din we, A-rin?"

"Yes, we did, Goochie. Yes, we did. But it was worth it, wasn't it?"

"Shore was. They was so much money on that plane, you guys even gave ol' Goochie a thousand dollars."

"And you earned it, Goochie, you earned it. Now, Goochie, do you remember, there was a box of papers that came in with the money on that plane. Do you remember that?"

"Ya, ah do."

"Do you know where that box is today, Goochie?"

"Ya, ah do. It's in the trunk of that old Chevy Rollie used to drive."

"I need that box, Goochie. You think you could find Rollie's old Chevy?"

"Shee-it, A-rin, I guess! That worthless rust bucket's parked out back of my trailer. Got birds' nests in it."

CHAPTER 119

Ever since he had given Tully the information on the bonus payments, Roger Kincaid had been having trouble with his conscience. As Comptroller of TLP, he was the only person outside the loop of the company conspiracy who could back Gary Long's story about the bonuses with facts and figures. But if he did so, he could kiss his job good bye, and any future prospects as well. If he needed any evidence of the ruthlessness of William Hargiss and his henchmen, their campaign against Gary provided it. If only there was some way to get the information out without anyone knowing it came from him.

He thought about copying some of the documents and sending them to Gary. But that wouldn't work. Once Gary or his lawyer presented them, it wouldn't take Hargiss more than two seconds to figure out where they had to come from. What he needed, he realized, was for someone from outside to come in and audit the books, someone who would know what to look for. While they were at it, they just might find some interesting things about how the balance sheets were put together.

What could he do, he wondered, to trigger something like that without giving himself away? Finally, one morning, he worked up his courage. At lunchtime, he left the office and drove to the Steuben County courthouse. From a phone booth in the basement, he dialed long-distance information and asked if they had a listing for an attorney in Chicago named Keith Parr. That was the name. It had been in the papers a lot.

He got the number and placed the call, punching in the 14 digits of his AT&T credit card. He asked Parr if he was the attorney representing Gary Long. Yes. Parr asked who he was.

"I want to remain anonymous," he said, "but I really want to tell you some things."

Parr agreed, and listened intently to what Kincaid told him. "G.T., Howard, just about all the top guys used the system," he heard the nervous voice say. "You need to get a court order or something and go through the books with a fine-tooth comb. If you do, you'll have evidence that Gary Long is telling the truth."

"Have you told this to anyone else?" Parr asked.

"No."

The line went dead, and Parr wrote out the conversation on his legal pad. "What do I do with this juicy little tidbit?" he asked himself out loud.

The operative listening in on the bugged phone knew exactly what to do with it. Within two hours, Admiral Decatur had a transcript of the conversation and the name on the credit card. He called Hargiss.

"You have a Roger Kincaid working for you?" he asked.

CHAPTER 120

Physically, Gary was fine. But his mind just couldn't deal with the world around him, or the world of hurt and shame inside him. Under the influence of whatever it was the doctors kept injecting, he slept a lot. When he awoke, Jenna was often there. She kept telling him to be strong, and recover, and that she loved him. Then, one day, she brought the boys. Gary awoke to find them all sitting there in the private room.

"Gary," Jenna said, softly, "Justin and Mark wanted to come and tell you how sorry they are that you're sick and how they want you to get better and come home so we can all be together again."

Justin walked over to the bed and put his hand in Gary's, which was lying limply beside him. "I miss you, Daddy," he said. "Please get better real fast." Gary felt the muscles in his arm tighten, and he squeezed Justin's hand.

"Go ahead," Jenna said to Mark, who dropped his head to his shoulder, and then slowly walked to the bedside.

"Daddy," he began, tears welling in his eyes. Then he turned, and looked sternly at his mother. He made a quick little motion with the palm of his hand.

"Justin," Jenna said. "Let's go out in the hall for a minute. Remember, Mark said he wanted to speak with Daddy alone."

Mark watched the door close, and then turned back to Gary. "Daddy," Mark said again, "I didn't tell our secret. But Mommy said it was in the paper about the divorce, and she said she wasn't going to divorce you. She said, 'Not now, and not ever,' and Granddad asked me if I'd heard anything that afternoon and I just shook my head and he said, 'Don't you worry,' and that you and Mommy weren't going to get a divorce and so you were right, Daddy, when you told me that." He dropped his eyes. "That made me happy, and now I just want you to get better and come home."

Gary felt his hand rise up and stroke the boy's head.

After that day, Gary started to improve, slowly. Each day, the inside and outside worlds seemed a little more tolerable. He started talking to Jenna, using words that were actually coherent. The doctors told her the crisis was over; it was just a matter of time.

Then one day, he felt good enough to go for a walk with her. There was a solarium, and they sat on a couch near the window and watched the late summer sun stream in. He asked where the boys were, and she told him they were back in school now, that things had quieted down a lot, and she had moved back into their house and was getting it ready for his return, as soon as he was able.

"How's the case going?" he asked. It was the first time he had mentioned it. She told him not much had happened, and that Keith Parr had forced the Justice Department to slow everything down as long as he was sick.

"Call Parr," Gary said. "Tell him about the tapes. The ones Ralph has."

She made the call that afternoon from her mobile phone driving back to Wonanonly.

Parr's secretary answered and quickly put Jenna through. "Mr. Parr, this is Jenna, I need to talk to you."

"How's Gary?"

"Better. Getting better."

"That's good to hear. Jenna, I've been hoping you'd call. We need to talk a little bit."

"What about?"

"Well, I had an anonymous call from someone who claimed that if I could get a court order to review the books at TLP, I'd find the evidence we need to prove that other executives got bonus payments, just like Gary's been saying. I'd thought about that before, but I figured they'd have everything buried and it wouldn't be worth it. Besides, I could never get a court order just to go fishing. But this call means I might have a chance. The guy sounded like he really knew what was there. Do you have any idea who it could be?"

"Maybe Roger Kincaid," she said. "He's the Comptroller, and as far as I know, he's not in on any of the corrupt stuff. At least not much."

"Kincaid, great, I'll look into that. Now, is there anything else you can think of that might help me substantiate Gary's claim?"

"Yes, there is," she said. "There are tapes, copies of tapes he gave to the FBI. I think one of them had G.T. talking to him about a bonus. And also, I don't know where things stand with the FBI, but there are tapes the FBI doesn't know anything about, with Gary talking to Sid Cox. Gary feels that Cox said some things on those tapes that would get the FBI in a whole lot of trouble."

"What?"

"I listened to some of them. Cox was telling Gary to do things he shouldn't have been doing. And there's one where Cox told him to destroy a tape he didn't want to be part of the case."

"Where are these tapes?"

"They're in Chicago at Ralph Sori's house. We sent him seven shoeboxes full of tapes."

"Ralph Sori, the ex-Bear?"

"Yeah, that's him. Gary used to work with him at TLP. We sent the tapes to him before the FBI came to pick up their equipment."

Parr was stunned. Who knew what those tapes contained? Whatever it was, it could help him negotiate a better deal. "I'm due in court in ten minutes," he said. "Call Sori right now and tell him I'll call him tonight. This might be Gary's ticket out of this mess."

Jenna gave Parr the Soris' phone numbers and then tried to call Ralph at his office. He was out, so she tried the home number, hoping Becky would be there. After five rings, the answering machine picked up, and Jenna left Ralph a message that Parr would be calling him, and to give him the tapes.

In the basement of Parr's building, NSA agents were high-fiving each other. What had started out as a wild goose chase was ending up striking paydirt. They called Decatur and played the tape of Jenna and Parr's conversation. When the tape finished, they could hear the smile in Decatur's voice. "Boys, we've hit the mother lode. Now we've got to get those tapes."

Over the next half hour, they set up a plan to get Ralph out of the house and three members of the team in to search for the tapes that night.

It was already 5:00 in Chicago. They had Sori's address in seconds, and two agents headed immediately to Park Ridge. A nice suburb, but not in the first rank. Two kinds of people lived there: those who never quite made it to the top, and those who were on their way up, but not quite ready for Winnetka or Lake Forest. Ralph Sori obviously belonged in the second category. They pulled into a park across the street and called their findings back to Washington. Decatur had searched the news for any events in Chicago that might be of interest to Ralph and his wife, but came up with nothing he had confidence in. Plan B was to get Ralph's boss on the phone and steal his voice.

The city directory listed Sori's job with a PR firm. The CEO's name was Edward Miller. Decatur placed a call. "Is Ed Miller in, please?" he asked.

"No, I'm sorry, he's out of town," the secretary answered.

"I'm looking for an agency to place a large block of media time, and your firm was recommended. Can you tell me if you handle any national accounts?"

"Oh, yes – Motorola, Biogen, WGN, several. Would you like to talk to our media director?"

"No, no, that's fine. I'd really like to speak to Mr. Miller. Can you put me into his voice mail, so I can leave a message?"

"Sure, and have a nice day."

Decatur nodded to the technician sitting beside him. It was show time.

Ed's voice came across the phone line. "This is Edward Miller. Well, I sure didn't want to miss *your* call, but I guess I have. So, the best thing now is, just leave me a message, and what time you called. I check in pretty regularly, so I should be able to get back to you before long. Hey, thanks for calling."

Decatur hung up as soon as he heard the beep, and turned to the tech.

"Do you have enough?"

"Sure do. He gave us enough vowels and consonants to fill a dictionary with pronunciations."

"I'll give you the script in a few minutes. Meanwhile you can start off with, "'Hello Ralph, this is Ed.' That should be pretty direct, right?"

"Yes, sir."

Decatur searched the directory for a restaurant in a suburb southwest of the city, and picked one in a town called Naperville. That should be far enough, he thought. Then he looked up the name of the investment relations manager for Motorola, wrote the script out, and handed it to the tech.

In five minutes it was ready, and as he listened to it, Decatur marveled at the ability of the computer to mimic a voice based on just a few words. It was one of the newest tools of the agency. "Send it." Decatur said.

The tech dialed the number and after five rings the answering machine picked up. He pressed a button: "Ralph, it's Ed. Jim Haynes from Motorola wants to see us tonight. Since I'm out of town, you need to meet Jim and his wife at the Rosebud in Naperville. Be sure to bring Becky. Eight o'clock. Sorry for the late notice. Thanks."

Two agents sat in a specially-equipped cable company truck, holding pictures of Ralph Sori they'd pulled out of cyberspace moments before. They watched as the man in the picture got out of a white Lexus, unlocked the front door and walked inside. No more than two minutes later, a dark green Pathfinder pulled into the driveway and stopped alongside the Lexus. A pretty blonde got out, went around the other side, opened the door and pulled out two bags of groceries. As she walked toward the door, Ralph opened it, motioned for her to hurry up and then closed the door behind her. He'd gotten the message. The two agents smiled at each other and called headquarters. It was 6:45.

At 7:02, the couple came out of the house, locked the door behind them, got into the Lexus and roared off. A Taurus pulled out of the park across the street and slipped in behind the Lexus at the next corner.

The cable company repair truck drove into the Sori's driveway and the two men exited and went around to the side of the house where they cut the phone line, checking to make sure they had the active line, and not a dummy line set up by an alarm company. Ralph's alarm, if there was one, was now disabled. They reappeared at the front of the house where two other men, who had driven at breakneck speed from Great Lakes Naval Base and arrived in Park Ridge only moments before, joined them. In less than a minute they were in the house.

They began their search in the bedroom, looking for anything that might resemble seven shoeboxes of cassette tapes.

Ralph and Becky took the exit onto the I-294 tollway, heading south toward Naperville. Ralph hated going into a meeting without any preparation, and decided to try to call Ed. Ralph knew he was in New York, and when he went there, he usually stayed at the Plaza, sometimes the Sherry-Netherland. The phone message was highly unusual. It wasn't like Ed. While Ralph drove, Becky dialed numbers on the car phone. She called New York information and got the number for the Plaza. He wasn't there. She called information again for the Sherry-Netherland.

"If we do get through to him," Ralph said, "let's try and call Jenna next, and see what her message was all about."

The switchboard operator at the Sherry-Netherland put Becky on hold. Then she came back on and confirmed that they had an Edward Miller registered. The whole process had taken ten minutes, but Ed's voice finally filled the car.

"Ralph? What do you want?"

Ralph was taken back by the tenor of his voice: it was almost like he was irritated, which in fact he was. Miller was at that moment trying to unhook the front snap of a bra, which happened to be attached to the stunning young advertising executive he'd met at the meeting. The ringing phone had certainly thrown a little cool water on the moment. He thought about letting the damn thing ring, but by the eighth ring, the mood had been broken, and he gave up and picked up the receiver.

"Hey, Ed, sorry to interrupt you, but can you fill me in a little on this meeting with Motorola?"

"What meeting with Motorola?"

"The one you called about tonight."

Ed disengaged himself from the busty brunette. "What the hell are you talking about?"

"I got your message about meeting Jim Haynes in Naperville. I was just calling to get a heads-up."

"Someone's played a hell of a trick on you, Bud. I didn't call you about anything."

Ralph knew better than to push this too far. He looked over at Becky and shrugged his shoulders. "Sorry to bother you, I guess I got a bad message somehow."

Ralph pointed the car at the next exit, looped around, paid the toll at the entrance booth and headed back. In the car behind him, the agent picked up the phone. "They've turned around, you've got another ten minutes max safe."

"You want me to try Jenna?" Becky asked.

"Nah, we'll do it when we get home."

The search of the bedroom proved fruitless, and the agents began spreading out into the other rooms, the spare bedroom, living room, basement, garage, crawl space, going through each, searching, examining, opening everything big enough to hide even one shoebox. Nothing. With five minutes left, one of the agents looked overhead and spied a pull-down trap door to the attic.

He reached up, pulled the door down, and clambered up the steps. Damn, he'd forgotten a flashlight. Pitch darkness. He called for a flashlight, more time lost. He looked at his watch, only four minutes left. The flashlight magically appeared in his hand. He popped back into the sweltering heat of the attic. There were a few boxes, and he searched them: nothing. From below came a call: "Two-minute warning. Guys, let's find these things."

He started down the stairs, giving the light one more quick sweep. Below him, someone shouted, "Time's up, we've got to get outta here." As he took the last step off the ladder, something registered in his mind. Damn it, was the insulation higher on the one side or was it his imagination?

Climbing back up the stairs, he shined the flashlight in the direction of the higher insulation. It *was* higher than its neighbors. Below him, he heard the cry, "Out! Now! Everyone out!" He heard the front door of the house open. Frantically, he headed toward the lumpy insulation. He pulled it up. Shit, there they were, shoebox after shoebox. He called for help, but everyone was gone. He pulled out the shoeboxes and piled them in his arms, pushing the insulation down as he went.

He reached the door hole, and heard the front door opening again, someone calling his name. He yelled back, "Come here, I've got 'em." Then the sound of pounding footsteps up the stairs. He handed four of the boxes down and climbed down the stairs with the other three, closing the door to the attic in one swift motion. Outside, the sound of the truck motor startled him – they were going to leave them behind! The two men flew out the door, slamming it behind them and diving for the open door to the cable truck.

As they pulled out of the driveway and onto the road, the white Lexus pulled around the corner. They'd made it with nothing to spare.

Inside the Lexus, Ralph turned to Becky. "Jeez, did you see that cable truck? Somebody must have been seriously pissed to get service this late at night." He shut off the car, and headed up to the door and put his key in the lock. Damn, that was funny, he thought he'd locked it, was sure he'd locked it.

When he got inside, he looked all around the house. Becky came up behind him and he put his finger to his lips telling her to be quiet, then motioned for her to stay put. Nothing was really out of place, just different, like a strong wind had moved everything around a little bit. He looked around the first floor and went upstairs. In the hall, there were paint chips and bits of insulation on the floor beneath the attic door. Somebody had been in the house. He picked up the phone to dial 911. Damn, the line was dead. "Becky," he yelled. "Call the police from your car. Someone's been in our house."

At that moment, Keith Parr was listening to a recorded message. "We're sorry," it said, "the number you have called is experiencing technical difficulty. Please try your call later."

The cable truck and two cars headed for Palwaukee Airport. As they were on their way, Decatur congratulated them, and ordered them to listen to the tapes on the flight to Washington, and told them what to listen for. Every hour counted. They boarded the jet and began the task of cataloguing and reviewing each tape.

Almost immediately, one of the men stumbled across a tape that piqued his interest. There were two male voices. One told the other "You've got to get rid of that tape. Take it home and put it in the garbage, throw it out of the car, burn it up, I don't care." They concentrated on the tapes from that box after their discovery, and the more notes they compared, the more amazed they became.

Conversations between the informant and the agent, begging for psychiatric help, asking for legal help, being told not to, even countermanding a prosecutor's suggestion that he show his immunity agreement to a lawyer. Racial slurs, and a confession that an agent had assaulted the witness. Even to seasoned NSA pros, it was incredible.

Gary had done his job well. Cox had trained him in techniques for getting people to talk on tape, and he in turn had used the techniques on the trainer.

In the conference room in Ft. Meade, Decatur gave the orders to listen to all the tapes, and transcribe the relevant sections. In the 34 hours they had left, they had just enough time.

Two officers of the Cook County Sheriff's Police walked through Ralph Sori's house, filled out their report, and left Ralph with the unpleasant task of telling Jenna the tapes were missing.

CHAPTER 121

At exactly 9:00 the next morning, Decatur placed his call to McWhorter, who didn't see the need for a face-to-face meeting. "I think we both know what's possible," he protested.

"Well, we've uncovered a few things I think you need to hear," Decatur argued.

"All right, Admiral, come over at your convenience."

"I'll see you ten-thirty."

Well, well, McWhorter thought. So Decatur has a few things he thinks I need to hear. Well, I've got a few things he needs to hear, too, thanks to Goochie Mudge.

"Mr. McWhorter, how are you today?" Decatur greeted him an hour later.

"Fine, and I hope you are as well," McWhorter answered in a voice that was just a little too comfortable and confident for Decatur's liking.

"Well, Admiral, what revelation do you have for me today?"

Decatur took 15 pages out of his briefcase and handed them to McWhorter. "These are transcripts of tapes that appear to be..." Decatur hesitated, "no, not 'appear' – that we're sure actually are conversations between your agents and Dr. Gary Long. Take a few minutes and read them over."

Dutifully, McWhorter read the transcripts. Finally he looked up. "Well, under normal circumstances these could present quite a problem. But these are not normal circumstances, are they?

"We kind of have a Mexican standoff here, Admiral. We've been doin a little lookin of our own," McWhorter said in his thick southern accent. "We've been lookin into some bank accounts, Interoceanic in the Caymans, Tracinda in Switzerland. What can you tell me about them?"

Then he sat back in his chair with a satisfied smile. Decatur hoped his panic wasn't evident. How much did McWhorter know? This was turning into a slop bucket if there ever was one.

"Mr. McWhorter, those are accounts, as I'm sure you know, that, in the interest of national security, I'm not allowed to discuss."

"Well then Admiral, it looks like we're back to square one. Here's the deal the A.G. will swallow, and I can tell you it's not a happy deal, but it's a deal we'll live with. Tamson-Long pays a fine of one hundred million dollars. Two

TLP executives go to trial; one of them can be Gary Long, the other needs to be either Binghamton or young Hargiss. You'll also need to turn over every tape that relates to this case, along with any transcripts or copies. Finally, you cease and desist from investigating anything whatsoever involving our fine President, turn over everything you have – and that means all of your files. We will respond likewise with everything we have regarding Interoceanic and Tracinda. What's your answer?"

Decatur thought a moment. McWhorter had sweetened his offer by only the tiniest bit, but it might be enough to satisfy Hargiss. "Let me be sure I understood you," he said. "I give you my China stuff, and the TLP tapes. You give me what you have on Interoceanic and Tracinda. As far as the case itself is concerned, you want either Binghamton or Howard Hargiss, not both, and we get to make the choice?"

"I had to do some fast talking on that last part," McWhorter said. "The prosecutors in Chicago were a lot more willing to give up Binghamton, because the stuff on Hargiss is juicier and better and there's more of it. But I figured the old man would want to save his kid, so I talked them into accepting one or the other. You see how much I'm trying to help you out here, Admiral?"

"You certainly are," Decatur said flatly. "I'll visit with the Director, and get back to you."

"Please give my compliments to the Director," McWhorter said.

The Director, of course, knew nothing about Decatur's China files, so they weren't part of his decision-making when Decatur presented him with McWhorter's offer.

"This whole thing's gotten to be a can of worms, hasn't it?" the Director told Decatur.

"A can of worms that could set our covert operations program back a decade, maybe even kill it altogether," Decatur said.

"Well, we can't let that happen, can we? You know, Jon, using this price-fixing stuff to finance those operations has been a godsend."

"When Hargiss first came to us with the plan, I didn't understand how it could work," Decatur responded. "I didn't see how there could be more money in anything than there was in the drug trade. But there is."

"And price fixing is so much less messy," the Director said. "It's just sort of like normal business."

"All in all, William Hargiss may be the most valuable operative in the history of the agency," Decatur said.

"I guess we were really lucky. If they knew how close they were to exposing the underbelly of our operations, we'd be up the creek."

"That's why we have so many layers of protection. Personally, I think they were just guessing about our involvement in those accounts."

"It was close enough. Call Hargiss before you call McWhorter back, give him a couple of minutes to absorb the news. If you need me I'll be available."

Decatur dreaded the call to William Hargiss, but it had to be done. "I think it's the best option available to us," he concluded after reviewing the bidding.

Hargiss thought about the offer for a few minutes before saying anything. At least that son of a bitch Long was going to stand trial, he thought. The filthy little rat. And his own name would be cleared in all the mudslinging. But still, it hurt him a lot to think of G.T. behind bars. At last he spoke. "How long would someone have to go to jail for?"

Decatur was surprised; he hadn't asked McWhorter that question. "I don't know, but I'll find out and call you back."

He called McWhorter who had clearly been waiting for his call. "Adrian, I'm sorry, but I forgot to ask you what they would be charged with and how long the sentence would be."

"Well, I guess we could drop it to one count of price fixing, that'd be two years. I'd be willing to limit the personal fine to something in the neighborhood of thirty-five thousand dollars if that'd help. Remember, we could go for treble damages and at least fifteen counts of price fixing."

"Where would the guy do his time?"

"An interesting question. You've got two minimum security prisons in the North Central region, Yankton and Duluth. Normally, they'd get one or the other. But I can pull strings and get young Hargiss or Binghamton into Pensacola or Eglin. An all-expense paid vacation to Club Fed in Florida."

"Thanks. I'll let you know in the next hour or so."

Decatur redialed Hargiss. "Bill, here's the deal. G.T. – or Howard, whichever – will have to plead to two years and a fine of thirty-five thousand dollars. They'll recommend sending him to Eglin or Pensacola."

Hargiss considered this for a few seconds. "Take the damn deal," he said. "I'll have to do some footwork with the board, but I'll get what I want. Take the damn deal."

CHAPTER 122

Keith Parr swore under his breath when Jenna told him the tapes had been stolen from Ralph Sori's house. It had to be the Justice Department, he thought. All his life, he had had nothing but respect for Federal prosecutors. As a native Chicagoan, he knew full well how corrupt local law enforcement and local state's attorneys could be. But for him, the Federal government had always stood above that sort of thing. He almost couldn't believe they would stoop to burglary.

In any event, the tapes were gone, and his hopes of exonerating Gary Long were pretty much gone with them. All he had left was the court-ordered audit. If this Kincaid, or whoever the anonymous caller was, knew what he was talking about, the audit could still save Gary's case.

He quizzed Jenna carefully about the exact sequence of events leading up to the tape burglary. When he finished talking to her, he had a sickening feeling in the pit of his stomach. There was only one scenario that made sense. He walked out of his office and took the elevator to the basement of the building. He told the man at the security office he wanted to check the telephone box. "There's something very suspicious going on," he said.

The man led him through dingy corridors to the place where the phone equipment was. "Holy smoke," the man said after they had looked and looked through the massive panels of wires. "You're right! Your phone's bugged!"

Just then, the head of security rushed into the room. "Vinnie, I'll handle this," he barked, and Vinnie made a quick exit.

"You know something about this illegal tap on my phone line?" Parr asked the man.

"I ain't saying nothin'," the man said, "except you need to get out of here. This is a restricted area."

"Yeah," Parr snorted, "well, it sure looks like somebody's been in this restricted area. I want that thing removed right now, and I want to know who put it there."

"I ain't saying nothin'," the man repeated.

"Mister, I am an attorney and a client in this building. If you don't remove that bug right now, I'll have your job, and your ass in jail by lunchtime."

"I'll take it off," the man said, moving toward the board and extracting a small screwdriver from his pocket. "But I ain't saying nothin'."

He did the work, and placed the bug in Parr's outstretched hand. "You better watch yourself," he said. "Somebody real big doesn't like you."

Parr went back up to his office and sat at his desk for a long time, looking out the window. He watched the traffic slipping by on Wacker Drive, across the river. The light turned green, the cars moved. The light turned red, they stopped. It was the law in action, at its simplest. Everyone knew they had to stop on red, and if they obeyed, it worked to everyone's benefit. He saw a city police car, lights flashing, cautiously ignore the signal and move through the Wabash Avenue intersection. The government was exercising its prerogative to be above the law, because, presumably, that was in the common interest as well.

But there have to be limits, he thought. He reached for his telephone, hesitated, felt the little bump in his shirt pocket where he'd put the bug, picked up the phone and called his friend Ted Asturian at the U.S. Attorney's office across the Loop.

"Someone wiretapped my phone," he told Asturian. "It has to be about the TLP case, and it has to be your office. I want an explanation."

When Asturian reached Susan Henry's office, she had just hung up the phone after a call from Adrian McWhorter.

"I'll call him," she said after she heard Asturian's story. Then she thought again. "No, you'd better call him. Tell him – and Ted, this is the God's honest truth – tell him the Department of Justice had absolutely nothing to do with that tap."

"Are you saying you know there was a tap?"

"I'm saying the Department of Justice had absolutely nothing to do with that tap."

Jenna couldn't decide whether or not to tell Gary that the tapes had been stolen. She didn't think he was strong enough for the bad news. But when she got to his room, he seemed to be almost his old self again.

They walked to the solarium, and talked for a long time. Finally, she told him. He stared at her intently, and she struggled to hold back the tears she felt welling up.

"Tell me again that you are not going to divorce me," he said, softly.

"Never, ever, ever, ever, ever."

His mind was clear now. He could almost feel the machinery of his brain humming again. For weeks, maybe longer, it had been clogged like the fermenters on the first day the Sugere plant had opened. Instead of crystalline thoughts, it had been pumping out big chunks of psychotic uselessness, which he had hidden under mental burlap. But he knew it was finally over.

"I am recovered," he told her. "I want to go home."

Through the oversized solarium windows, bright afternoon sunlight illuminated their long, loving kiss.

CHAPTER 123

Alex Bremerton boarded the JAL flight at O'Hare in the early evening. His marching orders were simple: use the video and audio tapes of Sumiko Numata and Sadaaki Hamanaka to extract a 50 million dollar fine and their cooperation in the case against TLP.

Gary Long's problems had eroded their case, and if it came to trial, they'd need the cooperation of another witness to be able to play the tapes as evidence. Alex was chosen for the trip because in a former life he'd been an army intelligence officer, assigned to Japan.

Eighteen hours after boarding the plane, he stepped off into the familiar world of Tokyo. After barking a few orders in Japanese to a very surprised cab driver, Alex settled in for the one-hour cab ride to the Imperial Hotel. After dropping off his bags, he climbed into another cab and rode the seven blocks to Nippon Kagaka.

He gave his card to the receptionist and asked to speak with Mr. Hamanaka. After a few whispered words on the phone, she escorted Alex to a teak-paneled conference room on the fifth floor.

Within two minutes, Sadaaki Hamanaka entered the room. He shook hands with Alex, who bowed and said, "Konichiwa." Hamanaka smiled and sat down. Alex explained the purpose of his visit in Japanese, and Hamanaka's brow furrowed into clear displeasure.

"We have been expecting you to visit us, and we knew that you would not bring good news. We did not expect you to request such a large penalty. Our attorneys did, however, expect you to request our assistance. I am authorized to tell you that in exchange for your releasing our company from any further penalty, we will cooperate. I have not been authorized to make a payment of the size you request. You must wait here while I visit with the other managing directors."

"Do you have a counter-proposal?" Alex asked. He had authority to go as low as 40.

"We could accept thirty-five million," Hamanaka said.

"I'll split the difference. Forty-two five. That's as low as I can go."

Hamanaka bowed and left the room. Half an hour later, he returned, and the deal was done. Alex guessed they were under extreme pressure from the Japanese government to settle the issue. Nothing else could explain the ease with which it had all been accomplished.

Across the Sea of Japan, in Seoul, Kim Jungwoo couldn't believe his good fortune. First, he'd gotten word from Washington that the U.S. Justice Department wasn't going to prosecute anyone connected with Daehan Hwa-Hak in the TLP case.

The call he had just received from Song Dian-Nuan was even better news. New World was completely out of the artificial sweetener business, and Song had offered to sell him his bug, his media and 50 million dollars worth of unneeded machinery for ten cents on the dollar. Market share to gobble up, and the means to gobble it. Life was good.

He looked up to see Park Soo-hee entering his office, a worried look on his face. Kim did not relish an interruption to his pleasant thoughts. "What is it?" he snapped at Park.

"I apologize," Park said, bowing and backing up a step. "I have just received a call from *The Korea Times*.

"Yes," Kim said, irritably. The *Times* was the English-language newspaper in Seoul, and an important publication.

"The reporter wanted to know if we were still paying patent royalties to Dr. Gary Long."

"Are we?"

"Yes. And the reporter knew something I did not. For several years, we have made the payments to an account at the Kookmin Bank, here in Seoul."

"The reporter knew that?"

"Yes, and when I checked, it was true."

Lee Cha at first refused to answer the reporter's questions. But he was so insistent, and she could tell that she was about to break down and tell everything. Frightened, she pleaded for time. "It is late at night," she said, almost sobbing. "You call back tomorrow, please."

When the man had finally agreed, she sat alone in her Itaewon apartment, the nicest home she had ever known. She tiptoed to the boy's bedroom and looked in on him, fast asleep in his comfortable bed. What would happen to them now? If the money was cut off, she would have to give all this up, go back to being a bar-girl. Frantic, she dug through her papers and found the telephone number in Madison, Indiana.

"Hello," she heard a woman's voice answer.

"Mr. Long is there?"

"No, he's at work. Can I take a message?"

"He can call me? In Korea? Is very important."

"Yes," Mary Lou Long said, puzzled at the unusual message, "I suppose so. What is it about?"

"Please to tell him Mrs. Cha call. Very important."

"All right. What is the number?"

Mary Lou Long sat still for several minutes after the call. Then she phoned Bert at the machine shop. "Oh, my God," he said when she gave him the message.

After speaking with Bert an hour later, Lee Cha spent the rest of a sleepless night packing clothing for her son and herself, waking him early and leaving Seoul for a small village in the southwest of Korea where her family lived. *The Korea Times* had to run its story without further comment from her, but it was an interesting story nonetheless, and *The New York Times* picked it up and made it the lead it the business section. "TLP Informant Implicated in Korean Paternity Case," the headline read. The article talked about a DNA match and a secret bank account. "Contacted at his home in Indiana," one paragraph read, "Dr. Long refused to confirm or deny the report, telling a reporter it was 'none of his business.'"

For William Hargiss, it seemed like the myriad loose ends were beginning to get tied down. Gary Long was going to jail. Ian Howes had been stopped in his mad attempt to compromise the secret espionage network. He and Howard were safe from prosecution. Still, he had two unpleasant tasks ahead of him.

The first was relatively easy, however unpleasant. A simple phone call to Tully would handle the really unpleasant part, and a busy weekend would clean up the rest of it.

The second problem, however, was something he would have to handle himself. There's no help for it, he thought.

CHAPTER 124

Roger Kincaid looked forward to the first of September each year – the opening day of dove season. This year, the chance to be alone with his thoughts and to vent a little frustration with each kick of his double-barreled 12-gauge Browning Citori Invector held special appeal.

Dove season opened at noon, and Kincaid had decided to make a day of the event. He'd neither seen nor heard anything to suggest that his call to Keith Parr had had any effect at all. That disappointed him, but maybe these things just took a little time. He drove to Wonanonly and ate an early lunch in the local café, famous for its wonderful pies. Finishing off a home-style meal of meat loaf, mashed potatoes and corn, Roger looked at his watch. He had enough time to order a piece of the incredible-looking blackberry concoction he'd seen in the pie safe.

In dove hunting, one's first choice would always be a good sunflower field, and second choice would be a wheat field that had been burnt off in the last couple of days. Third choice, still an excellent one, would be a pasture with cattle, and water running through it. Kincaid owned a prime example of the third choice, a property that had come down to him through his mother's family, and that he leased out to a local farmer. As a dove hunting spot, it had rarely disappointed him over the years.

The State of Indiana allows a hunter 15 doves a day, and frequently before sunset Kincaid had his limit. The birds were fast, and he usually burned up several boxes of shells.

As he drove toward the field, he did the math. Three boxes of shells cost ten dollars each; the hunting license was 15 dollars; a 40 mile round-trip drive at 21 cents a mile, make that 20 for rounding purposes – 53 dollars total. If he got his limit of 15 birds, they were a little over $3.50 each. Expensive poultry, but you couldn't really put a price on what it did for your mind.

Kincaid pulled off the road about 200 yards from where it crossed the creek. The wind was light, out of the south, so it'd be tough to predict which direction the birds would travel, although generally they would fly down the tree line bordering the creek. The line had just enough dead trees to welcome birds who wanted to stop for a little rest.

That also meant that finding the downed birds would be easy. Pasture on one side, tree line on the other; good cover and shade, Kincaid thought as he lugged his gear to a spot 300 yards in from the road.

After he set up his flutter poles, with their flat decoys that made the doves stutter just a second, long enough for him to get a little better shot, Kincaid placed a couple of decoys on the woven wire fence that went along a little mudhole to his right. The birds would probably be coming in to drink out of the mudhole as the day wore on. Then he turned his bucket over and sat on it, watching the sky for any sign of activity. Within ten minutes, he had five shots.

Hargiss's heads-up had given Tully enough time to put a tracking beacon underneath the bumper of Kincaid's car.

Tully had loosely tailed Kincaid as he drove down to Wonanonly, waiting in the car while he ate, and then staying back at least a mile while Kincaid drove out of town. When the signal started to weaken, he turned around and turned onto the first crossroad. The signal stopped getting weaker and started gaining strength. Tully pulled over to the side of the road to wait for another five minutes before going any farther. A car came toward him, and Tully quickly restarted the car and moved forward slowly. The last thing he wanted was to have anyone stop and ask if he needed help, a practice common in the back country of Indiana.

He waved at the capped figure behind the wheel of the pickup truck and drove toward the strengthening signal. One mile, two miles, the signal was nearly at full strength. He crested a rise, and there was Kincaid's car, 200 yards past the creek.

He got out of his car and looked around. Not spotting Kincaid, he looked in the car. Son of a bitch, this was going to be his lucky day! There on the front seat was a gun-cleaning kit, and the doors were unlocked. He reached in, pulled out the cleaning kit, threw it on his own front seat and pulled away. Tully decided to drive around the section. It wouldn't do to have anyone drive by and see his car parked next to Kincaid's. He turned right at the next intersection, drove down to a dirt road, turned right again and spotted a creek line. That had to be the same creek that exited on the opposite side of the section, and bonus of bonuses, he'd get to park on a dirt road that was obviously not well traveled.

Tully parked the car next to the creek, got out his shotgun, put on his green camouflage gear, put the cleaning kit into his backpack and started down the tree line. A quarter mile down the line, Tully heard the report of a shotgun ahead. A moment later, it barked again, and Tully had a good fix on where Kincaid was. He stood up and walked across the creek line and out into the pasture where he was sure Kincaid would spot him.

Kincaid smiled as he broke open the Browning and stuffed two more shells into it. This had been the best day he could remember. The doves had been flying like butterflies, and he'd already put ten into his game bag.

His shooting had been on the mark as well. He'd gone through less than a box of shells. As he brought the gun back to his side, he saw a movement along the edge of the tree line. What? Who the heck was that? he wondered.

Within a minute, he could tell it was another hunter, walking with his shotgun in hand, camo'd up and wearing a backpack. Nobody else had permission to hunt this pasture, but maybe the person was just passing through, walking to another field somewhere. No, that didn't make any sense either. Oh, well, better let him know I'm here, he thought.

Tully watched as Kincaid stood up and yelled a greeting, then, waving his hand in response, he changed direction and headed toward him. When he got within 20 yards, Tully called, "Roger, is that you?"

Kincaid was surprised that anyone would recognize him from that distance. He squinted into the sun, trying to figure out who was calling his name. When the man got closer, he saw who it was. He began to feel panic rising in his gut. "Tully, what're you doing out here?" he shouted.

"Well, I thought I'd try to do a little dove hunting, but I haven't had a shot in the past hour on the opposite side of the section. I kept hearing shots this way, and I thought I'd see who was doing all the shooting …you know, see if I could impose a little and join the hunt."

That was the last thing Kincaid wanted, but he couldn't bring himself to refuse. "Uh, okay, why don't you go down 50 yards or so back that way," he said. "I've seen several birds heading across the pasture from that hole."

"Great. Thanks. Hey, what are you shooting, is that a Browning?" Tully asked, pulling has backpack off and setting his shotgun down.

"Yeah, it's a lightning grade; I just got it a couple of years ago," Kincaid said, beginning to feel a little better.

"Mind if I take a look at it?" Tully asked.

"No, here. It really swings nice; it's the best feel I've ever had against shoulder. It almost seems to point on its own," Kincaid said, chuckling as he handed the shotgun over to Tully.

Tully took the gun from him and put it to his shoulder, aiming out toward the field. Softly, he pushed up on the safety, disengaging it.

Tully turned back around and bent over as if he was stumbling. In one swift motion, he put the butt of the shotgun on the ground. Aiming for Kincaid's chest, he pulled the trigger.

It all happened so quickly that Kincaid's face didn't even have time to register shock. A red splotch began to spread on his chest as he stumbled forward. He fell slightly in front of Tully, and Tully saw where the tiny birdshot had exited Roger's back. Behind him on the tree, bits of vital organs and a mass of blood began sliding down the trunk. It was a fatal shot, Tully thought, no question.

Kincaid was on his knees, wordlessly trying to get up, pushing himself away from Tully. Tully watched him struggle for a minute, then cracked open the shotgun, put a new shell in the lower chamber, made sure the switch was set to fire the lower chamber first, and pulled the cleaning kit out of his backpack. As he screwed the ends of the cleaning rod together, he watched Kincaid pulling himself along the ground, leaving a trail of mucus and blood as he crept.

Tully pushed the cleaning rod into the top barrel of the gun, found a stick to prop up the gun, and another to pull the trigger, then leaned the gun against the stick he'd just found. Standing just behind the shotgun, he pushed down on the trigger with the second stick, causing the gun to fire and tumble onto its side. Then he picked up the sticks, shoved them into his backpack and took another look around.

Kincaid had managed to pull himself about 75 feet before collapsing. Tully didn't even bother to check for signs of breath; he didn't want any extra footprints around. He pulled his gloves off, stuffed them into the backpack and headed back toward his car.

He drove back to the highway and called Hargiss. "Job done," he said.

"Very good," Hargiss responded. "I'll meet you Saturday at one o'clock."

"You got it, boss," Tully replied.

It took them all Saturday afternoon and evening, and a good part of Sunday, but eventually they had everything in order. The paperwork on each of the 107 bonus payments was neat as a pin. The six missing documents had been forged and carefully photocopied signatures affixed. For every payment, there was now a contract, an AFE and a cancelled check.

"We do an average of twenty-eight hundred AFEs a day," Hargiss said. "That means an auditor is going to have to review three million documents to go back five years. If they analyze each of them carefully enough to spot those six photocopied signatures, they deserve to catch us."

On Monday morning, three SEC auditors arrived in Steuben, armed with the court order Keith Parr had won. "You have our complete cooperation," Hargiss told them. "We have nothing to hide.

"It is unfortunate that our comptroller, Mr. Kincaid, isn't available to help you, but I'm afraid he met with an accident over the weekend. I'll be attending his funeral tomorrow, the poor man."

The auditors never were able to come up with anything incriminating.

CHAPTER 125

Buffy Carney chuckled to himself when he read the faxed copy of the story in the New York *Post*. It couldn't have come out better. He'd done exactly what William Hargiss had asked, so there was no way he could be held responsible; but the story had not quite come out the way Hargiss had intended.

It was just the sort of juicy stuff the *Post* loved. An illegitimate child. Hush money. A link to an international scandal. And most of all, a chance to gig their hotsy-totsy competition, the *Times*.

The *Post*'s stringer in Seoul, who shared an office with a private detective named Kang Pok-tong, had managed to find the elusive Lee Cha. When he asked her to confirm that the father of her son was Gary Long, she looked startled. "Oh, no," she exclaimed. "Not *Gary* Long! *Albert* Long!"

The *Post* story included information that Albert Long, of Madison, Indiana, Gary Long's brother, had been stationed in Korea, along with a statement from a respected DNA expert who testified that DNA testing could not prove which brother was the father. "It's just like the Jefferson situation," the scientist was quoted. "All those African-Americans who claim Thomas Jefferson as their ancestor could just as easily be descended from Jefferson's brother, Randolph."

At lunchtime, Buffy drove to Mailboxes, Etc. and faxed the story to Gary.

G.T. was surprised when William Hargiss came into his office that same Monday. Usually, if Hargiss wanted to see him, he called and had G.T. come to his office.

Since the night of the raid, G.T. had been a busy man. He'd taken personal control of the Bio-tech Division, and had moved quickly to bail out Armand Pomerleau on the Czech factory deal, keeping the project alive in spite of the acute embarrassment the Czechs had suffered by being in the wrong place at the wrong time.

He'd kept the lid on the company, making sure that the news didn't hurt production or sales. Along with Howard, he'd taken steps to cover all the price-fixing agreements and send appropriate signals that there was no need for panic, that business could go on, even if the agreements were now just informal. None of the prices of the fixed products had gone into a tailspin, at least not yet.

With Sugere, the news that New World was getting out of the sweetener business was a boon for the other companies. Of course, they couldn't talk to one another, but as if they were of one mind, they began to gobble up New World's market share in what seemed, at least so far, to be totals equivalent to the market percentages in the Steuben Agreement. The price of Sugere held steady.

G.T. had reason to be proud of what he had done.

At first, he was scared stiff he might have to go to jail, but William had assured him that everything would be taken care of, and as he watched the PR campaign against Gary Long unfold, he gained hope. Now he got through whole days without thinking about the prospect of facing charges.

Cathy was distraught at first. Her blood sugar imbalance made it hard for her to accept bad news, and G.T. spent many hours patiently comforting her. Eventually, he gathered the whole family and managed to sell them the company line: that the scandal had been cooked up by Gary Long in an effort to take over TLP before his embezzlement scheme was uncovered, that the truth would come out soon, and that he, George Thomas Binghamton, Sr. was innocent of any wrongdoing.

Carrie didn't understand a word her father said, but bought into it anyway. For her, Gary Long was still just Ralph Sori's friend, the scoundrel. Tommy asked some sharp questions, which impressed his father, who managed to answer them to the young man's satisfaction.

While the little family meeting was going on, Cathy just nodded, but once she and G.T. were alone, she murmured, "I just can't believe that nice young man was doing all those horrid things."

"I know," G.T. told her, "it is hard to believe."

William Hargiss sat down at G.T.'s little round conference table, and beckoned G.T. to follow him.

"Man, I just can't believe Roger's dead," G.T. said, picking up a cup of coffee from his desk and moving to the table. "As experienced a hunter as he was, I can't believe he made such a stupid mistake as to try to clean his gun with a shell in the chamber."

"Well, we all make mistakes," Hargiss said. "And some of them are fatal."

They sat in silence for just a moment, until Hargiss figured it had been long enough to convey a sense of respect for the deceased. "G.T., we need to talk," he began.

"We've been together forever. I need your help again." A deep furrow formed on G.T.'s forehead. "I've gotten the final word on the investigations,"

Hargiss continued. "We've got it down to where we're going to pay a fine of a hundred million. That's the easy part. That's less than two months earnings. Now the hard part."

G.T. shifted uncomfortably in his chair.

"Try as I might, I couldn't get Justice to drop all the personal charges. They want Killer and Dan Anthony, which of course I don't care about one way or another. But they've insisted on two senior corporate officers. They'll take Long as one of the two, but they want either you or Howard as the second person. Howard can't go to jail; I have to have someone who can take over for me when I retire. That leaves you."

"What are you talking about? Do you expect me to go to jail?" Hargiss could see the veins in G.T.'s neck popping out.

"Well, it's not really a jail, more like a country club. They want a two-year sentence, which means you'll be out in a year. I don't expect you to do it for nothing, G.T. I'll give you a couple million wherever you want it, and of course you'll receive full retirement from TLP. You should have several million set aside by now huh?"

"Well, yeah, but I'm not gonna take the rap for this thing, William."

He doesn't understand that he doesn't have a choice, Hargiss thought. "G.T., I want you to go home and really think about this. You tell me what it'll take to make you happy, well, not happy, but willing to go along. I'm heading to the West Coast on Wednesday, but I'll be back Friday, and we'll talk then."

G.T. got up, pushed his chair back and said, "William, I'll think about it, but I can tell you I don't feel like my loyalty is being very well rewarded."

He watched Hargiss closely.

"I know," Hargiss said. "Sometimes in life, you have to eat a shit sandwich. That's just the way it is. I'm sorry." He pushed his chair back from the table and walked out of the room.

G.T. couldn't believe what he'd just heard. He was expected to take the fall for the whole rotten mess, which William and Howard had more to do with than anybody, and which they were going to walk away from scot-free.

G.T. figured he had a reputation to protect, a family, a respected position in the community. Howard's reputation was such that a year in jail wouldn't lower it one bit. But Howard would get to go on fucking everything with legs in a skirt, while G.T. served time in the pen.

It wasn't fair, it wasn't even possible! How could William even think about doing this to him? The nerve he'd had, to ask him what it would take to make him willing to be the scapegoat. Well, at least he hadn't been ordered to do it. Maybe there was some way he could fight back. He'd always figured loyalty was one of his chief virtues, but if William Hargiss didn't have any loyalty, why should G.T. Binghamton? All those years of service, and this was what he got.

He picked up the blueprints he'd been working on so he could finish them at home, then thought better, threw them back down on his desk and left without even bothering to turn off the lights.

Cathy greeted him with her usual smile and asked him how his day was. On the trip home he decided not to say anything until he had a chance to sort it out himself. After all the time he had spent getting her back to something like normal, he didn't see how he could go through it all again. If she found out he was going to jail after all, she would simply fall apart. He went to his wine cellar and selected a 1989 Southern Rhône; it was one of his favorite vintages, and he would not normally have opened it just for himself. But this was not a normal day, and he felt a strong urge to do something just for himself. He poured a glass and sat down in a recliner to watch the evening news.

"Supper's ready," Cathy called out. G.T. folded the recliner down and lumbered into the kitchen. Mmm, the smell of her beef tip casserole wafted from the open oven door. That was something he'd miss in prison. Damn, the thought of prison made his stomach turn sour. He sat down at the table and tried his best to make small talk with Cathy and Tommy.

That night as he lay in bed, he thought about what it would be like to be a convicted felon. What amount of money could make that right? Cathy would be an outcast in the social world. Nobody would help her or do anything for her. Her warm body, filled with sleep, shifted against him. It had been decades since he'd slept alone for more than a few nights, and he wasn't sure he could do it. Whenever he was on the road, he had trouble sleeping, and when he was home, he needed to be touching some part of her every night. Whether it was his hands or his feet, or just their bodies being close and touching, it didn't matter, he had to have contact with her. There wasn't anything that could make a year apart acceptable. He'd have to find some other way.

By 6:00, when he got out of bed, his resolve had been strengthened. There had to be a way to convince Hargiss to change his mind and let Howard go to jail instead of him. Sure blood was thicker than water, but what was between him and Hargiss wasn't just water, it was decades of sweat, a commingling of intellectual and psychological fluids. As he pondered the problem, he thought about the times he'd seen Hargiss change his mind in the past. Once Hargiss started down a path he usually finished it, unless he was forced to turn around. But what could G.T. do to force Hargiss to retreat?

What would William do, he thought, if he were in my shoes?

He arrived at his office at 6:45 and reopened the blueprints on his desk. Then it struck him. The audacity of it! Nah, it would never work. G.T. discarded it. But it wouldn't leave him alone. Everywhere around him, bits and pieces of it floated in front of him. Maybe the report from Tully on Gary Long's credit card bills was what triggered it. Maybe it was the vial of Rophynol he came across in the back of his desk drawer, the one Howard had brought him from Paris. Maybe it was the vision of William Hargiss at one of his ugliest moments, but whatever it was, it wouldn't leave him alone. By 10:00 it oozed out of every pore.

He picked up the phone and called Tully. "Tully, it's G.T."

"Yeah, what the fuck you want?" Tully was reading and rereading the police report on Roger Kincaid's accident, looking for any hint that foul play was suspected, finding none. "It's not what I want, but what I can do for you." Very level tone, no excitement, G.T. thought.

"Huh, what do you know, you turning generous in your old age, G.T.?"

"Nah, I'm just the messenger. You did something for William a long time ago, and he wants to settle the debt. With all that's come down, he feels things are going to be a lot less loose and easy from now on, and he wants me to make things right for a few of his favorite people, especially you. He told me to go upstairs and get a case full of money and bring it to you."

"What the fuck for?"

"He wants the files on that job in Minnesota. You know, the thing about his brother."

"What do you mean?"

"He wants your files, pictures, notes, phone numbers, everything. You keep that here, or in Washington?"

"Nah, it's here. How much money did Hargiss tell you to bring?"

"A million dollars. He thought that'd be enough to settle the score." There was silence on the other end of the line. Finally Tully responded.

"I think he's got the right number. Tell him I appreciate it very much, but it isn't necessary."

"I'll tell him, but you know how stubborn he can be. Come on in here around seven, and we'll go somewhere to have a drink."

"Yeah, sure, I'll do that. I was going back tonight, but for a million dollars, I'll stay over. I'll get a room at the Chemical Club."

G.T. called Cathy, suddenly feeling much brighter. "Honey, can you meet me at the Chemical Club for lunch?"

"Sure, any special reason?"

"No, but you've got to come in town for the funeral anyway, and I thought we might as well have something pleasant in the day, so I figured we'd have time for lunch."

"What a nice surprise! Sure, I'll meet you for lunch."

At noon, Cathy pulled up in front of the Chemical Club, looking for G.T.'s car. She didn't find it and went inside. G.T. was in fact at that moment racing toward the club, having just stopped by the house and slipped two bottles of her insulin into his coat pocket along with a syringe and needle.

He parked on the street, around the corner, plugged the meter, and hurried inside the club.

They enjoyed a leisurely lunch of crab cakes and rice. G.T. told her his car had been acting up, and suggested he ride with her to Roger's funeral.

"Then I'll hitch a ride back to the plant with one of the other men," he said.

After they finished the meal, they got into her car and Cathy drove him toward the funeral home. "What time will you be home tonight?" she asked.

"Ah, well, I'll be late, what with being gone all afternoon. I've got a meeting and I've got to wait for a phone call from Australia, which won't come through until at least eight. Then there's a whole bunch of stuff I've got to sign, because with Roger gone, I'm the only one who can."

"Poor Roger," she said.

At 6:00, G.T. called up to the sixth floor to see if Hargiss's secretary had left. After six rings, he was satisfied and headed to the elevator.

Andrew Tully arrived at G.T.'s office at 7:00 on the nose. In his hand he had a brown manila envelope that he threw on G.T.'s desk.

"There it is, everything I have. You know, I never would have used that stuff against William. He's been better to me than anyone I've ever known."

"Oh, hell, Tully, he wasn't worried that you'd use it. He just wants it in his own possession. I mean, what if something happened to you?"

"Yeah, well, whatever."

G.T. smiled. "Care for a drink, Tully?"

"Yeah, sure. What've you got?"

"I think I've got almost anything you'd want."

"How about a Dewars, neat."

"Sure." G.T. poured the drink into a plastic cup laced with enough Rophynol to make sure Tully soon wouldn't be feeling anything, at least anything painful. "You know, I never really understood how the two of you got together."

"It's quite a story. How much do you really know about your boss anyway?"

"Quite a bit, but I'm sure you can tell me things I don't know."

"He's a real fuckin' hero. If the world could only know everything he's done."

"Whadda you mean, Tully?"

"Fuck, William Hargiss has saved the taxpayers of this country billions, no zillions of dollars, not to mention lives."

"How?"

"You really are clueless, aren't you? How do you think you've been able to get away with this little price-fixing game of yours all these years? Do you think you're just that damn good? Do you really think TLP can buy all that political muscle just by giving campaign contributions to politicians?"

"What are you talking about?"

"Price fixing, shit, that's just a little tax the American people pay they don't know about. They don't even miss it. I guess people can't protest what they don't know exists."

G.T. looked at Tully with genuine surprise on his face.

"I shouldn't be telling you all this, but what the fuck. With this payment I'm out of the game. Gonna move to a little island somewhere south where I can buy a couple of maids to clean my house and wash my dick for thirty dollars a month. Anyway, your boss was recruited years ago to be a field asset for the NSA...you know, National Security Agency. The politicians all call it No Such Agency because it operates below the budget line. They operate in the U.S., outside the U.S., doesn't make a fucking bit of difference to them. They're charged with making sure that anything that can be done to protect liberty here is done. They're a bunch of super-patriots."

G.T. gave Tully a blank look. "So what's that have to do with price fixing?"

"Well, for years they 'assisted' the drug trade, made a few million here, a few million there, and got enough Commies on drugs along the way to nearly destroy their civilization. They almost got caught, and for several years had to dip into their savings to pay for everything. Then Hargiss gave them the bright idea of financing their campaigns with a quiet tax, price fixing."

"How does that work?"

"You ever try to add up all of your divisions and see what the total profitability is?"

G.T. laughed. "Yeah, we never foot."

"Ever wonder why?"

"Not really. The boss moves things around to try and even up the quarter. Hell, he's got us way ahead of the competition in that area. That's one of the reasons our stock has always traded at a higher multiple than anyone else in the industry. Our earnings look like a straight line."

"Yeah, well one of the reasons it always looks like a straight line is that William has a series of buffer accounts. He's got it so complex no one could ever figure it all out. But one thing's for sure, it grows and grows because if you'd ever take all that money out and show it, the analysts would go crazy trying to figure out how a commodity business could earn that much money on razor thin production margins. You can show those straight-line earnings because you never report profits by division, and no analyst can understand every business you guys are in. That way it looks like when one division is sucking wind, another kicks in. Every once a while the NSA comes along with a special project and debits the accounts for what it needs."

G.T. shook his head. How could all of this go on right under his nose for twenty-five years? It was amazing, but then he was just the engineer who made sure the machinery got oiled.

"Whew, this Scotch is really starting to kick in," Tully said, shaking his head.

It was working. G.T. needed to keep him talking for another five minutes or so. "So besides the money, what makes William such a special guy anyway?"

"Shit, he had the perfect cover. Nobody would ever suspect him. He could start or stop wars by locating a plant someplace, buying a company and keeping the plant open to keep the people fat and happy while the country was getting raided. Hell, I don't know. Goddamn, G.T., I don't feel so good."

He'd stopped making sense in the last sentence, and G.T. knew the time was at hand. "You don't look good," he said. "How about I drive you to the Chemical Club?"

Tully managed a wan smile. "Yeah, yeah, okay. Let me carry the money though."

G.T. pulled up the bag and opened it up for Tully to see.

"Fuck, that's a pretty sight."

"Yeah, close it up and let me get you to your car. Where'd you park?"

"Out by the back entrance."

G.T. put on his coat and gloves and helped Tully to the car, picking him up when he stumbled against something. He started the car and drove out of the lot, barely slowing down at the guard shack.

On the way to the Chemical Club, Tully was silent, but suddenly he sat bolt upright. "If I didn't know better, I'd think you were trying to drug me. You're not doing that are you G.T.?" he asked, menacingly. G.T. didn't have to answer because Tully slumped back against the door and a gurgling sound came out of his mouth. When they got to the Chemical Club, G.T. pulled into a parking spot away from the lights and reached in his pocket for the insulin. In the condition Tully was in, the two vials were more than enough to cause the man's heart to give up and die on the spot.

He pulled out the first vial and loaded the syringe. He reached over and pulled up the sleeve of Tully's coat and was shocked when he got no response. All of a sudden it hit him: maybe Tully was already dead. Maybe he'd put more Rohypnol in the drink than he'd intended.

G.T. felt for a pulse and under Tully's nose for breath. He couldn't find any sign of life. The man was dead! Rohypnol wasn't supposed to kill a person! Just to be sure, he thought, I'd better inject him anyway. But if Tully was dead already, then the insulin wouldn't be transported by the blood system, it would just sit there, wherever he injected it, and the coroner would find it.

"Tully, damn it, are you dead or alive?" he whispered, shaking the limp body. Again he felt for a pulse. Nothing. By now he was shaking, and starting to feel creepy at being in contact with a dead man. It was time to get away, and just hope to hell Tully was dead. He had the envelope, what else did he need? He grabbed the satchel with the million dollars and checked to see if anyone was watching. Then he got out of the car, went around to the passenger side and opened the door, catching Tully, or what was left of him, as he fell.

Pushing him across the seat, he arranged Tully's body so that his feet were on the pedals and hands on his chest. Then he closed the passenger door and walked across to his car, still parked where he had left it at lunchtime. Heading straight back to the plant, G.T. replaced the money in Hargiss's vault and made copies of the information Tully had given him. Then he went home. He had the oddest feeling as he went to bed that night. He kept hoping he was a murderer, because if he wasn't, if Andrew Tully was still somehow alive, anything could happen.

The next morning, G.T. scanned the paper for any sign of news about Tully. There wasn't any. He couldn't afford to call anybody for fear of raising suspicion, so he got dressed and headed into work. To his surprise, William's car was already in its parking spot in the garage.

He went to his desk, gathered every bit of courage he could muster and headed up to Hargiss's office. When he arrived at the threshold, the door opened and a skinny black man wearing a Chicago White Sox hat came out. G.T. had never seen the young man before, and wondered what business someone like that could have with Hargiss. They brushed past one another, and G.T. could see William through the open door, sitting at his desk looking out the window. "I thought you'd be on your way to the West Coast this morning," G.T. said, walking into the office.

The old man's body twitched suddenly at the sound of G.T.'s voice, but he composed himself. "I had to cancel the trip," he responded.

G.T. threw the packet onto the desk much in the same offhand way Tully hand given it to him the night before. Then, after looking around the office, he sat down.

Hargiss's normally intense eyes looked blurry and bloodshot this morning. He moved to pick up the envelope, and, opening it, examined its contents. "Those are copies William; I've got the originals," G.T. said.

"Was that what Tully was doing here last night, delivering these to you?"

"Yeah."

"What are you telling me, G.T.?"

"I'm not going to jail, William."

"Well, I'm certainly not, either," Hargiss said. Then he sighed. Not the sort of sigh that might come from an athlete who was winding down from a tough game, but the tired sigh of an old man who was at the end of his life. He looked older than G.T. had ever seen him.

"I'm sorry I had to use this, William. I know you wanted your brother to stay dead."

"Yeah, well, he shouldn't have been talking about things he didn't have full knowledge of."

"A two-bullet suicide's kind of hard to cover up, I would think, but I guess Tully can make almost anything disappear, huh?" The message was clear, and both men knew there is no statute of limitations on murder.

Hargiss was briefly silent. "If I go first, make sure you destroy all this. I don't want Howard to ever see it," he said at length.

"Sure, William, sure thing."

"You'd better get your ass to work. That plant in Czechoslovakia isn't going to get built on good intentions."

"It's not Czechoslovakia any more, it's the Czech Republic. I got an earful when I made that mistake two weeks ago. And yeah, it's looking better. I think we'll be on schedule. Anybody you need me to be meeting with?"

It was as though nothing had passed between them, and yet everything had changed. Both of them knew it, yet both were unwilling to acknowledge it. The more things change, the more they remain the same, G.T. thought, as he walked back down the stairs to his office.

CHAPTER 126

"Oh, by the way, I've got something of yours," Mr. Paoletti, the dry cleaner, said.

"Something of mine?" Phil McLaughlin replied, watching the tall, wavy-haired man fumble under the counter.

"Yeah, you left it here a long time ago. We set it aside for you, but it slipped down behind the counter." He straightened and indicated with his left hand a small space between the counter and the wall. In his right hand he held a small plastic bag with a cleaning ticket stapled to the top. It had the word "McLaughlin" written on it in green Magic Marker.

In the bag, McLaughlin could see an audiocassette tape.

"Are you sure this is mine?" he asked in the instant before he recognized it. No, he thought, it isn't really mine. He had picked it up off the floor of a garage in Indiana, and somehow....

"I think so," Mr. Paoletti said, breaking McLaughlin's concentration.

"Well, yes, I guess it is mine," McLaughlin said.

He fingered the object as Mr. Paoletti wrote out the ticket for the shirts McLaughlin had brought in. Pressing the plastic against the side of the tape, he could read what was written on the label. "Tape 2 – Steuben Agreement," it read.

In his car, McLaughlin tore open the plastic bag and slipped the tape into the cassette player. By the time he got home, he knew he had William C. Hargiss dead to rights.

Once home, he went to the room he used for an office. Piled up in a corner was a stack of newspapers, mostly *Wall Street Journals* and business sections of the *Times*. It contained pretty much everything that had been in print about the TLP price fixing case.

He found the name he was looking for, and, after battling for a few minutes with an incredibly annoying mechanical voice at long distance information, managed to get the phone number from a human operator.

"Mr Parr," he said when the man answered. "I think I have a tape you'd like to hear."

CHAPTER 127

Sid Cox was apprehensive as he entered Jim Thompson's office, sniffling from the cold January weather. The sniffles seemed to have come on within minutes of his landing in Indianapolis, tanned and feeling refreshed after two months on administrative leave in Arizona. Now he'd been ordered back and told to prepare to move to a new assignment. Vacation or no, it had not been a good time for Cox. First, there was the matter of Gary Long's bonus money. The Bureau wanted to know why Cox hadn't found out about it long before he did. Then there were the tapes. Tapes of him – making racial slurs, committing obstruction of justice. He almost couldn't believe how Gary had actually gotten him to talk so much – even to discuss things that had already happened, just like Cox had taught him to do with suspects. "Hoist on your own petard," the agent Crowley had taunted him.

The only good news was that somehow none of those tapes had surfaced in the media. Whether Gary's lawyer really had them as he claimed didn't matter much. The one he did have was enough to close down the case, and fast.

From what Cox could figure out – he'd been told nothing officially – the tape must have been from the meeting in Steuben, and must have been too hot for Justice to handle.

The whole thing was a piece of crap, in his mind. He busted his butt to get not just the underlings, but the top dogs, too – Hamanaka, William Hargiss. But Hargiss was just as powerful as everyone told him, Cox decided, and once Keith Parr had forced the prosecutors to either charge Hargiss or drop the case against Gary, they'd cut the deal.

Oh, there were fines – big ones – of TLP and Nippon Kagaka, and Gary had to pay all the taxes he owed, plus interest and penalties. But nobody higher up than Howard Hargiss was in jail, not even G.T. Binghamton.

Not that Cox cared much. All he he'd ever really wanted, from the start, was to get out of the one-man office in Steuben, Indiana, head to a warmer climate and serve out his remaining ten years before retirement. The question of the day was, would he get to do that, or was this meeting to tell him he was fired?

"You wanted to see me?" he asked as he crossed Thompson's threshold.

Thompson didn't even look up from the papers he was holding in his hand. "Come on in and close the door, Sid." He had been waiting to savor this moment. He was so angry at Sid Cox, he almost couldn't see straight. As a result of Cox's screwups, Thompson could now go the bathroom twice as fast as before; such was the extent of the ass chewing he had received. Still, they wouldn't let him fire Cox. Put him where you can keep an eye on him, they told him.

Finally Thompson put the papers down, and looked at Cox for the first time. He didn't want to miss seeing what was to come. "You caused quite a stir in the Hoover Building, Sid," he said.

Cox merely nodded. He didn't think it was the kind of statement that required any discussion.

"Well, you've got your transfer." Cox was shocked; he hadn't expected any good news today. Maybe they really wanted him to stay quiet.

"I did?"

"Yup, you're going to Green Bay."

"Wisconsin?"

"Yup," Thompson smiled at Cox. "Nice town, right on the water. Maybe you can get Packers tickets. And if you don't like it, just remember that you're damn lucky to have a job, period. You pissed a lot of people off, Sid. A lot of people don't want you around at all."

"If Washington hadn't cut our budget to zero, maybe we would have had enough time and help to do things right."

"It's water over the dam, Sid. Keep your nose clean and put it behind you."

It sounded more like bull than advice to Cox. You didn't recover from something like this. Even with the convictions and fines they'd won, he would end up a bad footnote in a file somewhere, never receiving the proper credit for what he'd done. Green Bay, damn it anyway: 20 degrees colder than Steuben, maybe more. His stomach felt queasy. Thompson got up and stuck his hand out signaling the end of the discussion. As he walked out through the squad room, Cox could feel every eye on him. Somehow, everyone apparently had already heard the news.

CHAPTER 128

Howard reached into the bag and pulled out a nine iron. This approach shot gave him trouble every damn time. As he looked for the pin he saw it was at the back of the green. Good. That suited his shot from this lie much better.

His foursome today included a CPA from New York, a former Congressional staffer and a real estate developer from Atlanta. Betting wasn't allowed on this course, but all in all, it was a pretty pleasant way to spend a January afternoon – especially for a kid from Steuben, Indiana.

The rules at the Pensacola Federal Prison were simple: follow orders and don't do anything illegal. If you managed that, you served out your time comfortably at one of the gentlest correctional facilities on earth. Howard really didn't have a care in the world. When he got out, his father had promised him a life of plenty. Plenty of money, plenty of time to do what he wanted, and plenty of respect from dear old Dad for the great sacrifice Howard was making for the company.

The problem was it didn't feel so great. It felt like jail, even out here on the golf course.

Shit, he'd come so close. Of course, they all said that around Pensacola Federal Prison.

His dad hadn't come to visit him. There was always something in the way, but Mom sent him a care basket every two weeks. And he'd been allowed to have a fish tank in his room. Drugs and liquor were taboo, but not women. Conjugal visits were allowed whenever you felt like it, and Howard felt like it pretty often.

Why had it been him? But of course, it had to be him. Everyone at TLP knew he was the Price Fixer. When he'd left, his father had shaken his hand and told him he was sorry it had worked out like this, and he'd do what he could...to what? That hadn't ever been said.

He lined up over the top of the ball and swung, watching as the little white sphere arced high over a sand trap and plopped onto the green, ten feet from the pin. He'd been given 18 months; with good behavior that meant somewhere around 13 months, and all because he'd tried to make his father proud of him. The law against price fixing was stupid, anyway. But nobody gave a damn what he thought. His lawyers insisted the best way out of the trouble was to plead guilty. So he'd done it, with the promise of a life on Easy Street after he got out.

He figured he'd earn more than three million dollars during the time he was here on his golf retreat. He had stock, options, and a consulting contract that alone would be worth more than ten million dollars over the next five years. His dad had lined it up with a company Howard had never heard of, something called Interoceanic. What he'd be doing for that money he didn't know, didn't in fact really care. If he could endure this enforced vacation, life would be good again.

Like Howard, Leigh Curtis was in Florida that day, sitting in the sun in Naples. The day the plea bargains were announced, she gave her notice, in spite of Buffy's urging that she stay on and work for him. He'd asked her what she was going to do, and she'd said she was going to take some time off, go to Florida for a few weeks, see the sights and visit some old friends from Colorado who lived in Ft. Myers now.

He'd wanted to know where she was going to stay, and she said she didn't know yet. Then he'd reached into his pocket and pulled out a leather key case. He released a key from its clasp and set it on his desk. Then he took a piece of notepaper and wrote out an address. "It's my condo in Naples," he said. "Right down the road from Ft. Myers. Use it as long as you want."

She hesitated for just a moment, and then took the key. "Thanks, Buffy," she said.

"Hey," he replied, "it's the least I can do."

Before leaving TLP forever, she walked down the hall to Brad Redfoot's office. It was his last day, too. He'd been rehired by Nippon Kagaka; they were sending him to Thomasville, Iowa to try and get their operations there up to snuff.

Now she was seated in an open-air beachfront restaurant, talking to an attractive widower in his mid-60s. He owned the condo next to Buffy's. He seemed very nice, and had talked to her several times in the week she'd been there, so when he asked her to lunch, she said, "Sure."

Monoh paused at his task and drank cool water from the plastic bottle. He looked back at the hedge he was working on with the clippers. Almost half done, and the completed part was straight and square.

From the city below, he could hear the chant as the crowds followed Salah's bus through the streets. "Vooot, Sesay Salah," the people chanted. "Vooot, Sesay Salah." Again and again they chanted, joyous in their support of the candidate.

Yes, Monoh thought, the people will vote for Ahmad Sesay Salah, and there will be democracy in Sierra Leone. He rolled the strange word over and over, pronouncing it in the West African way, DEH-mo-crassy.

In his two years in the city, Monoh had learned much. As to whether this democracy could stop the smuggling, mutilating and killing, however, he was still unsure.

William Hargiss looked in the mirror in the bathroom next to his office. He'd lost so damn much face he felt he was lucky to see a reflection. The past six months had drained more out of him than ten years of bad business. But the recovery had started. The board was compliant: without Randolph Thad and Ian Howes, there was no independent leadership to challenge Hargiss. And no intellectual companionship, either.

After a huge drop in price, the shares of TLP turned upward again as soon as the plea agreement was announced. There were several shareholder suits, but Robert Aiken, Zack Brilley and Louie Cobb were finally earning their keep, and managed to limit the damage.

As for G.T. Binghamton, well, G.T. had shown more spunk than Hargiss thought he had. He was doing, as he had always done, a heck of a job for the company. He still could make the pipes fit better than anyone Hargiss had ever met.

On the agenda today was a meeting with Buffy Carney. Hargiss figured it would be the first of many; he had a lot to go over with Jim Carney's grandson. He wanted to fill Buffy in on all the details of what his grandfather had done, and what Hargiss had done as old Jim's successor. And at the end of the discussion, the two of them would map out a plan for Buffy to become the CEO of TLP, and the most important independent asset for the NSA. Hargiss was confident he'd found the man for the job. One thing about a PR guy, Hargiss thought: he sees all aspects of what's going on.

As he finished washing his hands, he looked again at the face in the mirror. He probably should feel bad about sending his son to prison, especially since it was all his fault. But he didn't feel bad. He felt good, powerful, like he'd just looked straight down the jaws of destruction and defeated them. He was, after all, a Giant of the Earth.

G.T. sat hunched over his desk studying the numbers for a new plant TLP was building in North Carolina. It was progressing on schedule, well, as much of a schedule as he ever had for building anything. TLP wasn't about to change when it came to moving quickly; he'd insisted on that. The new Corporate Governance Committee tried to flex its muscle a few times, but when push came to shove, William had helped them see the light.

G.T. felt William had a newfound respect for him, one that went even beyond his ability to get things done. At first, he was afraid his blackmail would forever taint their relationship. But it quickly became clear that William still needed him, and, after all, he needed William.

It was still a mystery what happened to Andrew Tully. The papers never carried a single word about a body being found at the Chemical Club, nor did William ever broach the subject. G.T. supposed he'd never find out – unless, of course, he ran into Tully in a dark alley somewhere.

As he pushed the plans across his desk he thought about the new product line. He never expected to be involved in fixing prices again, and for that he was thankful. The past months had given him a great deal of time to ponder what the price fixing meant.

Maybe it was true the American economy was going the way of the Wal-Marts: everything bigger and more efficient. If that was true, then TLP's actions were merely hastening the world down that path. That really was the bottom-line effect of price fixing. It forced everyone to go along to get along, or it forced them out. Everyone had to be crooked to survive. On top of that, it caused massive inefficiency.

The ringing phone jangled G.T. back into focus. "Huhh," he grunted.

"G.T., get your ass up here, we've got a problem in Louisiana." Hargiss's voice sounded tense.

"All right, I'll be right up."

G.T. hung up the phone and pushed away from his desk. As he stood up, he marveled at just how quickly business had gotten back to normal at TLP.

Outside Keith Parr's office in the Wrigley Building, snow was falling. Inside, Gary and Jenna were busy signing papers. "How come you didn't put those little yellow stickers on the places we have to sign," Gary asked Parr.

Because I don't want you to just leaf through and sign," Parr said, sternly. "You're going to read every damn word of this. You're going to know exactly what you're agreeing to. You're too trusting, you know. I think it's time you stopped just going along, stopped assuming what somebody tells you is right – whether it's your boss or an FBI agent or even your lawyer."

Gary grinned sheepishly. "How about my wife?" he asked.

"Her, you trust," Parr said.

When the three of them had worked their way through the stack, Gary and Jenna had signed away most of most net worth, but when she finally handed the last document to Parr, Jenna felt nothing but joy. She and Gary had no idea, yet, where they were going to live, or what sort of work he was going to do, but it didn't matter. For years they had lived in a pressure cooker, in which she woke up every morning and had at best ten seconds of normal thoughts before she felt the intensity of it. And she knew it was even worse for Gary.

Now all that was going to change. Life would be slower, simpler – better.

"Do I understand you're going to sell the house?" Parr asked.

"Dad's listing it today," Jenna said. "Probably out in the snow pounding in a sign right now."

"Somebody's going to get a real bargain on that place," Gary added. He was pensive for a moment. "With all the bad memories, though, I wouldn't have met her without it," he said.

He and Parr both looked at Jenna.

"True," she said. "But I want it gone. I don't ever want to see it again. Even when we go back to see Mom and Dad, there's no way I'm driving out that road."

"Job prospects?" Parr asked, looking at Gary.

"Some possibilities," Gary said. "Foremost is starting a new research arm in North Carolina, and Phil McLaughlin has made me a nice offer to be the number two person there. Ian Howes has invested in some sort of oil operation in Texas. I've got to follow up with him. Some guy in Denver wants me to take a teaching post at the University there. And then there's Alan Bishop...."

"The reporter?"

"Yeah, he thinks I should write a book on the whole case, and wants to help me with it."

"I think he could take any of the other jobs and still do the book," Jenna said to Parr.

"Actually," Gary said. "I tried to get started. But one thing keeps bothering me about it."

"What's that," Parr asked.

"There's a million things I still don't know," Gary said. "What really happened to me? Who stole the tapes? Why did they put Howard in prison, but not G.T. or William? And most of all, what's the real story behind TLP's profits? How can I write a book about something I may have been in the middle of, but don't understand to this day."

"Give it a try," Parr said. "I think you're story's pretty compelling. I don't know a lot of things, either, but I can probably fill in some of the holes for you."

They shook hands, and Gary and Jenna drove out the Kennedy Expressway to Park Ridge, where they had rented a house Ralph Sori had steered them to. It was just a temporary deal, but Justin and Mark had to finish the school year somewhere, and Jenna didn't want it to be in Wonanonly.

When the boys got home, shortly after Gary and Jenna did, she looked at them and noticed how tall they were getting, especially Justin, who was now taller than she was.

While she fixed a dinner of broiled chicken thighs, rice and frozen broccoli with cheese sauce, Gary found a legal pad, sat down in the living room, and began to write.

The End